ENGLISH RECUSANT LITERATURE
1558–1640

Selected and Edited by
D. M. ROGERS

Volume 315

RICHARD SMITH
An Answer to Thomas Bels
Late Challeng
1605

RICHARD SMITH

An Answer to Thomas Bels
Late Challeng
1605

The Scolar Press
1976

ISBN 0 85967 329 4

Published and printed in Great Britain by
The Scolar Press Limited, 59-61 East Parade,
Ilkley, Yorkshire and
39 Great Russell Street,
London WC1

1931603

NOTE

Reproduced (original size) from a copy in the library of the Brompton Oratory, by permission of the Provost and Fathers.

References: Allison and Rogers 771; STC 22809.

AN ANSWER
TO THOMAS BELS

LATE CHALLENG NAMED
BY HIM THE DOWNFAL
OF POPERY

WHERIN AL HIS ARGVMENTS

are anſwered, his manifold vntruths, ſlaunders, ignorance, contradictions, and
corruption of Scripture, & Fathers
diſcouered and diſproued:

WITH ONE TABLE OF THE
Articles and Chapters, and an other of the
more markable things conteyned
in this booke.

WVhat controuerſies be here handled is
declared in the next page.

By S. R.

Hieremiæ c. 50. verſ. 2.

Capta eſt Babylon confuſus eſt Bel,

Babylon is ſurpriſed, Bel is confounded,

S. Cyprian. lib. 4. epiſt. 9.

Amongſt men fallen, and prophane, and out of the
Church, from whoſe harts the holy Ghoſt is departed, what other thing can there be then a
wicked mynd, deceitful tong, venemous
hatred, and ſacrilegious lies?

AT DOWAY,
Imprinted by LAVRENCE KELLAM, at
the ſigne of the holie Lambe.

M. DC. V.

Controuersies handled in this booke.

TO
THE MOST HIGHE
AND MIGHTIE PRINCE,
IAMES

By the grace of God King of great Britanie,
France, and Ireland, Defendor
of the Faith.

 F S. Paul (Moſt Grati-
ous Soueraigne) being
accuſed of the whole
Synagog of the Iewes,
by their Orator Tertul-
lus of diuers heynous crimes, both a-
gainſt Gods and the Princes lawes,
found notwithſtanding ſuch equitie
in the heathen Preſident Feſtus, as
that he anſwered his aduerſaries, that
it was not the Romans cuſtome to cō-
demne any man before he haue his ac-
cuſers preſent, and place to make his
anſwer : and alſo ſuch fauour at the
Iewiſh King Agrippa his hands, as he
both licenced him to ſpeake for him
ſelfe, & afforded him fauorable audience. Much more cauſe haue your

Act. 25.

The like re-
porteth
Plutarch of
K. Alexan.
the great.
Act. 26.

a 2   Maje-

Maiefties Catholique Subie&s, being accufed of the minifters by a hyred fpokefman Bel, to expe& the like, yea greater fauor & equitie at your Graces handes. For if the Romans though Heathens, thought it iniuftice to condemne any particular man at the clamors of a whole nation, before his accufers were prefent and his defence were heard? And if King Agrippa, albeit a Iew & perfecutor of Chriftians, deemed it notwithftanding a Princes part to geue audience to one accufed of that Religion which he both hated and perfecuted : How much more wil a Chriftian Prince forbeare to condemne the vniuerfal caufe of his Catholique fubie&s at the flaunders and outcries of minifters & one hyred Pro&or, before their accufers be brought face to face, and they haue time and place graunted to anfwer for them felues? wherein we fhal account our felues more happy then S. Paul, becaufe we fh l plead our caufe, not before a Iew fh, but a Chriftian King, &
felues? wherein we fhal account our

He killed S. Iames and emprifoned S. Peter. Act. 12.

fuch

such a one as better knoweth the questions and customes of the Christians,
then King Agrippa did of the Iewes.

VVherfore seeing that of late Thomas Bel (a fugitiue once from Protestants religion, as he is now from Catholiques) hath not only accused, but
also malitiously sladered the vniuersal
Catholique cause, in a booke which
he hath dedicated to your Maiestie, &
termed it the *Dovvnefall of Poperie*, and
withal challengeth, dareth, yea adiu-
reth (in which case our B. Sauiour Matth. 16.
though with danger of his life made
answer) al English Iesuits, Seminary
Priests, and (as he speaketh) Iesuited
Papists to answer him. I haue presumed vpon your Gratious fauour to accept his chaleng, and am ready to performe it hand to hand, if your Maiestie graunt licence, and in the meane
time, to dedicate to your Name this
my confutation of his arguments and
slaunders. VVherin I speake not for
my selfe as S. Paul did before King
Agrippa, but for the religion of your

a 3   owne

owne Progenitors and Predeceſſors, for the faith of our Forefathers, for the cauſe of al Catholiques, and for the good (I dare ſay) of your Maieſties owne perſon & kingdoms. For though Bel calumniate Chriſtian Kinges and Emperors with opening the window to al Antichriſtian tyranny, and Catholiques generally, with thinking Chriſt to be killed a thouſand times a day and the like: yet eſpecially he ſlandereth the Popes with vſurping power proper to God, and to depoſe Princes, and diſpoſe of their kingdomes at his pleaſure, therby to alienate your mind from the Sea Apoſtolike. wherin he not onely abuſeth your patiéce with telling you vntruths, but greatly harmeth and endamageth your ſelfe and Realme, by endeuoring through his falſe ſlanders to auert your minde from the Popes, who haue bene the moſt ancient, moſt aſſured, and moſt beneficial frends, which the Kinges & Realme of England euer had. VVhich thing that I may make manifeſt vnto your

pag. 17.

p. 1. 22.

Vir Apoſta-
ta prauo co-
rde machi-
natur malú,
omni tem-
pore iurgia
Seminat.
Prouer.c.6,

your Grace, I humbly befeech you geue me leaue to fet downe fome praticular examples of the mutual amitie, kind offices, & benifites, which haue euer bene betwixt the Popes and the Princes of this land. VVherein if I be fomewhat longer then men in Epiftles vfe to be, I hope that the varietie and profit of the matter wil make requital.

The loue & benefits of Popes to England and Kings therof.

Not long after the Apoftolike Seat was fettled in Rome, S. Peter the firft Pope, about the 63. yeare of Chrift came hither (as not only Grecians, but Proteftants alfo confeffe) ftayed here a long time, conuerted many Nations to Chrifts faith, erected Churches, ordered Bifhops, and Priefts, and being admonifhed of an Angel, returned from hence to Rome to fuffer Martyrdome. Neither was this loue to our Countrie extinguifhed by death, but as he promifed to fome, fo he had it alfo in mind after his death, and miraculoufly affifted it in the greateft diftreffes. So that truly wrote S. Sergius I. Pope vnto our Kings of England

S. Peter P.

Metaphraft. tract.de Pet. & Paul. apud Lippoman. Cambden in defcrip. Britaniæ p. 52. And Nicephor. as he faieth.

2. Pet. 1.

Malmesbur. lib. I. Pont. Angl.p.209.

a 4 land

land almoſt a thouſand yeares agoe, that S. Peter was mindful of them: & Pope Alexander 3. to King Henry 2. that England was vnder S. Peters proteƈtion euer ſince Chriſts name was glorified there. For when our country about the yeare 611. began to Apoſtatate from the faith of Chriſt, and the Biſhops were determined to forſake the land. S. Peter appearing to Sainƈt Laurence Arch-biſhop of Canturbury did ſeuerly rebuke and ſcourge him becauſe he would abandon the flocke which I (ſaid S. Peter) cōmitted vnto thee. This miracle is ſo certaine as ſome Proteſtāts confeſſe it, & though ſome others wil not beleue it, becauſe they haue neither ſeene nor put their fingers into S. Laurence his wounds; yet it may ſuffice any indifferent man, that it was auouched by S. Laurence, beleeued by King Edbald & his people, who thereupon returned to the Chaiſtian faith, recorded by S. Beda aboue eight hūdred yeares agoe (who wrote nothing but what he knew him ſelfe

Eugubin. de donat. Cōſt.

Gadwin in the life of S. Laurence.

lib. 2. hiſt. c. 6. Malmesb. lib. 1. Reg. & lib. 2. Pont. Hunringt. l. 3. Marian. A. 693. al. 617. VVeſtman. 16.

felfe or receaued from credible men, whofe hiftory was approued by the King of his dayes & by the Proteftants now) and finallie it is contefted & deliuered by our beft Chroniclers.

Godvvin in life of Tatvvin.
Cambd. in Britania. p. 12.

Not long before, when the King had built a Monafterie and Church in honor of S. Peter, where now weftminfter ftandeth, S. Peter came from heauen and confecrated (as by miracle he confirmed) the fame church, promifing that there he would heare the prayers of the faithful. VVherupõ King Edward Conff: reedified that church of new & chofe it for the place of his fepulture; whom the moft of his fucceffors haue imitated, and bene there alfo crowned. Authors of this are Abbat Ealred, Malmesburienfis (a man highlie efteemed of Proteftants) P. Nicolas 2. and others. In like maner when England was fore oppreffed by the Danes, S. Peter was feene of Brithwald a holie B: of winchefter, in a vifion to anoint S. Edward Conff: King of England, and to fore-

In vit. S. Eduardi.
Malmesbur. l.1.de Pont.
See Sauil ep. ad Reg. Elizab. ante Malmesbur.
Epift. ad Eduard. R. apud Sur.
Baron. An. 610.

tel

tel the yeares of his raigne, and the end of the Danish fury, adding withal these most comfortable words. *The*

Loc.cit.Mal-
mesb.lib.2.
reg.cap.13.p.
91.
lib.8.histor.
Angl.

kingdome of England is the kingdome of God. This testifie the foresaid Ealred, Malmesbury, Polidor, and others. If Protestāts obiect againſt my Authors, that they were Papiſts, I muſt confeſſe (but to their shame) that I finde no proteſtāt writer before K. Henry 8. his time: yet such papiſts they are as pro-

Cambden
in Britan. p.
12. & in Dur-
ham. Stovv
A-726.
Bel in dovv
nefal p. 54.
of s Beda.
Sauil of
Mafmes-
bur. Hun-
ting. and
Hoveden.
epist. ante
Malmesbur.

teſtants account some of them *the ſin-gular ornamēts of England, eſpecial friends of truth, and renowmed through Chriſten-dom for vertue and learning,* and others they cal *faithful recorders of things done, good and diligent Authors, and moſt true guides of the times paſt.* Such alſo they are, as wrote long before proteſtants were, & therefore not vpon any ſplene againſt them: and finallie ſuch they are, as vpon their authority principal-lie dependeth al the credit of our En-gliſh Chronicles. Others perhaps wil ſay, that the foreſaid hiſtories are not in ſcripture. True: nor almoſt any thing

thing els in al our Chronicles. Shal we therefore beleue nothing but what God reporteth? I requeſt no more, but that the foreſaid matters be as wel credited, as other things are, which the ſame Authors report.

This affection and loue towards England was not proper to S. Peter alone, but deſcended vnto his ſucceſſors. For when the ſweet ſound of the Ghoſpel firſt preached here by him, had ſo increaſed, as it came to the eares of Lucius then King of this land, he ſending to Rome for preachers, P. Eleutherius about the yeare 156. ſent hither S. Fugatius and S. Damian, who baptized the King, Queene, and almoſt al his people. VVhereby our Country became the firſt, that publikely profeſſed the faith of Chriſt, and there vpon is called *Primogenita Eccleſiæ*. The like charitable office performed alſo P. Victor vnto Scotland about the yeare 203. ſending thither his legates at the requeſt of King Donaldus, who conuerted the King together

P. Eleutherius A. 156.
S. Beda lib.1. c. 4. Martyr. Rom. 26.
Ado & Marian. in chronic.
VVeſtmon. A. 188. Stow 179.

P. Victor. 203.
Boet. lib.6. hiſtor.Scot. Genebr. chron. in Victore.

gether with the Q. and nobility And about the yeare 324. Pope Siluester hauing perfectlie instructed our great Emperor Constantin, baptized him, and miraculouslie cured him of his leprosie, as the said Emp. and many others testifie. Afterward when the Christian faith in Britany began to be infected with heresie, P. Celestin about the yeare 432. sent hither S. S. German and Lupus for to expel and confute the heresies, which they accōplished. And the same P. in the yeare 434. consecrated Palladius a Bishop, and sent him to Scotland, where as yet was no B: & not forgetful of Ireland, sent thither S. Patrick, who with miracles cōuerted the Iland, & deserued (saith Cambdin) the title of Apostle thereof. Thus cōtinued the loue of the Sea Apostolicke towards our Coūtrey al the time that the Britōs possessed it.

But towards our English nation, after they had conquered this Iland, it was far greater. For whereas not only the Britons refused, but the Frenᴄh

P. Siluester.
324.
Constant. in edicto Me-
nolag. Græ-
cor. cal. Ion.
Huntingr. l.
1. hist. p. 306.
Acta liberij.
vita Silue-
stri.

P. Celestin.
A. 432.
Prosper in chron. An.
432. Baron.
429.
Prosper An.
434. Beda l.
1. c. 13. Plat.
in Celesti-
no. Baron.
Ann. 419.
Cambden in Hibernia.
Marian. in chron.
Cambd. in Hibern.

Beda lib. 1.
c. 11.

French alſo and other Chriſtian nations neglected , to preach vnto our
Engliſh aunciters, who euer vntil that
time had bene Pagans, & bondſlaues
(ſaith S. Beda) of Idols : only Rome
put forth hir helping hand to draw
the out of that darcknes & miſerie of
Infidelity. For no ſooner that bleſſed
& holie father S. Gregory (as Gadwin
calleth him) vnderſtood that the Angles or Engliſh (whom for their bewtie
and his tender affection he called Angels) were Pagans, but forthwith he
went to the P : (being him ſelfe yet
a monke) and deſired him to ſend
Preachers into England, and offering
him ſelfe to be one : And obtaining
licence came on his voyadge towards
England three daies Iourney, but was
recalled at the importunity of the Ro-
manes, who were vnwilling to forgoe
ſoe worthie a man, neuertheles he forgot not his holie enterpriſe. *For as ſoone*
(ſaith S. Beda l. 1. cap. 1.) *as he was*
high Biſhop ouer the vvhole vvorlde, he
made our nation the Church of Chriſt,
which

Gregor. lib.
5. epiſt. 58. 59.
Gadvvin in
liſe of S.
Auſtin.

lib. 2. c. 1.

P. Gregory
An. 596.
loc. cit

Beda lib. 2. c.
1. Malmesb.
l. 1. Reg.

Ioan. Diac.
in vit. Gre-
gor.

vvhich had bene euer vntil that time the box a slaue of Idols. And in the yeare 596.
sent hither S. Augustin with almost forty Moncks more to preach, who being receaued of K: Ethelbert in short time conuerted both him & his Coūtry. And that they preached the true faith and religion of Christ, appeared by the miracles they wrought in testimony thereof, which were so great, and many, *as it seemed* (saith S. Gregory) *that they imitated the vertues of the Apostles* by the miracles they wrought, and are withal so certaine, as they are not only testified by the said S. Gregory in diuers places, S. Beda & other ancient writers, and by the Epitaph of S. Augustins tombe, but cōfessed also by diuers Protestants. Againe in the yeare 601. he sent more Preachers and with them al things necessary for the furniture and seruice of the Church, *as holie vessels* (saith S. Beda) *Aultar clothes, apparel for priests and Clarcks, reliques of holie Apostles and Martirs, and many bookes,* and a Palle to S. Augustin

to vse

Beda sup. Stovv. An. 596. Godvvin. sup.

lib. 7. epist. 30.

lib. 9. ep. 56. 58. Beda lib. 1. c.31.l.2.c.2. Apud Godvvin. in vit. August. Godvvin. sup. Stovv An. 603. Cambd. in Britan. p. 704.

Beda lib. 1. n. 29.

to vse only (writeth S. Gregory) *at Masse,* Apud Bed: sup.
appointed also him to be ouer al the
Bishops and Priests of Britany, and
gaue him licence to institute 24. Bishopricks, whereof 12. should be
vnder his prouince, and 12. vnder
yorke. Besides he sent rich presents of Bed.lib. 1. e. 32. Gregor. lib. 9. epist. 59. 60.
diuers sorts, and letters vnto the King
and Queene, for to confirme them in
their faith : and sent order also into Gregor. lib. 5. epist. 10.
France to buy such English youths as
were there slaues, and to send them vp
to Rome there to be brought vp in
vertue & learning. VVherein he gaue
the example of the English Seminary
which not long after, our English
Kings founded in Rome. This was
the exceeding loue of this B. Pope towards our Nation, *vvhom vve may*
vvel, and must (saith S.Beda lib. 2.c.1.)
cal our Apostle, and may lavvfullie pro-
nounce of him that saying of the Apostle. 1. Cor. 9.
Although he vvere not an Apostle to others,
yet he vvas vnto vs: For the signe of his
Apostleship vve are in our Lord.

Neither was this great good so happilie

pilie begun and planted in our nation
by S. Gregorie and his Legates, neglected by the Popes his succeffors, but
rather diligentlie watered and furde-
red by them, as appeareth by the letters & Meffages of diuers of them fent
vnto our Princes and Bishops to that
purpofe. as of P. Boniface 5. in the
yeare 618. of P. Honorius in 633. of P.
Agatho 679. P. Zacharie about 746.
P. Adrian 789. P. Formofus 894. and
others. But moft of al it was increafed
by P. Honorius his fending hither in
the yeare 635. that Apoftolical man S.
Birin, who conuerted the weft Saxons: and by P. Vitalian, who in 668.
fent hither thofe holie and great learned men S. Theodor and Adrian, by
whofe teaching Englishmen in short
time became the rareft men, and beft
learned of their age, and the firft foun-
ders of the vniuerfities in Paris, and
Pauia, and confequentlie the chiefeft
fountaines of the learning which hath
bene fince in the weft. After this time
Eardulf King of Northumberland,
being

Bed.lib. 2. c.
10. 11. Hun-
tingt.l.3.
Bed.lib. 2. c.
17.Hunting.
fup.
Ped.lib.4. c.
18.Hunt. l.4.
p.335.
Malmesbur.
l.1.Pontif.p.
197.
VVeftm o-
naft. A.789.
Malmesb. l.
2.Reg. p. 47.
A. 804.
P.Honorlus
An.635.
Bed.l.3. c. 7.
Gadvv. in
vit. Birini.
P. Vitalian.
668.
Bed.lib.4. c.
1. 2. Gadvv.
in vit.Theo-
dori.
Antonin.tit.
14.c.4. para-
gr.14.Lazius
l. 3. de Cim-
merijs Ra-
mus & Poe-
ta German.
apud Cähd.
in Britan. p.
105. Polid.
lib. 5.

being driuen out of his kingdome & countrey, P. Leo 3. in the yeare 808. sent Card : Adalph his legate into England, who with the helpe of Charles the greats Embassadors, restored the King peaceablie vnto his kingdome. Not long after P. Leo 4. dispensed with King Ethelwal for to marry, which he being a Subdeacon could not do lawfullie : & at the same kings request crowned his sonne Alfred King, and adopted him for his sonne. who afterward, for his worthie deeds both in warre & peace was surnamed *the great*, and for al things became the rarest Prince that England (and perhaps Christendom) euer had. Soone after in the yeare 883. at the suite of the King Alfred, the great P. Martin 1. released the tribute which the English schoole or Seminary then in Rome paide, & sent to the King many guifts, among which was a good piece of the holie Crosse.

In the yeare 990, when Richard : Marques of Normandie had purposed

P. Leo 3. An. 808. Amoinus l. 4. c. 94. Regino in chron. Baron.808.

P. Leo 4. 855. Gathezelin in vit. S. Suithuni apud Sur. Baron. 855.

VVestmonast. 855. Baron, sup.

P. Martin. 1. 883. VVestmonast. & Baron. A. 883. Gadvvin in vit. Pleg-

b   to in-

P. Ihon. 15.
An.990.
Epift. apud
Malmesb. l.
2.Reg. c. 10.
Baron. An.
990.

P.Nicolas 2.
1059.
Epift. ad E-
duard. R. a-
pud Sur. in
vit.Eduardi.

P. Vrban. 2.
1094.
Malmesbur.
l.1.Pontif. p.
223.Gadvvin
in vit. An-
felmi.

Malmesbur.
fup. p. 208.
209.

to inuade England, and make warre
vpon king Ethelred, P. Iohn 15. fent
his Nuntio and letters to take vp the
matter, who happilie brought them to
agreement: and about the yeare 1059.
P. Nicolas the fecond granted to king
Edward Conff. and his fucceffors, *ad-
uocationem & tuitionem omniū totius An-
gliæ Ecclefiarum*, the aduouzon & pro-
tection of al the Churches in Englād.
And in the yeare 1094. P. Vrban 2. in
a councel at Bari, appointed that S.
Anfelme Archbishop of Canterburie
and his fucceffors fhould fit in Councels befides the Archdeacon cf Rome,
who fitteth before the P. adding thefe
honourable words *Includamus hunc in
orbe noftro tanquam alterius orbis Papam*,
wheras before it was vnknowne (faith
Malmesbury) what place belonged
to our Archibishop; & the fame place
did P. Pafchal 2. confirme in a councel at Rome about the yeare 1102. But
befids this, diuers other dignities haue
bene graunted to the Sea of Canturb:
by the Popes, as that it fhould be Pri-
mate

mate ouer al Britany, and the B : *legati nati*, and other like dignities.

Polid.lib. 19. Gadvvin in vit. Theo-baldi.

Moreouer in the yeare. 1098. the Scottiſh men (ſaith Genebrard out of Maior & Boethius two Scottiſh Chroniclers) obtained of P. Vrban 2. for their Prince, that he might haue the name, title, and anointment of a king (which the Hungarians and Polonians had obtained for their Princes, about the yeare 1000.) whereupon Edgar was then firſt anointed King of Scotland. And about 1107. P. Paſcal 2. writing to king Henry 1. among other things promiſeth ſo to fauor him and his ſonne, *as vvho* (ſaith he) *hurteth you or him may ſeeme to haue hurt the Church of Rome.* And in the yeare 1152. when K. Steephen (hauing vſurped the Crowne of England) would haue cauſed the Biſhops to Crowne his ſône Euſtace, thereby to exclude for euer the right heyre Henry 2. Pope Eugenius 3. ſent commaundement to the Cleargie not to medle in that matter, whereby it was hindered. In the yeare 1160.

Genebrard. chron. in Vrban. 2. Paſcali 2 Leone 9.

Baron. An. 1000.

P. Paſcal. 2. 1107. Malmesbur. lib. 5. Reg. p. 263.

P. Eugenius 3. An. 1152. Stovv An. 1152. Gadvvin in vit. Theobaldi.

P.Adrian. 4.
1160.
Stovv. An.
1160.

VVeſtmon.

P.Alexander
3.An. 1171.
Houeden.
p.1.Annal.p.
528. Polid.
lib. 13.
P.Lucius 3.
1185.
Houed.
p. 2. p. 628.

P.Vrban. 3.
An.1185.
part.2.p. 631.

Stovv. Ann.
1185.

P.Clement.
3.An.1189.
Hovved. p.
2. pag. 652.
VVeſtmo-
naſt.A. 1189.

1160. P. Adrian 4. gaue vnto King
Henrie 2. the dominion and regiment
of Ireland, and ſent vnto him the Bul
of his graunt with a ring of golde in
token of the inueſtiture : which graūt
at the requeſt of the ſaid K. P. Alexander 3. cōfirmed to him & his heyres.
And as for P.Lucius 3.ſucceſſor to the
ſaid Alexander, his good wil appeareth by the great praiſe which he giueth to our Engliſh kings, whom he
writeth to haue far exceeded the reſt
of Chriſtiā Princes in warlike prowes
and noblenes of minde. VVhich affection continued alſo in his ſucceſſor
P. Vrban 3. of whom (as Houeden
writeth) K : Henry 2. obtained many
things,whereof one was that he might
crowne which of his ſonnes he would
of the kingdome of Ireland, which he
confirmed by a bul,and in token of his
good wil & confirmation, ſent to him
a crowne. And laſtlie P. Clement the
third in the yeare 1189. when, not only
the French king, but alſo his ſonnes
and Nobles had conſpired againſt the
ſaid

said K: & inuaded his dominions with a far greater power then he was able to refist, sent a Cardinal to exhort them to peace, who excommunicated the hinderers of the peace, and threatned to interdict the French kings countrey vnles he made peace with England.

Likewise in the yeare 1193. when K: Richard Ceur de lyon was taken prifoner, as he came from the holie land by the Duke of Auftria, P. Celeftin 3. at the K:requeft excommunicated the D: and enioyned him to releafe the couenants which he had conftrayned the K: to make, and to fend home the pledges: who not obeying the Pope he foone after died miferablie, and was left vnburied vntil his fonne had fent home the pledges, and fworne to ftand to the iudgemēt of the Church. And in the yeare 1207. P. Innocent 3. fent to K: Iohn an eloquent Epiftle and diuers pretious Iewels. And in the yeare. 1215. when the Barons had extorted from the faid king certaine

P.Celeftin.3.
A. 1193.
VVeftmon.
Ann. 1193.
Stovv 1195.
Polid.l.14

P.Innocent.
3.An. 1207.
Stovv Ann.
1207.

char-

THE EPISTLE

charters and liberties, the P. at the Kings requeſt diſanulled them, and excōmunicated the Barons which had rebelled againſt him, & when the ſaid Barons had called in Lewis the Prince of France, choſen him their King, and yeelded the chiefeſt Citties & holdes into his hands, ſoe that England was in euident danger to be loſt, the P. ſent his Legate to aſſiſt kinge Iohn, and to forbid the French vpon paine of excōmunication to enter into England, which he ſtoutlie performed. Alſo in the yeare 1253. P. Innocent 4. beſtowed the Royal title and right of the kingdomes of Naples and Sicily vpon Edmond ſonne to K: Henry 3; and ſent by a Cardinal the inueſtiture thereof. And 1257. P. Alexander 4. ſent Meſſengers vnto Richard brother to the ſaid king, for to aſſure him of the Imperial dignity and to exhorte him to goe into Germany to receaue it, which he did, and was crowned king of Romans at Aquiſgran. And in the yeare *1292.* when the Barons had

Stovv 1195. 1296. 1297. Gadvvin in vit. Steph. Langton. Polid.lib.15. 16.

P.Innocent. 4.An.1253. Com in ventura nella relat.de Napoli. Polid. lib.16.Stovv A. 1254.

P. Alexander 4. Ann. 1257. VVeſtmon. An. 1259.

had wrested out of the said K. hands certaine liberties, P. Vrban 4. at the kings suite, sent a Legate to accurse the Barons that had rebelled in defence of the said liberties.

P. Vrban. A. 1262.
Stovv Ann. 1262.1264.

Againe in the yeare 1272. at the request of king Edward 1. P. Gregory 10. excommunicated Guy of Monfort for killing the kings Coosin German in a church at Viterbo, and condemned him of wilful and priuy murder, of Sacriledge and treason, declared him to be infamous, and incapable of any office in the commonwealth, and disherited his posterity vnto the fourth generation, and excommunicated al those that intertained him and interdicted their dominions. And in the same kings time was Cambridge of a schoole made an vniuersity by the P. & soone after in the yeare 1311. vnder king Edward the second P. Clement 5. appointed that in Oxford should be read two lectures of the Hebrew, Arabick, and Caldaick tongue, and authorized it for one of the famousest

P. Gregory 10. An. 1272.
VVestmon. An.1272. Polid.lib.17.

Cambden in descript. Cantabrig. p.435. ex Remington.
P. Clement. 5. 1311.
Clement.tit. de Magist. c. 1.

vniue-

P. Ihon. 22.
An. 1316.
Polid. lib. 17.
Stovv. An.
1316.

vniuerſities in Chriſtendome. Alſo in
the yeare 1316. P. Iohn 22. at K : Edward 2. his requeſt, ſent two Legates
to make peace betwixt England and
Scotland, and to reconcile Thomas
Earle of Lancaſter to the King, who
excommunicated the Scots, becauſe
they would not agree to peace. And
in the ſame yeare at the kings petitiő,
the P. confirmed al the ancient priuiledges of the vniuerſity of Cambridge,
which of long time they had enioyed

Stovv. 1317.

by the benefit (writeth Stow) *of the*
Popes predeceſſors.

P. Innocent.
8. A. 1489.
Stovv. Ann.
1486.

Moreouer in the yeare 1489. Pope
Innocent the eight ſent a Nuntio to
take vp the variance betwixt the King
of Scotland and his people, but before his arriual the King was ſlaine.
And about the yeare 1504. when there
aroſe a contention betwene K : Henry
7. & Ferdinand King of Spaine about

P. Iulio 2. A.
1504.
Valaterran.
Comin ven-
tura.
Stovv ib.

the precedence, P. Iulius 2. hauing
heard both their Embaſſadors gaue
ſentence for the King of England.
And in the yeare 1505. ſent to the ſaid
King

King a sword & Cap of maintenance, as to a defendor of the Church. But as no King of Englād deserued better of the Sea Apostolick then K: Henry 8. did for a long time, so none receaued more honor from thence then he did. For he receaued not only from P. Iulius 2. in the yeare 1514. a sword and Cap of maintenance, for defending him against the French king; But also of Pope Leo 10. in the yeare 1521. the most honourable title of *Defendor of the faith*, for defendig by writing the Catholique faith against Luther. VVhich title as it is more honorable then the titles of most Christian, or Catholique, giuen likewise by Popes to the French K: and K. of Spaine: so was it euer highlie estiemed of K. Henry, and by him caused to be engrauen on his tombe, where he left the title out of his Supremacie.

And though Q. Elizabeth had vtterly cast of the Popes friendship, yet he forsooke not hir. For Pius 4. supposing that she had reuolted from that

Sea,

Stovv 1514.

P.Leo 10. A. 1521.
Stovv A.1521
Onuphr.
chron.1520.

Stovv did see it. An. 1547.

P. Pius 4. A. 1560.

Sea, rather for feare left her title to the crowne might be called in queftion, becaufe one P. had before declared her birth, to be vnlawful, then for diflike of the religion which in her father and fifters daies fhe had profeffed, fent a Nuntio to promife her al fauor touching her title to the crowne: And foone after an other, to requeft her to fend her diuines to the Councel of Trent with promife of al fecurity and liberty. Neither may I leaue your Maieftie out of the number of the Princes of this land, who haue tafted the loue & frindfhip of the Sea Apoftolike: Becaufe out of your owne grateful mind, you haue publiquely profeffed, your felfe behoulding vnto P. Clement 8. for his temporal carriadge, and diuers kinde offices towards your Maieftie. Befides he hath (as it is reported) cenfured al fuch as fhal moleft your grace, and hath often times profeffed that he would willinglie giue his life for the eternal good of our countrey. VVhich is the greateft loue that one can beare

(as our

Margin notes:

1560.

1562.

P. Clement. 8. 1603.

Proclamat. A.1.regni.

(as our Sauiour teftifieth) vnto his friend. Oh how great enimies are they vnto England, who feeke by falfe flaunders to make fuch freinds odious vnto vs.

By this which hath bene faid (omitting much more for breuity) your Maieftie clearlie feeth, how greatlie and how continually the Sea Apoftolique hath euer fauored the Chriftian Princes of this land : how many and how great benefits both fpiritual and temporal, Popes haue beftowed vpon them, and in their dangers and diftreffes according to their power affifted them. VVeigh (I befeech your grace) in the ballance of your Princely wifdome, the forfaid benefits, with fuch as your felfe or Auncitors haue receaued from the reft of Chriftendom, and *Popes haue* you fhal finde that the Sea Apofto- *benefited* licke alone, hath more benifyted En- *then al* gland, then al Chriftendom befides, *Chriftendo-* and confequentlie that the forfaking *me befyds.* of the Popes friendfhip hath more endammaged your Realme, then if it

had

had forsaken the rest of Christendom. But especiallie (I humblie beseech your Maiestie) weigh them with such as Bel, or any minister can shew you to haue receaued, from their two seats of pestilence in witenberge and Geneua. VVhat kingdomes haue they bestowed vpon you? vnto what imperial or Royal dignity haue they exalted you? from what Paganisme haue they conuerted your land? what enimies haue they appeased? what assistance haue they afforded you in any need? what good, litle or great haue they brought to this land? Now what mischeefe haue they not brought? That one Apostata, and fierbrand of seditiõ Knox, sent from Geneua, brought more mischiefe to your Grandmother, your B. mother, to your father, and Kingdom of Scotland, then I can rehearse, or your Maiestie without great griefe can remember. Ministers pretend the loue of the Ghospel, as the cause of persuading you from friendship with the Pope: But yet

Bel in his owne iudgemēt vvas both an Apostata and Traiter vvhiles he vvas Preist.

disswa-

diſſwade not from friendship with the Turke. They pretend alſo your graces ſecurity: But the true cauſe indeed your Maieſtie deſcried & diſcouered in Knox, to wit their owne ſecurity & aduaūcement, which they fear would be endangered, if you kept your ancient, and ſureſt friend, and therefore with your loſſe (as your maieſtie perceaued in your Grandmothers caſe) they worke their owne wealth and ſecurity. And thus much of the Popes.

See Conſer. at Hampton Court. p.80.81.

As for the Chriſtian Princes of this land, though they haue bene of foure different, and moſt oppoſite nations, to wit Britons, Engliſh, Danes, and Normans, yet haue they al agreed in keeping the league of friendſhip with the Pope, being officious vnto him, & accoūting him their eſpecial friend. Of the British kings of this land firſt is King Lucius, whoſe particular affection towards the Sea Apoſtolick, is euident, by that he neglecting other Chriſtian Churches neare vnto him, he ſent ſo far as to Rome for Preachers.

The laue & benefits of the Britiſh Kings to the Sea Apoſtolik. Note this.

K. Lucius A. 156. Beda lib. i. c. 4.

chers. As for Conftantin the great (the immortal glory of the Britifh kings) his extraordinary loue and affection vnto the Sea of Rome is more notorious then I need rechearfe. For he not only gaue vnto the Pope the gouernment of Rome, and of a good parte of the weft (as befides him felfe, and Latin hiftoriographers, both Greecks and Iewes profeffed enimies to the Pope do teftifie) but alfo ferued him as a lackey houlding his ftirrop and leading his horfe by the bridle. Cadwallader alfo the laft Britifh king in England, hauing lefte his countrey went no whither but to Rome, and there ended his daies. And if the hiftories of thofe anciét times were more perfect, or the Britons had raigned longer in this Iland, no doubt but we fhould haue more examples of their deuotion to the Sea of Rome, as appeareth by Salomon their King in litle Britany, after they had bene driuen hence by the Saxons; who writing to Pope Adrian

drian the second beginneth his letter thus. *Domino ac beatiſſimo Apoſt: ſedis Rom: Hadriano, Salomon Britanorum Rex flexis genibus inclinatoque capite.* And ſendeth him his ſtatua in gold, with diuers rich guiſts and money, promiſeth a yearlie penſion, and acknowledgeth his Royal title to haue bene giuen to him by Popes. This was the loue of the British kings vnto the Sea Apoſtolike.

To the Britiſh kings ſucceeded the Saxons or English, as wel in their loue and reuerence to the Sea of Rome, as in their kingdome. For king Ethelbert at the very firſt receaued S. Gregory his Legats very courteouſlie, prouided them of al things neceſſary, and freelie licenſed them to preach, vſing theſe gratious words worthie to be imitated of your Maieſtie in the like caſe. *For ſo much as you are come ſo far to impart vnto vs ſuch knovvledge as you take to be true, vve vvil not trouble you, but rather vvithal courteſie receaue you.* After him king Oſwin hauing

The loue & benefits of the English Kings.
K. Ethelbert An.596.
Beda lib. 1. c. 25.

K. Oſwin. A.665.

uing perfectly learned that the Church of Rome (saith S. Beda) was the Catholique and Apostolicke Church, sent thither in the yeare 665. a Priest to be consecrated Archbishop of Canterbury. And in a conference about the obseruation of Easter, hearing that the keies of heauen were giuen to S. Peter, concluded thus. *I vvil not gaine say such a Porter as this is, but as far as I knovv and am able, I vvil couet in al points to obey his ordinance. And in the* yeare 670 *he bare* (saith S. Bede) *such loue and affection to the Apostolike Sea of Rome, as if he might haue eskaped his sicknes, he purposed to goe to Rome, and to end his life in those holie places there.*

But what he could not through death performe, the valiant Prince King Cedwalla did in the very flour of his age and prosperity. For in the yeare 689. *forsaking his kingdome* (saith S. Beda) *he vvent to Rome, thinking it to be a singular glory, and renovvme for him to be regenerated vvith the Sacrament of Baptisme at the Sea Apostolicke. And vvith-*

Lib. 5. c. 19.

Bed. lib. 3. c. 25. Bar. An. 664.

Lib. 4. cap. 5.

K. Cedualla. An. 689.

Beda lib. 5. c. 7.

vvithal conceaued hope, that as soone as by baptisme he vvas cleansed from sinne, he should depart from this vvorld to immortal ioy. VVhich by Gods prouidence was perfourmed, and he honourablie buried by the Pope in S. Peters Church. Not long after him, to wit in the year 709. two English Kings Coenred and Offa forsooke their kingdomes, went to Rome, and there became Moncks, *continuing (saith S. Beda) at the Apostles tombes in praying, fasting, & dealing almes vntil their dying day.* Ina al. Hun successor to K. Cedwal in his kingdome, succeeded him also in his deuotion to the Sea Apostolike, *for after he had raigned (saith S. Beda) 37. years he gaue ouer his kingdome, & vvent him selfe to the tombs and monuments of the Apostles in Rome, as in those daies many English both of the Nobility and Commons, spiritual and temporal men and vvoemen vvere vvont to doe vvith great emulation.* Neither went he only to Rome, but became there a Monke, and was the first that paied the Peter pence, appointing that euery

K. Coenred and Offa. 709.

Lib.5.cap.10. Baron. 709. Huntingt. l. 4.p.137.Malmesb.t.re3. c.6.Marian. chro.VVestmonast.710. Sigeb.707. Polid.lib.4. Fox.l.2.
K. Ina. An. 716.
Lib.5. cap.7. Baron. 716. Ethelvvead l.1.c.13.Huntingt. l. 4. p. 358. Malmesbur.l. 1. Marian. chron. Stovv 685. Fox. l. 2.
VVestmon. An. 727. Geneb.741.Polid. lib. 4. Stovvv in Ina.

c   house-

householder of his kingdome, who had thirty penyworth of Cattel of one fort, fhould pay yearlie one penny to Rome: which money was partlie for the P. partlie for the maintenance of an Englifh fchoole or Seminary which he then built in Rome for bringing vp of Englifh youths there in vertue and learning.

Not long after about the 750. yeare S. Richard K. forfooke his kingdome, & leauing his two fonnes in Germany with S. Boniface an Englifhman the Popes Legate there, went him felfe in Pilgrimage to R. but dying in the way at Luca is there honourablie buried. And the yeare 775. King Offa though a warlike Prince, gaue ouer his kingdome, went to Rome, and there became a Monke: and imitating the example of King Ina, increafed the Englifh Seminary begun by him, and impofed the like penfion of Peter pence vpon his kingdome of Mercia: as Charles the great about the fame time impofed vpon France the like tribute

to be

Marginal notes:

English Seminary in Rome almoft 900. years agoe.

VVeftmon. A.727.794.

S. Richard K.A.750. Sur. 7. Februar. Baron. 750.

K. Offa An. 775. Fox l.z. Martyr.

See Malmefbur. l. 2. reg. c.2.p.38. VVeftmon. An.794. Bar. 775 Polid. l. 4 Hunting. l.4.p.342. Greg. 7 l.8. ep ft vlt.Baron.A.782.

to be paid to Rome. The loue and affection of King Kenulph, a worthie Prince, and succeſſor to King Offa, appeareth by his redeeming the Popes Legate taken of Pirats in the yeare 808. and by his ſubmiſſiue letter to the Pope, wherin he humblie craueth his bleſſing, as al his predeceſſors had, deſireth to be adopted for his ſonne, as *I* (ſaith the King) *loue you like a father, & embrace you vvith al obedience.* And proteſted to be willing to ſpend his life for the Pope.

K. Kenulph. An.808.
Annal. Fran. Baron.808.
Malmesbur. 1.Reg.c.4. p. 30. 33.

After him King Ethelwolph in the yeare 855. went to Rome, tooke with him his beſt beloued ſonne Alfred, for to be inſtructed (ſaith weſtmonaſter) *of the Pope in manners and religion,* where he abode a whole yeare, and procured his ſonne to be crowned of the Pope and adopted of him for his ſonne, he alſo notablie repaired the Engliſh Seminary at Rome, which had bene burnt a litle before, and confirming guifts of K. Ina, and Offa, impoſed the penſion of Peter pence vpon al England,

K. Ethelvvolph. An. 855.
VVeſtmon.
Baron. 855.
Ethelvverd lib. 3. cap. 3. Stovv Ingulphus.

Malmesb. l. 2.cap. 2.p.38. Stovv Ann. 839.

Malmesbur. ſup. Marian. 877. Platina in Leone 4.

land, which was afterward paid vntil the later end of K: Henry 8. About the same time King Burdred leauing his kingdome went to Rome, and was there buried in the English schoole. Neither would King Canute, though a Dane be found vngrateful to the Sea Apoſt: but went to Rome in the yeare 1032. confirmed the payment of the Peter pence, gaue great guifts of golde ſiluer, and pretious things to S. Peter, & obtayned of Pope Iohn immunity for the Engliſh Seminary. And finally K. Edward Conf: the laſt but one of the Saxon bloud, would haue gone to Rome in Pilgrimage, had not his people vpon feare of the Danes inuaſion hindred him, yet ſent he Embaſſadors to the Pope with great preſents, and confirmed al the dueties & cuſtomes belonging to him in England. And thus continewed the Engliſh Kings al the time of their raigne in ſingular affection, and deuotion to the Sea Apoſtolicke.

To whom as the Norman Princes
ſuc-

K. Burdred.
Ethelvvead
l 4. c. 3. Mal
micsb. l. 1. c.
4. p. 33. In-
gulph.
Stovv 875.
K. Ganute a
Dane 1032.
Malmesb. l.
2. cap. 1. In-
gulph. Po-
lid. l 7. Hun-
tingt. lib 6.
Stovv in Ca-
uute. Ma-
rian. A. 1033.

K. Eduard.
Conf. A 1.
1056.
Ealred in
vit. eius.

The loue &
benefits of
the Normā
Kings.

succeeded, so they followed them in their piety and religion. For beside that they paid the Peeter pence, in particular K. william Conqueror hauing subdued England, and slaine K. Herald in the yeare 1066. sent straight his standard to the Pope, as to his peculiar friend. And K. Henry 1. professed by his Embassadour to P. Paschal 2. that England was *a peculiar prouince of the Church of Rome, and paid vnto her yearlie tribute.* King Henry 2. about the yeare 1180. together with Lewis King of France ledde P. Alexanders horse, and with great pompe conducted him through the Citty Tociacum. K. Richard Ceur de Lion at the exhortation of the P. went in person to the holy land, with an army of 30. thowsand foote, and fiue thowsand horse: in which voiage he conquered the kingdome of Ciprus, & citty of Ptolemais, and ouerthrew the Souldan in a great battel; and the like enterprise afterward vndertooke K. Edward the first in the yeare 1241. King Henry 3. placed

K. VV. Conqueror. An. 1066. Stovv in Herald.

K. Henry 1. Malmesb. l. 1. Pont. p. 116.

K. Henry 2. An. 1180. Genebr. in chron. 1180.

K. Richard 1. Polid. lib. 14. Genebr. 118. Stovv.

K. Henry 2. An. 1241. Stovv An. 1241.

c 3

placed the Popes Legate in the moſt honourable roome of the table at a publique banquet in Chriſt-maſſe betwixt him ſelfe and the Archebiſhop of yorke : And afterward *vvith great pompe* (ſaith Stowe) *and innumerable company of Nobles, and trumpets ſounding before, brought him to the Sea.* How deuout K. Richard 2. and Engliſhmen in his time were to the Sea of Rome, appeareth by their building an hoſpital there, for receit of Engliſh Pilgrims (inſteed of the foreſaid Seminary which as it ſeemeth was deſtroyed in that great burning of Rome in the yeare 1084) in the place where S. Thomas of Canturbury had before built a chappel in honor of the B. Trinity. This hoſpital was afterward in the raigne of K. Henry 6. and Henry 7. reedified, and much encreaſed, and laſtlie in the yeare 1570, was much bewtifyed and augmented both in buildings and reuenews by P. Gregory 13. and by him conuerted to the auncient vſe of a Seminary, retayning ſtil the obli-

K. Richard 2. Stovv An. 1407.

the obligation of an hospital.

The affection of K. Henry 4. ap-peareth by his letter to the Pope A. 1409. which he beginneth thus. *Most holy father our humble recommendations in filial vvise premised.* And afterward, *hauing taken vvith our said sonne, and also vvith our Prelats and Nobles mature deli-beration, vve beseech vvith al humility & require your clemency (vvhose state and honor vpon diuers causes as a deuout sonne of the Church so far as vve might vvith God, vve haue euer embraced and do em-brace) by the expresse and vvhole assent of the estates aforesaid &c.* And as for King Henry 5. he in the yeare 1416. sent his Embassadors to the general Councel at Constance, at whose procurement *it vvas there ordained that England (* saith Stowe*)should obtaine the name of a nation & be said one of the fiue Nations that ovve their deuotiõ to the Church of Rome, vvhich thing vntil that time men of other Nations for enuie had letted.* Behould what an honor K. Henry 5. the Alexander of England, and Conqueror of France,

K. Henry 4. A. 1409. Stovv Ann. 1409.

K. Henry 5. An. 1416. Stovv Ann. 1416.

Note this.

c 4   and

and England in his moſt floriſhing &
triumphant time, accoūnted it to owe
deuotion to the Church of Rome.
VVhich now Miniſters would accoūt
ſo diſhonourable. And as for K. Henry
7. your Maieſties great grandfather,
his affection is euident by the ſword
and cup of maintenance ſent to him
from the Pope, & ſpoken of before.

But none of the kings of the Norman bloud euer ſhewed ſo great ſignes
of loue & affection to the Sea Apoſtolike as K. Henry 8. did for a long time
for firſt in the yeare 1511. he wrate to
the French K. to deſiſt ſrom moleſting
Pope Iulius 2. and in the next yeare
ſent an army of ten thouſand men into
France for the Popes defence. And in
the yeare 1513. wēt him ſelfe in perſon
with a royal army & conquered Tur-
win and Turnay. And not content to
defend the Pope with his ſword , in
the yeare 1521. wrate an excellēt booke
in his defence againſt Luther. And
againe in the yeare. 1527. when Pope
Clement 7. was taken priſoner by the
Empe-

K. Henry 7.
An. 1505.

K. Henry 8.
A. 1511. 1521.
Stovv 1511.
1512. 1513. O-
nuphr. in
Iul. 2.

Stovv An.
1521.

Emperors souldiers, he gaue moneth- Stovv An. 1532.
lie 60. thowsand Angels to the maintenance of an armie, for the Popes deliuery. And in this singular affection
towards the Sea Apostolik contine-
wed he vntil the 22. yeare of his raigne Stovv 1530. & deinceps.
An. 1530. when not vpon any iniury
offered by the P. or dislike of his religion, which (except the matter of supremacy) he defended to his death,
and persecuted the Protestants , but
only *vpon occasion of delaie* (saith Stowe)
made by the Pope in his controuersie of de-
uorcement, and through displeasure of such
reports, as he heard had bene made of him
to the court of Rome , and thirdlie pricked
forvvards by such counsellers to follovv the
example of the Germanes , he first forbad
the procurement of any thing from
Rome, and soone after prohibited al
payments and appeales to Rome, and
lastlie tooke vpon him that supremacy
which al his Christian predecessors
had acknowledged to be in the
Pope.

Thus your Maiestie seeth how long,
how

how honourablie, and how profitablie also vnto both parties, hath the mutual amity and league of friendship, betwixt the Sea Apost. and the Princes of al the foure Nations, that haue swaied the Scepter of England continewed and flourished: & how of late it was broken by one Prince vpon meere passion, contrary to the example of al his Predecessors and Successors also, except one childe and a woeman. VVhat dangers and troubles he and his kingdome incurred thereby, and how his progeny (according as Frier Pœto did then foretel him) is now consumed, and his Crowne translated to an other Royal lyne, against which in his time he made sharpe war, I need not heere declare. Only I wil say, that him selfe being after more free from passion, laboured to be reconciled to the Sea Apostolike and employed therein B. Gardener (as he professed in a sermon at Paules Crosse) and had easelie obtained it, if he would haue acknowledged his

fault

fault and done penance. VVhat remaineth for me to conclude this
long epiftle, but proftrate at your Maiefties feet humblie to befeech you
for your owne good, and in the name
of the forefaid Chriftian Princes, that
as you are the head of the fieft Nation, which (according to Gods pro-
uidence foretolde by a holy man Hunting.l.6, p. 359.
many hundred years agoe) hath attai-
ned to the rule of this land , fo you
would continew that moft auncient,
honourable, and proffitable league
of friendfhip , which was betwixt
them al and the Sea Apoftolicke;who
(I befeech your grace) wil giue you
more faithful councel , then your
owne Progenitors and forefathers?
who can giue you more fafe and fe-
cure directiō in gouernement of your
kingdome , then your owne Prede-
ceffors, who foe happily, and fo long
time gouerned it? who are fo worthie
to giue you example, or whom can
you with fo much honor imitate, as
fo many, fo valiant, fo prudent Princes?

ces? and yet they al with one voice, counsel and request you, to follow in this so importāt a matter, not so much them selues, as the councel of the wisest King that euer was, yea of God himselfe in these words. *Thine ovvne* *friend and thy fathers friend see thou for-* *sake not*, especiallie such a one, as hath euer bene not only your owne friend, and particularly your B. mothers friend, but of al your Christian 'forefathers. VVho as they haue lefte vnto your grace their Crowne and kingdome; so haue they also bequeathed their faith religion & friendship with the Sea Apostolick, as no smal portion and stay of their inheritance. VVe e-stieme your publique acknowledging of Rome to be the Mother Church, and your selfe to be behoulding to P. Clement 8. *for his temporal cariadge and* *kinde offices*, as sparks of a greater fyer of loue inkindled in ycur Princely hart towards that Sea, which we be-seech almighty God so `to increase, as it may one day burst forth to your

owne

Prouerb.
27.

owne good, and the vniuerſal ioy of
Chriſtendome. Our Lord Ieſus long
preſerue your Maieſtie with al grace,
health, and proſperity

Your Maieſties dutiful Subiect
and daily Oratour.

S. R.

S no water (Christian Reader) waxeth so could, as that which hath bene once hot: no enemies become so cruel to a common wealth, as Rebels who haue bene once subiect: So none are so eager aduersaries to Gods Church as Apostataes, who heue once bene her members, and children. Amongst Heretikes none more earnest against the Apostles then the first Apostata Simon Magus, who dared to encounter hand to hand with the principal Apostle S. Peter, and labored to seduce by his magik, whom he by myracles had conuerted. Amongst the Tyrants, and persecutors none more cruel then Iulian the Apostata, who by blood endeuored to wash away his Christendom, and both by sword, & pen laboured al he could, not only to extinguish the religion, but also the very name, and memory of Christians. Amongst Philosophers none more vehement then Porphyry the Apostata, who writ fifteen books against Christian religion, and for his

S. Maximus serm. de Apost.

S. Hieron. de Scriptor. in Petro.

Baron. Annal. An.68.

Nazianz. orat. 1. in Iulian.
Theodoret. lib.3.c.21.

Porphirius & Iulian. rabidi in Christum canes.
Hieron.

his singuler hatred therof was syrnamed *tou Christianon polemios* the Christians aduersary. And in these our miserable daies none haue bene so spiteful, so malicious, so vehement againt Catholiques ether in persecuting, speaking, or writing, as they who haue bene once Catholiques. And in England now none sheweth him selfe, so forward, or so vehement againt Catholiques as the Apostata Bel, daring, challenging and adiuring al Papists iointly, and seuerally to the combat with him, being desirons as it seemeth of the tytle of *ton catholicon polemios*. The Catholiques aduersary.

These Apostaraes be like to him, who being deliuered of one diuel, the house clensed with beesoms and trimmed vp, was afterward possessed with seauen diuels worse then the former, and his end made worse then his beginning. For such is the estate of this miserable caitiue Bel, who being once deliuered from the diuel of Heresy, clensed with the beesom of confession, and Penance, and trimmed with patient sufferance for the Catholique faith, falling afterward to idlenes, and dissolute life, wherof him self since hath boasted, is possessed again of his old diuel of Heresy accompained with seuen other wicked sprits of blasphemy, railing, pride, slaundering,

Luc. 11. v. 25. 26.

See S. Ireney lib. 1. c. 13.

dering, lying, diſſembling, and abuſing of Gods and holy Fathers words, and his end becomme far worſe then his beginning was. His ſpirit of blaſphemy he deſcryeth in many places as p.149. where he ſaith that *God hath giuen vs thoſe commandements which we can not poſsibly keep.* This the holy Father S. Hierom both calleth, and accurſeth as blaſphemy in theſe words. *VVe curſe their blaſphemy who ſay that God hath commanded to man any impoſsible thing.* And no ,maruel. For what reaſon can ther be in God to command a thing which he knoweth can not be done? what fault in vs not to do that which can not be done? what iuſtice in him to punish, and that with eternal death, the not performance of that which can not be performed? If neuer there was man ſo void of reaſon as would commãd a thing, which he knew could not be done, neuer Tyrant ſo cruel as wold punish with temporal death the vnperformance of impoſsible matters, shal we think it no blaſphemy to God, to atttribute that to him which we can not imagin that any man who hath any ſpark of reaſon, or humanity wold attempt? Hauing thus blaſphemed againſt God no meruail if he blaſpheme againſt his Church of late daies ſaying. p. 134. that she is no ſufficient witnes of his truth, & p. 41.

S.Hieron. e-piſt. ad Da-maſc. de expoſi.ione fidei.

Quod ratio-nem non habet dici non debuit. S.Eugenius apud Victo-rem de per-ſecut. van-dal, l. 2.

againſt

againſt our iuſtification calling it *ſuppoſed holy* wherby he giueth vs to vnderſtand that as he is fallen from God and his Church, and loſt holy iuſtification, ſo he is an enemy to them al.

His railing ſpirit he could ſo il maiſter, as in the very firſt period of his epiſtle to the King, without reſpect of his Maieſtie he muſt needs cal vs *the curſed brood of traiterous Ieſuits,* and ſtreight after ſpeaking *ex abundantia cordis,* and reuiling eſpecially againſt the Ieſuits, who haue bene his maiſters, he auoucheth them to be *traiterous, ſeditious, brutiſh, barbarous, cruel, villanous, moſt bloody, treacherous, prowd, cruel, tyrants, firebrands of al ſedition, theeues, murderers, right Macheuels, cooſiners, malicious, and dependers vpon the diuel.* And of this Rhetorik I expect good ſtore for my part, but the more the merrier, ſuch reprochful terms in this quarrel ſhal be to me *ſuper millia auri, & argenti.* His pride is more notorious then I need ſhew it. For if it were pride in Golias though a Gyant to challenge any of Gods hoſte, what is it in this puny, not only to challenge, but to adiure al Papiſts ſeuerally and iointly, being him ſelfe not worthy to cary the books after many of them, as ſhal appeare by his manifold ignorance, not only in deuinity, but alſo euen in Latin, principles of Logik,

Epiſtle to the King.

See the Index.

d   Hiſto-

Histories, and Preaching, as shal be made manifest in this anſwer.

pag: 17. His ſlaūders reach euen from the higheſt to the loweſt, Kings and Emperours he ſlaundereth with no les matter then ope-Bels ingra-ning the window to al Antichriſtian ty-titude.ranny. Popes (who long tyme manteined p. 16. 40. him at ſchool) with challēging powre equal 106. to God, with diſpenſing with one to marry his ful ſiſter, with burning the Scriprure, p. 22. and the like. And Papiſts he ſlaundereth with killing Chriſt a thouſand tymes a day, with affirming that the Pope can depoſe p. 1. Kings and Emperors, and tranſlate their Empires and regalities at his good wil and pleaſure, with attributing to the Pope p. 16. powre equal to God, thinking the breach p. 130. of Lent to be a greater ſin then adultery periury, or murder. His other three ſpirits, of lying, diſſembling, and abuſing Gods word euery where ſhew them ſelues in his books, and now and then are noted in my anſwer.

No maruel therfore if one poſſeſſed of ſo many, and ſo wicked ſpirits be ſo forward, ſo ſpiteful, ſo malicious, againſt Catholiques, as to callenge, & adiure them al iointly or ſeuerally to the combat with him. Oh that it would pleaſe his Maieſtie to admit this combat, that Bel, & I (the weakeſt of many

of many thousands of Gods soldiers) might
try the truth, not by writing, which blu-
sheth not (as Tully said) but face to face as
the Bishop of Eureux, and Plessy did before
the French King. I doubt not but if there
were any blood in Bels body, or any shame
of men in his minde, I shold make it appeare
in his face. But whiles this combat must be
fought a far of, only by paper shot, and writing and our writings kept from the view
of the people, no meruail if Bel feare no
shame of men, whiles they may see him
fight, & florish, but must not behold ether
defence or blowes of his aduersary.

If he be so confidét in his Heresy (which
he once vomited forth, and now like the
dog hath lickt vp again) as he maketh shew
of, why hath he not in al this tyme of his
Apostasy procured lycence for publike dis-
putation? or at left, why neuer repaired he
to the Catholique Priests in prison? Let
him procure but one such safe conducte
for Priests as the councel of Trent graunted Sess. 13. 15.
three or fowre to Protestants (when none 18.
of our English Ministers durst accept it)
& he shal not need to challenge, or adiure,
but shal be dared at his owne dore. For
Priests who willingly spend their blood in
testimony of the truth which they teach,
wil far sooner spend their breath in defence
therof,

therof, & are ready (to make the like offer
as Bel doth in a different matter) to iustify
it before indifferent iudges against him, or
what Protestant soeuer vpon peril of their
liues, if their aduersaries wil aduenture the
like peril. And vpon this condition Bel I
challenge thee, and adiure thee, accept it if
thou darest. What more could haue bene
done to bring this so weighty a matter,
wherupon dependeth the eternal saluation
of so many millions of soules to tryal face
to face, then hath bene done of Catholiques
by speaking, by writing, by petition, by
supplication ? Puritans vpon one only supplication haue bene admitted to Conference, Catholiques can vpon none. And
this is that which maketh Bel so bold to
challeng vs to the open combat, when he
knoweth we can not appeare in open shew,
but vpon hazard of our liues. And I wold
to God that with danger, yea with losse of
life we might be lycéced publikly to try this
truth so important to the eternal life of our
dearest countrimen. But seeing there is no
hope of this, when I red Bels challenge it
seemed to me not only an vnlearned thing,
patcht vp of obiections gathered out of Bellarmin, and learnedly answered by him, but
a witles challenge of some coward, who
seeing his enemy commanded vpon pain of
death

death to keep his house, callengeth him to the open field, and more like to condemne the Author of folly, and vanity; then the Catholique religion of falsity before any discreet, & iudicious Reader. Neuertheles because (as I vnderstood some monthes after the publishing of it) some vnaduised Protestants hearing Bels glorious vaunts and challeng, had conceaued great hope of this their Champion, & thought his booke vnaswerable, I took it in hand not knowing as then that any other wold vouchsafe to medle with it, & haue left to my knowledg no one point therin vnanswered, attending more to solue what he obiecteth, then to cōfirme what Catholikes mantein, though this also I haue done sufficiently (as I hope) for my intended breuity. *Author of the Fore-runner of Bels dovv-nefal.*

He termeth this challeng a downfal of Popery and yet in the greatest part therof impugneth no point of Popery, but ether perticuler opinions of priuat men, or (which is worse) false imputations of his owne, being so desirous of quarrelling, as he figh-teth with his owne shadow. And what he impugneth he doth with so good successe, as almost in euery Article he ouerthroweth what he meant to establish, and confirme. So that if he had giuen his booke the right name he shold haue called it the downfal of *VVhat Bel impugneth.* *VVith vvhat suc-cese.*

d 3   Bels

Bels foolery. Of these eight Articles which he hath pickt out as most aduantagious for him self, & in which there are some things, which as S. Austin speaketh l. de vtil. cred. c. 1. to. 6. *may be impugned to the common peoples capacity, but not be defended by reason of their difficulty but of few*. In the first he impugneth the Popes superiority ouer al Princes on earth, and his powre to depose them at his good wil, and pleasure. wherof the first is but the opinion of some few Canonists commonly reiected of al Catholiks, and disproued at large by Bellarmin, whose doctrine Bel accounteth the Popes owne doctrin, & saith it is approued by him. The second no Catholik holdeth, but it is Bels faulse slaunder of Catholiks. In the second omitting the question of the being of Christs body in the blessed sacrament, he impugneth the being of his quantity therein as a thinge (saith he) held of al papists as an article of their faith, which is vntrue, as is declared in the answer. In the third he inueigheth against the Popes powre to dispense in matrimony before it be consummated, which likwise is an opinion of Canonists, & commonly refuted of Catholik deuines. In the fift omittinge true merit which is a point of faith, he impugneth condigne merit as a thinge defined by the Councel of Trent which

s. Austin.

pag: 1.

p: 19.

pag: 37.

p: 75.

which it is not. In the seuenth Article in
steede of Traditions conteining things necessary for mans saluation, which in the
beginning of the article he proposed to impugne, he impugneth an erronious opinion *p. 131. 132.*
of Papias about Chrifts reigne after his iud- *133.*
gement, and an other of S. Ireney about
Chrifts age, one history about Zachary S.
Ihon Baptifts father, & an other concerning
Conftätins baptifme, a probable opinion of
Popes priuate teaching the same doctrin
with S. Peter, and an other concerning our
Ladies Coception without fin. In the eight
he oppugneth the keeping of Gods com-
mandments in fuch a fenfe as no Catholik
dreameth of. So that though he had flong
down al thefe matters, yet ther had bene no
downfal of Popery. Is not this fellow think
you a iolly challenger of Papifts? a goodly
downfeller of Popery? Is not he one of thos *1. Timoth. 1*
of whom S. Paul faith willinge to be Do-
ctors of the law, know nether what they
fay, nor of what.

But if we marke the fucceffe which this
Champion hath, whiles he yet florisheth
by him felf, before his aduerfary enter the
field, and like Vergils Bul. *AEneid.*
12.

    ---- *beates the winde withal his might*
And cafting fand doth florish to the fight.
it is admirable. For, omitting particuler co-

tradi-

tradictions, almost in euery Article he flin-
geth down the very main point which he
wold establish. As art. 1. he wold proue that
the Pope hath no superiority ouer Princes,
nor power to depose them: and yet affirmeth that *some Kings, and Emperors haue hum-*
bled them selues, yeelded their soueraign rights to
him, and that Popes liued in duetiful obedience
vnder Emperors vntil the year 603. which he
proueth by S. Gregory, and yet no les then
six Popes did in that tyme excommunicate
their Emperors, & S. Gregory was the first
that decreed the deposition of Kings and
Princes. In the second article after he had
talked long against the real presence and sacrifice of the Masse he falleth to cal the *sa-*
crificing of (Christs) *flesh with Preists hands,*
golden words, and to say that *if we wold be*
iudged by a doctrin of Bellarmins, (which a litle
before he had said was the Popes doctrin)
the controuersy about the real presence wold be at
an end. In the fourth article after he had
long labored to proue inuoluntary motions
of the flesh to be formal sin, and called the
contrary damnable doctrin, he both affirmeth and proueth such inuoluntary motiós
in S. Paul to haue bene no sin, because they
were against his wil. In the fift Article after
he had spent many leaues to fling down
condigne merit, at the last he auoucheth,
that

pag. 17.

pag 2.

S. Fabian.
S. Innocent.
1.
Symmachus
S. Felix 2.
Anastasius
2.
Vigilius.

p. 26. 27.

pag. 48.

that if we wold be iudged by Bellarmins & *p.78. 79.* others doctrin published in print, that controuersy wold be ended, & yet immediatly before he had affirmed that Bellarm. taught his doctrin of merit, (which is the very some which commonly al Catholiks hold) *after mature deliberation, and graue consultation with al the best learned Iesuits in the world , and with the Pope himself.* What is this but to confesse that in vain he impugneth the Popes doctrin of merit? Such is the force of truth (saith S. Austin) *that it. is more forceable to* Lib. cont. *wring out confeßion, then any rack or torment.* In Donat. post collat.c.24. the sixt Article he admitteth the distinction *pag.* 81. of mortal and venial sin in a godly sense (as he saith) and yet streight after concludeth absolutly that al sins are mortal , and saith that we flatter our selfs in our cursed deformed venials. In the seuenth article after he had spent 27. leaues to fel down Traditions, called them falshoods , and vanities p. 93. and pronounced them accursed of S. Paul who receaue them: at last him self p. *p.* 134. 135. 134. and 135. accepteth one Tradition about the Bible whither it be Gods word or no; wherby he beateth down whatsoeuer before he had set vp against the Traditions of the Church. In the last he graunteth that Gods commandements are possible to be kept in a godly sense, and yet afterward absolutly

solutly concludeth that we can not possibly keep them. Thus we see this silly fellow as he hath bene of opposit religions and professions, so playing ambedexter, now the minister now the Priest, now the Protestant now the Catholik. what aduersary need such a challenger who is so great an aduersary to him self? what successe is he like to haue of a mean aduersary, who hath this euil euent of his own brauado?

He promiseth to subscribe if one argument which he maketh vpon S. Austins words be answered, or if any could conuince him ether to haue alleadged any writer corruptly or to haue quoted any place guilfully, or to haue charged any other falsly. But al this is fraudulently done only to gain credit with the simple, and ignorant Reader of a sincere and inuincible challenger. For himself wel knoweth how often that argument out of S. Austin hath bene solued by Catholiks, against which solution because Bel cold not reply he wold quite dissemble it. And his allegations of Authors is too too shamful as shal appeare in the processe of this answer. Scripture he alleadgeth but as the Diuel did, when he brought it against our Sauiour, corrupting ether the words, or meaning. Fathers he bringeth but quite against their wil, and mea-

p. 149.

pag. 31. Preface to Iesuits Seminary Preistes.

See S. Hilary lib. ad Constant. S. Hierom cont. lucifer. vincent. lyrin. cont. hereses.

meaning and no maruel for he forbeareth
not his professed aduersaries such as in our
daies haue written against Protestants, and
wil make them wil they nil they turne Protestants, as he hath done, & like the spider
suck poison out of sweet flowers. And I
doubt nothing more, then that if he find
this answere so strong for him to impugne,
he wil ether proclaime me a Protestant as
his breethren do Bellarmin, or procure him
self (as his Father Iewel did) to be quit by
proclamation, against my book. But Bel,
if thou didst meane sincerely to repent if
thou beest conuinced, *remember whence thou*
art fallen and do penance: or if thou intendest
obstinatly to fight it out, harken to S. Hierome, and *take some shame becoming a man*, *if*
thou wilt haue none belonging to a Christian,
and deale plainly, set downe the Catholike
doctrin truly, alleadg Authors incorruptly,
cite the places rightly, answer directly yea
or no to euery thing obiected, and then in
Gods name *verte omnes tete in facies & contra-*
he quicquid, siue animo siue arte vales: and I
dare warrant thee, it shal be answered.

Daue of
Recusancy.
pag. 22.

Apoc. 13.

Hieron. a-
polog. cont.
Ruffinum.

AEneid.
12.

But thee (my dear Countryman) seduced
by Bel & such like, who *walking in craftines*
adulterate Gods worde, for whose sake al this
pain is taken, I beseech for Christs sake,
haue some care of thy saluation, consider
how

2. Cor. 4.
v. 2.

how of late your Church seruice and discipline hath bene condemned by more then
a thowsand ministers of *enormities, & abuses
not agreable to Scripture, and want of vniformity of doctrin,* al your English Bibles (the
very foundation of your faith) adiudged *to
be il translated,* and some to contein *very partial, vntrue and seditious notes, and too much sa-
uoring of dangerous, and traiterous conceits,* and
order taken to make a new translation. Alas
what certainty can you haue of that religion, which more then a thowsand of your
Ministers professe to haue no vniformity
of doctrin, and abuses contrary to Scripture? what goodnes can there be in that
faith, which is builded of an euil foundation, as by your owne iudgmēts your Bibles
hitherto haue bene? yea what faith at al can
there be in this mean tyme, whiles the old
Bibles are condemned as naught, and a new
not yet made? If these Ministers had once
deceaued you in a mony matter, you wold
beware how you trusted them again, and
wil you beleeue them stil, they hauing by
their owne confession, hitherto deceaued
you both in your Church seruice, & Bible,
commending the one to you as diuine seruice, and the other as Gods pure word, and
now condemning them both. Open your
eyes for the passion of Christ, and seeing

publike

*Petition ex-
hibited in
April.
1603.*

*See Confe-
rence at
Hampton
Court.
pag. 45. 46.
47.*

publike conference wil not be graunted,
where we might lay open vnto you the de-
ceits of your Ministers, help your selfs as
wel as you may, read with indifferency such
books as are written for this purpose, make
earnest intercession to God to see the truth,
& grace to follow it when you haue found
it, which God of his goodnes graunt. Fa-
rewel. 2. Februar: 1605.

Thy seruant in Christe
I E S V.

S. R.

A TABLE OF THE ARTI-
CLES AND CHAPTERS.

Bels

ARTICLE VIII.

Of keeping Gods commandements.

THE

THE FIRST ARTICLE
OF THE POPES
SVPERIORITY.

CHAPT. I.

Bels arguments against the Popes Supe-
riority answered, diuers his vntru-
thes and dissimulations therin
discouered.

E L like a man in great choler
and very desirous to encounter
with his enemie beginneth his
chalenge very abruptly & ha-
stily , yet not forgetting his
scholerschip or ministerie he geueth the
onset with a syllogisme ful charged with vntruthes & dissimulacions. *You Papistes* (saith
he) *tel vs that the Pope is aboue al powers and*
potentates on earth, that he can depose Kinges &
Emperours from their royal thrones and translate
their empires and regalities at his good wil and
pleasure: But this doctrin is false, absurde, & no-
thing else but a mere fable : And consequently
Romish Religion consisteth of meere falsehoods,
fables & flat leasinges.

2. Not without cause (gentle Reader)

A   hath

3. *Vntru-*
thes.
2. *dissimu-*
lations.

hath Bel proposed these bloudy **questions** of the Popes supremacie and deposition of Princes in his first article, and placed them in the forefront of his battel, for he hopeth that they wil be his best bulwarke and surest defense in the combate, & that in such lystes he shal not fight alone, but assisted with the Princes sworde, wherein he dealeth with Catholiques *as Puritanes* (which his Maiesty prudently obserueth) *doe with protestants, who because they could not otherwise make their partes good against protestants, appeale to his supremacie.* And as the old Arians did, who euermore accused the Catholiques as iniurious to the Prince, which they al learne of the Iewes, who being vnable to disproove Christs doctrine endeuoured to bring him into the compasse of treason, and at last procured his death as enemy to Cesar. Wherfore ymitating the example of our Sauiour, when the like question was propounded to seeke his bloud, I answere Bel briefelie. That what is Cesars, we ought to geue to Cesar, and what is Gods, to God, and what is Gods Vicars, to Gods Vicar. Onely because Bel in his said syllogisme chargeth Catholiques most falsely, & withal dissembleth the opinion of protestantes touching the supremacie and deposition of Princes. I wil disproove his vntruthes, and

discouer

Conference at Hampton Court. pag. 82. 83.

Ambr. epist. 32. victor lib. 1. de prester. vandol.

Matth. 22. v. 17.

Luc. 20. v. 25.

difcouer his diffimulations; and afterward
compare the opinion and practife of Pro=
teftants & Catholiques touching this matter together: whereby the indifferent Reader may, by Bels euil and corrupt dealing
in the very beginning of his chalenge take
a tafte of the reft of his proceedings. for, as
Tertullian faith well, *Vvhat truth doe they* Tertull.l. de
præfcript.
defend vvho begin it vvith lyes?

3. I demand therfore of Bel who they are
whome he chalengeth, to whome he fpeaketh, and whome he vnderftandeth by,
You Papifts; Surely I fuppofe he writeth in
English to none but fuch as vnderftand English, whome in his preface he termeth
English Iefuyts, Seminary Priefts, & Iefuy=
ted Papifts. Yf thefe (Maifter Bel) be they
whome ye meane, I tel you in their name,
that as your propofitiõ hath two parts, viz.
the Popes Superiority ouer al Princes and
of his power to depofe them, fo it contei=
neth three (to vfe your owne tearme) flatte
leafinges.

For though, concerning Chriftians, they
beleeue the Pope to be fpiritually fuperiour
aboue al whatfoeuer accordinge to Chrifts
words fpoken to the firft Pope S. Peter,
Matth. 16. viz. *Thou art Peter, and vpon this
rocke vvil I buylde my Church,* and Io. 21. v. 17.
Feede my sheepe, which sheepe conteine and
A 2   inclu-

include as wel Chriſtian Princes and potentates as ſubieċts and vnderlings. And, concerning infidels, they alſo beleeue that the
Pope ought to be ſpiritually aboue them,
and they vnder him in that they be bound
to be Chriſtians: neuertheleſſe, vntil theſe
be Chriſtened, he is not aċtually their ſuperiour : vntil they be made members of
Chriſts Church, he is not *de faċto* their head:
vntil they be in Chriſts fould, he is not
their sheape hearde. For, as Bellarmin writeth; whoſe teſtimonie (ſaith Bel) is moſt
ſufficient in al Popiſshe affaires, *Chriſt was
aboue as wel infidels as faithful, But to S. Peter he
committed onely his sheepe, that is the faithful.*
Wherefore S. Paul as not acknowledging
that he had any ſuperiority or iuriſdiċtion
ouer infidels ſaid, *what belongeth it to me to
iudge of them that are without?* 1. Cor. 5. And
although the Pope may preach him ſelfe
or ſend others to preache to infidels without their licence, yet this argueth no more
but that the commiſſion which he hath
from God to preach the Ghoſpel vnto al
nations is independent of the infidels, and
that they ought to be vnder his iuriſdiċtiō.
Wherefore vntil Bel doe prooue that there
are no powers or potētates on earth which
are infidels, I muſt needs tel him that he
vntruly auoucheth vs to ſay that the Pope
is ſpi-

Bellarm.lib.
5. de Rom.
Pont.c. 7.
Bel p. 29.
125.

is spiritually aboue al powers and potentates on earth.

4. And much lesse did we euer tel you that the Pope hath temporal superiority ouer al Princes on earth, but teach the quite contrary with, *VValden, Bellarmin,* and others. For as two most auncient Popes, *Gelasius* 1.and *Nicolaus* 1. taught vs, the Pope by his Pontifical dignity chalengeth neither *royal soueraignity . nor imperial name,* But what royalties he hath either in the Popedome or els where, he chalengeth by the guift of Christian Princes whereof. *Some (as your selfe confesse) haue yeelded vp their soueraigne rights , vnto him.* And what superiority we thinke him to haue ouer Christian Princes, he should haue though he were not Lord of one foote of land, but as poore, as he that said Math. 19. v. 27 *Behould vve haue forsaken al.* For his Papal superiority and authority is not temporal or of this world, nor the weapones of his warfare carnal, but (as S. Paul speaketh) mighty to God, vnto the distruction of munitious destroying Counsels, and al loftines extolling it selfe against the knowledge of God, and hauing in readines to reuenge al disobedience. Wherupon P. Innocent. 3. professeth that the Pope hath ful power in temporal matters, only in the

VValden. tom.1. lib.1. art.3.c.78.
Bellarm.lib. 5. de Rom. Pont. c.4.
Gelas. 1. de vincul. Anathematis.
Nicol. 1. de 96.Can.cum ad verum.

Pag. 17.

S. Mathew

S. Paul. 2. Cor.10.

Cap.per venerab. extra qui filij sunt legitimi.

A 3　　Pope-

Popedome, and that *Kings acknowledge no superior in temporal affaires.* And this also teach S. Ambros de Apol. Dauid c. 4. & 10 Gloss. Lyra in psalm. 50. and others. By which it appeareth how much he is abused who is made to beleue, *That the Pope present, challengeth an imperial ciuil power ouer Kings, & Emperors, or that English Papists do attribute vnto him any such power.* For neither doth Paulus 5. challeng more authority, then Innocent 3 did, nor English Papists attribute vnto him other authority ouer Kings then spiritual. But do with tong, and hart, and with the Popes good liking professe: *That our Soueraigne Lord King Iames hath no superior on earth in temporal matters.* If Bel reply that some Canonists haue affirmed the Pope to be temporal Lord ouer the world, let him challeng them & not like a wise man strike his next fellows the English Papists, who mantayne no such opinion.

5. The second parte of his Proposition touching the Popes deposition of Princes at his pleasure, though he repeat it thrise is most vntrue. For no Catholiques, English or strangers, teach that the Pope can depose Princes but for iust causes, yea *ordinarily* (saith Bellarmin) *not for iust causes, but when it is necessary for the sauing of souls.* And surely otherwise Princes shold be but his tenants at wil,

Margin notes:
S. Ambros. tom. 4.

pag. 1. 4. 17.

Bellarm. lib. 5. de Rom. Pontif. c.6.

at wil, and he haue more power ouer them,
then they haue ouer their subiects. which
is far from al Catholiques imaginations, let
vs see therfore how Bel proueth vs to teach Bel p. 2
this doctrin.

6. *Becaufe* (faith he) *Bellarmin setteth it downe*   Bellarm. de
in thefe words, If therfore any Prince, of a sheep or   Rom. Pon-
a ram become a wolfe, that is to fay, of a Chriftian   tif. lib. 5. c. 7.
be made an heretike, then the Paftor of the Church   4. vntruth.
may driue him away by excommunication, and
withal command the people not to obey him, and
therfore depriue him of his dominion ouer his fub-
iects. Behold (good Reader) the forfaid vntruthes proued with an other. Becaufe
Bellarmin calleth the Pope Paftor of the
Church, Bel auoucheth him to think the
Pope to be aboue al Princes, & Potentates
on earth; as if there were no Princes infidels, or out of the Church: and becaufe he
teacheth that the Pope may excommunicate, and depofe Princes for Herefy, that he
may depofe them at his pleafure, as if matters of Herefy (which is one of the greateft
finns that is) were the Popes pleafure. An
indifferent reader would rather haue inferred, that becaufe the Pope is Paftor of the
Church, he is not aboue any infidel, Prince,
or fubiect; which Bellarmin teacheth in   *Bellarmin.*
expreffe words in the fame booke c. 2. &
6.4. And becaufe he can not excõmunicate,

A 4   fo ne-so neither depose Princes for his pleasure, which Bellarmin euery where supposeth, yea in the same book c. 6. auoucheth. That *ordinarily he can not depose Princes euen for iust causes.*

Anatomy of Popish tyrany in the Caueat to the Reader and lib. 2.cap.4. §. 10.& c.9.
1. Contra-diction.

7. But let vs heare Bel disproue him self; *Secular Priests* (saith he) *write plainly and reso-lutly that the Pope hath no power to depriue Kings of their royal Scepters, and regalities, nor to giue away their Kingdomes to an other. In which opi-nion like wise the French Papists do concurre, & iump with them.* Item. *The Seculars, although they acknowledge the Popes power supereminent in Spiri-tualibus yet do they disclaime from it in tempora-libus when he taketh vpon him to depose Kinges from their empires and translate their Kingdo-mes.* And least we should thinke these few Priests, who wrote so, were no Papists, Bel him self testifieth that they are *the Popes deare*

Epistle to the King.

Vassals and professe the selfe same religion with other Catholiques.

8. The third vntruth conteined in the proposition is that we teach the doctrine of his proposition as a pointe of our faith: wherevpon he inferreth in his conclusion, our religion and faith to be false. Becaufe we teach no such doctrine at al and much lesse as a point of our religion or faith. And the grauest & best learned amongst Catho-liques attribute to the Pope onely spiritual supe-

superiority ouer Princes, and power to depose them in that cafe wherin our Sauiour
faid Math. 18. that it were better for a man
to be caft into the fea then to liue, to wit,
when they fo fcandalize others as their depofition is neceffary for the faluation of
foules as I haue already shewed out af Bel- Bel. parag.
larmin, whofe teftimony in this matter Bel   29.
can not refufe feing he calleth him the
mouth of Papifts and auoucheth his doctrin to be the Popes owne doctrin. And
this doctrin good Chriftiã Princes account
no more preiudicial or iniurious to their
eftates, then they do the like doctrin of S.
Paul 2.Cor.10. where he profeffeth him felf
to haue power to deftroy al loftines extolling it felf againft the knowledge of God,&
to be ready to punish al difobedience.

9. Wherfore, to requite Bel with a fyllo-
gifme like vnto his owne, I argue thus: you
Bel tel vs that we Papifts faie, the Pope is
aboue al powers and potentates on earth,
that he can depofe Kings and Emperours,
and tranflate their empiers at his good wil
and pleafure, But this your tale is a very tale
falfe, abfurd, and nothing elfe but a mere
fable: and confequently your late chalenge
confifteth of mere falfehoods fables & flat
leafings. The propofition is your owne
wordes, the truth of the affumption appeereth

reth by my anſwer to your argument. **And**
thus much touching Bels vntruthes vttered in his propoſition and proofe therof,
now let vs come to his diſſemblinge.

Chap. II.

The opinion of proteſtants touching Prin-ces Supremacie, ſet dovvne.

Luther. lib.
cont. ſtat ec-
cleſ. in pro-
logo, & in
gloſſa cont.
decreta Cæ-
ſar.
Ex Sur. An.
1531. 1539.
Pope of Re-
cuſamy p.
31. 32.
Magdeburg.
præfat. Cen-
tur. 7.
Caluin in c.
7. Amos.

L VTHER an Euangeliſt (as he termeth
him ſelfe, or as other accompte him,
an Apoſtle, a prophet, a third Elias, a beginner of proteſtantiſme, in his booke of
ſecular power condemneth thoſe Princes,
*who preſcribe laws to their ſubiects in matter be-
longing to faith and the Church.* Magdeburgians his firſt, and cheefeſt childeren write
thus. *Let not Magiſtrats be heads of the Church,
becauſe this Supremacy agreeth not to them.* Caluin ſaith, they were blaſphemers who attributed the ſupremacy, to King Henry 8.
And leſt we ſhold think that only forayne
Proteſtàts are of this opinion. Antony Gil-

Gilby.

by in his admonition to England and Scotland calleth King Henry a monſtrous bore
for taking the ſupremacy, that he diſplaced
Chriſt, was no better then the Romiſh An-

VVillet cõ-
tract. 791.
part. 1 and
3. p. 269.
270.

tichriſt, made him ſelfe a God. And lately
Willet auoucheth. That *Biſhops and Paſtors
haue a ſpiritual charge ouer Kings, & that Kings
ought to yeeld obedience to thoſe that haue ouer-*
                                            ſight

sight of their *soules.* That *Heathen Princes had
the same power, and authority in the Church
which Christian Princes haue,* and yet soone
after affirmeth. That *heathen Princes cold not
be heads of the Church, that is to haue the soue-
reingty of external gouernment* Againe. That
*the King is nether mistical nor ministerial head
of the Church, that the name of head is vnproper-
ly giuen to the Prince, and if any think it to great
a name for any mortal man we wil not* (saith
he) *greatly contend about it.* So we see he denyeth both name, and authority of the head
of the Church to Kings.

*Kings not
so much is
ministerial
heads of the
Church by
vvillet.*

2. And his Maiesty perceaued that Rea-
nolds, and his fellows aymed at a Scottish
Presbitry (which agreeth with a Monarch,
as wel as God, and the diuel page 79.) and
acknowledged his supremacy only to make
their partes good with Bishops, as Knox &
his fellow ministers in Scotland made his
grandmother head of the Church therby
to pul downe the Catholique Bishops. Yea
that the whole English Clergy is in their
harts of the same opinió, appeareth by their
open profession to agree in religion with
forayne Protestants, who plainly deny the
supremicy of Princes: by their writing and
teaching, that Christ alone can behead of
the Church: by their condemning Catholiques for attributing such authority to man:
and

*Conference
p. 82. 83.*

*Apologia
pag. 28.*

and finally by their Synodical explication
of the article of supremacy: which they expound thus. *That Princes should rule al estates*
and degrees committed to their charge by God
whether they be Ecclesiastical, or temporal, and
restrayne with the ciuil sword the stubborne, and
euil doers, wherein we see no power in Ecclesiastical causes granted to Princes, but
only, ouer Ecclesiastical persons. And we
deny not that Princes haue any power ouer
Ecclesiastical persons, yea in the very canon
of the Masse, as priests pray for *Papa nostro*
N. and *Antistite nostro N.* for our Pope and
Byshop, so they pray for *Rege nostro N.*
acknowledging the one to be their King
as the others to be their Prelates, and consequently both to haue power ouer them. For
as S. Augustin said, and it is euident, *Rex à*
regendo dicitur, a King is so called of power
to gouerne. And as ecclesiastical persons be
ciuil or politique members of the common
wealth. wherein they liue, so haue they
the same politique or ciuil head which that
commonwealth hath: for otherwise either
ciuil members should haue no ciuil head at
al, which were monstrous, or not be vnder the head of that body, whereof they be
members, but onely vnder a ciuil head of
an other body, which is impossible. Wherefore, what some say that Clergie men be
exem-

Lib. 39. Artic.
art. 37.

Augustin in
Psalm. 44. &
67.

See Stapel-
ton rele-
ctione Con-
trouersia 2.
q. 1. a. 1. ad
2.
Victoria re-
lectione de
potesta. ec-
clesiastica
sect. 7.

exempted from the power of Princes, is
not to be vnderftood vniuerfally but of
their coactiue power which they haue to
punifhe the laity. And of late Bilfon Super-
intendent of Winton confeffed to certeine
Catholiques, (if I be not mifinformed) that
the King is but *a ceremonial head*, that is
either a head onely for fafhion fake, or
onely in matters of ceremonies, not in al
ecclefiafticall caufes. And albeit they fub- *supplicat.*
fcribe to the fupremacie, yet perhaps they *to the King*
doe that onely in refpect of time, as a thou- *in April*
fand minifters teftifie, that diuerfe of them *1603.*
did to the communion booke, fome vpon
proteftation, fome vpon expofition, fome
with condicion, albeit it conteyned (as
they fay) enormities, and abufes not a-
greable to Scriptures, rather (forfooth)
then the Church fhould be depriued of
their labours, but in deede rather then
they fhoulde be depriued of the Churches
lyuings.

3. The true difference therfore betwixt
Catholiques and English Proteftants (if
thefe durft vtter their mindes as ftrangers
doe) would not be, whether the Prince or
Pope, but whether the Pope or minifters
ought to be head of the Church, wherein
I appeale to any indifferent mans iudgement, whether be more agreable to Gods
                                    word,

Matth. 16.
Ioan. 21.

word, that the successour of S. Peter, vpon whome Christ built his church and committed his sheepe vnto, should be head of the Church, or they who are successours to none but beginners of them selues, who (as

Cyprian. lib.
de simpl.
prælat.

S. Ciprian writeth) no man creating them Bishopes, made them selues Bishopes. And wether be more secure to Princes that he

Constant. in
edicto Con-
stant. 5. Pho-
cas.
Iustinian. C.
de summa
Trinit. l. vlt.
Valentinia-
nus epist. ad
Theodosii.
See cap. 6.
parag. 6. 7.
Conference
p. 79. 4.
and 20.

should be accounted head of Gods Church whom the whole Christian world hath euer acknowledged for such, and vnder whome the mightiest Monarches haue and doe liue as securely as any Protestant Prince whatsoeuer ; or they, who if they were permitted would erect such a Presbitrie, *as agreeth with a Monarchy no better then the diuel with God, who haue kept Kings without state and honor &c. and of whom some beardles boies haue braued Kings to their faces,* and excommunicated them when they came within ther parish.

CHAP. III.
The opinion of Protestants touching deposition of Princes.

Germany.
Luther.
See Surius
An. 1525.
Prodromū
Staphil. p.
75.

LIKWISE touching the deposition of Princes, Luther as Sleidan testifieth wrote to Princes: *That subiects neither cold, nor would, nor ought any longer, to suffer ther gouerment.* And benig asked his opinion touching

the

the league of Protestants against their Emperor *Charles 5.* answered. *Because at this time so*
doubtful, & perilous, many things may hapen, that
not only right it seife, but necessity of conscience may
reach vs weapons, We may make league for defence,
Whether the Emperor him selfe, or any other make
War. And alitle before his death said; *VVho*
taks not armes whils he may, vseth not things giuen
him by God. And the Protestant Princes in
their rebellion against the Emperor, set
forh Proclamation wherein they write; *Be-*
cause the Emperor endeauoreth to dostroy religion &
liberty, he giueth vs cause to assaile him with good
consience And againe *we renounce* (ô Emperor)
the faith and duty wher with vve are bound vnto
thee. This did German Protestants.

Sleidon l. 8. Sur.An. 1531.

Sur.An. 1546.

Sleidon l. 21.

lib. 17.

  2. In Swiserland Zwinglius teacheth vs.
That *vvhen the King shal deale perfidiously and*
beside the rule of Christ, he may in Gods name be de-
posed. Againe *VVhiles naughty Kings are not de-*
posed the vvhole people is punished of God. And as
for the Protestants of Sweudland their opinion is manifest by their excluding the Catholique King of Polad from succeding his
late father : And the Holandish Protestants
wholy, or cheefly defend their long rebellion against their Prince by coolor of religion.

Svviser-
land.
Zvvingl. to.
1. art. 42.

Svveneläd.

Mercur.Gal-
lobelg. An.
1603.
Holland.

  3. In France Caluin their Arch-maister
teacheth that *who reigneth not to serue Gods*
glory,

France.
Caluin. in e-
pist.ante lib
institut.

glory, ruleth not but playeth the theefe. **And in**
an other place. *Earthly Princes depose them
selues whyls they rise against God, yea are ʋn-
worthy to be accounted men.* And his scholer
Beza accounteth them Martyrs who dyed
in batel against their King for religion, and
at *Cabilon* in France 20. Ministers in a Synod decreed to distroy the Church, Nobility, & Magistrats. And againe at *Berna* 1572.
set forth Canons of this matter and decreed
Can. 3. *That in euery City al swore that they &
their posterity shal obserue firme and inuiolated
the points following.* Can. 40. *Vntil it shal please God in whose hands are the harts of Kings to
change the hart of the French tyrant, and restore
the state of the Kingdome to better order, & raise
ʋp some neighbor Prince, whom we may know
by his ʋertue & notable marks to be the deliuerer
of this miserable people, in the meane tyme euery
Citty shal choose a maior to gouerne them as wel
in warre as peace* Can. 40. *Let al the Captains &
leaders haue this axiome, as an ʋndoubted and
most certain Oracle, neuer to trust to them* (the
King and his) *who so often, and so notoriously
haue broken their promise, the publike peace and
quietnes. Nor euer let them lay downe weapons,
as long as they shal see them persecute the doctrin
of saluation, and the disciples of the same.* Item
*But if the euil be incurable, if Gods wilbe to roote
them* (natural Princes) *out, then if it please*
God

In cap.6.Da-
niel.

Beza in Præ-
fat. Bibl.
1564. Panta-
leon.
Responsum
trium ordi-
num Burgū-
diæ 1563.
Michael Fa-
britius ep.
de Beza fal.
62.
Goodly Ca-
nons of Mi-
nisters.
Protestants
svvorne to
rebel & de-
pose Prin-
ces.

God to raise some Christian Prince to take reuenge of their sinnes, and deliuer his people, let them subiect them selues to that Prince, as to an other Cyrus sent to them from God. In the meane space let them gouerne them selues by these rules which we haue prescribed vnto them as laws. Behould the verdit of French ministers assembled in Councel. O if such rules had bene made in Seminaries, what traitors and rebels had the authors bene ? What exclamations would Bel and his fellow ministers haue made against them ?

4. In Scotland Knox vttereth his, and his fellow ministers mind herein, in his appellation to the nobility & people of Scotland. *That I may say bouldly, the nobility, gouerners, iudges, and people of England ought not only to resist, and withstand. Mary Iezabel, whom they cal their Queene, but also put to death her, her Priests, and al others that ayded her, as soone as openly they began to suppresse Christs Gospel.* And he setteth downe titles of books which he would after publish, whereof the third is this. *If the people haue rashly preferred one manifestly wicked, or ignoratly chosen, such a one, who afterward sheweth himselfe vnworthy of gouernment ouer Christian people (for such are al Idolaters and cruel persecutors) the same people may most iustly depose, and punish him.*

5. Finally in England if we had asked our

B

Scotland.

Knox. p : 36.

Protestants bond to kil Princes by Knox.

p : 72.

England.

our miniſters of what minde they were, while the Septer and ſword was in Catholique hands. Goodman in his booke intituled how we ought to obey ſuperior Magiſtrats, telleth vs: *But if they (Prince & Magiſtrats do boldly tranſgreſſe Gods lawes, and command the ſame to others, then haue they loſt that honor, and obedience which otherwiſe ſubiects were bound to giue them, nor are hereafter to be accounted Magiſtrats, but to be puniſhed as priuat men.* But who muſt puniſh them? he anſwereth the common people. *If the Prince and al Magiſtrats do reſiſt Gods law, you people haue expreſſe teſtimony of Gods vvord for your part, and God himſelfe wilbe your Captaine, & leader, vvho commandeth not only Peers, and Magiſtrats to take euery euil from them ſelues, whither idolatry, blaſphemy or open iniury, but requireth this of the whole multitude to vvhome the ſvvord of iuſtice is in part committed. VVherfore if al Magiſtrats together vvil deſpiſe iuſtice and Gods lavves, it is your part (o comon people) to defend and conſerue them vvith as much violence and ſtrife as you can againſt Magiſtrats, and al others. For this God requireth of you.* Exod: 17. *this burden lieth vpon the whole people to puniſh euery idolater vvhatſoeuer none is excepted, vvhither King, Queene, or Emperor.* And a litle after *That fact is recounted number 25, it is a perpetual example for al eternity, and a certayne and ſure*

Goodman c.
9.p .118.

See Couel of
Church go-
uernment.
cap.4 p. 55.
hovv this
doctrin.
vas Caluins
& the lear-
nedeſt Pro-
teſtants of
that tyme.
c.13 p.180.
181. 184.

Princes
muſt be hã-
ged accor-
ding to
Goodman.

sure denouncement to the people that in like reuoult from the vvorship of God, they do carry to the gallous, and hang their gouernors, vvho lead them from God.

6. And in particular touching Wyats rebellion he saith. *None but Papists can accuse VVyat of treason, or disobedièce, it vvas the duty of VVyat & al others that amongst you professe Christs Gospel, to take in hand that vvarre, and they vvere true traytors, vvho ether kept not promise to him, or ayded not his part. O most noble VVyat thou novv liuest vvith God, and these noble men vvho dyed vvith thee in that cause. Yea noble men and Counsellers did not you condemne your selues as manifest and base minded traytors not only to VVyat, but euen to God him selfe? O Gospellers is this the loue of Gods vvord you pretend, haue you so learned the Gospel?*

l.14 p.103.

Protestants duty to rebel according to Goodman.

Traiters vvho do not rebel according to Goodman.

7. And albeit ministers hauing now gotten the Prince on their side, do in words condemne Goodman, yet that their minde abhorreth not from this opinion, may appeare *by the partial, vertue and seditions notes, & to much fauoringe of dangerous, and trayterous conceipts as of allovving disobedience to Kings, and taxing Asa for deposing his mother, and not killing her* which his Majesty obserued in their English Bybles, And thus I hope the Reader seeth that Bel had litle cause to charge Papists alone with deposition of Princes, but

Conference p. 47.

much

much better wil he fee it, if we compare
Papifts and Proteftants opinions herein together.

8. Catholiques fay, Kings may be depo·
fed , Proteftants fay, they may be depofed
and hanged : Catholiques fay, it fhould be
done after due tyme, and admonition giuen,
& the Lateran Councel prefcribeth a years
refpit : Proerftants fay, fo foone as they begin to fuppreffe Chrifts Gofpel: Catholikes
fay, it muft be done by the Pope the Kings
fpirituall Paftor and Father: who as a Father
louingly, and as a Prince aduifedly, and as a
ftranger difpaffionatly, wil proceed in fo
weighty a matter; Proteftants fay, it may
be done by cómon people the Kings owne
fubiects, who as common people rafhly and
headely, and as fubiects infolently and paf-
fionatly, are like to behaue them felues in
controuling and correcting their Prince, as
the lamentable examples herefter touched
can teftify. Befides what Catholiques fay of
Kings, the fame they fay of the Pope, that
he may as wel be depofed for herefy, or infidelity, as Princes; and what they fay vnder
an heretical Prince, they defend vnder a Catholique. Whereas Proteftants change their
tune according as the Prince fauoreth or
disfauoreth their religion. Now let vs fee
the practife of Proteftants.

The

Margin notes:
1.
Knox Good man. fup:
2.

Lateran : 3. c.3. de Hært: Knox fup:
3.

Goodman. fup:

4.

Note this in differency of Catho-liques and partialitty of Proteft-ants.

Chap. IIII.
The practise of Protestants touching deposition of Princes

CONFORMABLE to their doctrin haue bene the practises of Protestants. For in Germany vnder pretence of religion, first the common people being Protestants rose against the nobles, in which insurrection there were an hundred thousand of the common people slayne, many castles and towares spoyled, and burnt. And soone after the nobles rose against their Emperor, gathered an army of eighty thousand foote, ten thousand horse, and 130. feeld peces. And George Duke of Saxony wrote to Luther, that there was neuer more rebellions against Magistrats then through his Gospel: And Erasmus a holy Confessor in Foxes calender, giueth this testimony of them. *Many disciples of Luther are so vnapt to publike quiet, as the Turk is said to detest the name of Luthereans for sedition: Testimonium hoc verum est?*

2. In Swiserland Zwinglius togeather with Protestantisme sowed sedition, and brought his country to three pitcht battels in one moneth, and was him selfe slayne in one of them. In Denmark Protestantisme

Germany.

Sleidon. l. 4. 17. 19. Sur: An: 1522. 1525.

Sur: An: 1530. 1534.

Apud Sleid. Et sur: 1526.

Erasmus l. 3. de lib: arbit:

Swiser-land.
Sur: An: 1531.

Denmark.

Staphil. a-
pol. art. 3.
was no sooner settled, then the Commons
rose against the nobles & the nobles against

Sur.An.1532.
their King, whom they deposed, and after
long banishment cast into prison, whereas

Svveuland.
Mercur.Gal-
lobelg. An.
1603.
it is reported they poysned him. In Sweuland the Protestants haue lately excluded
their natural, lawful, and crowned Prince,
the present King of Pole-land, and chosen

Holland.
his vncle. In Flanders, they elected Francis
Duke of Alanson for their Prince, and haue
depriued two of their lawful Princes, from
a great part of the Low countries, & made
watre against them almost 40. yeares.

France.
3. In France Protestants haue rebelled
against three of their natural and anoynted

Genebrard.
chron.
Sur.An.1563.
Furores Gal-
lici.
Michael Fa-
britius in e-
pist. de Be-
za.
Kings, Francis 2 : Charles. 9. Henry 3. they
tooke by treason, or force, many of their
cheefest cities, Roane, Orleans, Lyons and
others, made league with the enimies of
France, and giuen townes into their hands,
they haue leuied great armies of subiects,
brought in great bands of Strangers, and
fought foure mayne battels against their
King, they deposed their King and chose an
other, and coyned money in his name with

Sur.An:1560.
title of *the first Christian King of France,* They
opened the tombs of two of their Kings &
burnt their bones. They conspired to murder the King & two Queenes, his wife and
his mother, with his brethren & nobility,
and

and had executed their defignments, if they
had not bene preuented by their maffacre.
They flew the King of Nauar, Father to the *Fabritius*
French King now regnant. And their hor- *fup. fol. 61.*
rible outrages in al kinde of dishonefties *66.*
cruelties, and Sacrileges are vnfpeakable.

4. In Scotland the Proteftants firft took *Scotland.*
armes againft the Queene dawager, Grand *Sur. An. 1560.*
mother to his Majefty, then regent of Scotland; and by their rebellions, and tumults
haftened her death, which his Majefty great *Conference*
ly lamented in the conference. Likewife af- *p. 81.*
ter infinit indignities, and perils they driue
Queene Mary of bleffed memory his Ma-
jefties Mother, their natural and lawful
Prince out of her kingdome, and country,
forced her to furrender her crowne and
Scepter to a baftard, murthered her hufband
his Maiefties Father, and therof infamed
her wrongfully (as was proued at her iudgment in England) had murdred both her
felfe and his Maieftie then in her womb, if
a charged piftole put to her womb would
haue giuen fyer. And at laft by Proteftants
she was put to death againft law of nations,
And his Maiefty cófeffeth of him felfe that *Confer. p. 4.*
in Scotland *he vvas a King vvithout ftate, vvith-* *and 20.*
out honor, vvithout order, vvhere beardles boyes
vvould braue him to his face, and keept for the moft
part as a yvard. And in what prefent danger
B 4 he was

he was of being murdered by the Proteſtant Earle Gowry and his brethren, no man is ignorant. And otherwhere gratiouſly acknowlegeth, *That he found none more faithful to himſelfe, then ſuch as had bene faithful to his mother* (who were Papiſts) *and them he found faithles to himſelfe, vvho had bene ſuch to his mother:* and an honorable perſon yet liuing and worthy of credit, and hard it, can teſtify that Queene Eelizabeth did oftentymes ſay to my Lord Moūtague a famous Catholique of worthy memory. *That if ſhe fel into danger, ſhe vvould ſooner put her life into his hands, and others of his profeſſion, then of any other ſubieċt ſhe had.* And if Queene Elizabeth (though ſhe were far more ſeuere towards her Catholique ſubieċts then al Proteſtant Princes together haue hiterto bene towards theirs) did neuertheles put more affiance and truſt in them, euen after ſhe had bene depoſed of the Pope, then in any Proteſtant, what aſſurance may that Prince haue of the loyalty and fidelity of Catholiques, who hath vſed great lenity towards them, and nether is, nor like to be depoſed of the Pope.

5. Finally in England Proteſtants rebelled twiſe, & that in one yeare againſt their Queene Mary ; once vnder the conduċt of the Dukes of Northumberland, & Suffolk, ereċt-

Baſilicon doron.

Q. Eliʒab. vvoords & confidence of Catholiks.

His Maieſties ſpeech to the Parlament 19 Mart. 1603. England.

erecting a falfe Queene, & fo excluding as much as lay in them, the Succeffion of his Maiefty. And againe vnder Wyat, and at both times she was defended by Catholiks. The things I rather touch then relate, becaufe they are fresh in memory of many, or to be found in many hiftories.

6. Now let vs compare the practife of Proteftants touching the depofition of Princes, with the practife of the Pope, fince the tyme that Proteftants began. They haue within this 70. yeares partely depofed partly attempted, as far as lay in thir power, one Emperor, three French Kings, two Kings of Spaine, one of Denmarke, one of Pole-land, one Queene of England, and one of Scotland. They haue flayne one King of Nauar, one of Denmarke, one Queene of Scotland, one Queenes hufband, and burnt the bodies of two other Kings, & attepted to murder one French King, two French Queenes, & one King of Scotland. Whereas the Popes neuer flew any Prince at al, but haue faued the liues, & kingdomes of many, & fince Proteftats began, haue depofed one onely King Henry 8. and one Queene Elizabeth and fpared both King Edward, the 6 & many Kings of Demark, & Sweuland, befids a great number of German Princes. And his Maieftie is fo far from danger of being

Proteftants and Catholiques practife compared.
1 Carolus 5.
2 Francis 2.
3 Carolus 9.
4 Henricus 3.
5 Philippus 2.
6 Philippus 3.
7 Chriftiernus.
8 Sigifmundus.
9 Maria Ang.
10 Maria Scot.

see D. Gifords commission and Monf. Bethunes letters.
Proclamation 22. Februar. anno 1.
Note this.

being depofed by him, as he hath already cenfured al thofe that molefte, or difturbe his maiefty; and his maiefty, gratefully acknowledgeth him felfe *beholden to the Pope for his temporal cariage, and diuers kind offices towards him,* euen then when ther was leffe caufe of fuch kindnes, then now is. Yea which is a point worthy of confideration. Neuer did any Pope depofe any King, or Prince merely for not profeffing the Catholique religion, if he had not before embraced it; If any obiect, that the Pope hath befide King Henry, and Queene Elizabeth depofed the prefent French King, I anfwer that it was before he had the Crowne of France, and was onely *titulo tenus* King of Nauar; befids that the Pope vpon his amendment hath both reftored him to his dignity, and shewed him many great, and extraordinary fouors. And thus much of Bels diffembling the opinion, and practife of Proteftants, touching the Supremacy or depofition of Princes. Now let vs come to his proofs of his Affumption.

CHAP. V.
Bells proofes of his Affumption answered.

BELLS proofs of his Affumption I might let paffe, as nothing pertayning to vs, to vs, feeing we teach no fuch doctrin as he therin affirmeth to be falfe : Neuertheles becaufe the Reader may iudge, wbither he be a more fond difputor or falfe reportor, I wil fet them downe and anfwer them feuerally. His firft proofe is out of *their famous* (faith he) *Pope Gregory the great* lib: 2. epift. 61. where writing to the Emperor Mauritius, he calleth him. *Soueraigne Lord, and profeffeth him felfe fubiect to his command, and to owe him obedience.* Whereupon Bel inferreth that for 600. years after Chrift, Popes liued vnder Emperors in al dutiful obedience, that is (as he vnderftandeth) in al caufes Ecclefiaftical and ciuil.

2. Marke (good Reader) how many and how groffe errors he committeth in this one filly proofe. Firft he fheweth fmal skil in chufing Authors for his purpofe, becaufe none make more againft him in this matter then S. Gregory. For he is the firft P. whome we find to haue made a flat decree touching the depofition of Princes in thefe words. *If any King, Prelat, Iudge, or feculer perfon of what degree or highnes foeuer* (do violate the priuileges of S. Medards monaftery) *let him be depofed.* And vpon the 4. al : 5. poenit: pfalme he writeth that no reafon alloweth him to be King who alienateth men from Chrift and enthralleth his Church : and sharply

Bel p. 2,

lib. 12. epift.
vlt.lib. 11, epift. 10.

sharply inueigheth againſt the Emp: for
vſurping right of earthly power ouer the
Church of Rome, which he calleth the
head of al Churches and Lady of Nations,
and telleth him that it were better for him
to acknowledge her his Lady, and ſubmit
him ſelfe to her according to the example
of godly Princes.

Anſvver.   3. And as for the place which Bel citeth
he ſpeaketh not there of the ſubiection
duty, or obediéce of a ſubiect to his Prince,
but of a ſeruant to his Maiſter (as he had
bene to Mauritius whiles they were both
priuat men) which him ſelfe plainly profeſſeth in the beginning of his letter in
theſe words. *In this ſuggeſtion I ſpeake not as*
Bishop, nor as ſubiect, by reaſon of the common
wealth, but by priuat right of my owne, becauſe you
haue bene my Lord ſince that time when as yet you
were not Lord of al. And therfore by the for-
ſayd words he meaneth no otherwiſe, then
a louing ſeruant doth, when vpon curteſie
to his old Maiſter though he haue left him,
yet he ſtil calleth him Maiſter, and offereth
him ſelfe and his ſeruice at his command.
His ſecond error was, in inferring vpon the
bare words of one P. ſpeaking of him ſelfe
alone, not onely his dutiful obedience, but
alſo of al his Predeceſſors for 600. years together. He would eſpie his error, if I ſhould
                                            infer

infer the same of al. S. Greg: his succeſſors
for 600. years after him. And though euery
Engliſh Prieſt do cal his Maieſty Soueraigne
Lord, profeſſe them ſelues ſubiect to his
commande, and to owe him obedience, as
far as Bel can shew that euer S. Gregory did
to the Emp: yet wil he not ſuffer me to infer
that they liue in al dutiful obedience to
their Prince, but wil condemne them al of
high treaſon. For with him (as of old with
Donariſts) *Quod volumus Sanctum eſt.*

4. His 3. error is, in granting that Popes
for 600. years after Chriſt, liued in al dutiful
obedience to Emperors, wherein he quite
ouerthroweth what he ment to proue in
this Article. For if that be true, he can not
thinke that to excommunicate or depoſe
Princes vpon great cauſes, is againſt the
duty of Popes. Becauſe (to omit S. Ambroſe
his excōmunicating of the Emperors Theodoſius & Maximus, & S. Babilas his excō=
municating an other Emp: whom *he droue*
(ſaith S. Chriſoſt) *out of the Church as if he had
bene a baſe ſlaue & of no account*) no fewer then
fiue or ſix Popes haue excōmunicated their
Emperors in that time. As S. Fabian excōmunicated Phillip the firſt Chriſtian Emperor S. Innocent 1. the Emperours Arcadius
and Eudoxia, P. Symachus & P. Anaſtaſius,
and (as ſome ſay) P. Gelaſius excommunicated

Contradict.
Gelaſ. epiſt.
ad Anaſtaſ.
Theodoret.
lib.5. cap.18.
Sozom. l. 7.
c.24. Paulin.
in vit. Am-
broſ.
Lib. cont.
Gentil.
Euſeb.lib. 6.
c.26. Niceph.
lib.13. c 39.
Gelaſ. d. 96.
con. Duo
ſunt. Georg.
Patriarcha
in vit. Chry-
ſoſt.
Symach. ep.
ad Anaſtaſ.
Stapleto. de
Eccl. Rom.
Platina in
Gelaſio.

Baron. An. 84.
Contradict.
cated the Emperor Anastasius, and P. Vigil
the Empresse Theodora. And S. Gregory
him selfe proceeded further (as you heard)
euen to depose Princes. Moreouer Bel writeth p: 8. that Barbarians possessed al Italy
from the yeare 471. vntil Charles the great
801. How then saieth he here that Popes liued vnder Emperors vntil 603.

5. His fourth error is in cōfessing S. Gregory the great to be ours, that is, a Papist,
wherupon follow many things to his vtter
confusion. First that the old Rom, religion
(for I hope what is aboue a 1000. yeares old
is old) which him selfe p: 83. confesseth to
be *Catholique, sound, & pure*, is Papistical. 2.
That the first Christian religion which our
English Anceitours (hauing bene euer before bondslaues (saith S. Beda l. 2. c. 1. of
Idols) receaued from S. Gregory by his legat
S. Austin, was Papistical. 3. That al Christendome was in S. Gregories time, Papistical, becaufe it communicated with him in
faith and religion as is euident by his Epistles written to al partes of Christendome.
Thus we see this mans smal wit in prouing his vntruthes : Now let vs see his
good wil.

Bel pag. 3.
S. Ignat. ep.
ad Mariam
Caffab.
6. Very loth he is to graunt the Pope the
name of Pope, which Saints, Councels,
Princes, Catholiques, & Schismatiks haue
euer

euer giuen him. *Bishops of Rome* (faith he)
now called Popes. And when not Syr ? did not
S. Ignatius who liued in the Apoſtles tyme
cal S. Anacletus Pope?did not alſo S. Iuſtin
euen as the Magdeburgians confeſſe ? did
not S. Auſtin, S. Hierome, S. Ambroſe,
Vincent: Lirin: & others aboue a thouſand
yeares a goe ? did not the Councel of Calcedon,ot Carthage, of Mileui of Epirus ? do
not the Grétians cal the Bishop of Rome
Pope. Was he not alwaies called Pope as
wel in England as in al Chriſtendome els
vntil the 26. yeare of Henry 8. when hauinge reuoulted from the Popes obedience,
he commanded this name to be razed out
of al writings calendaries, & Holy Doctors
whatſoeuer.

7. And a maruailous thing it is to con-
ſider the contradictious ſpirit of Proteſtants. They wil cal vs nothing but Papiſts
(as Arians called Catholique Romans) and
our religion Popish , which are bynames
inuented of them ſelues, and deriued from
the name of Pope ; and yet wil they not cal
him Pope, which hath bene his name euer
ſince the Apoſtles time. And thus much touching Bels proofe of his Aſſumption out of
S. Gregory.

8. Next he alleadgeth S. Ambroſe ſaying
Dauid being King was ſubiect to no human law.
But

S.Iuſtin. ep.
ad zenam &
ſeren.
S.Aug.epiſt.
92.95.261.
S.Hiero. ep.
ad Damaſ.
Amb. ep. 81
Vincét.cont
hæreſ. libe-
ratus in bre-
uiar.cap.22.
Concil. Cal-
cedon.aſ.16.
Carthag. &
Mileuil. a-
pud Auguſt.
ep.90.& 92.
Epirot. ep.
ad Hermiſ-
Conſtantin.
in edicto.
Galli Placi-
dici epiſt.ad
Pulcheriam
Choniatas.
Vide epiſt.
trium Con-
cil.Africon.
ad Damaſ.
to.1.Camil.
*Proteſtants
cal vs Pa-
piſts of the
Pope & yet
vvil not cal
him Pope.*
Victor de
perſecut.vā-
dalica.lib.1.
Bel p.3.
Gregor. Tu-
ron.de glor.
mart.cap.25.
30.& 79.

But (besids that the word (*human*) is not in that place) S. Ambrose freeth Kings onely from penalty of ciuil or temporal lawes. For how subiect he thought them to be to Ecclesiasticall lawes, appeareth by his excommunicating the Emperors Thodosius, and Maximus; beside that Constantin and Valentinian professed them selues to be vnder Bishops. And doubtles the human lawes enacted by the Apostles Act: 15. v. 18 and 1. Cor: 7 v. 12. exempted no more Princes then priuat persons; S Hierome, Bel affirmeth to teach the same that S. Ambrose: but neither alledgeth his wordes, nor quoteth ether booke, or chapter, perhaps becaufe he made leffe shew for him.

Bonus imperator intra non supra ecclesiā est. Ambr. epift. 32. Theodoret. lib.5.cap.18. Sozomen. l. 7.c.24. Paulin.in vita Ambrof. Ruffin.lib.1. c.2. Theodoret. lib.4.cap.5.

9. Euthimius he citeth becaufe he writeth. *That Dauid as a King had God onely iudge ouer his sinnes.* But he meaneth of a temporal iudge as doe alfo the Glosse, and lira cited by him. And though S. Thomas proue of fet purpofe. That the Pope may depofe Princes, yet is not Bel ashamed to cite him becaufe he faith 1. 2. q. 96. art. 5. *That a King is not subiect to compulsion of his owne lavvs.* As if therfore he were subiect to no law. Hereafter the Reader neede not maruail to fee Bel citing Scriptures, and Fathers for his purpofe, feing he abftayneth not from his profeffed aduerfaries. For with him al is fish that

Bel p. 3. Euthym. in Pfalm. 50. Gloffa ordin. & lyra in Pfalm.50. S.Thom.2. 2.q.12.art.2.

comes to net, and as litle make the one for
him, as the other. Laftly he citeth Hugo
Card : writing . *That God alone is aboue al* Hugo Card.
in pfal.50.
cap. 1.
Kings. But this is ment in temporalibus as
before we cited out of Innocent. 3.

10. After thefe proofs of his Affump- Bel p. 4. 5.
tion Bel hudleth vp fix vntruthes togeather
faying. *The good Kings Iofue, Dauid, Salomon,* Vntruthes
Iofaphat, Ezechias, and Iofias knew right wel they 5. 6. 7. 8. 9.
had authority aboue al Priefts : and therfore tooke 10.
vpon them not onely to command & control them;
but alfo to depofe euen the high Priefts them felues.
For proofe of thefe vntruthes he referreth
vs to his Golden Balance, and I refer him
for confutation of them, to Doctor Staple-
tons Conterblaft againft Horns vaine blaft,
& his Relection con: 2.q: 5: ar.1. Onely I fay
that Iofue was no King, nor the Scripture
affordeth any colour of faying that any high
Prieft was depofed by any of the faid Kings,
except Abiathar by Solomõ 3. reg: c. 2: v. 35.
et. 27. And yet (as it is gathered out of the 3. Reg. 4.
7. 4.
4. chapter where he is accounted Prieft in
Salomons raigne) Salomon depofed him
not, but onely for a time confyned him to
his howfe for his confpiracy with Adonias,
and fo debarred him from executing his
Prieftly function. And though he had depofed him he had not done it as King , but
as Prophet fulfilling as the Scripture tefti-
C   fyeth

3.*Reg.* 2.*v.*
27.
fyeth the Prophify againſt the howſe of Hely, from whence Abiathar deſcended. And this is al which Bel obiecteth againſt the Popes ſuperiority ouer Princes Now let vs ſee how he anſwereth one obiection of Catholique in anſwers wherof he ſpendeth the reſt of this article.

CHAP. VI.
Bels anſwer to an argument of Catholiques for the Popes authority, confuted.

Bel p. 5.

BEL for better ſatisfaction (as he ſaith) of the vulgar ſorte propoundeth one obiection of Catholiques, but yet ſo nakedly, and without al forme or faſhion of argument (ſetting downe an Antecedent without any conſequent) that therby one may gheſſe he meaneth nothing leſſe then to frame (as he promiſſeth) a plaine, and ſincer ſolution vnto it. And yet the obiection though ſo ſillily propounded, not onely much trobleth many vulgar people (as he ſaith) but puſſeth him ſelfe ſo, as after ſeuen leaues ſpent to diuert the Readers minde, & to make him forget (as Heritiks vſe to do) the argument, which he can not anſwer, he ſyndeth no better ſolution, then to graunt what the Antecendent con-

The manner of Proteſtants in anſwering Catholiks.

contayneth and to fay nothing to the con-
fequent following therof.

2. Wherfore becaufe Bel was fo trobled
with the matter of this obiection, as he
forgot the forme, I wil fupply his default,
and argue thus in forme. He by whofe authority the Empire was tranflated, the electors of the Emperor appointed, and the
elected is confirmed, and whofe fuperiority
ouer them many Emperors haue willingly
acknowledged, hath fome fuperiority ouer
Emperors : but the Pope is fuch, as by his
authority the Empire &c. Ergo the Pope
hath fome fuperiority ouer Emperors. The
forme is fyllogiftical and good. The Propofition is manifeft, for no power or dignity
can be truly tranflated, or confirmed by in-
feriors or equals, but onely by fuperiors :
none (efpecially) willingly acknowledge
as fuperior, whome they thinke is not.

3. The Affumption contayneth three
parts expreffed in the Propofition, wherof
the firft vz. That the Empire was tranflated
by the Popes authority Bellarm: l. de tranfl: *Bellarmin.*
Imper : c. 4 proueth by the teftimony of 33.
writers & c. 5. by the confeffion of 11. Emperors : and Princes, and c. 6. by affertion
of 7. Popes. Yea Bel (though with much a
doe) confeffeth it page. 12. faying. *That
Charles the great* (to whome the Empire was

firſt tranſlated) *was made Emperor by Pope
Leo 3. for reſtoring him to his place, and dignity,
being driuen out by the Romans,* though ſoone
after he condemne the Pope of treaſon for
this tranſlation. But differing the queſtion
of treaſon til a non (which hindreth not
the verity of the tranſlation if the tranſlator
haue power to transfer : as a ſouldier may
by gift, or ſale truly, and yet trayterouſly
tranſlate his armes, and munition to the
Enemies) I ask of Bel, whether the Pope
did truly tranſlate the Empire, or no. If he
did, then hath the Pope power to tranſlate
Empires: If he did not, then was nether
Charles the great, nor any of his ſucceſſors
to this day true Emperors. And if the Pope
be Antichriſt (as Bel auoucheth) for depoſing ſome few Emperors for iuſt cauſes; Bel
may be wel accounted Lucifer, for depoſing at once, and for no fault at al, the Emperors of the weſt, which haue bene theſe
800. yeares. But Proteſtants haue great
cunning in making and vnmaking Emperors, according as it redoundeth in their
opinion to the grace or diſgrace of Popes.
For when the Pope depoſeth them, they be
true Emperors, but when he maketh them,
they haue onely (as Willet writeth) *the name
title, and image of Emperors.* But let them anſwer this dilemma. Theſe Emperors whom
the

p. 13.

Proteſtants
can make
& vnmake
Emperors
vvhen they
liſt.

Willet Cō-
tract. 4. q.
10.p.178.

the Pope depoſed ſince Carolus Magnus, were true or falſe Emperors? If falſe, he did a good deed in depoſing them: If true, then hath the Pope authority to make true Emperors, and tranſlate Empiers.

4. The ſecond parte included in my Aſſumption vz. That the Pope appointed the electors of the Emperor, and confirmed the elected, touching the apointing of electors is confeſſed by Bel pag. 14. and touching the confirmation is conteſted by many hiſtriographers, and practized by as many as are crowned Emperors. The laſt parte vz, that Emperors haue acknowledged the Popes ſuperiority Bel him ſelf confeſſeth page 17. where he ſayth, *That ſome Chriſtian Kings and Emperors haue ʋpon a blynd Zeale humbled them ſelues to the Pope*, yea (which is more) *haue yeldeed ʋp their ſoueraigne rights to him.* And ſhal not the Pope be ſuperior to them, who haue humbled them ſelues & yeelded their ſoueraingties vnto him?

5. But what ſhift hath Bel to auoide this? forſooth that thoſe Chriſtian Princes were blynd. O moſt blynd anſwerer? not ſeing that he graunteth more then his aduerſary requireth. Catholiques argue that Kings, and Emperors haue acknowledged Popes their ſuperiors, this Bel graunteth in confeſſing their humiliation to Popes, which is

C 3 neuer

Likevviſe vvhen vvillet liſt the imperial authority is in the Pope loc.ſcit. But vvhen he liſt not,he is no tempo-ral Prince. ib. q. 8. p. 154 155.

pag. 17. O dolor fraudata ſunt tali magiſterio tempora antiqua. Auguſt. lib. 1.cont. Gaudenſ.c.19.

neuer done, but to Superiors. and addeth
that they haue yeelded vp their Souereigne
rights, which is more then the obiection
contayneth. And what he addeth of blynd
zeale maketh nothing to the purpose. Because the question is not vpon what cause
Kings, and Emperors humbled them selues
to the Popes, but whither they did or no.
And because they haue so done (as Bel confesseth) Catholiques infer the Pope to be
their Superior. Vnles perhaps Bel think
blynd zeale to disanul euery fact, or gift,
and so say the Iewes persecuted not the
Church, because they did it vpon blynd
zeale. Ro. 10. v. 2. nor our Catholike aūce-
tors gaue any liuings to Churches, because
they did it vpon blynd zeale (as Bel must
think) for maintenance of Papistry. Neuertheles because the Reader may see whither
is more likly to be blind, a dooble turne
coate Minister, or so many Princes as haue
humbled them selues to Popes, I wil name
onely a few Emperors, omitting for bre-

Cassiodor. uity sake both Christian Kings, and the
Miscell. vid.
Baron.anno heathen Attilas miraculously made to reue-
452. rence Pope Leo.
Euseb.lib. 6.
c.25. 6.   Philippe the first Christian Emperor
Nicephor. about the yeare 246. reuerenced Pope Fa-
lib.13.c.34.
Bel p. 113. bian. Constantin worthely (saith Bel) syr-
Edictū Con- named the great held the stirrop to Pope
stantini.
                                        Siluester

Siluefter about the yeare 323. Soone after in S. Ambrofe and S. Chrifoftomes tyme as them felues witnes *Emperors bowed their necks euen to Priefts knees and layd their heads vnder their hands*, the fame teftifieth Pope Gelafius of Anaftafe Emperor of his tyme, and S. Gregory of Emperors before his tyme. Iuftin about the yeare 525. humbled him felf to the ground to Pope Ihon 1. Iuftinian 534. humbled him felf to Pope Agapet and worshiped him. Iuftinian the fecond about the yeare 710. kiffed the feet of Pope Conftantin. Ihon Paleologus wold haue kneeled to Pope Eugenius 4. in the yeare 1438. And thus did the Emperors of the Eaft.

7. Of the weftern Emperors Charles the great about the yeare 773. cold not be held by Pope Adrian I. from kiffing his feete. Lewis his fone fent the honorableft of his court to meet Pope Steuen 4. him felf went a myle and as foone as he faw him, lighting from his horfe, with great veneration brought him into the city in the yeare 817. Lewis 2. went a myle to meet Pope Nicolas 1. and putting his hand to his horfes brydle brought him into his Camp about the year 860. Henry 3. 1077. barefooted in the depth of winter attended vpon Gregory 7. Henry 4. IIII. kiffed the feet of Pope Pafcal 2. Frederick 1. about the year

S. Ambr. de dignit. facerd.c.2.
Chrifofto. hom.4. & 5. in illud Ifaiæ. vidi Dominum. *The like* S. Hilary. l. cont. Conftant.
Gelaf. 1. ep. ad Anaftaf.
S.Greg.in 4. Pfal.pænit.
Baron.anno 536. ex Anaftaf.Mifcell. zonora. Naucler.General.18.
Platina in Coftantino. Naucler.general.24.
Concil. Florent. per Iouerium.
Platina in Adrian.1. Naucler. general.26.
Centur. 8. c. 10.col.724.
Platida in Stephan. 4. Naucler.general. 28.
Platina in Nicolao 1. Plat na in Gregor.7. Naucler. general. 36.

Platina in
Pascali 2.
Naucler. ge-
neral. 38.
Platin. in A-
drian. 4. Ale-
xand. 3.
Naucler. ge-
ner. 40.
Onuphrius
in chron.
Plat. in Ioã.
22,
Naucler. ge-
neral. 48.
Surius in cõ-
mentar.

1155. held the stirrop to Pope Adrian 4. and 1177. kissed the feete of Pope Alexander 3. Sigismund 1418. prostrate on the ground, with most great veneration kissed the feete of Pope Martin 5. Charles the 5. 1530. 1538. kissed the feete of P. P. Clement 7. & Paul 3. and wold haue held the stirrop of Pope Clement 7. of al these Christian Emperors it is recorded in publik histories how they humbled them selues to Popes, and of no Catholique Christian Emperor is written that he refused to do the like.

8. Let now any indifferent Reader be iudge, whither the Pope haue reason to think him self to be Superior to Christian Emperors, seing so many, and they the most wise, most valiant, and most famous, of al, euen the very first and last of them, haue acknowledged him their Superior. And whither it be likly that. Bel shold see, and al these Christian Emperors together with their Counsellors, Nobles, Prelats, Diuins, & Commons, be blind; yea so blind as they shold not see that their humiliation

p. 17.

to the Pope *opened the window* (sayth Bel) *to al Antichristian tyrany.*

9. Vsual it is for Heretiks to condemne not onely former Catholiques, but euen Heritiks of blindnes if they disagree from them: So the Caluinist condemneth the Lu-

See S. Au-
stin lib. 2.
cont. Iul. c.
10. to. 7.

therian,

therian, the Puritan faith the fame of the
Proteſtant, the Brouniſt of the Puritan. And
King Edward, ſixtimes códemned K. Hen-
ries religion of blindnes, and thoſe found
the like meaſure in Queene Elizabeths *Petition ex-*
time, and ſhe had fared a like, if more then *hibited to*
a thouſand miniſters, who condemne her *his Maieſty*
proceding of Enormities, Superſtitions and *1603.*
abuſes contrary to Scripture, had obtayned
their petition. But of them al we may ſay
as Tertullian ſaid of Heritiks in his time. *Tertull. lib.*
To theſe alone, and to theſe firſt was the truth re- de præſcrip.
uealed forſooth, they obtayned greater fauor, and
fuller grace of the diuil. For light they haue but *2. Cor. 11.*
ſuch as cometh from him who *transfigureth* *v. 14.*
himſelfe into an angel of light, and brag of it *Conference*
til as the Kings maieſty ſaid of the Scottiſh *p. 71.*
miniſters) *they goe made with their owne light.*
And thus much of the Catholiques obiection and Bels anſwer therto. Now let vs
come to his ſleunderous vntruthes.

Chap. VII.
Some of Bels ſlaunderous vntruthes diſproued.

BEL perceauing that the ſlightnes of his
forſaid anſwer would haue eaſely appeared, if it had bene ſet down immediatly
after the Catholiques obiection, without
daze-

dazeling the Readers eyes before with some
other matter, though best before he answered it to slander both Pope and Papists,
and to tel the Reader a long tale of steps de-
uised by him selfe, in an imaginary ladder of
his owne. *Many absurd things* (saith he) *haue*
bene affirmed by Popes parasits for aduancement of
his primacy. If one aske him? what these absurd things are, & who were these parasits.
He nameth none. For *dolosus versatur in gene-*
ralibus. But let vs heare him proue his saying
As Victoria doth testify in these words. Sed glos-
satores iuris hoc dominion &c. The glossors of the
law haue giuen this dominion to the Pope, they
being poore in substance, and learning.

2. Here in steed of proofs I find an vntruth. For nether doth Victoria in these
words speaketh of many things, but onely of
this dominion (meaning temporal ouer
the world) nether yet doth he cal it absurd.
This want therfore Bel thought to supply
of his owne store, and therfore Englishing
Victorias words, he addeth (*and these lordly*
titles) and then as hauing a sure foundation,
he rayseth his lie somewhat higher, saying.
That Victoria affirmeth, ignorance and pouerty
were the beginning of al lordly Popery. Wheras
Victoria speaketh onely of temporal dominion ouer the whole world, and Bel him
selfe herafter maketh Kings and Emperors
　　　　　　　　　　　　　　　　　　　authors

pag 5.

11. *vntru-*
the.
Victoria de
potestate
ecclesiæ re-
lect.1.sect.6.

VVhen he
speaketh a
lye he spea-
keth of his
owne.
Ioan. 8. v.
44.
12 *vntruth.*

Bel p. 17.
4. *Contra-*
dict.

authors of the Popes dominion.

Bel p. 7.

3. Hauing thus dealt with Victoria he falleth to slander the late Popes saying. *That they haue challenged more then human, and royal power euen that povver vvhich is due & proper to God alone.* True it is that both late & ancient 13 *vntruth.* Popes haue challéged more then human, & royal power. For such is al spiritual power as shal hereafter be proued. But most false it is that any Pope ancient or late, challengeth any power proper to God, or that any Catholique attributeth such power vnto him. As his brother willet telleth him in these *VVillet cōtrad.* 544. *prel.* 3. *p.* 210. words *The Pope by their owne confession can not do al that Christ did.* But what say you Sir to Caluin attributing duine power to Magistrats? And to Protestants *arrogating greater,* *Caluin 4. instit. c. 20. parag. 4. Magistratus præditi sunt diuina authoritate.* *more intolerable, and les excusable authority and power, then euer the Pope did, as Melanthon* writeth, or to other calling Princes Gods, as *Melancthon apud Sur. 1501.* you shal heare a none. Now let vs see what proofs he bringeth of his slander. Gerson *Bel p. 6. Gerson de potest. eccl. confid. 12. p. 3.* (saith he) *reporteth that some Popish parasits say that Christ hath giuen al that power in heauen and earth, to S. Peter, and his successors which was giuen to himselfe, and that he hath written in the Popes thighe King, of Kings, and Lord of Lords.* And that there is no power Ecclesiastical or temporal but from the Pope.

4. Behould good Reader Bels euil dealing

ling with Popes. He chargeth al late Popes
with challenging power proper to God,
which is a moſt heinous and Luciferian
crime, and for proofe therof bringeth not
one word, or deede of any one of them, but
ones report of ſpeeches of ſome nameles
fellows, without proouing that any Pope
ether allowed, or liked, yea heard of ſuch
ſpeeches. Were ſuch dealing with any priuat man tolerable? And how much les with
ſo great Princes as Popes (at leaſt) are. Sup-
poſe paraſits had attributed to Popes power
proper to God, doth it therfore follow that
they challeng it? Doe al Princes challeng
what their flatterers impoſe vpon them?
Did Q Elizabeth challég to be a Goddeſſe
becauſe Caſe Cambden and other Proteſtants called her a Goddeſſe ? ſhe (ſaieth
Cambden) is *the onely Goddeſſe of Britans. She*
shalbe my Goddeſſe, the groũd wher she was borne
is rather to be adored then adorned she is Numen
to be worshiped of the whole word. Or doth his
Maieſty challeng to be *head of the Church of*
France, or Toby Mathew to be the *ornament*
of learning, and religion, becauſe Bel ſo tearmeth them? did S. Paul and Barnaby challég to be Gods, becauſe the Licaonians did
ſo account them? doth not the Pope profeſſe him ſelf to be Chriſts Vicar, and ſeruant of his ſeruants? How ſtandeth this
                                                with

Proteſtants
cal Princes
Goddes.

Caſe in ep.
ſuop Poli-
corum.
Cambden in
Berqueria,
in Natis ad
lectorem. in
Cantic. & E-
piſt.
Bel in his
epiſtles to
the King
& to B. of
Durhom.
Act. 14. v. 10.
11. 12.

with the challeng of equality.

5. But I deny that euer any Catholique attributed to the Pope power proper to God: let vs therfore confider Gerfons report. The firft point *is, that Chrift hath giuen al the power in heauen and earth to S. Peter, and his fuccefsors which was giuen to him felf.* But befide that, thefe words concerne no les the Ancient then the late Popes, namely S. Peter him felf, though Bel be afhamed to charg them with this ftaunder, are thefe woords of Popifh parafits? doe they giue to men power proper to God alone? Then was S. Chrifoftome a Popifh parafite, and gaue to Priefts power proper to God, when he faid. *Priefts haue al power of heauenly things, and the very felf fame al kind of power which Chrift had of his Father.* S. Bafil fayth, *that Chrift gaue this authority to others.* S. Leo writeth *that S. Peter had thofe things by participation, which Chrift had proper by power.* or doth Bel think that our King in creating a deputy in Ireland, and giuing him authority to gouerne that Kingdome, giueth him power proper to Kings? Are deputies Kings are they no more fubiects? True it is that the power which Popes haue, came from God alone as the authority of deputies cometh from Kings, but fuch power by commifsion is no more proper to God, then the

like

Bels flander toucheth as vvel S. Peter and the auncient Popes as the late.

S. Chryfoft. lib. 3. de facerdot.

S. Bafil. homil. de pœnitent.
S.Leo ferm. 2. de Natali Pet.& Pauli.

like in deputies is proper to Kings.

6. The second point in Gersons report is that the forsaid nameles persons cal the Pope _Lord of Lords, and King of Kings._ If these be parasits Words and make men equal to God then was Daniel a parasite, & he made Nabuchodonozor equal to God in calling him _King of Kings._ Vnles Bel allow this title in a heathen Prince and account it blasphemy in a Christian. Besyds the Scripture it self doth apply the very names of Christ and God vnto men. And S. Bernard no parasite but a holy writer (in Caluins opinion) calleth the Pope _Prince of Bishops, leader of Christians, hammer of tyrants, father of Kings, Vicar of Christ, Christ of the Lord, and God of Pharao._ And thus spoke S. Bernard euen in those books, where (according to Caluins iudgment) _he spoke it so as truth it selfe semed to speake._ And albeit the Pope do not entitle him selfe King of Kings but _Seruant of Gods seruants_, which is a more humble stile , then any Prince vseth : yet rightly might he , becausͤ he hath twoe Kingdomes, vz. Naples and Sicily , Feudatary , and temporally subiect vnto him, as he had also Ireland , before he gaue it vnto the crowne of England in K. Henry 2. time.

7. But because Bel is so hard a corstruer of some Catholiques words, let vs heare, not

Daniel. 2. v. 37.

Exod. 7. psal. 81. Io. 10. psal. 104. Esaiæ 45. S. Bernard. l. 2. & 4. de cõsiderat. Caluin. lib. 4. instit. c. 7. paragr. 22.

Caluin. l. 4. c. 11. paragr. 11.

The Pope gaue Irlãd to the King of England. Stovv. ann. 2171.

not a parasite, but a Protestant Prelat, speaking not in absence but in presence of the King and realme. Bilson in his late sermon at the Kings coronation saith *Kings be Gods by office, they haue the society of his name, are in his place, their very robes are sanctified, euery thing belonging to them is sacred, are pertakers, with Christ in the power, honour, and iustice of his Kingdome on earth, and partake with Gods homage.* Behould he calleth Kings Gods, and partners with God in his name, power, honour, and homage, and yet no Catholique chardgeth Protestants that they attribute to the King, or that he challengeth power proper to God alone.

Bilson.

8. The third point reprehended by Bel in Gersons reporte, is that ecclesiastical and temporal power is said to come from the Pope. *This* (saith Bel pag: 16.) *is to make the Pope author of al power, a thing proper to God.* This say I is for Bel to vtter two vntruthes at once: for neither do they speake of al power, but only of power in earth, which they deuide into ecclesiastical & temporal, besides which there is power in heauen of God, and Saints: neither do they make the Pope, author of al power in earth, but only saie it commeth from the Pope, which is not to make him author therof, vnles Bel wil make euery officer author of what he

14. vntruth
15. vntruth.

doth

doth in the Princes name, euery instrument author of the effect it worketh by vertue of the cause. And thus much touching this slaunder of Popes, imposed by Bel. Now let vs come to others, for no other stuffe we are like to hear hereafter in this article.

Chap. VIII.
Certaine false steps of a ladder vvhich Bel *imagineth the Pope had to climbe to his superiority, disproued.*

Bel pag.17.

BEL hauing vpon the foresaid words of some nameles Catholiques, taken occasion to slaunder Popes, goeth on in like sorte for many leaues together, setting downe steppes in a ladder, which (as he imagineth) the Popes had to climbe to their superiority. *The first steppe* (saith he) *was the departure of the Emperour Constantine from Rome to Constantinople* : but if he had better considered, he should haue found that as the cittie of Rome decaied by Constantines departure, and Constantinople increased : So the Sea of Rome rather fel therby in external dignity, and the Sea of Constantinople rose, then otherwise. For wheras before Constantines going to Constantinople (which was about the yeare. 330. that church was but new, and a parish of another

Euseb. & Hieron. in chron. Conc. Constant. epist. ad Damasc. Gelas. ad Episcop. Dardaniz.

other church as Gelasius witnesseth, soone after in the yeare 381. it was made a Patriarchate next to Rome, and in the yeare 451. the Grecians gaue it equal priuiledges with Rome. And not content with this, about the yeare 600. that Patriarch arrogated the title of Oecumenical, that is ouer the whole worlde. And finallie in the yeare 1054. claimed the place of the first Patriarch, alleadging the Pope to haue lost his primacy by adding *filióque* to the Nicene Creed.

Conc. Constantin. c. 5. Concil. Calced. act. 16.

Sigebert. in chron.

2. *But Constantine* (sayth Bel) *at his departure did as the Popes parasites tel vs, giue lardge guifts to the Pope, euen his whole power, dominion, and territories, both in Rome, Italy, and al the west.* Behould a man (as the Prouerbe is) hauing a wolfe by the eare, which he dare neither hould nor yet let goe. For if he graunt, that Constantine gaue the Pope his whole power and dóminion ouer Rome, Italy, and al the west, he must needs graunt that the Pope of right hath imperial power ouer al the west. If he deny it, he sheweth not how Constátins departure was a steppe for the Pope to climbe to higher authority. Besides that, not Constantins departure, but his guifte should haue bene made the steppe. Notwithstanding choosing rather to condemne him selfe, of not shewing how Constantins departure was a steppe

pag. 7.

D for

for the Pope to climbe, then to graunt that
the Pope hath so good right to imperial
power ouer the west, he inclineth to denial of the guift, & citeth Valla, Volaterran,
Cathalan & Cusan, fowre late and obscure
writers against it, and tearmeth them Po-
pishe parasites who affirme it.

3. But against these foure late writers I
oppose foure most auncient, Isidor, Photius or Balsamon, Gratian, & Iuo, & many
late writers, besides two Iewes Rabby A-
braham, and Aben Esra, who al auouch
Constantins guift, whereof Photius and
the Iewes were professed enimies of the
Pope : and Bel him selfe confesseth that
some Emperours haue giuen the Pope their soue-
raigne rights. In which kinde no Emperour
excelled Constantine. yet *Bellarmine* (saith
Bel) *seemeth to doubt of this, and such like dona-*
tions. Wherein Sir ? In these words (saith
he) *there are extant at Rome the authentical eui-*
dences of these and the like donations, and if there
were not, prescription of eight hundred yeares
would aboundantlie suffice. For Kingdomes vn-
iustlie gotten are in proces of time made lawful.
as he proueth by the Romane Empier gotten by Cesar, the Kingdome of England by
Saxons, and others. What shew is in theis
words of doubt? or rather not of certainty?
For Bellarmin affirmeth that the Pope hath

two

Bellarmin.
lib.5. de Ro-
man. Pont.
c. 9.

Prescrip-
tion of 30.
yeares suf-
ficeth by ci-
uil lavv.

two iuſt titles to hould his eſtate: The firſt
is free guiſt of Princes , whereof he can
ſhew authentical euidences: the other pre-
ſcription of time.

4. *The ſecond ſteppe* (ſaith Bel) *was the fal*   *pag.* 8.
of the Empire in the weſt, in the yeare 471. *and*
vacancy theroffor almoſt 330. *yeares.* But how
this fal and vacancy of the Empire was a
ſteppe for Popes to climbe, neither he ſheweth nor any can imagin, eſpecially if (as
he writeth ſtraight after) *in this vacancie of*
the Empire Rome was ſpoiled with fier & ſword,
and the verie walles throwne downe to the
ground , and al Italia poſſeſſed of the Barbares
vntil Carolus Magnus, who was the firſt Emperour after the vacancie, if in this vacancy
Rome was deſtroied, and al Italy poſſeſſed
by Barbares (who for the moſt part were
heathens, or heretiks) how could it bee a
ſteppe for the Pope to climbe , and not
rather to fal?

5. Euident it is out of hiſtories of thoſe
times, that Popes in that vacancy were
ſometime vnder Barbares , ſometime vnder
Emperours of the Eaſt , according as the
one preuailed againſt the other (for falſe it
is that Barbares poſſeſſed al Italy vntil Carolus Magnus yea Bel before ſaid that *Popes*   *pag.* 2. 3
liued vnder Emperours vntil the yeare 603.) and
betwixt both liued in great daunger, ſubie-

   ćtion,

Siluerius.
Iohannes 1.
Martinus 1.
Leo 3.
Sergius.
Gregorius 2.
vid. Plati-
nam in vit.
Pont.

&ction, and mifery. Three of them died in banishment or prifon, one pitifullie mang-led and beaten, others should haue bene imprifoned and murdered, and diuers were ftraictlie befieged of their enimics. And for a long time none could be freelie elected without confent of the Barbares, or Empe-rours. And can we thinke that this was a time for Popes to climbe to greater authori-ty? I omit, that before Bel faid *Popes liued*

5. Contra-
dict.

in duetiful obedience vnder Emperours vntil the yeare 603. how doth he now faie that they climbe to tiranny from the yeare 471.

pag. 8. 9.

6. The 3. *fteppe* (faith Bel) *vvas the volūtarie Charter vvhich Conftantin the Emperour of Con-ftantinople made to Pope Benedict. 2. vz. that vvhofoeuer the Cleargie people and Romane foul-dires should choofe to be Bishoppe, al men should beleeue him to be the true Vicar of Chrift, vvith-out any tarying for any authority of the Empe-*

16 vntruth

rour of Conftantinople, or the deputy of Italie, as the cuftome and manner vvas euer before that day.

Platina in
Benedict. 2.

Thus (faith he) writeth Platina. *And the Popes almoft for the fpace of* 700. *yeares could haue no iurifdiction, nor be reputed true Ei-*

Vbicunque
eft impu-
dentia ibi
eft vltio.
Chrifofto.
hom. 4. in il-
lud Efai. vi-
di Dominū.

shoppes of Rome, vvithout the letter pattēts of the Emperour.

7. Behould the impudencie of this fel-low. Platina faith, *Vt antea fieri confueuerat,* Bel affirmeth him to fay, *it vvas the cuftome*

euer

euer before that daie. where is in Platina the worde (*euer*) where (*til that daie*) Nay doth not Platina faie that Pelagius the fecond was created *iniuſſu principis* without commaund of the Prince, that Siluerius was made Pope *iubente Theodohato* at the commaund of Theodate a Gothishe King? Did not Bel him felfe tel vs that *Barbarians ruled in Rome, and poſſeſſed al Italie for* 330 *yeares, vntil Charles the great*? How then could it be, that before Benet the fecond neuer Popes could haue iurifdiction, and be accompted true Bishops of Rome without letter patents of Emperours, who were profeſſed enimies, and made warre vpon moſt of thefe Barbarians? or is Bel fo mad euen to imagine, that Pope Anaclete (to omit S. Peters want of Neroes letter patents) could haue no iurifdiction, or be reputed true Bishoppe of Rome, without letter patents of Domitian the Emperour, Clement without Traianus? Cornelius without Decius? Cuius without Diocletian? or the other holie Popes that were martyred vnder heathen Emperours, without their letter patents?

8. What therefore Platina faieth had bene wont to be done before, about expecting the confirmation of the Emperour, or his deputie in Italy, he vnderſtood of the time fince Pope Vigilius (excepting Pela-

Platin.in pelagio & in Siluerio.
Nauclerus general. 18.
Bland. Dec. 1.l.3.

pag. 8.

gius

gius 2.) vntil Benedict the second; for Iustinian the Emperour hauing in the yeare 553. quite subdued the Gothes, and recouered Rome and Italie, which had bene lost to the Barbares in the yeare 475. or 476. (Bel

pag. 8.

wronglie saith 471.) imitating the tiranny of the Gothish Kings, who being Arians much oppressed the Popes, appointed that they after their election, should expect the Emperour or his deputies confirmation, before they were consecrated, or vsed their function. And this order endured from Pope Vigilius his time, vntil Benedicte the second, for more then one hundred years,

Placin. sup.

at what time Constantine the fifth, in the yeare 684 moued (saie the writers) at the holines of Benedicte 2. abrogated the said order, permitting as wel the consecration, as the election of Popes vnto the Romane Cleargie, and people.

9. Hereby wee see, that the creation of Popes without Emperours consent, was no new thing begun first in Benedict. 2. but an auncient libertie begun euen with the Popedome it selfe, and continued vnder Constantine the great and other Christian Emperours vntil the time of the barbarous Gothish Kings, & restored againe by Constantine the fifth. but marke good reader how Bel before confessed Gregory the great who

Papistry aboue a thovvsand years ould yet nevv gvith Bel. pag. 2.

(who died about the yeare 604) to haue bene a Papiſt, and here acknowledgeth the Emperour Phocas in the yeare 607 to haue declared Rome to be the head of al Churches: likewiſe Conſtantine the fifth in the yeare 984. to haue declared the Pope to bee Chriſts true vicar: yet neuertheles wil haue Papiſtrie, and Popes ſupremacie to be new things. So to him a thowſand yeares are as one daie.

10. The fourth ſteppe Bel maketh the depoſition of Childrick King of France by Pope Zacharie, which (he ſaith) the Pope did for hope of aduauncemēt. But as for the depoſition, it was moſt iuſt, for it was done, not only with the conſent of the whole realme of France , no man reclaiming, but at their requeſt as teſtifieth Sabellius æneid 8. & Blandus Dec : 1. lib: 10. out of Alcuin : Paule and others, at what time the Sarazins poſſeſſing al Egipt, Siria, Affrick, & Spaine, had not long before inuaded France , with many hundred thouſands of men, & Childrick being extreamlie ſlouthful, & careles of the commonwealth, not only France, but al Chriſtendome was in great daunger to be ouerrunne with thoſe Sarazins.

11. And that Pope Zacharies intention was iuſte, appeareth by his great holines of life, who (as Anaſtaſius and others write)

The ſame declared Iuſtinian about the year 532. epiſt. ad Ioā. P. and Valentinian ep .ad Theodoſium lōg before. pag. 83. 2. Pet. 3. v. 8.

This Childrick was ſurnamed the Idiot or ſenſles. Claud. Paradin. Annal. Frāc. Naucler. general. 25. Platin. in Gregor. 3.

was ſo

was so good as he would not requite euil with
euil, and much leſſe for his owne aduaun-
cement wrongfullie depoſe a King, as Bel
vpon meare malice, without al proofe doth
calumniate him, taking vpon him to know
the ſecrets of harts, and *Iudge an others ſeruant.*
Beſides, that neither was he any way ad-
uaunced by Pipin, nor can it be iuſtlie pre-
ſumed, that he expected to be. But for what
end ſoeuer it had bene done, it could be no
ſteppe to the Popes ſuperiority ouer Princes, but an act of ſuch authority already
gotten,

12. Whereupon Bellarmin out of this ſo
auncient example, aboue eight hundred
yeares agoe, proueth Popes to haue ſuch
authority, whereat Bel ſo ſtormeth that he
ſaith, *Ieſuits teach that the Pope can ſet vp, and*
pul downe Kings at his pleaſure, and that they are
grand maiſters, and Architects of ſeditions, rebel-
lious, and bloudie treaſons, which are but falſe
ſlaunders of his owne. *Et quis innocens erit ſi*
accuſaſſe ſufficiat. And aduiſeth Chriſtian Princes that *if the Pope ſend any into their dominions,*
with his Buls and excommunications, they deale
with them as Phillip the faire dealt with Boniface
the eights Nuncio, vyhom he impriſoned, and bur-
ned their buls : and as Charles the ſixt, vyho gaue
ſentence that the buls of Benedic. 13. *ſhould be rent*
in pieces, the bearer ſet on the pillarie, and traduced
in the

Marginalia (left):

1. Paralip.
6.
Roman, 14.

Bellarm.lib.
5. de Rom.
Pontif. c.8.

pag 10.
17 vntruth
18 vntruth

pag. 11.

in the pulpit. But withal he forgot to tel what befel to Phillip for his euil dealing with Boniface, vz. That he him selfe was killed with a fal of his horse, his three sonnes vntimelie died, their wiues shamefullie taken in adultery, and the crowne translated from his Issue to an other line. Of Benedic 13. no meruaile if he and his messenger were so handled, because he was no true, but a false Pope; and thus much of Bels first oure steppes, now let vs see the rest.

Genelrard. in chron. Antonin. 3. part. art. 20. paragr. 20.

Chap. IX.

The rest of Bels false steps, and slaunderous vntruths in this article disproued.

THE *first steppe* (saith Bel) *vvas the decaie of the Empire in the East about the yeare 756, at vvhat time Pipin being called into Italie by Pope Steeuen 2 to deliuer Rome from the siedge of Lombards, and ouercomming them gaue vp the gouernement of Italie into the Popes handes.* Here Bel hudleth vp store of vntruths. *That the empire decaied in the East about the yeare 756.* For it decaied long before about the yeare 635. vnder the heretical Emperour Heraclius, when the Sarazens conquered Palestin, Siria, and Egipt, and about the yeare 697. al Affrick, & went more & more decaying according as it reuolted from the faith and obedience

Bel pag. 11.

19 vntruth

Onuphr. in chron. Platin. in Honorio 1. art. 623. Balmerin. in chron. 639. Onuphr. in chron.

of the

of the Romane Sea, vntil in the yeare 1452.
it was vtterly extinguished, Conftantinople
being taken by Turks, and the Empetour
flaine. And about 756. wherof B. I fpeaketh,
the Eafterne Empire loft little or nothing,
except a verie fmal piece of Italie, called the
exarchate which the Lombards had conquered in the yeare 751.

2. *That Pipin gaue vp Italy into the Popes
hands.* Whereas Pipin fubdued only that part
of Italie which the Lombards held : *that in*
21 vntruth. *Pipins conqueft ended the vvhole povver of the Emperours Lieutenants in Italy.* This is doubly vn-
true. Firft becaufe Pipin conquered nothing
from the Emperour but from the Lombards, who foure or fiue years before, had
taken the exarchate of Reuenna from the
Empire. Secondly becaufe, befides that
which Pipin then conquered, or the Lombards had before taken from the Empire,
Naucler. ge- the Emperours had both then, and long
neral. 27. after great dominion in Italy, vz almoft al
Platin. in
Leone 3. the kingedome of Naples which he gouer-
Bland. Dec. ned by Lieutenants.
2. lib. 1.

3. But what was the end of this vntruth?
forfooth that we should Imagine, that in
Pipins time the Pope became Antechrift.
pag. 12. For *novv* (faith Bel, *vvas he taken avvay, vvho*
2. Theff. 2. *as the Apoftle teacheth vs hindred the comming
of Antechrift,* meaninge the Emperours do-
                                                       minion

minion in Italie. Marke good reader in the
yeare 476. or as Bel faith 471. not only al
Italie, was taken from the Emperour, by
the Herules, but he alfo depofed, and the
weafterne Empire vtterlie diffolued. And
albeit in the yeare 553. the Grecian Emperours recouered Italy againe, yet foone after in the yeare 568. they loft a great parte
therof to the Lombards, which they neuer
recouered. And in neither of thefe times
Bel thinketh the hinderance of Antichrifts
comming, whereof S. Paul fpake, to haue
bene taken away , becaufe then he findeth
no coulour to make the Pope a new Antechrift.

4. But when the Grecian Emperours loft
to the Lōbards the exarchate of Reuenna (a
petit dominion of fiue Citties, & one shire
called Emilia, though they helde ftil a good
part of Italie) then the hindrance of Ante-
chrifte was taken away , becaufe forfooth
foone after, that exarchate being taken by
Pipin from the Lombards , it was by him
giuen to the Pope , who therby became
Antechrift , as if Bishops become Ante-
chrifts by temporal liuings, a reafon fmel-
ling ranckely of a puritan fpirit , which
would pul downe Bishopricks; but if temporal dominion made the Pope Antechrift,
he was long before Pipin ; for in the yeare
699.

Baron. an-
nal.
Onuphr. in
chron.

Onuphr. in
chron.
Palmer. in
chron. 572.

Naucler. ge-
neral. 16.

Ado in
chronic.
Bland. Dec.
1. lib. 10.
Magdeburg.
cent.8.c.10.
Regino Ado
Sigebert. in
chron.Mag-
deburg. su-
pra.

699. Aripert King of Lombardy gaue to him
the Coctian Alpes where Genèua is, which
donation confirmed King Luithprand in
the yeare 714. as the Magdeburgians confesse. and King Pipin in the yeare 755. added the exarchate, and a good piece of Italy
which he had conquered from the Lombards.

5. As for the hindrance of Antechrists
comming whereof S. Paule speaketh, it
was not the petit dominion which the Emperours had in the exarchate of Reuenna,
but the Romane Empire it selfe; as testifie

S. *Chrisost.*
S. *Ciril.*
S *Hierom.*
S. *August.*
tom.5.

S. Chrisostome, and others vpon that place,
S. Ciril Catech. 15. S. Hierom q. 11. ad Al-
gasiam: S. Augustin lib. 20. de ciuit. c. 19.
and other fathers who out of that place affirme, that Antechrist shal not come vntil
the Romane Empire be quite taken away,
which is not yet I let passe a contradiction

Contradict.

of Bel saying, p. 8. *that Barbarians possessed al
Italy vnto Carolus Magnus,* and pag. 11. *that in
Pipins time VVhoe VVas Carolus his father ended
the power of the Emperours Lieutenants in Italy.*
For how could the Emperours haue Lieutenants in Italy vntil Pipin, it Barbarians possessed al Italy vnto his sonnes time.

6. But the quicke sight of this fellowe,
whoe before called so many Kings & Emperours blinde, I can not let passe. He wri-
                                          teth

teth (pag. 11.) that *Pipin gaue vppe the gouernment of Italie into the Popes hands, a thing* (faith he) *fo apparant as it can not be denied,* and yet (pag.14.) confeffeth, *that he can not fee how the Pope vvas King in Pipins time.* So blinde he is that he can not fee, that to giue vp the gouernment of a Kingdome into ones hands, is to make him King. Againe he can not fee, hovv if *Pipin as Sigebert vvriteth* had Italie in *his poßeßion in the yeare* 801. and *Bernard made King thereof by Carolus Magnus* 812. *that the Pope vvas either then or novv any King at al.* Surelie Bel is either fhort fighted or ftarcke blinde. For what Sigebert writeth of Pipin, he meaneth not of Pipin Carolus his father and giuer of the exarchate, who died 768. but of Pipin Carolus his fonne: and neither his poffeffing Italy 801. nor his fonne Bernards kingdome therof 812. doth preiudice the Popes regalitie ouer the exarchate and Coctian Alpes, giuen him before by King Pipin & Aripert, any more then it doth preiudice the regality and dominion which the greeke Emperours had at the fame time ouer a great parte of Italie, vz. From Naples and Manfredonia to the fea of Sicily.

7. For befides that Lombardy (whereof Pipin and Bernard were kings) was then called Italie, as is euident out of Charles his teftament, where he faith. *Italie which is alfo called*

pag. 14. *His brother vvillet controuerf.* 4. q. 10 *p.* 7. *pag.* 178. *faith that the imperial authority is in the Pope.*

Naucler. general. 26. Palmerius in chronic. Paradin des allian- ces Genealo- giques.

Nauclerus general.17. Platina in Leone 3. Bland. Deci 1.l.1.

Nauclerus general. 18.

called Lombardy, becaufe they alone in **Italy**
were then called Kings, and poffeffed the
beft parte thereof, they were intitled of the
whole: as the Kings of England were before the vnion of Scotland by ftraungers
called in latin Kings of Britanny. And as
for Charles the great, he was foe far from
taking from the Pope, what his father Pipin had giuen, as he added thereto (faith
Nauclerus) *the ile of Corfica, and what is from*

Leo Oftien-
fis lib. 1.
chron. Caf-
finen.

Luna to the Alpes confines of Italy, and what be-
twixt Parma and Luca, together with the Duke-
domes of Spoleto and Beneuent.

8. But yet far greater blindenes it is, not
to be able to fee how the Pope can be now
any Kinge at al, if others were Kings of
Italie 800. years agoe, can he not fe how
kingdomes may be altered not only to different families, but euen to diuers nations
in leffe then eight hindred years ? are not
the Normans and their difcent Kings of
England becaufe they were not 800. nay
600: years agoe? are not Spaniards Kings in
Italie, becaufe they were not 400. yeares
agoe ? could not the Popes in eight hundred years fpace come to a kingdome either
by guifte of Princes or by iuft ware, or at
leaft by prefcription of time, which they
had not before.

9. As for the Popes befides the guifts of
Con-

Conſtantine, Ariẛhpert, Pipin, and Carolus Magnus before mentioned, Ludouic
Pius Emperour and ſonne to Carolus Magnus confirmed the donation of his grandfather Pipin , and afterward Counteſſe
Maud, gaue to the Pope Liguria and Tuſ-
cia in the yeare 1079. of which guifts the
authenticall euidences (ſaith Bellarmin)
are extant in Rome. which ſuffiſeth to let
Bel ſee how the Pope may be now a King,
though he were none in the yeare 812. beſides that (pag : 17.) he could ſee *how ſome*
Chriſtian Kings and Emperours haue yeelded vp
their ſoueraigne rights to the Pope, and (pag 11.)
how *Pipin gaue vp the gouernment of Italie into*
his hand, and is he ſtricken blinde in the
mideſt, ſo that (pag : 14.) he could not ſee
how the Pope is now any King at al. Thus much
of Bels blindnes out of his owne confeſſion. Now let vs ſee as much of his ſmal
credit by the like confeſſion.

10. *Bellarmin* (ſaith he) *muſt be credited at*
leiſure, when he telleth vs that Pipin gaue Rauenna,
and Pentapolis to S. Peter & S. Paul, meaning
the Pope, and yet him ſelfe telleth vs (pag :
11.) *that Pipin gaue vp the gouernement of Italie*
into the Popes hands. If Bellarmin muſt be credited at leiſure, for ſaying Pipin gaue to the
Pope a ſmal parte of Italie, though he proue
it by many witneſſes, and Bel confeſſe it to
be ſo

Marginal notes

Gratian. d.
63. can. ego
Ludouicus.

Leo lib. 3.
chron.c.48.

Bellarm. de
Rom. Pont.
c. 9.

Bel pag.14.
Bellar. ſup.

Ex Adone
loc. cit. &
l'b.3. c. 3. ex
regione &
Sigebert. in
chron.
Bland. Dec.
1. lib.10.
Magdeburg.
cent.8.c.10.

Bel p. 12
Bel not to
be credited.

be so *apparant that it can not be denied.* Surelie
him selfe must not be credited at al, for saying without al testimony, yea contrary to
his owne testimony (pag: 13.) *that he gaue
Italie to the Pope.* I omit a petit vntruth of his
saying that Meroueus was the first christian
King of France. So blinde he is that he
can not discerne the grand-father from the
grand-childe, Mercueus from Clodoueus,
a heathen from a christian.

Annal. Gall.
Claude Pa-
radin des
Alliances
Gnealogi-
ques.
Bel pag. 12.

11. The sixt steppe, Bel maketh the translation of the Empire by Pope Leo 3. from
the Greekes to the French, or Germans in
the person of Charles the great, of this
translation we haue spoken before, and it
is rather a notorious act of the Popes superiority ouer Emperours, then a steppe
thereunto. But because Sigebert in recoun-
ting it saith *Romani animo desciuerant ab Impe-
ratore Constantinopoli.* Which Bel Englisheth
reuolted from the Emperour, he inferreth
diuers vntruths: first *that Popes were subiect to
Emperours* 800. *yeares after Christ.* Secondly
*that the translation of the Empire implied flat trea-
son in the Pope, and Romans.* Thirdlie *that Sigebert saith they surrendered the right of their soueraigne to an othor.*

Sigeb. chro-
nic. 801.

pag. 13.

23 vntruth.

24 vntruth.

25 vntruth.

12. To disproue the two first vntruths
I need no other witnes then Bel him selfe,
who (pag: 8.) affirmed that *from the yeare*

Bel dispro-
ued by him
selfe.

471.

471. *Vntil Carolus Magnus* (which was 801.)
Barbarians possessed al Italie. If from 471. vntil
801. Barbarians possessed al Italie, how
were Popes 800. yeares vnder Emperours?
how committed they treason against Emperours, in making Carolus Emperour,
if at that time, & aboue 300. yeares before,
they were not vnder Emperours, but vnder
Barbarians.

Contradict.
7.
Contradict.
8.

13. The truth is that Barbarians possessed Italie from the yeare 476. for more
then 80. yeares, after which time the Grecian Emperour in the yeare 553. recouered
al Italie, and albeit they lost shortly after in
the yeare 568 a great part therof, yet they
kept Rome vntil about the yeare 726.
Onuph saith 731, when both Rome and
Italie reuolted from Leo 3. Emperour of
Constantinople for his heresie against I-
mages, and would then haue chosen an o-
ther Emperour against him, if Gregory the
second then Pope had not disswaded them.
Since which time Rome was neuer vnder
the Emperours of Constantinople. And
therefore neither were the Popes subiect
to Emperours 800. yeares after Christ : nor
did Pope Leo commit any treason against
the Grecian Emperors, by creating Charles
Emperour in the yeare 801. which was almost a hundred yeares after the reuolt of

Baron. in annal.

Onuphr. in chron. Baron. in annal.

E   Italy

Italy from the greekes. As for the third vntruth it is euident, becaufe Sigebert doth
not cal the grecian Emperour foueraigne to
to the Romans: And the word *defciuerant*
fignifieth any forfaking or leauing of one,
whether he be his foueraigne or no.

Bel pag. 13.   14. But Bel goeth on in erring the Pope
not to be true King of Italie, becaufe wri-
ters agree not about the Pope to whom, or
time, when this regality was firft graunted.
Marke good reader, him felfe before affir-
pag. 12. 13.   med that *King Pipin gaue vp the gouernement
of Italie into Pope Steeuens hands and that this*
Bel denieth   truth is apparant by the teftemony of many re-
rvhat him   *nowm'd Cronographes, and can not be denied,*
felfe faieth   and now in the next page denieth both the
cannot be   fact, and conteftation of hiftoriographers.
denied.   What wil he not deny, who denieth that
Onuphr. in   which him felfe faith can not be denied?
chron.
Nauclerus   15. The truth is that Pipin gaue not the
general. 25.   exarchate to Greg. 3 who died in the yeare
An. 750. Clau   741 or as other write 740, fourteene yeares
dius Parad.   before Pipins entrance into Italie, neither
des allian-   was Pipin then a King, but made afterward
ces Genealo-   by Zachary fucceffor to Gregory as Bel te-
giques.   ftifieth page 19. but to Pope Steeuen 2. as is
Ado Regino   apparant (to vfe Bels words) by the tefti-
Sigebert. in   mony of many renowmed Cronographers,
chron.   though fome cal him Steeuen 3. becaufe
Blond. Dec.   they reckon his predeceffour, whom others
1 l. 10. Mag-   omit,
deburgenf.
cent. 8. c. 10.
Leo Often.
lib. 1. chron.
c. 9.
Onuph. fup.

omit, becaufe he liued but foure daies, likewife al writers agree that Lewes pius confirmed the donation of his grandfather Pipin vnto Pafchal. 1. and his name is in the
donation, as alfo that Counteffe Maud
gaue Liguria, and Tufcia vnto Gregory the
feauenth.

Apud Gra-
tian. dift. 63.
can. ego Lu-
douicus.
Leo Oftien.
lib.3. chron.
c. 48.

16. And Bels prouing the hiftoriographers
to difagree, becaufe Blondus and Platina
(faith he) write that Pipin gaue the exarchate to Gregory the third, Regino referreth
it to Steeuen, and Sigebert faith Pipin had
Italy in his owne poffeffion in the yeare 801.
is like the reft of his proceedings. For that
of Platina is a manifeft vntruth, for he faith
Pipin gaue the exarchate in Pope Steeuen
the fecond his time, and Sigebert meaneth
not of King Pipin the giuer of the exarchate
who died 768, but of his grandchild fonne
to Carolus Magnus, and how his poffeffion
of Italy doth not preiudicate the Pope, is
before explicated. Regino faith that which
is truth, for beft authors agree, that Pipin
gaue the exarchate in the yeare 755. at what
time Steeuen 2. al. 3. was Pope.

Bel pag. 13.

Platina in
Stephan. 2.
Naucler. ge-
neral. 26.
Palmerius
in chronic.
Claud. Para-
di. in Pepin.
paragr. 6.7.
8.9.

17. But fuppofe writers did not agree
about the Pope to whome, and time,
when Pipin made his guift of the exarchate, muft we therefore needs deny the
guift in which they al agree? So wee

might

might deny that Christ was borne, because writers agree not about the time: is it
not vsual for historiographers to agree in
the substance of the narration, and yet differ in some circumstance of the person, or
time ?

18. Last of al least we should thinke the
Grecian Emperors, acknowledged Charles
Bel pag 14.   made by the Pope to be true Emperour,
Sigebert.   he telleth vs out of Sigebert, that they had
A.a. 805.   indignation against Charles, and therefore
he with often Embassages procured their
friendshipes: yea *Blondus and Platina* (saith
he) *affirme constantlie that Charles agreed with
Irene, and afterward with Nicephoras, that with
their fauors the might rule ouer the west.* Behould
the drift of Bel, to make vs thinke that
Charles became Emperour, not by creation
of the Pope, but by graunt of Grecian Emperors : so loath he is to confesse the Pope
had so great authority aboue 800. years
agoe. Wherein the silly foole ouerthroweth
what he before said. For if the Pope did not
translate the Empire, then was it no steppe
to his tiranny, as he imagineth.

19. But let vs heare how he proueth,
that the Grecian Emperours did not ac-
hnowledge Charles the great for true Emperour, first forsooth *because Sigebert saith, they
had indignation against Charles*; what then ?
are ne-

are neuer Emperours offended for any
thing lawfullie done, especiallie if they
thinke it preiudice their estate & dignity?
and albeit Sigebert affirme, that some Grecian Emperours (who them selues came
vnlawfullie and by tiranny to the Empire,
and that after Charles was crowned Emperour) had indignation against Charles;
yet none write that Irene (who was the
only & lawful Empresse at that time, when
Charles was created) was offended with
his creation, but rather content, as may be
gathered by hir purpose which (as Zonoras
and Cedrenus write) she had to marry him,
Yea Nauclerus saith, she was deposed for Naucler. ge-
the fauor she bore to Charles, besides the   neral. 28.
indignation of those Emperours vz. Nicephorus, Michael, and Leo, was not so much
for the Imperial dignity taken by Charles,
as because, as writeth Eginhart, Charles Eginhart in
his secretary, *they greatlie suspected least he* vita Caroli.
should take the Empire from them ; which they
might iustlie feare, because by tirany and
deposition of their predecessors , they had
gotten it, and yet notwithstanding their indignation, of their owne accord they sent
Embassadours to Charles, and made league
and friendshippe with him, as the same
Eginhart, Ado, and others testifie. Yea the
Magdeburgians adde, that the *Grecians in a*
E 3   *manner*

manner conſented to Charles his Empire.

20. His other proofe out of Platina con-
Platina in
Leone 3.
taineth an vntruth, for Platina writeth that
Charles being made Emperour, Irene ſent
Embaſſadours to make peace and league
with him, & to deuide Italie betwixt them,
which league Nicephorus renued : but he
hath no word of Charles his ruling the weſt
with their fouours, more then of their ruling the Eaſt with his. And the like ſaith
Blond. Dec.
2. l. 1.
Blondus.

Bel pag. 14.
21. *The ſeauenth ſteppe* (ſaith Bel) *was the
conſtitution of the ſeauen Princes electors of the future Emperour by Pope Gregory 5. by the fauour
and free graunt af Otho then Emperour.* But this
was rather an act of ſuperiority in the Pope
ouer Emperours, then a ſteppe vntil it. And
ſeing this conſtitution hath euer ſince bene
inuiolablie obſerued, and the Emperours ſo
elected accompted as true Emperours
throughout al Chriſtendome, a ſigne it is
that Chriſtians thinke the Pope hath authority to appoint Electors , who may
chooſe what Emperour they pleaſe, by the
authority giuen them from the Pope. Wherfore I would Bel anſwered me this dilemma. The ſeauen Electors haue authority to
chooſe an Emperour, or not ? If they haue
then the Pope who gaue them that authority , had the ſame, becauſe none can giue
what

what he hath not him felfe; it not, Bel de-
pofeth at once more Emperours and Princes, then al Popes haue done.

22. *The eight and higheſt ſteppe of this ladder* Bel *pag.* 15.
(faith Bel) *did reach vp euen to the higheſt hea-*
uen, and to the verie throne of our lord Ieſus. here
is a great cry! now let vs fee *quid dignum*
tanto fert hic promiſſor hiatu? becauſe (faith he) Extrauag.
they challenge the royal right of both ſwords Bonif. 8. v-
throughout the Chriſtian world, and haue made nam fan-
thereof a flat decree. But firft I deny that the obedientia.
Pope, as Pope, challengeth royal right of *vntruth.*
either ſword. For his right to the ſpiritual
ſword is not royal, but of a different nature, as is euident, & ſhal be declared hereafter: and his royal right to the material
ſword, is neither ouer al chriſtendome, as
Bel vntruelie auoucheth, but only ouer the
Popedome: nor he challendgeth it by his
Papacie, yea (as Pope Gelaſius wrote) *Popes* Gelaſius de
haue not challendged royal ſouraigntie, but by vincul. ana-
the guifte of Princes, who as Bel faith haue Nicol.1.dec.
giuen their rights to them. And albeit the 96. can.cum
decree doe (after S. Bernard) giue to the *pag.* 17.
Pope right of the material ſword; yet nei- Bernard.lib.
ther hath it the word *royal,* nor meaneth of 4.de confi-
Royal right, as is euident becauſe it tea- deratione.
cheth, that this ſword is not to be drawne,
or vſed by the Popes hand (as no doubt it
might, if he had royal right vnto it) but

by the

by the hand of the fouldier, at the commaundement of the Emperour, and becke
of the Pope. Whereby we fee, that the decree attributeth royal right, of the material
fword, only to the Emperour, who is to
commaund the fouldier to draw, and vfe it,
and to the Pope only authority to direct
the Emperour in his commaund and vfe of
his fword.

23. But fuppofe that Popes did challenge
royal right of both fwrods, throughout the
chirftian world, is this to climbe to the
higheft heauen and to Chriftes throne? doth
the chriftian world reach to the higheft
heauen? or yet to the bounds of the earth?
doth Chriftes throne rule no more then the
chriftian worlde? or doth royal authority
vnder him, reach to his throne? furelie Bel
hath a bafe conceipt of Chriftes kingdome,
if he imagine that Popes, or Princes by
their authorities, reach to his throne, who

Ad Ephef.
c.1.v 21.

(as S. Paul faith) *is aboue al powers and prince-*
domes, thrones and dominations, and aboue eue-
rie name which is named, either in this world or
in the next. but marke good reader, how Bel
condemneth that for horrible blafphemie
in the Pope, which him felfe accoumpteth
as highe treafon to deny to other Princes.
For what is fupremacie in both ecclefiaftical & ciuil caufes, but (as he fpeaketh) royal
right

Bel condem-
neth that in
the Pope for
blafphemie,
which he
iudgeth
treafon to
deny to
Princes.

right of both swords, and to deny this to
temporal Princes, he deemeth no lesse then
highe treason.

24. Secondlie he proueth his foresaid
slaunder out of Pope Nicholas 1. his words, *Christ committed to S. Peter the right both of heauenlie and earthlie empire.* which Bel seemeth
to vnderstand of spiritual, and temporal
power. *Answer.* Suppose the words were
meant of spiritual & temporal power, they
make nothing for royal right, but may be
wel expounded according to the meanig of
the foresaid decree. That S. Peter had from
Christ right to both empires, vz. to gouerne the one, and to direct the other, but of
royal right there is no word in P: Nicholas:
yea he professeth *that Christ distinguished eclesiastical and imperial* power by distinct acts
and dignities, that in spiritual matters the
Emperour should need Bishops, & in temporal, Bishops vse Emperourrs. But indeed
Pope Nicholas meaneth not of temporal
power at al, but only of spiritual giuen to S.
Peter, which he calleth both earthlie and
heauenlie dominion, becaufe according to
our Sauiours words (Math : 16. to which
he alludeth what he loofeth in earth is loofed in heauen.

25. I omit a glofe cited by Bel, becaufe it
only faith that the Pope hath both fwords,

vz, in

pag. 14.
Dift. 22. can
omnes.

Nicol. 1. ep.
ad Michael.
Imper.

Gloffa F. Cæ
leftis.

vz, in the sense before explicated. But what
he bringeth out of an obscure appendix of
P. Boniface his making a constitution,
wherein he affimed him selfe to be spiritual and temporal Lorde in the whole
worlde, is vntrue, as is euident by the constitution, and words before cited out of it.
And Pope Clement 5. declared extrauag.
meruit Chariſsimi: de priuilegys: that Pope Boniface his constitution did nothing preiudice the kingdome of France. But what
the appendix saith of Boniface his sending
to Phillip King of France to haue him acknowledge, he helde the kingdome of him,
may wel be expounded by that Platina writeth vz. *That Phillip hauing againſt the law of*
nations impriſoned a Biſhop, whom Boniface ſent
vnto him to perſwade him to make ware againſt
Infidels, the Pope ſent the Archedeacon of Narbo
to procure the Biſhops libertie, and othervviſe to
denounce, that the kingdome of France vvas fallen
to the churches diſpoſition, for the offence of the
Kinge.

26. But let vs goe on with Bel. *Since this*
ladder (saith he) *was thus framed. Popes haue*
tiranized aboue meaſure , depoſed Kings and
Kingdomes, and taken vpon them authority, per-
taining to God alone. Omittirg Bels ſtraunge
phrase of depoſing Kingdomes: it to depoſe Kings for neuer ſo iuſt cauſe be to
tiranize,

Appendix
Fuidenus.

Clemens 5.

Platin. in
Bonifac. 8.

Bel pag. 16.

tiranize, Proteſtants haue tiranized far more in the ſpace of 70. years, then the Pope hath in theſe 300. years ſince that decree was made. For in al theſe 300. yeares, beſids one or two Kings of Naples, who were his liege men, I finde depoſed by the Pope one Schiſmatical and heretical Emperour of Greece Andronicus Paleologus, and one other doubtful Emperour Ludouick the Bauarian, two French Kings Philip. 4 and Ludouick 12 and one King of Bemeland George, and one King of Nauarre, beſides King Henry 8. and Queene Elizabeth, and theſe al for heynous crimes. whereas Proteſtants in 70. years (ſetting aſide the iniuſtice of their quarrel) haue as much as laie them, depoſed one Emperour, ſix or ſeauen Kings, & two abſolute Queenes, ſlaine two Kings, one Queene, and one Queenes husband, as before hath bene tolde. c. 4. paragr. 6.

Hovv many depoſed by Popes in 300.yeart. Clemens 5. extrauag. ad Certitudinem.

Hovvmany by Proteſtants in 70.yeai s.

27. And Bel who ſo much obſerueth the depoſition of Emperours and Kings by the Pope, and omitteth both their iniuries to him, and his benefits done to them, sheweth him ſelfe to be no indifferent man. For omitting almoſt 33. Popes put to death by heathen Emperours, Chriſtian Emperours, Princes, and others, haue murdered ſix Popes vz. *Felix* 2. *Iohannes* 11. *Iohannes* 15. *Benedi-*

Sacerdotes nunquam tyranni fuerunt, ſed tyrannos ſæpe ſunt paſſi: Amb. ep. 33.

vid. Platinam in vit. Pont.
Six Popes murdered.

Benedictus 6. *Clement.* 2. *Victor* 3. besides *Gregory* 2. and diuers other whome they haue attempted to murder. They haue banished

Foure banished.

foure vz. *Liberius, Sieuerius, Vigilius, Martin I,* besides many others whom for feare of their liues they droue into banishment.

Six emprisoned.

they haue imprisoned six vz. *Iohannes* 1. *Iohannes* 9. *Paschorlis* 2. *Boniface* 8. *Vrbanus* 6. *Clement.* 7. besyd *Sergius* 1. & others whom they attempted to imprison. They haue deposed as much as they could sixteene vz.

Sixteene deposed.

Iohannes 12. *al.* 13. *Benedict.* 5: *Gregory* 5. *Benedict.* 8. and 9. *Alexander* 2. *Gregory* 6. and 7. *Gelasius* 2. *Innocent.* 2. *Alexander* 3 *Iohn* 22.

Platin. in Alexand. 3.

Vrban 6. *Martin* 5. by *Alphons* King of Arra-

Liberality of Popes towards England.

gon , *Eugen.* 4. by procurement of *Philip* Duke of Millen & *Iulius* 2. whereas on the

Stovve an. 1171. Polidorus lib. 16. Comin. ventura in relation. de Napoli.

contrary side (to omit spiritual benefits) Popes haue bestowed the Empire vpon almost al them Emperours whom they deposed, and haue refused to take the Empire from the Germans though they haue bene much sollicited thereto by the Grecians, and to let passe their liberality to other

VVhen vvould Luther and Caluin haue giuen three Kingdomes to England.

Princes, they haue bestowed the Kingdome of *Ireland* vpon Henry the second , and of Naples and Sicily vpon *Henry* 3. and the most honourable title *of defender of the faith* vpon *Henry* 8. Kings of England: hereby may the indifferent reader (euen setting

aside

aſide the iuſtice of the cauſe, and conſide-
ring only the fact) clearly perceaue, whether Chriſtian Emperours and Princes haue
more tiranized ouer Popes, then Popes
ouer them, now let vs come to Bels proofe
of his ould ſlaunder here againe renued, of
the Popes taking vpon them power proper
to God alone.

28. *A Gloſſe* (ſaith he) *affirmeth the Pope* *Bel pag.*14.
to haue celeſtial arbitrement, to be able to alter Gloſſ. lib. 1.
the nature of things, applying the ſubſtance of one tit.7.c.3.
to an other, and to make ſomething of nothing:
and the Pope (ſaith Bel) *is wel pleaſed therewith.*
Anſwer. As for the Pope being pleaſed with
the foreſaid words, it is more then Bel knoweth, but ſure I am he deteſteth them, if
they be meant of power to create, or proper to God alone. But wel I ſee that which
doth not diſpleaſe Bel, if it be giuen to
Princes; he condemneth as intolerable blaſ-
phemie, if it be attributed to Popes. For the
foreſaid words are al in the ciuil lawe, and
by the Emperours applied either to them
ſelues, or to the Pope: as the Emperours
Gratian, Valentinian, and Theodoſius de ſum. *Three Em-*
Trin. lib. 1. affirme the Popes to haue ce- *perours ſay*
leſtial arbitrement, and condemne them *the P. hath*
as infamous hereticks, who follow not the *celeſtial ar-*
religion of Pope Damaſus: and his arbitre- *bitrement.*
ment in ſpiritual matters, may be called
heauen-

heauenlie, becaufe his authority therein came from heauen. That of altering the nature of things, and applying the fubftance of one to an other, the Emperour Iuftinian *C. communia de leg. lib.* 2. applieth to him felfe and meaneth of ciuil contracts, as legacis and feoffees in truft, which by his imperial power, he can alter and change. and the like power (faith the gloffe) hath the Pope in contracts pertayning to fpiritual matters. But of altering the nature of natural things, neither the Emperour, nor the gloffe dreamed.

Of what things Popes or Princes can alter the nature.

29. But the words which Bel moft vrgeth are, *that the Pope can make de nihilo aliquid fomething of nothing.* For (faith he) *it is a thing proper to God to make fomething of nothing in al cafes and at al tymes.* But befides that the gloffe neither faith that the Pope can make *de nihilo aliquid,* but *de nullo aliquid,* neither yet in al cafes, and al times, as Bel addeth: the forefaid words are taken out of Iuftinian. *C. de rei vxor. act. lib.* 1. where the Emperour faith, that becaufe he can make to be accompted a ftipulation, where none is, much more he can an infufficient ftipulatiõ to be fufficient: & the like authority in humane contracts touching fpiritual matters, the gloffe attributeth to the Pope? & this he meant when he faid, the Pope can *de nullo fecere*

Of what nothing Popes or Princes can make fomething.

were *aliquid* of no contract make one. which
Bel would applie to creatiõ & making crea-
tures of nothing as God made the world.

30 Secondlie he proueth his slaunder,
out of Gersons report before answered, and
thirdlie out of Gregory 9. saying. *Ad firma-* Gregor. 9.
mentum Cæli &c. to the firmament of heauen that lib.1.decret.
is of the vniuersal church, God made two lights, tit.33.c.6.
Pontifical authority, and power Roial, that we may
knowe there is as much difference betweene Pope &
Kings, as betwixt sunne & moone. Is here any
word of authority belonging to God? or yet
of deposing Kings? but only a cõparison, of
Pontifical & Royal power with the sunne
& moone (allowed by the publique letters *Written*
of three Princes electors) and a preferring 1279. *and*
of the Pontifical before the Royal, which if *one extãt in*
Bel had any feeling of Christianity in him 10.an.996.
he would not deny. Is not the loosing and *Matth.16.*
binding of sinns in heauen & earth, of prea- *vers.19. &*
ching the ghospel, admnistring the sacra- 18.
ments, of feeding Christs sheepe, and the 15 16.
like, which belongeth to Bishops, as is eui- *Act.20.v.*
dent out of scripture, far more excellent 18.
then Royal power? which as wel woemen *Matth.28.*
and children, as men: infidels, as Christians *v.19.*
may haue.

31. The sunne & moone are of the same *Royal po-*
nature and quality, differing only in more *wer far in-*
or lesse light, but Royal power is both of *ferour to*
Pontifical
nature

nature and quality far inferiour to **Pontifi-**
cal: thas is more humane and begun by
men, this supernaturall and instituted by
God: that common to Infidels, this proper
to christians: that passeth not earth, this
reacheth to heauen: that concerneth only
the body, this the soule: that helpeth men
to worldlie and transitorie quietnes, this to
heauenlie and euerlasting rest. Bel could not
abide Pope Gregory saying Pontificall authority excelled Royal as far as the sunne
excelleth the moone, nor the glosse saying, it
excelled it 47. times, how then wil he abide
S. Chrisostom saying *it excelleth the kingdome*
as much as the soule doubth the body, or S. Ambrose
saying *that nothing can be equal to Pontificall dig-*
nity, and that Royall glorie, and Princes crownes, are
far more inferiour to it, then lead is to glistering
gould. And againe *nothing in this world is more*
excellent then priests, nothing higher then Bishops.
or S. Ignatius saying *that nothing is more honou-*
rable in the church then Bishops, and that we owe
the first honour to God, the second to Bishops, the
third to Kings. he exclamed against the glosse
for affirming the Pope to haue celestial ar-
bitremer, what wil he say to S. Chrisostome
(worthely in his own iudgment Sirnamed
the goulcē mouthed doctor) auouching *that*
the Priests throne is in heauen, that he hath authority
to iudge of celestiall busines, and that God hath put
　　　　　　　　　　　　　　　　　　　the

Constantin
called Bi-
shops Gods
and profes-
sed him self
vnder them
Ruffin.lib.t.
hist.c.2.

Chrisost.l.3.
de sacerd.
Ambros.lib.
de dignit.
sacerd.c. 2.

Ibid. cap. 3.

Ignat. epist.
ad Smirnen-
ses.

Chrisosto.
hom.5. in il-
lud Esaiæ
vidi Domi-
num, & ho
mil 4. item
hom. 60. ad
populum.

the verie *Princes head vnder the hands of the priest*,
to teach vs that the priest is a Prince greater then he. And in an other place affirmeth
a Deacon to haue greater power then an Emperour,
and aduiseth vs that who dispiseth the Priest, *at*
length falleth to contemne God. and S. Gregory
writing to the Emperour him selfe saith
priests are certaine Gods amongst men, and
therefore to be honoured of al euen of
Kings. But Bel in debasing priesthood, and
too too much exalting Princes , sheweth
him selfe to be a right Apostata from priesthood, and a right heretike, who, as Themistius said , *honour not God but Princes.* And
thus much of Bels eight steppes.

hom. 83. in
Matth.
Hom. 2. in
2. in Ti-
moth.
Gregor. lib.
4. epist. 31.
S. Ciprian.
l. b. 3. epist. 9.
noteth that
the begin-
ning of
Schismes
& Heresies
is by con-
tempt of
Priests and
Bishops.

32. Thus thou seest Christian reader that
of these eight steps, which Bel imagined the
Pope had to climbe to his superiority ouer
Princes, two of them to wit the first and
secōd were steps rather to fal, then to climbe
by, three vz. the fourth, sixth, and seauenth, were euident acts of such authority
alreadie enioyed, & acknowledged by Princes, the third was but a recouery of his aun-
tient libertie, the fieft is no more a step for
the Pope to climbe, then temporal liuings
are to other bishops. And the eight and last
is a manifest vntruth. But the true step he
omitted, which is Chrifts promise to S. Peter to build his Chruch vpon him. and his

Themistius
in l. consul.
apud Socra-
tem. l. 3. c. 25.
Arian Bi-
shops more
for the pa-
lace then
for the
Church.
Hilar. l. cōt.
Constant.

Matth. 16.
v. 18.
Ioan. 21. v.
17.

F   com-

commiſſion to feed his sheepe, by vertue whereof, al S. Peters ſucceſſours challendge to be ſpiritual ſuperiour to al that are in Chriſts church, or be his sheepe, be they Princes, or ſubiects, as is euident out of the foreſaid decree of Boniface 8.

33. Bel hauing thus (as you haue heard) ſlandred Popes, thought not to let ether Kings, or Emperors paſſe free, but ſaith that *ſome of them haue opened the windovv to al Antichriſtian tyrany.* Greater iniury he could not do to Chriſtian Princes, then to accuſe them of ſuch horrible impiety of opening the window not to ſome, but to al Antichriſtian tirany. No maruel if he ſpare neether Pope nor Prieſt, who thus handleth Princes? If one ask proofe of his ſlander, he bringeth none, but it ſuffizeth that he hath ſaid it, his word alone is ſufficient to condemne many Kings, & Emperors. This is the reſpect Proteſtants beare, euen to the greateſt Monarches, when they are againſt their proceedings. So Luther ſaid *Princes for the moſt parte were ether the verieſt fooles or arranteſt knaues.* And againe. *The Turk is ten tymes better and wiſer then the Emperor, and other Princes whome he cals idiots doults, madde, furious, and frantik fooles,* and namely King Henry 8. he reuileth with ſuch ſhameful, ſuch ſpitful, and ſcurrilous tearmes as I am aſhamed to write.

Bonif. 8. extrauag. vnã ſanctam. de maioritate & obedientia.
Sed epiſt. Ioan. 2. ad Iuſtinianum Imper. Gregor. lib. 1. epiſt. 24.
Bel pag. 17.
Bel ſlandereth Princes.

Luther. lib. de ſæcular. poteſt. edit. 1523.
lib. cont. duo edicta Cæſaris 1524.
Lib. cont. Hentric. Regem Angl.

to write. And amongſt Proteſtants nothing
more vſual then to cal Princes, Antichriſts,
and ſlaues of Antichriſt.

34. Bel not yet ſatisfied with iniuring *pag. 17.*
the Pope, addeth *that he hath made it ſacriledge* *vntruthe*
to diſpute of his povver , which is a manifeſt *26.*
vntruth diſproued by him ſelfe art : 2. p :
26 where he affirmeth that *the Pope alloweth*
Bellarmins vvorks, who at large diſputeth of
his power. And becauſe Sigebert (whome *vntruthe*
Bel vntruly calleth the Popes deare fryer, *27.*
for he̱ was his vtter enemy, and to his *Trithem. in*
power fauored the ſchiſmatical and Excom- *Sigebert.*
municated Emperor Henry 3, in whoſe be-
halfe he fained diuers things as Baron. pro- *Baronius.*
ueth tom. 9. An. 774.) reprehendeth them,
who taught the people that they owe no
obediēce to euil Kings, Bel inueyeth againſt
Catholiques. Whereas Catholiques vtterly *Art.15. dam-*
defie ſuch Doctrin, & condēned it lōg ſince *nat. in Con-*
in the Proteſtants great grandfather wicliſe *cil. Conſtan-*
and haue learned of the firſt Pope S. Peter *tien.*
to be ſubiect in al feare, not onely to good and mo- *1. Pet. c. 2.*
deſt maiſters , but alſo to vvayvvard. But Pro- *v. 18.*
teſtants teach that and worſe Doctrin, as *Cap.3.parag.*
appeareth by what hath bene ſayd before, *4. 5. 6.*
and by Godman, who (as Couel writerh)
publiſhed to the vvorld , that it vvas lavvful to kil *Couel of*
vvicked Kings, and whitingham a deane of no ſmal *Chnrch go-*
account, in his preface before Godmans booke, af- *vernment.*
  F 2   *firmed* *c 4. p 35.*

firmed it to be the doctrin of the beſt learned, meaning (as Couel thinketh) *Caluin and the reſt.*

35. Finally becauſe the end of this article should not be vnlike the beginning he concludeth it with three vntruthes as he began it, ſaying. *That the Popiſh religion hath bene alwaies condemned of great learned Papiſts.* If he had named the men, and points of religion, as he told the tyme, the three vntruthes wold haue appeared in their likenes. As I gueſſe he meaneth of the Popes power for depoſing Princes, which I confeſſe ſome Papiſts haue denyed, but nether were they the greateſt learned men, nor alwayes were there any ſuch, nor hath he proued it to be a point of Popiſh religion; And thus much of Bels firſt Article. *VVherfore remember (Bel) from whence thou art fallen and doe pennance.* Apoc: 2.

***

THE

THE
SECOND ARTICLE
TOVCHING THE
MASSE.

PREFACE.

Bel deuideth this Article into foure members, in the firſt wherof he impugneth the real preſence of Chriſt in the Euchariſt; in the ſecond the ſacrifice of the Maſſe; in the third he inueigheth againſt the recantation which Berengarius made when he adiured Bels hereſie; and in the fourth he treateth of apparent contradictions which (ſaith he) are in the Maſſe. And the like method we wil keepe in our anſwer.

Chap. I.

Bels reaſon againſt the Real Preſence of Chriſt in the B. Sacrament anſwered, his vntruth and diſſimulation therin diſcouered.

. Paul prophetied. *That in the laſt tymes ſome ſhal depart from the faith, attending to the ſpirits of errors and doctrin of diuils.* Which prophecy is moſt manifeſtly fulfilled in theſe heretiks who impugne the Catholique do-

1. *Timoth.* 4. *v.* 1.

F 3   ctrin

&ctrin of the B: Sacrament. For of Berengarius (first publike enemy of this Sacrament) Malmesburienses an English Chronicler of his tyme, writeth, that when he came to visit S. Fulbert B: of Charters lying on his death bed, *the holy Bishop commanded him to be put forth, protesting that he did see a huge diuil standing by him, and corrupting many to follow him by his flattering hand and alluring breath.*

2. Luther him selfe confesseth l. de Missa Angul: to:7: fol:228. to haue disputed visibly with the diuil and bene perswaded by him to abrogate Masse. And of this his conference with the diuil, besides others, Erasmus a ioly confesser in Fox his calender is a most sufficient witnes. To Carolstadius a great frend at the first of Luther appeared a diuil as he was preaching as testifieth Erasmus Alberus. Zwinglius an eger enimy of the real presence testifieth of him selfe l. de subsid: Euchar: That about the Eucharist he was instructed of a spirit *which* (saith he *I know not, whether it was black, or white.* And Luther l. cit: writeth that he thinketh Oecolampadius, & others to haue bene choked by the diuil. And the Lutherans cal the Zinglians diuilish heretiks, possessed and obsessed of diuils and their opinions diabolical.

3. Fi.

Berengarius

Malmesbur. lib.3. in Guilielmo 1. p. 114.

Luther.
Sainctes repetit. de Euchar.c.10.
Bellarm. l.1. de Missa c.5.
Surius in comment. 1534.
Genebrard. in chron.
Erasm. cont. epist. non sobriam Lutheri.
Carolstadius.
Zuinglius.
Lindan. ep. dissuasor. p. 114.
Oecolampadius.
Brent. in Recognit.
Iezlerus lib. de dioturn. belli euchariст.

3. Finally Caluin, epist : ad Bucer. confesseth that he had a familier, to which he
imputeth his vaine of curting. Thus we
see the very Fathers of Protestantisme to
haue bene haunted , and instructed of diuils. Who therefore can doubt but their
doctrin is the doctrin of diuils , and
they, such as hauing departed from the
Catholique faith, wherein they were chri-
stend, and bred , did harken to the spirits
of errors, and teach the doctrin, which
they had learnd of the diuil appearinge
in visible forme. Now let vs see how Bel
like a good scholer defendeth his black
maisters and oppugneth the Catholique,
doctrin.

4. He beginneth his second Article as he
did the first, with a syllogisme with dissi-
mulation, and vntruth. *Aquinas* (saith he)
*Bellarm : the Councel of Trent, and the rest of the
Romish brood hold constantly, as an article of their
Christian faith, that the true organical and natural
body of Christ, which is localy in hauen, is also
truly, and really vnder the forme af bred and wine
in the sacrifice of the masse : but this* (saith he) *is
impossible, as which imply th flat contradiction !
ergo &c.* I accept Bels confession of the Catholiques constancy in their faith, which is
a vertue far from him selfe, who hath twise
altered his religion.

5. Bels

Caluin.

Genium.

Bel pag. 19.

31. vntruth.

Conc. Trid.
sess. 13 can 1.
Aquinas 3. p.
76. art. 1.
Bellarm. l 1.
de Euchar.
c. 2.

Catholi-
ques con-
stant in
their faith.

3 . *diſſimu-lation.*

5. Bels diſſimulation is euident, for he could not be ignorant that Luther, and his Lutheriſh brood hold the real preſence of Chriſts body, and blood in the Euchariſt, no les then Catholiques, though otherwiſe

Luther. in præfat. lib. Sueuarum. In poſtrema confeſ. fidei de cæna Domini. Et theſti . 15. & 27.

then they doe. For Luther accurſeth them and accounteth them blaſphemers, and damned foreuer, and in plaine teatmes defineth them to be *heretiques and out of Gods church, who denie the body and bloud of Chriſt to be receaued with carnal mouth in the venerable Euchariſt.* This was Luthers ſentence & iud-

Ioan. Laua-therus. Ioan. Iecle-ſus.

gemēt vpō them that deny the real preſence, which his brood defend with tooth and nayle, as is euident by their endleſſe and mortal warres againſt the Zuinglians and Caluiniſts, whereof two Proteſtants haue written two bookes.

6. Bells want of fidelitie appeareth in this propoſition whereof he maketh no doubt. For albeit al Catholiques beleue as a point of their faith, that Chriſts true and natural body and the very ſelfe ſame which in heauen is organical, is in the B: Sacra-

Conc. Trid. ſeſſ 13.can.1. S.Thom.3.p. q.76.art. 1. Bellarm.lib. 1.de Euchar. c. 2.

ment : yet nether the Councel of Trent , S. Thomas nor Bellarmin in the places quoted by Bel, affirme as a point (and much leſſe as an Article) of their faith,that it is there organical. For organization being an accident of the body depending of quantity, they

hold

hold no otherwise his organization, then they do his quantity to be in the Sacrament. The Councel onely defineth whole Christ, that is euery substantial part of him to be in the Eucharist, without any mention of his quãtity or other accidents as appeareth by the words of the Canon. *If any shal deny the body and blood together with the soul & Diuinity of our Lord Iesus Christ, and consequently whole Christ to be in the Eucharist &c. be he accursed.* And in the same sense sayd S. Thom: 3. p: q. 76 ar: 1. that according to the Catholique faith whole Christ is in the Sacrament. And though art: 4. he teach that Christs quantity is also in the Sacrament, yet affirmeth he it not as a point of faith. In like forte Bellarm: in the place which Bel citeth teacheth, and truly, that Christs quantity is in the Sacrament, but not with Bels addition, as a point of faith. And though l 3. de Euchar: c. 5. he cal it the common sentence of the Schooles and Church, yet condemneth he not the contrary as heretical, but onely as false and erroneous. And as for Durand accom Gabriel Maior, and Satus also as Sainctes reporteth (whome Bel can not deny to be of the Romish brood as he scornefully speaketh) they thought that Christs body had not his quãtity in the Sacrament and consequently must

Durand.4.d. 10. q. 2. Occam 4.q.4.& tract. de Eucharist. c.29. maior. q. 2. Gabr. art. 2. concl.2.& lect. 43. in Can.

must needs thinke that it was not there organical. And to difproue Bel,Iuel in his apo-
logie writeth, that fome Papifts affirme
Chrifts quantity to be in the Eucharift, o-
thers deny it. For fome being perfwaded in
Philofophy, that quantity eſſentially requireth aptitudinal commenfuration to place,
fo that if it be put in a place it muſt needs
be coextended to the place,& thinking that
they cold fufficiently verifie Chrifts words
by teaching the fubftance of his body to be
in the Sacrament denied his quantity to be
there, faying that God fupplieth the effeſt
therof fo far forth as is neceſſary for the foule to informe the body,as in al Deuines opinion, he fupplieth the effeſt of coextenfion
to place, which alfo is a natural difpofition
required to life and information of a body
or matter. But other Deuines of greater
learning and grauity (iudging it an incon-
uenient thing to graunt Chrifts liuely body
to want in the Sacrament his quantity and
figure, and confidering better of the nature
of quantity, found that no commenfuration
to place was eſſential vnto it, but onely a
natural propriety, and therefore feparable
by Gods power from it, as light is from the
Sunne) taught that Chrifts hath his quantity in the Sacrament as a natural accident
accompaning his body. And albeit this be
a certaine

a certaine truth and not onely the common opinion of Schooles but seemeth also to be the common sense of Catholiques, yet saith Suarez a learned author Tom : 3 in 3. part. *Suarez.* disput : Si stec: 2. *It is to hard a censure to condemne the contrary of heresie.* For (saith he) *I find nether expresse definition nor irrefragable testimony of Scripture against it, nor yet any thing which can be conuinced out of reuealed principles, and al the reasons made against it, are deduced out of Philosophical Principles, true and certaine but not altogether euident.* In like sorte Claudius de Sainctes repetit. 4. de Euchar: c 4. testifieth *Sainctes.* that this matter is not clearly defined by the Church or Scripture. What shame therfore must it be to Bel to auouch that al Catholiks hold as a point of their faith that Christs body is organical in the Eucharist, and declining the principal question about the being of Christs body in the Sacrament (which is an vndoubted point of our faith, and against which his cheefe argument, which as he saith al the Papists in England can not answer taketh no hold) to impugne the being of Christs quantity in the Eucharist.

7. Neuerthelesse because it is a thinge most true and most agreable to our faith. I willingly vndertake the defense therof. Let vs see therfore how Bel disproueth it. For
soot

pag. 20.
Reason the
ground of
Bels faithe.

sooth *because it implyeth contradictiō for a greater body as Christ is to be cōtained in a lesser as in a cake.* Behould the foundation of Bels faith, the best weapon of this stout challenger, the

Scripture.
Matth. 26.
v.26 28.
Marc.14.v.
22.24.
Luc. 22. v.
19.20.
1.Cor.11.v.
24.25.

Ioan. 6. v.
55.

1.Cor.11.v.
29.

strong reason which al English Papists can not solue. We bring Christs expresse words auouching that what he gaue to his Apostle at his last supper *was his body giuen , and his blood shed for remission of sinnes,* which vndoubtedly he ment of his true body and blood. For he neuer gaue bred, nor shed wine for remission of sinnes. We obiect also his other words where he calleth his flesh *truly meat and his blood drinke,* as it were , preuenting the figuratiue exposition of Caluinists. Besids the words of S. paul testifying, that *who receaueth vnvvoorthily the B: Sacrament is guilty* (not of bread and wine il receaued) but *of the body and blood of our Lord.*

Fathers.

8. To these testimonies of holy writte we adioyne the vniforme consent of Fathers, who not onely continually cal the Eucharist the body, and blood of Christ,

Damasc.l. 4.
de fid.c.14.
7. Synod.
Act. 6.

and not once a bare figure, but withal some of them affirme that *it is no bare figure, but the very body,* and damne the contrary, *as abhominable and extreme madnes,* contrary to tra-

Chrysosto.
hom. de Eu-
char. in En-
cenijs.Cyril.
catech.3.

dition *of Apostles, and Fathers, and against the verity and propriety of Christs vvords.* Others deny it *to be bread albeit our taste so iudge.*

Others

Others ſay *that the nature of bread is changed, that bread changed in nature, not in ſhevv ; is by the omnipotency of God made fleſh : that bread and vvine are turned ſupernaturally into the Verity of Chriſts proper fleſh.* Others ſay *vve eate Chriſts fleſh and drink his blood vvith our mouthes, that vvhat vve beleiue vvith faith vve receaue vvith mouth.* Others auouch *that Chriſt at his laſt ſupper carried him ſelfe ſecundum literā* (that is truly & really) *in his hands.* Finally others ſay that *as Chriſt is the true ſonne of God, ſo is it true fleſh & blood vvhich vve receaue and drinke.* Theſe kind of ſpeeches and many other of the like ſort can neuer be verified, vnleſthe real preſence of Chriſt in the B. Sacrament be defended.

Niſſen. orat.
mag. catech.
c. 37. Cipria.
ſerm. de Cæna. Cyril. Alex. ad Calo
ſyr.
Chryſoſto.
hom. cit.
Damaſ. ſup.
Auguſt. lib.
2. cont. aduerſ. legis &
Prophet. c.
9. tom. 6.
Leo ſerm. 6.
de ieiun. 7.
menſis
Aug. ſerm. 1.
in pſalm. 33.
tom. 8.
Hilar. 8. de
Trinitat.

9. Againſt al theſe irrefragable teſtimonies of Gods word, and holy Fathers, Bel oppoſeth humane reaſon, though he expound them figuratiuely, becauſe he dare not deny them in bare words which hath bene euer the ſhift of hereriques. For ſo the Arrians being vrged with theſe words, *I and the Father are one* expounded them figuratiuely, becauſe they durſt not deny them, and their reaſon could not conceaue how two perſons ſhould be one nature. Likwiſe the Marcionits vnderſtood thoſe words. *The vvord vvas made fleſh* figuratiuely becauſe by reaſon they could not vnderſtand how

Quod intelligimus debemus rationi quod
credimus
authoritati.
Aug. l. de vtil. cred. c. 11.
*Heretiques
ſhift to expound ſcriture figuratiuely.*
Ioan. 10. v.
30.
*Heretik be
figure ſlingers.*
Io. 1. v. 14

how two natures shold be in one person.
And for the self same cause Bel and Protestants vnderstand these words, *This is my body giuen for you, my blood shed for you in remission of sinns,* figuratiuely. For these words doe as playnly teach the verity of Christs body and blood in the Eucharist, as those other teach the verity of his Godhead or humanity, yea more plainly, because in these words it is expressed what body, and blood is in the Eucharist, vz. that which was giuen for vs and shed in remission of sinnes, which kind of addition is not in those other words.

10. But as S. Austin saith *If an opinion of error haue preoccupated the mind, vvhatsoeuer is othervvise affirmed in Scripture men vvil vnderstand it figuratiuely.* Hereupon Caluin said *that the reuerence of Gods vvord vvas no. sufficient pretence to reiect his reasons*: And calleth it *foolish stubbernes to contend vpon the vvords of Scripture, and them catchers of sillables, foolish, superstitious, vvho stick fast to Christ vvords.* What is this good Reader but to make reason the rule of faith, and not to captiuate our vnderstanding to Gods word, but to captiuate it to our reason, and make it speake properly, or figuratiuely, according as reason can comprehend it. Truly therfore wrote the Magdeburgian Protestants of
such

such as deny the real presence. VVith philosophical reasons they so make voyd the testament of
God, that the body and blood of Christ concerning
the presence and communication therof according
to Christs owne most clere, most euidēt, & most po-
vverful words, they wholie remoue, & with mar-
uelous perplexity of words doe coulorably deceiue.

11. But to come to Bels reason. How
proueth he it to be cōtradiction for a greater body to be conteyned in a les. Surely not
at al, but as Pithagoras *autos epha* or as Fau-
stus the Manichist who as S. Austin writeth
sayd it, and avvay. Should not he want al
reason, who for such a reason proposed
without al proofe, should forsake Christs
expresse words, and plaine testimonies of
holy Fathers? Breefly I might answere with
S. Ambrose. *VVhat seekest thou the course of na-*
ture in Christs body, seing he vvas against natures
order borne of a virgin, and admonish Bel of
the faithles Capharnaits asking. *Hovv can he*
giue his flesh to be eaten? For to what other end
tendeth Bels reason then to aske. How
can God giue vs his flesh? Let him harken
to S. Chrisostome, S. Ephrem and others,
aduising him not to be curious but faithful,
not to trust to humain sense, and reason,
which is oftētymes deceaued, but to Christs
word. *He hath said* (writeth S. Chrisostome)
This is my body, let vs haue no doubt, albeit it seeme
absurd

S. Aug. l. 14.
cont. Faust.
c. 9.
S. Ambros.l.
de initiatis.
c.9.tom. 4.
Ioan. 6. v.
52.
Omnes hæ-
reticorum
& Gentiliū
quæstiones
eædem sunt
quia non
Scriptura-
rum aucto-
ritatem sed
humanæ ra-
tionis sen-
sum sequū-
tur. Hieron.
in Osee 7.
S. Chrisost.
hom. 60. ad
populum &
83. in Matth.
S. Ephren.
lib. de natu-
ra Dei mini-
me scrutan-
da.
Chrisosto.
sup.

absurd to our sense, and reason, which he sayth
let his vvord in al matters, but espetially in the
sacraments ouercome our sense, and reason, vvhich
is oftentymes deceiued, as Bels is here.

Hovv it is
contradi-
ction for a
greater bo-
dy to be in
a les, and
hovv not.

12. For albeit it be contradiction for a
greater body occupying a place proportionate to it greatnes, to be contayned in a
les (for so it should be both contayned,
and not conteyned in the les:) yet no contradiction at al it is for a greater body retayning it greatnes, to be so coarcted by Gods
omnipotency, as it fil a place far les, then
is naturaly due, or proportionate to it greatnes. For in this case it followeth not, that
it shold both be contayned, & not contayned in the lesser body (as in the former case)
but contayned onely. And thus we say hath
Christ disposed of his body in the sacramēt.
And that God cā thus dispose of bodies, we
doe not onely barely affirme, as Bel doth the
contrary, but can proue by many waies.

Proofs that
God can
put a grea-
ter body in
a lesser.
S. Beda in
Lucam.
S.Auguſt. de
hæreſ. c. 8ɪ.
tom.6.
Ambr.cp.8ɪ.
Leo ſer.ɪ. &
ɪ.de natiu.
Niſſen. ſer.
de occurſu
Domini.
Damaſc.l. 4.
de fid.c.14.

13. First because Christs body in his natiuity opened not his virgin mothers womb.
Ergo then it occupied not a roome naturally
proportionat to the greatnes. The consequence is euident. The Antecedent I proue,
because it is a point of the Catholique faith
as testify S. Bede and S. Austin, and appeareth by vniuersal consent of al Fathers as
S. Ambrose: S. Leo: S. Niſſen, S. Damascen:
and

and others, and professed in our Creed, that Christ was borne of a virgin, which vndoubtedly is ment of a perfect virgin, as wel in body, as mind. And the contrary was the heresie of Iouinian, who (as S. Austin writeth) affirmed that our Ladies virginity was lost *pariendo* by child bearing, which he could not otherwise vnderstand then by the Childs opening her womb, becaufe virginity can not be otherwaies lost *pariendo* by child bearing, and sure it is she lost not virginity by conceauing.

Ideo clausa quia virgo. Ambr. de instit. virg. c. 7. August. sup. & l. 1. cont. Iul. c. 2. to. 7. *Iouinian sayd Chrifts body shold be a phantafme if our lady had remayned a virgin in her trauail.*

14. Moreouer holy Fathers proue this truth out of that prophecy of Ezechiel 44. v. 2. *of a gate shut and not opened by vvhich the Lord alone should paffe* vnderstanding by this shut and vnopened gate the virginal womb of our B: Ladie. And Albeit some Fathers vfe the word of opening the womb in their speech of our Ladies child birth, yet they meane not properly, but vfe the name of the effect for the natural caufe therof. For becaufe children naturally do open their mothers wombs, both Scripture, and Fathers do fometymes cal child bearing opening the womb, and barennes shutting the womb. Of Scripture this is euident out of Gen: 20: 29: 30. & 1. reg: 1. of Fathers it is manifest by S. Hierome who though he say Chrift opened the gate of the virgins womb,

Aug. cont. Iul. cit. Hieron. in Ezechiel. 44. Ambr. of. lib. de instit. virginis c. 7. Aug. serm. 18. de tempore.

S. Hierom. dial. 2. cont. Pelagian.

G

womb, yet he addeth *that it continually re-mayned shut* , wherby he explicateth how before he took the opening vz. of Child bearing without any proper opening, for otherwife the womb could not remayne ftil fhut.

15. Neuertheles Proteftants , becaufe it maketh for the Catholique Doctrin of the B: Sacrament, deny the Antecedent, and Willet proueth their denyal, becaufe as S. Luke faith, *Chrift vvas prefented in the temple according to the layv. Euery male opening the matrice fhalbe holy to the Lord.* But by the like reafon he might proue that Chrift was con-ceiued by mans feed, becaufe S. Luke in the fame chapter writeth that our Lady was purifyed according to Moifes law, which was as we read leu : 12. of *a vvoman which hauing receaued feed had borne a male child.* The anfwere to both places is the fame. Becaufe naturally women conceiue by receauing feed,& children are borne by opening their wombs, therfore the law vfed thefe termes. But as the one law affirmed not, that no woman could conceiue without receauing feed,fo nether the other,that no child could be borne without opening his mothers womb. And as willets herefy made him to open our Ladies wób,fo his cófcience made him to fhut it againe. For why fhould he
teach

VVillet
cont. 13.p.
453.
S.Luc. 2.v.
23.

teach that it was shut after her deliuery, if he did not thinke the opening did preiudice her virginity ? The like proofe might be drawne out of Chrifts entring to his Apoftles the dores being shut faith S. Luke, and of his iffuing out of the fepulchar before the Angel had remoued the ftone.

See S. Hilarie lib. cont. Conftant. prope finé.

16. Secondly God can by his omnipotency bring a Camel through a needles eye as wel as a rich man into heauen : but he can bring a rich man to heauen keeping his riches, Ergo a Camel keeping his greatnes through a needles eye. The Propofition is euident out of our Sauiours words Math. 19. v. 24. 26. The Affumption is manifeft and approued by S. Auftin epift. 89. quæft. 4. And the fame S. Auftin lib. de fpir. & lit. c. 1. and Nazian. Orat. 36. affirme that it is poffible for God to draw a Camel through a needles eye. Thirdly God made the fornace of Babilon, though neuer fo hote, not to heate , yea to refresh the three children, why then can he not make a great body to occupy but a fmale roome ? For to occupy place is an effect and accident of quantity, as to heate is of heate. Moreouer nature by condenfation doth make a body to occupy leffe roome then is due vnto it, as appeareth in the freefing of water , and this it doth with out deftroying any quantity therof,

S. Auguftin. tom. 2.

S. Gregor. Nazianz.

Daniel. 3.

G 2   as ma-

as many excellent Philosophers euen by natural reason do gather. And can not God
work the like effect without condensation
by some other supernatural meanes? Finally
Bel teacheth that euery sinne of it nature
excludeth grace, and yet God of his power
maketh some sinne to stād with grace: why
then can he not make quantity to exclude
no body out of the place, though of it nature it should so doe. And thus much touching Bels reason. Now let vs see his authorities.

Bel art. 6
p. 81.

Chap. II.
The Authorities alledged by Bel against the Real Presence ansvvered.

Bel pag. 20.

AFTER the forsaid reason he alledgeth
some few authorities. The first is of
Caietan who *affirmed as Angles* (saith he) reporteth. *That ther is no text that conuinceth the Rea-*
der to vnderstand these words. This is my body pro-
perly. But Bel greatly wrongeth both Caietan and Angles, in changing the word *He-*
retik into *Reader.* For Angles in 4. q. 4. attributeth that opinion to Caietan onely concerning Heretiks, and addeth q. 5. that *he see-*
meth to haue recalled it. But how conuincent
the Scripture is in this point let Bel learne
of Luther writing. That *he vvas willing to*
deny the real presence and endeuored vvithal his
                                        povver,

Luther. ep.
ad Argenti-
nenses. vid.
Bellarm. lib.
1. de Euch.
c. 1.

povver, but could not satisfy the Scripture.

2. But suppose Caietan had said as Bel alledgeth. what then? Doth he therfore deny
the real presence, or think those words not
to be vnderstood properly? no surely? yea
he plainly auoucheth both. Or doth Bel
think that euery point of faith is so euidētly
delyuered in Scripture, as the very words
suffice to cōuince any reader though neuer
so obstinate? why then are not al heretiks
cōuerted by reading Scripture? yea why ad-   *Bel p. 134.*
mytteth he a tradition which is not at al in   *135.*
Scripture? If not, why inferreth he the Scripture not to teach the real presence if it
teach it not clearly?

3. The second is S. Tho: Aquinas *whoe*   S. Thom. 4.
(saith he) *affirmeth constantly. Corpus Christi*   d.10.q.1.art.
non esse in pluribus locis simul, secundum proprias   1.
dimensiones, that Christs body is not in many places   *Bel p. 20.*
at once, according to the proper dimensions therof.
Whose assertion (saith Bel) is my flat position. But Bel herein 1. contradicteth him   *Contradict.*
selfe 2. belyeth S. Thomas 3. vnderstandeth   9.
him not. He contradicteth him selfe, for   *vntruth 32.*
before he said Aquinas held constantly as
an article of the Christian faith, that the
true body of Christ is truly and really in the
Sacrifice of the Masse: & now he saith that
he affirmeth constantly an assertion which
is Bels flat position to the contrary. How

G 3   can

can Aquinas hold conftantly two contra-
dictory points? He belyeth Aquinas, for
he is fo far from maintayning Bels pofition,
as in the very place which Bel citeth, his
conclufion is this. *Vnder the Sacrament of the*
altar, is contayned the true body of Chrift which
he tooke of the virgin, and to fay the contrary is
herefie. Laftly he vnderftandeth not Aquinas.

Bel vnder-
ftandeth
not Aqui-
nas.

For he thinketh that Aquinas by the forfaid words meaneth, that Chrifts body can
not be in many places at once with his proper dimenfions, & therupon inferreth, that
Aquinas thinketh Chrifts body can not be
in many places at once, becaufe (faith Bel)
it can not be without thofe dimenfions which na-
turally pertayne vnto it. But (to omit Bels impious affertion, that God can not keep a
body without his natural appurtenances)
Aquinas meaning is playne and euident vz.
That the total caufe of Chrifts body being
in two places at once, is not his owne dimé-
fions alone, but they together with the dimenfions of the body conuerted into his
body. For he thinketh Chrifts owne dimenfions to be the caufe of his being in
that place where he is naturally, and the dimenfions of the body which is tranfubftan-
tiated, the caufe of his being, where he is
Sacramentally. Which opinion of his, about
the caufe of Chrifts being in many places,
maketh

maketh nothing to this purpose.

4. Thirdly he citeth Durand whom he *Bel p. 20.* saith holdeth the very same opinion. But in *Contradict.* this also he both contradicteth him selfe, *10.* & belyeth Durand. For in the fourth mem- *vntruth 33.* ber of this article, he telleth vs, that Durand *p. 34.* *holdeth the forme of bread to be changed* vz. into the body of Christ. True it is that Durand (as before I cited) thinketh the quantity of Christs body not to be in the Eucharist, yet neuertheles most constantly, he both affirmeth and proueth the substance of his body to be there.

5. Fourthly he alledgeth S. Austin wri- *pag. 20.* ting. *That Christ as man is in aliquo loco Cœli prop-* *S. Aug. epist.* *ter veri corporis modum : in some place of heauen* *57. ad Dar-* *for the manner of a true body.* Again. *His body* *danum.* *must be in one place* Item. *He can not be at once in* *De confe-* *the Sun Moone and on the crosse according to corpo-* *crat. dist. 2,* *ral presence.* But in al these places he speaketh *con. Prima* of the natural manner of bodies being in *quidem.* place, as appeareth both by those words *lib. 20. cont.* (*propter veri corporis modum*) and becauſe *Fauſtum. c.* he diſputeth againſt the Manichiſts, who *11. tom. 6.* douted (as the Proteſtant vbiquiſts doe *Ex Auguſt.* now) that becauſe Chriſts body was vnited *epiſt. cit.* to his Godhead, it therby became euery where as God is, which (ſaith S. Auſtin) *Ibid.* is to deſtroy the nature of a true body, nether fol- loweth it (ſaith he) *that vvhat is in God be*

G 4   *euery*

euery vvhere as God is.

6. But that Chrifts body being naturally in one place, might be Sacramentally in an other S. Auftin neuer doubted, yea exprefly affirmeth fer: 1. in pfal: 33. where, he faith. *That Chrift at his laft fupper carried him felfe in his ovvn hands fecundum literam* (that is truly and properly) *and us no other man can carry him felfe.* And lib: de cur: pro: mort. c. 16. He doubteth whether Martyrs be at once in different places which argueth that he thought they could be. And S. Chrifoftom hom: 17. in epift: ad hebr: *In many places is offered not many Chrifts, but the fame Chrift euery vvhere, here and there vvhole, one body not many bodyes.* And thus much of Bels firft member of this article againft the real prefence. Now let vs proceed to the fecond againft the Maffe.

S.Auguftin. tom. 8.

S.Auguftin. tom.4.

S. Chrifoft. tom.4.

CHAP. III.
The Maffe proued, Bels argument againft it anfwered and his manifold vntru- thes therin difproued.

S. Ignatius epift. ad Smyrnen. writeth of old heretiks. *That they admit not obla- tion and Eucharift, becaufe they confeffe not the Eucharift to be the flesh of our Sauiour which fuffered for our fins.* And therfore no maruel if Bel hauing in the former member impugned

S. Ignatius apud Theo- doretum. dialog. 3.

pugned the real preſence, do in this inueigh
againſt the oblatió or ſacrifice of the Maſſe,
where, according to Chriſts owne action
and inſtitution, his body and blood vnder
the formes of bread and wine, are offered
vnto almighty God. That Chriſt at his laſt
ſupper made an oblation to God is proued
many waies.

Chriſt offe-
red ſacriſi-
ce at his laſt
ſupper.
1.

2. Firſt becauſe he did then giue his
body vnto ſome, for his Apoſtles: But to
no other then to God. Ergo to him he then
offered his body. The propoſition I proue,
becauſe he ſayd not this is my body which
is giuen to you, but for you, and al the
Greek and Engliſh Bibles haue in the preſent tenſe *which is giuen, which is shed.* Therfore then did he giue his body, and shed
his blood to ſome perſon for his Apoſtles,
though ſoone after he gaue, and shed them
after another manner on the Croſſe. Secondly becauſe in S. Luke it is ſayd of
the Cup that is was powered out for remiſſion of ſins: but at the paſſion there was no
Cup powred out. Ergo at ſupper the Cup
was powred out for remiſſion of ſins. The
propoſition is out of the Greeke text, wher
the word *powred out* agreeth with the Cup,
and with none els *touto to poterion en to aimati*
mou to ecchunomenon. The aſſumption is
playne for ther was no Cup at the paſſion.
Thirdly

2.
Luc. 22. v.
19. 20.

3. Thirdly at the same tyme when Chrissts
body was broken, it was giuen, and his
blood shed for remission of sins 1. Cor. 11.
v. 24. But it was in no sort broken on the
Crosse as appeareth by S. Ihon. 19. v. 36.
and in some sorte broken at the supper, because it was really vnder the forme of bread
which was broken, therfore then his body
was giuen for remission of sins.

3. Many things more might haue bene
said in defence of Masse which are largely,
and learnedly handled by Bellarm. in his 2.
booke de Missa to. 2. and somthing shalbe
added hereafter as breuity wil permit, and
occasion shal serue. Onely here becanse the
Reader may perceiue from what spirit the
hatred of Masse proceedeth I aduertise him
that Luther writeth of him self, that he had
said Masse 15. yeares togither thinking it
had bene a holy thing, vntil on a time Sathan appearing visibly vnto him, and dis-
puting with him against Masse, perswaded
him to deteft it. From this spirit proceeded
first the hatred of Masse, and this confession God wold Luther shold him self make,
and publish in print, that al Christians who
had any care of their souls, shold deteft such
doctrin, which the cheefe precher therof
professeth he learnt of the diuel, & highly re-
uerёce that which the diuel so much hateth.

4. On

Denial of
Masse pro-
per doctrin
of deuils.
Luther. l. de
Missa angul.
to.7.fol.228.
Sainctes re-
petit. 1. de
Eucharist.
c. 10.
Bellarm. l.1.
de Missa c.5.
Surius com-
ment. 1534.
1517.
Genebrard.
in chron.
See Erasmus
cont. epist.
nô fobriam
Lutheri.

4. On the other syd S. Iames his Masse is yet extant, and Iewel in his sermon at Pauls Crosse 1560. confessed *that the Masse had Chrjsts institution*. Which is breefly to confesse that Masse was instituted by Christ and the Apostles, and that our Masse is good, which in substance is al one with that of S. Iames. Likwise the Masses of S. Basil and S. Chrisostome ate yet extant and at this day vsed of the Grecians, as the Masse of S. Ambros is vsed in Milan where he was Bishop, and of him self he writeth thus. *I abode in my function and began to say Masse.* S. Austins vse and reuerence of Masse appeareth by his words serm. 91. de temp. *In the lesson vvhich shalbe read to vs at Masse &c.* and by his complaint ser: 251 of some that compelled the Priest to shorten the Masse and by his testimony of a miracle wrought, by offering the Sacrifice of Christs body l. 21. de ciuit: c: 8: which Sacrifice saith he con: 1. in psal: 33. 17. de ciuit: c. 5 & li: de fid: ad Pet: is frequented in al the world.

5. S. Gregories deuotion to Masse, him selfe testifyeth in these words we *euery day say Masse in veneration of Martyrs.* l. 7. epist: 29. Indict 1: And to omit the Councels of Ephesus, Agatha, Mileuit, & others, which approue Masse; it may suffice for Englishmen that certaine it is that S. Austin who
first

S. Iames Masse.

Rastal in confutat. p, 156.

S. Basil and S. Chrisost. Masse

S. Ambros Masse.

S. Ambrof. L 5. epist. 33.

S. Augustin. tom. 10.

S. Gregory.

Councels.

Tom. 1. Con ciliorum. S. Beda lib. 1. histor. 23. 24. & 26.

first conuerted our English nation to Chrifts faith, both faid Maffe and wrought miracles in confirmation of that faith & feruice of God which he preached. And in honor of Maffe haue our Anceftors named diuers principal feafts of the year as Chrift-maffe Candle-maffe Michael-maffe Martin-maffe, builded Churches, erected aultars, founded Monafteries, and endued Bifhopricks and benefices, and liued and dyed in vfe and honor of Maffe. And not onely they, but al the Chriftian world as Grecians Armenians, Ethiopians, Moronits, Syrians, Ruffets & others, as teftifyeth Chytreus a Proteftant. And Caluin confeffeth that the whole world beleued Maffe to be a propitiatory Sacrifice, & that in this the Fathers are againft him. And who is fo careles of his faluation as to forfake the Fathers togeother with the whole world, and follow one lewd Minifter condemned of buggery, as the authentical proceffe yet extant in Noioun doth record.

England nameth the feafts of the yeear of Maffe.

Proteftants cöfeffe that al Chriftians vfe Maffe.
Chytreus orat. de ftatu Ecclefiæ in Grætia.
Caluin. l. 4. c. 18. & parag. 1. & 11.
Lindan. ep. diffuaforia. p. 108.

Bel p. 22.

6. Now then let vs heare Bels or rather the diuels arguments againft Maffe. *The Apoftle* (faith he) *telleth* v*s that Chrift rifing from the dead dieth no more : The Papifts tel* v*s that Chrift dieth euery day, nay a thoufand tymes a day in the daily Sacrifice of their Maffe.* But better might we fay that Bels tale of the Papifts, con-

vntruthe 34.

conteyneth a thouſand vntruthes. For Papiſts (as Caluin confeſſeth) l. 4. inſtit. c. 18. paragr. 5. profeſſe . *That they nether vvil nor can kil Chriſt.* But ſay with Bellarmin. *That it is ſacriledge to ſay that Chriſt dieth at Maſſe.* Yet wil Bel wring the contrary out of Bellarm: as water out of a flint. Firſt becauſe he graunteth. *That a Sacrifice implyeth intrinſecally the conſumption of the thing ſacrificed.* But this is anſwered out of Bellarmin teaching that Chriſt hath two kinds of being to wit naturally and Sacramentally. And the conſumption of his Sacramental being, in the Maſſe, is no killing, becauſe it is not by real ſeparating his ſoule & body, but onely by conſuming the Sacramental formes in which he was Sacramentally.

7. Againe *Bellarmin* (ſaith Bel) *telleth vs that Chriſts body and blood are offered truly and properly in the Maſſe.* True: and the like ſaith S. Auſtin, S. Ambros, S. Chriſoſtome, and others. But doth Bel think euery thing offered to God to be killed? then was Chriſt killed when he was offered in the temple, Samuel, when he was offered by his mother, and bread, wine, and frakincenſe offered in the law , were killed . Thirdly he proueth it out of Bellarmin, writing *that fleſh and blood are not fit for meat vnles the beaſt* (as Bel tranſlateth) *dye or be ſlayne,* Here Bel

cold

Caluin.

Bellarm. l.1. de Miſſa. c. vltimo.

pag. 22. Bellar. ſup. c. 2.

Sup. cap. vltimo.

Auguſt. lib. 13.de ciu.c.5.

Bel p. 22. Sup. cap. 13. S. Auguſt. l. 2.q.euangel. q.3. S. Ambroſ. in pſal.38. & in 1.Luc. S. Chriſoſt. hom. 24. in 1. loc. & hom. 17. ad Hebr. Luc. 2. v. 22. 1.Reg.1. v. 25. Leuit. c. 2. Bellar.l.1.de Miſſa c.12.

cold not imagin that Bellarmin spake of
Christ (as in deed he doth not) vnles he
think he called Christ a beast. But becaufe
flesh and blood of beasts are not fit for our
meat before the beasts be killed, he proueth
by parity that Chrifts flesh and blood were
not fit to be propofed in manner of meat
before he was facrifyced. And therupon gathereth that he did Sacrifice him felfe at his
laft fupper in an vnbloody manner, and
after the order of Melchifedech before he
gaue his flesh, and blood as meat & drinke
to his Apoftles. Which reafon he tooke out

S. Gregor.
Niffen. ho-
mil.1.de Re-
furrectione.
Sup.cap. vlt.

of S. Gregory Niffen: whofe words shalbe
alledged herafter. And of Chrifts body Bellarm: profeffeth. *That it taketh no hurt, nor*
leefeth his natural being, when the Euchariſt
is eaten.

Bellarm l. 1.
de Miſſa. c.
vltimo.

8. His fourth proofe is out of Bellarm:
when he faith. *That a true and real Sacrifice re-*
quireth true and real killing quando in occiſione

Bel pag.22.
Falfe tran-
ſlation.
vntruth 35.

poniturʃentia ʃacrificy, which Bel tranflateth
thus *Seing the eſſence of a Sacrifice conſiſteth in*
killing, which (faith he) *is the conſtant doctrin*
which *S. Paule inculcateth to the hebrews* : 9 : *v.*
17. 25 : 26. 27. 28. But this proofe relyeth
onely vpon Bels falfe tranflating the word
Quando Seing which he should haue tranſlated *when.* And Bellarmins mynd is that
the true Sacrifice requireth true killing,
when

when the essence therof consisteth in killing, as it doth in al bloody Sacrifices. But as for the Masse, he auoucheth it to be *no Sacrifice but Sacriledge to say that Priests really kil Christ.* And most false it is that S. Paul euer thought the essence of sacrifice to consist in killing. For beside the vnbloody Sacrifice of Melchisedech, he was not ignorant of diuers vnbloody Sacrifices in the old law, as of incense, for which there was a special aultar, and of bread and wine. And in the places quoted by Bel he affirmeth that it was necessary for Christ to dye, & by once dying to redeeme the world, which maketh nothing to this purpose.

Loc.iam cit.

9. These proofs out of Bellarmin he confirmeth by *a constant position, and general receaued axiom* (as he saith) *in the Popish Church, that by vertue of the words of consecration Christs body is put a part from his blood, and his blood from his body, and he so slain.* But omitting Bels fond inferring Christ to be killed, if his body and blood be put a parte how soeuer, because not to put body and blood a parte where they were not before, but to separat them where they are vnited, is to kil : Els God should kil a man, if he created a soule and body a part. Omitting I say this fond illation, a manifest vntruth it is to affirme, that to be a constant position and gene-

Bel pag. 23.

vntruth 35.

general axiom in the Popish Church which she condemneth as heresie in these words. *Accursed be he who shal deny that whole Christ is contayned vnder ether forme of bread and wine.* And the contrary is his Maister Luthers doctrin as testifyeth Bellarm:l.1.de Euchar:c.2.

10. But let vs heare what coulor he hath of this so notorious vntruth. *Bellarm* : (saith he) *teacheth. Ideo in cena seorsum consecratur corpus, & seorsum sanguis &c.* which Bel thus Englisheth. *Therfore is the body consecrated a parte in the supper, and the blood asunder, that we may vnderstand the presence of the body , and blood in the supper, to be there after the manner of a body slayne, and dead.* But what ? is to consecrate a parte, to put a parte ? But Bellarm : telleth him that it is a far different thing , and that albeit Christs body and blood be seuerally consecrated, yet they are not seperated, nor one without the other in the Sacrament, because as the Coūcel of Trent saith, they are so naturally, and necessarily vnited in his resurrection, as they can be no more disioyned. Which vnion because they wanted in the tyme of Christs death, if then Masse had bene said , they had not onely bene consecrated seuerally but also put a parte. But what incōuenience inferreth Bel hereof ? None at al. And thus much of his first argument against Masse.

The

Conc. Trid. sess.13.cau. 3. & c.3.

Bel p. 23. Bellarm.l.1. de Missa. c. 12.

Conc. Trid. sess.13.c.3.

S.Thom.3.p. 476.art. 1.

CHAP. IIII.
The reſt of Bels arguments againſt
Maſſe confuted.

HIS ſecond argument conſiſteth of
many abſurdities, and groſſe impie-
ties, which (ſaith he) follow of the Maſſe,
& he reckeneth diuers. Firſt *that Chriſt at his
laſt ſupper was both ſitting at table, and borne in
his own hands.* But if this be abſurd and impious, impious, and abſurd was S. Auſtin,
when he ſaid that Chriſt at his laſt ſupper
carried him ſelf *in his hands ſecundum literam*
that is properly, *and therin did more then any
man can doe.* But what abſurdity is it more,
then for a body to be in twoe places? for
that being once done, one may carry him
ſelf as wel as an other. As the ſoule becauſe
it is in al parts of the body, as it is in the
legges carrieth it ſelfe as it is in the body.
The ſecond abſurdity is *that Chriſt at his laſt
ſupper was both liuing and dead.* But this followeth not, for he was a liue in the Sacrament, though there he ſhewed no acts of
life, and as long as he is a liue according to
his natural being, he is neuer dead in the
ſacrament, becauſe his ſacramental being is
a memorial of his natural being repreſen-
ting, and depending of it.

   2. The third abſurdity is *that Chriſt was*

H   both

both visible and inuisible . Nether doth this
follow. For though he were inuisible in the
Sacrament, yet it is not true to say absolu-
tely, he was inuisible, because he was there
visible in his proper forme. But that he was
visible in his proper forme, and inuisible in
the sacrament, is no more absurd, then
that after his resurrection he was visible to
the Apostles, and inuisible to the Iewes, visible to S. Paul, and not to his Companions
Act. 9. v. 7. Willet saith that S. Paul did see
no man. But we wil rather beleue Ananias
saying that *Christ appeared to him in the way.*
Act. 9. v. 17. The fourth absurdity is, *that
Christ was at his supper long and short, broad and
narrow, light and heauy.* But rather these follow, for what length bredth or weight
Christ had in his proper forme, the same
he had in the sacrament, albeit it had not
there the like effects of filling roome, or
weighing; as nether he had when he was
borne, and walked vpon the Sea.

3. The fift is, *that Christ was a sacrifice for
our sins before he dyed for vs.* This which Bel
condemneth of impiety, we haue before
proued it out of Scripture to be certayne
verity, & for such the holy Fathers auouch
it, let Bel heare one or twoe for al. S. Gregory Nissen. orat. 1. de Resurrect. *Christ offereth him self an oblation and hoste for vs being
both*

Math. 29.
Mar. 16.
Luc. 20.
Ioan. 20.
21.

VVillet Cō-
trou. 4. q.3.
p.115.

Math. 14.
Marc. 6.
Ioan. 6.

S. Gregor.
Nissen.

both the Prieſt, and the lamb of God. VVhen was
this? when he gaue his body to be eaten and his
blood to be drunk to his diſciples. For it is manifeſt
to euery one.that man can not eate of a sheepe vnles
ſlaughtering goe before eating. Seing therfore he
gaue his diſciples his body to be eaten , he euidently
shewed that the ſatriſizing was already perfect,
and abſolute. S. Chriſoſtome alſo hom. de S. Chryſo-
proditione Iudæ. tom. 3. ſaith. *On that table* ſtom.
was celebrated both Paſchaes of the figure , and of
the verity. Againe *Iudas was preſent , and parta-*
ked of that ſacrifice. And the Fathers are ſo
playne for this matter , as Kemnitius con- Kemnitius.
feſſeth they vſually ſay *that Chriſts body and*
blood was at this ſupper a ſacrifice, an oblation, an
hoſte and victime , and he could not eſcape
their authorities, but by caſting of a figure.

4. The Sixt and laſt abſurdity or impietie which Bel inferteth is *that al Chriſts*
ſacrifice at his ſupper was imperfect, or at his paſ-
ſion needles. But nether this followeth. For
Chriſts ſacrifice at his ſupper was a moſt
perfect vnbloudly ſacrifice according to
the order of Melchiſedech, and yet his ſacrifice on the croſſe was needful, as the pe-
culier price which God exacted at his handes, for the redemption of the world, that Hebr. 2. v.
as the apoſtle ſaith, by death he might de- 15.
ſtroy him, who had the Empier of death.
For albeit not only Chriſts whole body and
H 2 blood

blood in the Euchariſt, but euen the leaſt
drop of his blood, had been a ſufficient ſacrifice to redeeme the whole world: neuertheles God, partly to shew his great hatred
towards ſinne (wherof Chriſt bore the punishment : partly to manifeſt his infinite
loue towards man kinde, for whoſe ſaluation he would not ſpare the life of his only
ſonne: partly for many other cauſes, exa-
&ed of Chriſt the ſuperaboundant price,
and ranſome of his bloody ſacrifice on the
croſſe. But let vs heare how Bel diſproueth
this.

5. He citeth fowre places out of S. Paule
Heb 9. and 10. to proue that one oblation
of the croſſe was ſufficient to take away al
ſinns in the world, and that by it once made
we are made holy, and after it once donne
Chriſt ſitteth at the right hand of God. But
what is this to the purpoſe. For we affirme
not Chriſt to haue offered ſacrifice at his
laſt ſupper , becauſe his ſacrifice on the
Croſſe was not ſufficient , or we not made
holy by it: but becauſe the ſcripture and
fathers teach ſo, and Chriſt therby executed the fun&ion of his prieſthood , accordinge to the order of Melchiſedech , and
applyed vnto his apoſtles the vertue of his
bloody ſacrifice , as he applyeth it vnto vs
by the dayly ſacrifice of the Maſſe: and
did

did not make perfect and conſummate his
bloody ſacrifice, as Bel falſly chardgeth vs
to thinke. As Bellarmin (whom onely I
cite becauſe Bel accounteth his teſtimony
moſt ſufficient) ſheweth at lardge lib. 1. de
Miſſa cap. 25. Wher alſo he anſwereth Bels
arguments. But he should do wel to obiect
the aforeſaid wordes of S. Paul againſt Caluin blaſpheminge lib. 1. inſtit. 16. num. 8.
& 10. *That nothinge had been done for* vs *if Chriſt* Caluin.2. in-ſtit.c. 16. pa-ragr.10.
had only ſuffered corporal death, but we *needed a*
greater, and more excellent price. For this is
plainly to ſay, that the oblation of Chriſts
body once was not ſufficient, nor that
Chriſt perfected al by one oblation, which
is expreſly againſt S. Paule Hebr. 10. v. 10. *Hebr.*
11. 14. And thus much for Bels ſecond argument againſt the Maſſe.

6. The third is this, *The Euchariſt is a teſta-* Bel p. 24.
ment. ergo either no ſacrifice at al, or of no value
before the teſtators death becauſe S. Paule Hebr. 9. *Hebr.*
v. 17. *denieth a teſtament to be of force before the*
teſtators death. Anſwer. The Antecedent we
grant with S. Luke 22. v. 20. though Bel
him ſelfe deny it ſoone after. The conſequence we deny? for as the blood of calues,
wher with the old teſtament was confirmed, was both the peoples ſacrifice to God
and his teſtament to them as appeareth
Heb. 9. 20. and Exod. 24. v. 8. ſo Chriſts
H 3　　　blood

blood at his supper was both his sacrifice to his father, and his testament to his apostles: And as a sacrifice it tooke effecte immediatly, because a sacrifice is an absolute gifte made to God, dependinge of no condition to come: as the sacrifice of Abel and Noe pleased god immediatly. But as a testament it was not of force, til (as S. Paule saith) it was confirmed by death; because a testament is a deed of gift, not absolute, but vpō condition that the giuers death ensue.

Gen. 4. & 8.

Hebr. 9. v. 17.

7. Bel hauinge (as you haue heard) labored to proue the Eucharist to be no sacrifice, because it is a testament, strayght after inferreth thervpon, that it is not really Christs blood, because it is not really a testament. For (saith he) *as Christ sayd in S. Mathevv. This is my blood of the nevv testament: so he said in S. Luke this cup is the nevv testament in my blood: But it is not really the nevv testament, because remission of sinnes is referred to sheddinge of his blood, vvhich vvas on the crosse, not at supper. Ansvver:* The proposition I grante, & deny the assumption: for not onely the last wil of the testator, but euen the authentical euidence thereof is properly called a testament. So we cal the Bible the testament, and Circumcision is called a testament, Ecclesiast. 44. v. 21. and a couenant Gen. 17. And Christs blood is the authentical euidence

II. Contradict.

Bel pag. 25.

Math. 26. v. 28. *Luc.* 22. v. 20.

dence of his last wil, or els he made none.

8. And Bels reason maketh quite against him selfe. For Christs blood was shed at his supper for remission of sinns, as we proued before, and him selfe testifieth sayinge then in the present tense, *which is shed for remission of sinns*, as the Euangelists both in Greeke and English bibles testifie. But because it was not shed or powred out then in a bloody manner, and proper forme, Bel wil not verefie Christs words in that tense wherin he spake them, not consideringe that euen then Christs blood being in a chalice in forme of wine, was in that forme powred out into the mouths of the Apostles for remission of their sinns; and his testament therby made, as the old was by the sprinkling of Calues blood vpon the Iewes: though the ratifying and confirmation therof, was afterward by his death.

Bel reasoneth against him self.

How Christs blood was powred out at the last supper.

Exod. 24. v. 8. Hebr. 9. v. 20.

9. Bels fourth argument is out of S. Paul Heb. 10. v. 18. *ouc eti prosphora peri hamartias. There is not hence forth an oblatiō for sinne*, Some Catholiques answer that the Apostle meaneth an other oblation in substance, as the oblations of the Iewes were, who offered dayly different beastes, and the oblation of the Masse is in substance al one with the oblatiō of the Crosse. This Bel impugneth, *because then the Masse sacrifice should be of infinit*

Bel pag. 25.

valeyr,

vntruth 36.

valevv, vvhich no Papiſt dare auouch. Here is an vntruth for many learned Papiſts auouch it, as Caietan, Silueſter, Canus, Ruard, Soto: and others, though they grant the effect therof to be finit, as the paſſion, and interceſſion of Chriſt are of infinit valewe, though the effect they worke be but finit, becauſe *fevv are ſaued.* But others as Thomas, Scotius, Gabriel, Bellarmin: and deuines commonly deny Bels illation. for though the hoſte offered in Maſſe be of infinit valew, yet the offeringe of it by men, is of finit valew. Becauſe al mens actions haue that valew which God by his grace giueth to them, which is but finit. And Bel by the widdowes offeringe Luc. 21. might know that the valew of the offering is not alwayes correſpondent to the valew of the thing offered. For rich mens giftes exceeded her 2. mytes, and yet their offering was inferior to hers. And much more inferior is mens offerings to the offering of Chriſt, though they offer the ſelfe ſome hoſte.

10. But in deed the Apoſtle in the place cited by Bel, doth not ſo much deny an other oblation in ſubſtance, as an other ful and perfect partakinge of Chriſts oblation, teaching the Hebrues (as he had done before and as agayne in this Chapter v. 26.)

that

Caiet.3.part.
q.79 art.5.
Silueſt. verbo Miſſa. q.
9.Can.12. de locis. c. 13.
ad 10.
Ruard. art.
16.parag. 2.
Soto 4.d.14.
q.2.art.2.
S. Thom. 4
d.45.q.2.a.4.
Scot.quodl.
20.
Gabriel lect.
26.in Con.
Bellarm.l.2.
de Miſſa c.
4.
Scholaſtici
4.d.45.

that if after they haue bene baptized they
returne agayne to the old lawe and Apofta-
tate from Chrift, they cannot haue the like
aboundant remiſſion of finns applyed to
them as was in baptifme. And this he ment
by thofe words, *vvhere there is remiſſion of thofe*
(finns) *novv ther is not an oblation for finne,*
which he vttereth more playnely v. 26. *If*
vve finn vvillingly after the knovvledg of the truth
receaued, novv ther is not left an hofte for finns, but
a certaine terrible expectation of iudgment. Becaufe God hauinge once pardoned by baptifme both offence and punishment, afterward vfeth not the like mercy, but pu-
nisheth finne.

11. After this Bel turneth to his old cu- Bel pag.26,
ftome of iniuringe his Mayfter Bellarmin,
charginge him with denial of the Maſſe to
be truely and properly propitiatory, becaufe Bellarm.l. 2,
he faith, *that Chriſt being novv immortal can* de Miſſa c.4.
neither merit nor ſatisfie. Wheras Bellarmin cap. 2.
fpendeth one whole chapter of that booke
to proue Maſſe to be a propitiatory facrifice. And ftrayght after thofe wordes which
Bel cyteth aproueth Maſſe to *be a ſatisfactory* cap. 4. cit.
facrifice, becaufe by it, Chriſts paſsion according to
his inftitution, is applyed to take away the temporal
paynes of the liue and dead. And by the wordes
which Bel citeth, onely meaneth that Maſſe
is not properly propitiatory as it proceedeth

deth from any acte which Chrift now hath,
becaufe now he can neither merit nor fatisfy. Wherefore falfly Bel doth accufe.
Papifts that with them Maße is one while a pro-
pitiatory facrifice and an other while not. For
the Tridentin Councel whom they al fol-
lowe, hath defined it to be *truely a propitia-*
tory facrifice. And Bellarmin proueth it at
lardge out of Scripture, Fathers, and Coun-
cells. See Origen hom.13. in Leuitt. S. Chrifoftom. lib. 6. de facerd. & hom. de prodit.
Iudæ S. Auftin q. 57. in Leuit. S. Beda lib. 4.
Hift Chap. 22.

12. His fift and laft argument againft
Maffe is taken out of the decree & gloffe de
confecrat D. 2. Can. *Hoc eft* thus tranflated
by Bel. *As therefore the heauenly bread, which*
is the flesh of Chrift, is after it manner cald the
body of Chrift, when in deed it is the Sacrament of
Chrifts body, of that body which is vifible, vvhich
is palpable, mortal, & nayled on the crofse. And
that oblation of flesh, which is made by the hands
of the prieft is called Chrifts death, and Crucifix-
ion, and not in truth of the thinge, but in a mi-
ftery fignifyinge the thinge: fo the Sacrament of
faith by which baptifme is vnderftood is faith.
Hetherto the decre now the gloffe therof:
The heauenly Sacramēt which reprefenteth Chrifts
flesh truely, is called the body of Chrift, but impro-
perly, wherefore it is faid after it manner, but not
in the

Conc. Trid. fefſ.22.c.2.& can.3, Bellarm. c. 2. cit.
Origen.to.1. S. Chryfoft. tom. 5. & tom. 3. S. Auguftin. tom. 4.
Bel pag.26.

in the truth of the thinge, but in the thing: signi-
fied that this may be the sense, it is called Christs
body (that is to say) it signifieth his body. These
(saith Bel) *are golden wordes (as God would)*
by pens of Papists deliuered.

13. I accept his confession. First then S.
Austin and S. Prosper are Papists, for (as
Gratian out of whom the decree is také testifieth) the words of the Decree were first
deliuered by S. Austins pen, and after recorded by S. Prosper. Secondly I hope Bel
hereafter wil allowe of sacrificinge or offering flesh by the hands of the priests, because these are part of the golden wordes of
that decree. For this so gentle confession, I
wil dissemble with a litle fault of Bels trans-
latinge, *quod visible quod palpabile mortale in*
cruce positum est. Thus, *which is visible palpable*
mortal & nayled on the crosse. When he shoud
haue said , which being visible palpable
mortal was nailed on the crosse. Now let
vs heare what he gathereth out of the
aforesaid words *to the confusion* (as he saith)
of Papists but he should haue said to his
owne.

14. 1. *That the blessed bread of the Eucharist is*
called the Body of Christ. What is here against
Papists? who willingly so cal it, but rather
against Protestants who seldom or neuer
cal it so. 2. *That it is also called the passion and*
death

Gratian. de
consecrat.d.
2. can.Hoc
est.

S. *Austin*
and S. *Pros-*
per Papists.
Sacrificing
of flesh by
Priests háds
allovved by
Bel.
2, *False*
translat.

pag. 27.

37. *vntruth*

death of Chrift. This is an vntruth : for not bread of the Euchariſt, but the ſacrificing of fleſh with Prieſts hands is ſo called. 3. *That it is not Chrifts body truely.* This is moſt true, for the bread or rather the forme therof, in the Euchariſt, is not Chriſts body truely & properly 4. *That it is Chrifts body as the Sacra-ment of Baptiſme is fayth.* This is nothing a-gainſt vs, who confeſſe bread (or rather the forme therof, called bread becauſe it ſo ſeemeth to ſenſe) to be but a Sacrament of Chriſts body.

15. 5. *That it is not Chrifts body in truth but in ſignification.* This S. Auſtin ſaith not but onely that *the oblation of the fleſh of Chriſt by the prieſt is his death and paſſion not truly but in a miſtery ſignifyinge his death,* which maketh nothing againſt vs or to this purpoſe. The gloſſe in deede ſaith that *the Sacrament is not Chriſts body in truth, but in ſignification* and the same ſay al Chatholiques namely Bellarmin l. 1. de Eucha. c. 14. *The Sacrament of the Eu-chariſt is not Chriſts body but contayneth Chriſts body, for a Sacrament is a ſenſible ſigne,* and this ſenſible ſigne of bread and wine, is that which the gloſſe ſayd is not in truth Chriſts body but is improperly ſo called : which is ſo far from being the vpſhot of the contro-uerſy, or not admitting any ſolution, (as Bel fondly boaſteth) as in mans ſight that hath

Bellarm.

Bel pag. 27.

hath eyes, it requireth no ſolution. For who wil thinke that one denieth Chriſts body to be truely in the Sacrament, becauſe he denieth the Sacrament (which is the ſenſible ſignes of bread and wine) to be truly his body? So Bel may gather that a body containeth not a ſoule, nor a place a body, becauſe the continents, are not the thing conteyned. But (ſaith Bel) *if Chriſts body were in the Sacramēt really it ſhould be there in rei veritatē truely.* As if the gloſſe had denyed that Chriſt is in the Sacrament in rei veritate. Suerly this sheweth that Bel neuer ment to deale *in rei veritate.* And thus much of the 2. member of this Article. Now let vs go to the third.

Chap. V.

Berengarius his Recantation explicated and S. Auſtins authority anſwered.

P O P I S H *decrees* (ſaith Bel) *tel vs a long* Bel pag. 28. *tale of one Berengarius ſome tyme Deacon of a church in Gaunt.* No maruail if this tale ſeeme long to Bel, which recounteth the foyle of his hereſie againſt the real pre- ſence, in Berengarius the firſt brocher therof, in a general councel at Rome vnder Pope Nicholas the ſecond, aboute the year of Chriſt 1060. wher he recanted publikly and

Berengar. condemned of 113. Biſhops.
Lanfranc. de Sactam. Euchariſt.

and (as him selfe saith) willingly, *denoun-ceinge al such to deserue eternal curse, who denyed Christs body and blood to be really in the Eucharist.*

Bel lacketh latin.

Bel maketh him Deacon of Gaunt, wheras he was Archdeacon of Angiers in France, not being able to distinguish Andeauum from Gandauum Angiers from Gaunt; and because he abiured his heresie, Bel termeth him *a silly Deacon*, though his brother Buck-

Bucleis ans-wuer to 8. reasons p. 62.

ly cal him *an excellent and holy man.* In deed he found more mercy at Gods hands then I read of any Arch-hereticke, and dyed a penitent Catholike. For dying, on twelf

Malmesbur. l. 3. histor. Angl. in Gabriel. 1. p. 114.

day said (as Malmesbur. an English author at that tyme writeth.) *In this day of his apparition my lord Iesus wil appeare to some, to glory as I hope for my repentance, or to punishment as I feare for others seduced.* The like repentance I pray God send to Bel ere he dye, that as he hath imytated Berengarius in heresie, and in abiuration also of it at Rome (if I be not deceaued) he may likewise imitate him in repentance and penance.

2. But because Berengarius in his recan-tation, which was afterward put amongst

Distinct. 2. cit.

the Decrees, professed *that Christ in the Eu-charist sensualiter manibus sacerdotum tangitur, frangitur, & dentibus fidelium atteritur, is sensibly touched with hands of Priests, broken, and chewed with the teeth of the faithful,* Bel exclaymeth
migh-

mightely, calling his recantation (but yet
without al proofe)*cruel, barbarous, villanous,
blasphemous, and horrible impietie*. Gladly he
would haue the reader beleeue, that Catholiques professe Chrifts body to be in it felfe
broken, and torne in peeces one member
from an other, though him felfe foone
after not only alleadge Bellarmin to the
contrary, but confesse alfo *that by the Popes*   *p.* 29.
*doctrin Chrifts body can not be broken or torne
truely, and in deed*, and cite the Glosse vpon
the faid decree faying, *that it were a worfe*   *pag.* 30.
herefie to thinke we made parts of Chrift, then
to deny him to be in the facrament. And this is
euident by the Masse it felfe where we fay,
Chrift nether broken , nor deuided is receaued   Missa de
whole, and *no cuttinge is of the thing, the breach*   corpore
is onely in the figne.   Chrifti.

3. Neuertheles Chrifts body is faid to
be toucht, broken, and chewed in the Eucharift, becaufe the figne of bread in which
it really is, is fo vfed. As God is faid to haue
bene crucified, becaufe the humanitie in
which he was, was fo handled, and Chrift
touched when his garment was touched.
And thefe kind of fpeaches we learnd of
the holy Fathers. For S. Chrifoftom. fpea-   S. Chryfoft.
kinge of the facrament faith exprefly *that* hom. 24. in
Chrifts body is broken, In other place *we fee,* 1.Cor.to.4.
feel, eate, and haue Chrift within vs. Agayne Math.to.3.
                                  Chrift

Hom.46.in
Ier.to.3.&
61. ad po-
pulnm to.5.
Tertul. l. de
Idolatria.

*Christ gaue him selfe to vs to touch, to eate, and
fasten our teeth* (marke Bel) *on his flesh.* Tertullian inueighinge againft vnworthy re-
ceauers faith *Corpus Christi lacesſunt*. They
vex Chrifts body. S. Ciprian of the fame

S. Ciprian.
ſerm. de la-
pſis.

affirmeth: *They vſe violence to Chrifts body and
blood and with their moutkes do offend him.* And
they learnt theſe ſpeeches of Chrift him

1.Cor.11.v.
24. in the
greeck.

felfe faying: *This is my body which is broken.*
Wil Bel now condemne Chrift and theſe
holy fathers of wickednes, villany, blafphemy, and horrible impietie? Surely they
vſe the very wordes of touching, breaking,

Bel pag.30.

and faſteninge, or chewing with teeth. Nay
wil he condemne both English, and many

Bel admit-
teth Chrifts
body to be
conſumed.

forrayne Proteſtants *whoſe conſtant doctrine*
(ſaith he) *is that Chrifts body is broken torne &
conſumed with mouth and teeth.* Behold good
reader. for Papifts to ſay Chrifts body is
touched, broken, and torne, is villany wickednes, blaſphemy and horrible impiety:
but for Proteſtants to ſay the ſame and adde
conſuming too, is good doctrine.

Bel pag.29.

4. But Bel wil ſay that he addeth, that al
theſe are to be vnderſtood ſignificantly and
ſacramentally. True. And the ſame adde
wee. For as him ſelfe citeth out of Bellar-

Bellarm.

min lib. 2. de Concil. c. 8. *It is and al wayes
was certayne that Chrifts body being now vncor-
ruptible can be nether broken nor torne but in a*
                                                    ſigne

figne or sacrament. But the difference is in the vnderstanding. For we say Chrifts body is broken in a figne, which really, and truely contayneth it; and Proteftants say it is broken in a figne, from which Chrift is as far as heauen is from earth, and to expreße this difference, and to exclude the fenfe which Berengarius vfed, and the Proteftants haue learnt of him, the Pope and Councel made him to profeße. That he beleeued this to be *in rei veritate* in the vérity of the thing. Not as if Chrifts body weare in it felfe fo handled, for therof there was neuer doubt, but that it was not handled fo in a bare figne, but in fuch a figne as in *rei veritate* truely contayneth Chrifts body. As the woman Luc. 8. did *in rei veritate* truely touch Chrift when she touched his garment, in which he truely was: as appeareth by his words ib. v. 46. *Some body hath touched me:* But the Crucifiers, when they parted the fame garments, did not touch him *in rei veritate* truely, becaufe then he was not truely in them. And hereby appeareth how the contrariety, which Bel noteth betwixt the Councel and Bellarmine, is none at al, and how proteftants can not vefifie the breakinge of Chrifts body, fo wel as Catholiques can, and leaft of al can (as Bel imagineth) verify Chrifts wordes of his body

I giuen,

Catholiques and Proteftants agreement and difference about the breaking of Chrifts body.

S. Luke.

S. Ihon. 19. v. 23.

pag. 19.

giuen, & blood shed for remiſſion of ſinns, becauſe neuer was any bare figure giuen or shed for remiſſion of ſinnes.

pag. 30.

5, But a ſinguler note (ſaith Bel) and worthy to be marked, is gathered out of the gloſſe vpon the foreſaid decree, when it aduiſeth vs, *That vnles we vnderſtand Berengarius words ſoundly, we may fal into worſe hereſie. Marke theſe words* (ſaith Bel) *for they teach vs playnly, that it is a moſt dangerous thing to rely vpon Popish decrees; euen then when they pretend to reforme the Church and condemne hereſies.* But better may we ſaye marke this note, for it diſcouereth Bels malice, and folly, & teacheth vs plainly that it is a moſt dangerous thing to rely vpon heretikes, euen when they promiſe to auouch no vntruth

pag. 22.

of any man, as Bel did a litle before. For what aduiſeth the gloſſe, againſt the relying vpon Popes decrees, and not onely againſt miſunderſtanding them. May we not in like manner ſay of the ſcripture, that vnles we ſoundly vnderſtand thoſe wordes, Ihon 6. *except you eat the fleſh of the ſonne of man, and drinke his blood, you ſhal haue no life in you,* but groſly as the Capharnaits did of eating it

Ciprian. de cæna Domini.
S. Auguſtin.
tract. 27. in Ioh.

ſodde or roſted, or cut in peeces (as teſtify S. Ciprian and S. Auſtin) we ſhal fal into greater hereſie, then that of Berengarius was. What now Syr Thomas? may we ther-

therfore infer that it is a moft dangerous thing to rely vpon fcripture?

6. Finally Bel concludeth this third member of his article with an argument drawne out of S. Auftins words: *illi mandu- cabant panem Dominum, illi panem Domini con- tra Dominum.* They (the Apoftles) eat the bread our lord, he (Iudas) eat the bread of our lord againft our lord. Out of which wordes Bel frameth an argument fo inuin- cible in his conceypt, as he promifeth to fubfcribe, and neuer more to write againft any parte of Papifts doctrine, if it be anf- wered. Marke therfore I pray thee gentle reader his argument, and my anfwer, and iudge, whether he be not bound to turne his coate the third tyme, if he wil performe his promife. The argument he propofeth out of forme, but it may be reduced to this. Iudas receaued but *Panem Domini* the bread of our lord, and not *Panem Dominum* the bread our lord: therfore in the Eucharift is not *Dominus* our Lord. The Antecedent (faith he) *is playnly auouched by* S. *Auftin*, the confequence is cleere, becaufe if in the Eu- charift weare our lord, doubtles Iudas in receauing of it, fhould haue receaued our lord. Before I anfwer this argument I muft aduertife the reader of three things: firft how flenderly this fellow is grounded in

Bel pag. 30. 31. S. Auguftin. tract. 59. in Ioan.

I 2   his

his faith, who promiſeth to ſubſcribe to
the contrary, if one onely argument, grounded vpon one ſaying of one father can be
ſolued. Euident it is that he hath neyther
playne ſcripture, nor conuincent reaſon,
nor the teſtimony of other fathers for his
religion, who for anſwering of one fathers
word, wil forſake it. Albeit this be les mar-
uelous in Bel, becauſe hauing already twiſe
altered his religion, he wil find les difficulty to change the third tyme. 2. I note the
extreame blindnes of this fellow, who biddeth *vs note and marke ſeriouſly that S. Auſtin*
telleth vs, that the bread vvhich the Apoſtles eate
vvas our lord. I would Bel had marked this
him ſelfe, for it is the very vpſhot (to vſe
his owne tearme) of this controuerſy, and
vnanſwerable by any Proteſtant. For if (as
Bel noteth out of S. Auſtin) the bread
which the Apoſtles eate was our lord, how
can proteſtants deny it, and ſay it was bare
bread? Or if (as S. Auſt. ſpeaketh) they eate
bread our lord, how can Bel ſay they eate
not our lord, but bare bread? Can one eate
fleſh mutton, if the fleſh he eate be no
mutton?

7. Thirdly, I note his notorious abuſing S. Auſtins authority. For firſt in Engliſhing his words he addeth to them, though
in a parentheſis, theſe words (*Not our lord*
but,

Bel noteth
a point
quite a-
gainſt him
ſelf.

Bels abu-
ſing of S.
Auſtins
vvords.

but) afterward he ſaith S. Auſtin telleth vs, *that which Iudas receaued was but the bread of our lord,* then, as imboldened to lye, auoucheth that *S. Auſtin affirmeth moſt conſtantly, that Iudas receaued barely Panem Domini* bread of our lord, and laſtly as cocke ſure not to be tript in lying, profeſſeth that *S. Auſtin playnly auoucheth that Iudas receaued not Panem Dominum bread our lord.* Wheras S. Auſtin ſaith no one of al theſe, but onely, that the Apoſtles receaued bread our lord, and Iudas bread of our lord, without *but* or *barely,* or denyal of the other. Marke ther'ore good reader his ſteps. Firſt his vntruth is cogged into S. Auſtins words with a parentheſis, then is it put with a *but,* afterward with *barely,* and laſtly playnly auouched. Theſe ſteps might Bel haue found in his ladder of lying, better then he deuiſed the like before, in the Popes ladder to his ſupremacy. But here may the reader take a taſte of the vntrue dealing of heretiques. For who would not haue ſworne, but that Bel would haue dealt truely in an argument, wherof he counteth ſo much, as if it be ſolued, he wil recant the third tyme: But now to come to his argument.

8. I anſwer directly by denying the Antecedent. for S. Auſtin ſaid not, that Iudas **eate** *but,* or *barely Panem Domini,* bread of

vntruth 38.

vntruth 39.

vntruth 40

Bels ſteps of vntrue dealing.
1.
2.
3.
4.

our lord, and much les said he eate not *Pa-*
nem Dominum: but onely said that the Apostles did eate *Panem Dominum* bread our lord,
& he *Panem Domini* bread of our lord. Wherfore the doubt can be onely why he altered
his speech , calling that bread our lord,
which the Apostles eate, and that bread of
our lord which Iudas eate . The reason
wherof can not be, because he thought the
Apostles and Iudas receaued a bread of different substance; for Epist. 162. he expresly
writeth that Iudas receaued *pretium nostrum*
our price which in substance is *Panis Domi-*
nus bread our lord , and S. Chrysost. hom.
de prodit. Iudæ affirmeth, that Christ offered to Iudas the blood, which he had sold.
and Theodoret. in 1. cap. 2. Cor. that he
gaue to Iudas his precious body and blood,
The reason therfore is that which S Aust.
him selfe insinuateth in the words immediatly following *ille vitam, ille pænam* they
eate life , he punishment, vz because the
bread had a different effect , and operation
in Iudas, then it had in the Apostles. For as
him selfe proueth lib. 11. cont. Faust. cap.7.
one thing of different effects or operations
may haue different names. What maruaile
then if he called that which the Apostles
receaued bread our lord , because it was
both in substance and operation food, and
life

8 . *Austin*
saith Iudas
eate our
price.to. 2.
S. Chrysost.
tom.3.

Buccella
Dominica
ven enum
fuit Iudæ.
See S.Austin
l. 2. cont. lit.
Petil. c. 47.
tom.7.
S.Augustin.
tom 6.
Corruptio,
carni hoc
nomen im-
ponit Aug.
l. 1.cont. ad-
uersf. legis.
Et prophet.
c.6.to.6.

life to them, and that which Iudas receaued bread of our lord, becaufe though in
fubftance it was the fame, yet through his
malice, in operation it was poyfon and
death vnto him And here by the way wold
I propound one choife to Bel, whether he
wil beleeue the Euchariſt to be *Panem Dominum* with Catholiques, or bare *Panem Domini* with Proteſtants. If the firſt, he may
eate *Panem Dominum* with the Apoſtles, if
the fecond, he may eate *Panem Domini*, but
it ſhalbe with Iudas.

*A choife
for Bel.*

9. But fuppofe S. Auſtin had faid (as he
hath not) that Iudas did not eat bread our
Lord, Bel could not therof infer that the
Euchariſt is not truly our Lord, feing he
auoucheth that the Apoſtles (who vndoubtedly receaued the Euchariſt) did eat bread
our Lord : but at moſt, that what Iudas receaued, was not the Euchariſt ; which diuers think, and it is a far different queſtion,
and maketh nothing to this purpofe : But
nether could Bel infer this, becaufe S. Auſtin
other where affirmeth Iudas to haue recea
ued the Sacrament, and our price which in
fubſtance is bread, our Lord, and becaufe it
is vfual to him to deny the name to a thing
if it want the accuſtomed quality or operation. So lib. 11. cont. Fauſt. c. 7. he faith.
In refurrection there ſhal be no flesh, and

*S. Hilar. can.
30. in Math.*

*S. Auguſt. e-
piſt. 162 to.
2. tract. 26. &
62. in Ioan.
tom. 9.*

*S. Auguſtin
tom. 6.*

I 4   ferm.

ferm. 5. de verb. Apoft. c. 12. There shalbe not the fame body, becaufe it shal not be mortal. Which kind of fpeech he vfeth other where, and proueth it out of 1. Cor. 15. and 2. cor. 5. The moft therfore that Bel can infer (and he may wel do it) is, that the bread which Iudas eate was not in operation our Lord, and life to him, but iudgment, and death: which I willingly graunt, but it maketh nothing for his purpofe. Let now euery indifferēt Reader iudge whether this argument out of S. Auftin, be not fufficiently anfwered, and Bel if he wilbe as good as his word, bound to recant yet once againe. And thus much of this member.

Chap. VI.
Bels imaginary contradictions in the Maffe anfwered, and true Contradiction in his Communion shewed.

Bel pag. 32. THE fourth member Bel maketh of the apparent contradictions which are (as he faith) in the Maffe. The firft is that Catholiques fay that Chrifts body is the fame in the Maffe which was on the croffe, & yet confeffe it to be a figure therof. Bellarm. l. 1, de Euchar. c. 3. This he proueth to be a contradiction becaufe a figure muft needs be inferior to the thing figured as Bellarm: profeffeth, and

S. Paul

S. Paul teſtifieth. Anſwer. Firſt I deny al figures to be inferrior to things figured: ſome be both figures & verity, as God the Sonne figure of the ſubſtance of his Father. Heb. 1. v. 3. and yet true God. And Seth, an image of Adam Gen. 5. v. 3. and yet true man. And ſuch figures are equal to the things figured, and ſuch a figure of Chriſt is the Euchariſt; Others be bare figures, as images are of men, and the Sacraments and Sacrifices of the ould law were, wherof S. Paul and Bellarmin ſpake, and the Apoſtles Heb. 10. v. 1. calleth ſhadowes of goods to come. And theſe I graunt to be inferior to the things figured. But this maketh nothing againſt vs.

2. Secondly I deny that to be ſuperior and inferior, is contradiction : for, as euery logician knoweth it is relatiue oppoſition, which may agree to the ſame thing in different reſpect. As the ſame ſoule as it is in the head, is locally ſuperior to it ſelfe, as it is in the foote; a man as he is learned, is inferior in valew to him ſelfe as he is vertuous : And a token as it is from a friend, more worth thē it is of it ſelfe. And hereby appeareth the error of Proteſtants inferring the Euchariſt not to be Chriſt, becauſe it is a figure or remembrance of him. For wel may one thing repreſent it ſelfe. As a King in a triumphant

shew

S. Paul.
Hebr. 10.

VVhat figures be inferior to the things figured vvhat not.

Bel ignorant in logick.

One thing may figure or repreſent it ſelfe.

shew may represent, how he behaued him
selfe in Battel. And Chrifts body and blood,
as they are vnder the formes of bread and
wyne, which are a sunder, represent them
selues as they were a sunder in their proper
formes on the crosse.

3. Thirdly I returne Bels argumét vpon
him selfe. Figures must needs be inferior to
things figured : Ergo the Euchariftis some
nobler substance then bread. The Antecedent is his owne, the Consequence I proue,
because the Paschal lambe was a figure of
the Eucharift as S. Chrisostom S. Cyprian S.
Hiero. S. Austin S Leo S. Gregory & others
affirme, and may be gathered out of S. Paul
saying Heb. 10. v. 1. That the law had a shadow of goods to come, and by Chrifts insti-
tuting the Eucharift immediatly after the
eating of the Pascal lamb. Whereby (saith
S. Chrisostome) *in one table both Paschals of*
the figure and verity was celebrated.

4. His second, and third contradiction
is of a greater body being conteyned in a
lesse, and of Chrifts body broken, and not
broken, which haue bene answered before.
His fourth is, that *if Chrifts body be made pre-*
sent in the Eucharift by vertue of these words this
is my body, ether the body is there before the last
words be pronounced, or no, if before ? then the
last is superfluous, if not ? then ether al the body is
                                                    made

S. Chrysost.
hom. de
prodit. Iudæ
tom. 3.
S. Cyprian. l.
de vnit. ec-
clef.
S. Hieron. in
26. Math.
S. Auguft. l.
2. cont. lite-
ras Petilian.
c. 37. to. 7.
S. Leo serm.
7. de Paffio-
ne.
S. Gregor.
hom. 22. in
Euang.

pag. 32.
Chap. 1. pa-
rag. 12. 13.
Chap. 5. pa-
pag. 2. 3. 33.

made by the laſt word, and ſo the three firſt ſtand for cyphers, or parte of his body by one word, and parte by an other? and ſo Chriſts body is torne in peeces. O worthy challenger ignorant of the principles of logicke. What ſhew of contradiction is there here, though we ſhould grant any one of the three points inferred? But this good fellow is more skilful in making contradictions, then in knowing what contradiction is.

Bel ignorāt in logick.

5. Briefly I anſwer, that nether Chriſts whole body, nor any parte therof, is in the Euchariſt before the pronounciation of the laſt word, yet are not the former words ſuperfluous, For the laſt worketh the traſmutation, not by his owne vertue alone, but with the vertue of them alſo, or rather God worketh al when the laſt word is pronounced. For (as S. Chriſoſtom ſaith) *It is not man that by the conſecration of our Lords table, maketh the things propoſed, the body and blood of Chriſt, but that Chriſt who was crucifyed for vs. The words are vttered by the Prieſts mouth, and conſecrated by the power of God.* And the like anſwer muſt Bel make for diuers matters.

S. Chryſoſt. homil. de prodit. Iudæ tom.3.

6. For in baptiſme one may aske whether a child be chriſtened, before the name of the holy Ghoſt be pronounced, and then it is ſuperfluous, and may be left out; or parte by the name of the father, parte by
the

the name of the ſonne, and parte by the
name of the holy Ghoſt, and then is the
child chriſtened by peece meale: or onely
by the name of the holy Ghoſt, and then the
other twoe names are cyphers. And the
like argument may be propounded in diuers other matters, but I wil propound it
in a matter more intelligible, and perhaps
more proportionate to Bels capacity out of
his owne name *Thomas*. When one calleth
him by that name, ether he is al called by
Tom, and then *As* is ſuperfluous: or parte
by *Tom*, and parte by *As*, and then is he
called by peece meale: or al by *As*, & then
is *Tom* : bnt a cypher, and *As* is al Bel, and
ſo by conuerſion, al Bel is an *As*. Let Bel
ſtudy to ſolue this argument, and I doubt
not, but he wil finde the ſolution of his
owne.

pag. 34. 7. The fifte contradiction which this
contradictious fellow findeth in the Maſſe
is, that Durand, Caietan, and foure Catholiques more, before the Councel of Trent
did otherwiſe explicate the manner of
Chriſts real preſence in the Euchariſt, then
was truth, and ſince the Church hath defined, and explicated in the ſaid Councel. Is
not this a goodly contradiction in the Maſſe?
Bellarm. l.3.
de Euchar.
c. 11. & 12. did Bel find al theſe mens opinions there,
or rather gathered them out of Bellarmin,
　　　　　　　　　　　　　　　　as he

as he hath done almost al his arguments?
Or what maketh it against Masse, that three
or foure Catholiques did in a difficult matter, before it was defyned and explicated by
the Church, dissent from the rest? Let Bel
if he can shew this diuersity now since the
Councel. As for Protestants, Sainctes aboue
20. yeares agoe, gathered aboue 80. different opinions of theirs about these foure
words, *This is my body*. And an other since
hath collected twoe hundred. This far exceedeth the confusion of tonges at Babel, for
there was but 72. tongues, but here be 80.
yea 200. to expresse foure words. There one
man kept one tongue, but here they alter
speaking sometymes Lutherish, sometyme
Zwinglianish, and otherwhyle Caluinish,
and yet seing such horrible confusion, wil
not giue ouer building of their Babilonian
tower of heresy.

8. The sixt contradiction is that when
the Priest proposeth the B. Sacrament to
the people, they must adore it, *albeit* (saith
Bel) *if the Priest haue no intention to consecrate,
or omit, or miscal any word of consecration it
remayneth but bread, and the worshipers commit
idolatry.* A ioly contradiction no doubt, do
we think Bel wanted not his wits when he
proposed such matter for contradictions?
Catholiques thinke in deed that when the

Priest

Lindan. Ca-
talogo sa-
cramentor.
Sainctes de
Euchar. Re-
petit. 1. cap.
vlt.
1577. ex Bel-
larm. lib. 1.
de Euchar.
c. 8.
S. August. l.
16. de ciuit.
c. 6. tom. 5.

pag. 34.

vntruth 45

Prieſt wanteth both actual, and virtual intention, or omitteth any eſſential word,
that there is no conſecration, and the Prieſt
ſinneth therin greeuouſly; but the people
worſhiping erroniouſly vpon inuincible
ignorance offend no more, then did S. Ihon
when he worſhiped an Angel as God, thinking (as ſaith S. Auſtin) it had bene God
him ſelf, or as did Iacob, when he lay with
Lia who was not his wife, thinking verely
it had bene his wife *Rachel*. But to ſay that
there is no conſecration when the Prieſt
omitteth any word at al, or miſcalleth any
words, ſo as the ſenſe be not altered thereby, is not Catholique doctrin, but Bels
vſual falſe dealing.

Si conſcien-
tia propte-
rea lædi nō
potuit quia
neſciuit &c.
Aug. lib. 2.
cont. Creſ-
con. cap. 26.
to. 7.
Apoc. 22.
ᵥ. 8. c. 19.
ᵥ. 10.
S. Auguſt. q.
61. in Gen.
to. 4.
Geneſ. 29.
ᵥ. 24.

pag. 34.

9. His laſt contradiction is, that *vvhen
many Prieſts are made together in Rome, they al
pronounce the vvords of conſecration*. This is
true but what then? *Papiſts* (ſaith he) *can
not tel hovv many Gods, or hovv many times
God is made in a peece of bread. O accuſator fratrum.* Where dideſt thou heare of many
Gods amongeſt Papiſts? Where of making
of God? we ſay after S. Hierom and S.
Pontian that Prieſts *conficiunt Corpus Chriſti*
make Chriſts body, but dreame not of making God. Theſe be the ſlanders malitiouſly
obiected to Catholikes againſt thine owne
knowledge and Conſcience. But where is
the

S. Hieron. e-
biſt. ad He-
liodor.
S. Pontian.
epiſt. 1. De-
cretali.

the contradiction? Forſooth becauſe *Innocentius holdeth that al ſuch Prieſts do conſecrate, Durand thinketh that he only who firſt pronounceth the words, and Caietan is of an other opinion.* I graunt theſe contradict one an other. But what is this to the Maſſe? are theſe contradictions in it? You promiſed to ſhew vs contradictions in the Maſſe, and twiſe you haue told vs of durand & Caietans contradictions, & as often of other matters, which had no ſhew of Contradiction. Beſides that the matter in which theſe three Authors contradict one other is no point of faith. For with Catholiques it is no more matter of faith, whether al the ſaid Prieſts or one only conſecrate, then it is with Proteſtants, whither al or one ſhould chriſten a child, if many at once ſhould dippe him into the font, & pronounce the words of Baptiſme. So the letter be wel ſealed, it ſkilleth not whither one or many be thought to make the print, when many together put their hands to the ſeale.

10. But if Bel when he looked vpon the Maſſe booke, had looked on his communion booke, and with the like eyes and affection, he ſhould haue found other ſtuffe in it then he did in the Maſſe. For beſyde that it is made out of our breuiary and Miſſal (wherupon Gilby called King Edward
the ſixt

Bel deceaueth his Reader.

Gilby admonition to England and Scotland. fol. 70.

the sixt his booke, an English mattins pat-
ched forth of the Popes Portesse) more
then a thousand Ministers (whome the
vniuersity of Oxford acknowledged to be
their brethren, and fellow laborers in the
Lords haruest) in their petition exhibited
to his Maiesty, say that they groan vnder a
burden of humaine rites and ceremonies,
finde enormities in their Church discipline,
and in their Churches seruice, want of vniformity of doctrin, Popish opinions, and
honor prescribed to the name of Iesus with
diuers abuses, which *they are able* (say they)
to shew not to be agreable to Scripture. Thus Syr
haue your owne ministers deminished the
credit of your communion booke. And
Reynolds (an excellent ornament saith
Buckley) in the conference at Hampton
court 1. proued the communion booke to
contradict twise the Byble, & the Bishops
were faine to amend it. 2. he argued it to
contradict the 25. Article of their faith. 3. to
conteyne manifest errors, directly repugnant to Scripture: 4. he requested it to be
fitted to more encrease of piety. 5. professeth that vrging men to subscribe vnto it,
is a great impeachment to a learned ministery, wherof he giueth diuers reasons, as
the repugnancy therin to Scripture, the
corruption of Scripture, the interrogato-
ries,

Ansvver to the Petitiõ.

Exhibited in April 1603.

A thou-sand mini-sters censure of the com-munion booke.

Ansvver to 8. rea-sons. Confer. p. 63. 86. pag. 25. pag. 59.

pag. 23.

pag. 58.

ries, and ceremonies in baptiſme, and certayne words in matrimony. Thus ſyr the excellent ornament of your Church hath adorned your communion booke, and this black verdict hath he giuen therof.

11. And if I ſhould but reckon the contradictions in Proteſtants doctrin about the Euchariſt, I ſhold neuer make an end, only I wil requite Bel with ſome few. 1. how Chriſts body (ſaith Willet) ſhold be verily preſent, and yet not really. Can there be *verum* and not *res*, or *ens*: *vere*, and not *realiter*? 2. how there can be a real preſence of Chriſt in the Sacrament (as ſaith Perkins) and yet Chriſt no otherwiſe preſent, then a thing to it name. 3 How God giueth Chriſt in this Sacrament (ſaith the ſame Miniſter) as really and truly as any thing can be giuen to man, and yet he is giuen by only faith 4. How (as Caluin teacheth) the Euchariſt is no empty ſigne, but hath the verity of the thing vnited to it, and yet Chriſt is only in heauen. 5. How there is (ſaith Caluin) a true and ſubſtantial communication of Chriſts body, and blood in the Euchariſt, and yet Chriſt no more there, then he was in the Sacraments of the Iews, which were before his body was any ſubſtance. 6. How Chriſts body is truely really, and ſubſtancially in the Euchariſt (as Beza wrote in his

K con-

D. Reinolds cenſure of the communion booke.

○

Proteſtants contradictiōs about their communion.

1.
VVillet Toſtoſtyl. col. 2. part. 3. p. 82.

2.
Perkins Reform. Cath. p. 185, 189.

3.
Perkins ſup.

4.
Caluin. 4. inſtit. c. 17. paragr. 10.

5.
Caluin. ſup. parag. 19. & 15.

6.
Sainctes de Euchar. repetit. 6. c. 1. p. 208.
Mich. Fabrit. ep. de Beza.

confession exhibited to the Count Palatine
and vttered publikly in the difputation at
Poyſi) and yet withal as far from the Euchariſt, as heauen from earth ; Surely ſuch
fellows as theſe haue *yea* , & *no*, in their religion, or els *walking in craftines adulterat* (as
the Apoſtle ſpeaketh) *Gods worde*. For if
their words be vnderſtood as they ſignify, & purport, they include manifeſt contradiction,and thus
much of the ſecond Arti-
cle. *VVherfore be myndful
(Bel) from whēce thou
are fallen and do pe-
nance* Apoc. 2.

⁎

THE

*Surius An.
1556.*

*2. Cor. 1. v.
17.
2. Cor. 4.
v, 2.*

Apocal.

THE
THIRD ARTICLE
OF THE POPES
DISPENSATIONS.

CHAP. I.

BEL beginneth this Article as he did *Bel pag. 36.*
the two former with vntruthes, and
diſſimulatiós. His vntruths appeare in that
he chargeth S. Antonin, and Auſtin of An- Antonin.z.
cona,with teaching the Pope to haue equal part.tit.22.e.
5.paͅag. 8.
powre with God. Becauſe S. Antonin wri- vntrnth 42
teth. *That ſeeing the Pope is Chriſts vicar, none* vntrnth 43.
can lawfully withdraw him ſelf from his obedien-
ce: And that Chriſt hath giuen him moſt ful
powre, as S. Cyril (ſaith he) *teacheth lib. theſaur.*
which proofe out of S. Cyril this honeſt
challenger left out. Auſtin of Ancona affir- Auguſtin.de
Ancona in
ſumma p.
meth: that *The Pope as Chriſts vicar hath vniuer-*
ſal iuriſdiction ouer al Kingdoms and Empiers. 152.
Did euer man ſee greater impudency, what
word is here of equal powre with God?
Nay expreſſe word of inequality, if vicars
be vnequal to principals: deputies to Kings.
Did Chriſts humanity when it receaued
moſt ful powre. Math. 28. v. 18. and autho- S. Matheͷ.
rity ouer al kingdoms, and bounds of the
K 2 earth.

Dauid.

earth, pfal. 2. v. 8. receaue equal powre to
God? And if the powre of Chrift as man
(though neuer fo ful, and vniuerfal) were
create, and vnequal to Gods powre, who
can imagin the powre giuen by Chrift as
man to a pure man to be equal to Gods? I

Ioan. 12. li-
ued 956.
Auguft. de
Ancona
1305. Onuph.
in chron.

omit Bels error in affirming that Auftin of
Ancona dedicated his booke to Pope Ihon
the twelft who was dead almoft 400. years
before him. But he shold haue faid Ihon
22. and this error can not be laid vpon the
Printer feeing the number is fet downe not
in cyphers but letters.

Diffimula-
tio 4.

2. His diffimulation is euident. Firft becaufe he concealeth that the opinion (That
matrimony only contracted may be vpon
vrgent occafion diffolued) is held but of
fome Canonifts, and of very few deuines,
who commonly hold the contrary. But im-

Bel impug-
neth an opi-
nion of Ca-
nonifts and
of Prote-
ftants as a
matter of
faith.
5. Diffimula-
tion.
Surius Ann.
1540.
Vid.Lindan.
l.de concor-
dia Hæreti-
cor.p.69.

pugneth it, as if it were held of al Catholiques, and as a point of their faith. Secondly
he impofeth the faid opinion vpon Catholiques only, diffembling that Proteftants
think not only matrimony contracted, but
alfo confummated by carnal copulation
may be diffolued, & impugne Catholiques
for not admitting any caufe of diffoluing
fuch matrimony.

3. Luther the Proteftants firft Father
writ a booke 1540. where he auoucheth it to
be hard,

be hard, and vniuſt, that the innocent perſon may not marry an other after ſeparation made for adultery. Caluin calleth it a moſt vniuſt law. Likwiſe Bucer in cap. 19. Math. Melancht. de loc. tit. de coniugio: Kemnitius in 2. part. exami. And Willet in name of Engliſh Proteſtants. Al theſe affirme that adultery is a iuſt cauſe why euen conſummated marriage may be diſſolued, and a new contracted. Luther addeth other cauſes as the one perſuading the other to ſinne: much debate betwene them : and long abſence of the one party, which if it be done of malice ſeemeth iuſt cauſe to Willet, and therto he citeth Beza 1. Corinth. 7. and other Proteſtants. And this was practized in K. Edward 6. tyme, when Syr Ralf Sadler hauing maried one Mathew Baro his wife in his abſence, though Baro had begotten children of her, yet could not recouer her, but by Parlament ſhe was adiudged to Sadler. Caluin addeth want of conſent of parents, if the parties be yong, and Bucer addeth incommodious behauior, of ether party to be a ſufficient cauſe.

Caluin. 4. inſtit. c. 19. paragt. 37.

VVillet controu. 15. q. 2. p. 526. 527.
1.

Luther. in c. 7. ad Corinth. edit. 1523.
2.
3.
4.
VVillet ſup.

Caluin. Bucer. ſup.
5.
6.

4. Wherfore if the Pope by diſſoluing contracted matrimony (which he doth very ſeldom, and vpon vrgent occaſion, & weighty cauſe) challenge (as Bel ſaith) powre equal to God. Surely Proteſtants by

Bel pag. 37.

K 3   diſſol-

diffoluing confummated matrimony often,
and vpon fo many caufes wherof fome are
very fmale, and not fufficient to diffolue a
meere ciuil contract, do challenge powre
aboue God. But let vs fee how he againft
fome Catholiques, and generally al Proteftants, proueth that contracted matrimony
can not be diffolued, but by God alone for
any caufe whatfoeuer.

pag. 38.   5. His reafon is becaufe Chrift faid Math.
c. 19. v. 6. *what God hath ioyned let not man fe-
perate,* and Luc. 16. v. 18. *Euery one that putteth
away his wife, and marieth an other committeth
adultery.* And S. Paul 1. Corinth. c. 7. v. 10.
*Thofe that are ioyned in matrimony command not
I but our lord, that the wife depart not from the
husband, but if she depart, abide vnmaried, or be
reconciled to her husband.* To this the Canonifts anfwer. That Chrift and his Apoftle
fpake only of confummated matrimony:
becaufe Math. 19. Chrift forbiddeth feperation
of fuch, as immediatly before he had
faid to be made one flesh, which is by con-
fummation of matrimony. And likewife
Luc. 16. prohibiteth mariage after difmif-
fion of a wife carnally known, as is gathered out of Math. 5. v. 32. where he vfeth the
fame words, and citeth the law of diuorce
Deut. 24. v. 1. which fpeaketh of a woman
carnally known faying. *If a man haue taken a*
wife

wife and had her, and she haue not found fauor in his eyes for some filthines, he shal &c. And hereby are answered the words of S. Paul, in which he referreth him self to the precept of Christ. Besids that S. Thecla virgin was by him *soluta à nuptys* losed from mariage as writeth S. Epiph. hær. 78. which fact S. Ambros. lib. 2. de virg. commendeth, and it argueth that the Apostle tought vnconsummated mariage might be dissolued.

6. Against this answer Bel bringeth many replies in number, but none of force. 1. *That if contracted matrimony were not de iure diuino the greatest Popish Doctors wold not deny the Popes dispensation therin.* Lo here when it maketh for his purpose, he confesseth the greatest Catholique Doctors to think contracted matrimony to be indissoluble. Why then doth he impugne the contrary as an Article of our faith ? To his argument I answer, that though al Catholiques beleeue the institution of contracted matrimony to be of God, and Deuines for the most part probably thinke the continuance also therof to be *iure diuino*, and commanded by God: yet neuertheles Canonists do probably teach that the continuance of it is not absolutly, and in al cases commanded by God, but may vpon

K 4   great,

S. Epiphan.
S. Ambros.

pag. 38.

great, and vrgent caufes be diffolued by
the Church.

7. Secondly he replyeth that *Chriſt ſpea-*
keth abſolutly, and maketh no mention of copula-
tion or popiſh conſummation. Anſwer. Though
in that verſe he ſpake abſolutly, yet immediatly before he made mention of copulation. And wil Bel forbid vs to expound a
ſentence of Scripture by the antecedents,
or conſequents? But I maruel much why
he tearmed conſummation, or copulation
popiſh. Me thinketh he ſhold rather cal it
Miniſteriſh. For Papiſts can ſay with S. Auſtin lib. de bono coniug. c. 13. tom. 6. *VVe*
haue many brethren and companions of the hea-
uenly inheritance of both ſexes, vvho are continent,
ether after experience of mariage, or are free from
al ſuch copulation, ſuch are innumerable. But for
Miniſters their firſt father Luther imitating
the beaſtly Valentinians, writeth that it is
as neceſſary to haue a wife as to eat, drinke,
or ſleepe : and how wel miniſters practice
this doctrin let al England be iudge.

8. His third reply is that *Papiſts thinck matri-*
mony contracted to be a Sacrament ergo (ſaith he)
perfect before copulatiõ & indiſpenſable by man.
For *as Canus ſaith : The holy Ghoſt and grace of*
Sacrament is not giuen by copulation. Anſwer,
graunting the Antecedent I deny the conſequence. For though it haue the eſſence,
yet

S. Auſtin ſee
lib. 5. cont.
Fauſt. c. 9.

Luther. lib.
de vit. con-
iugali 1522.
See S. Iren.
lib. 1. c. 1.
Raro hære-
ticus diligit
caſtitatem.
Hieron. in
c. 7. Oſeæ.
pag. 38.

Canus lib. 8.
de locis c. 5.

yet hath it not the perfection of the Sacrament before copulation. Because before, it signifyeth only the spiritual coniunction of Christ with a soule by grace, as S. Thomas, and Innoc. 3 teach, which as it may by man be dissolued, so also may matrimony before consummation; but after, it signifieth also the coniunction of Christ to the Church by flesh, which as man can not dissolue, so nether can he dissolue matrimony after consummation. And as a seal is the parfection of a bargain making it more hard to be broken then otherwise it shold be: so copulation is as it were the seal of the couenant of wedlock made betwixt man & woman, & maketh it more indissoluble then otherwise it should be.

S. Thom. 4. d.27.q.1 art. 3.q.1.

Innocent. 3. c. deinctum de digamis.

9. As for Canus he meaneth of sinful copulation betwixt persons only affianced when *they* (saith he) *after spousals company together*. But as for coniugal copulation after matrimony is contracted, if it be done in that manner and for that end it should be, it giueth grace, and is meritorius, as appeareth by S. Austin l. de bon. coniug. c. 21. 22. tom. 6. where though he prefer the chastity of single life before the chastity of mariage, yet he compareth Abrahams merit in his holy vsage of mariage with S. Ihons merit in liuing single. Besides lawful copulation

See S. Austin l. 1. de nupt. & concup. c. 12 13. 14. 15. tom.7.

is a

Artic.5.p.61. is a good worke as I hope Bel wil not deny, but according to his owne doctrin art 5. euery good worke is meritorius or imperratorius of Gods fauor, & reward. His fourth reply vz, that matrimony should not be fully perfected in the Church, if copulation do perfect it, containeth no new difficulty.

pag. 39.

10. Fiftly he argueth it to be absurd. That *matrimony beginneth to be a Sacrament by* 44 *vntruth* *copulation, and was not by the Priests action.* But more absurd it is to vtter vntruths. For See Bellar.l. 2. de Monachis.c.;8. *The contrary is a particuler opinion of Canus l. 8. de loc. c. 5.* Conc. Trid. sess. 14. c. 1. de Reform. *Pag.* 39. Catholiques say not that it beginneth to be a Sacrament by copulatió, or by the Priests action: but that it beginneth by the mutual consent of the parties, and is perfected by their copulation, though that it be lawfully contracted, the Priests presence be required. His sixt obiection is that *Matrimony was perfect in Paradise betwixt Adam and Eue.* But this is to assume that which he was to proue. His seuenth reply is: *If contracted matrimony were not de iure diuino both parties agreeing, they might dissolue it themselues, as they can dissolue spousals, because as the law saith euery one may yeeld vp his right.* Answer. Contracted matrimony is a Sacrament instituted by God, and therfore can not be dissolued but by such as succeeding the Apostles are S. Paul. dispensers of Gods misteries 1. Corinth. 4. v. 1.

v. 1. The like reason is not of spousals, nor of any other contract instituted by man.

11. Eighthly he replyeth. That mariage betwene the B. virgin and Ioseph was perfect, where doubtles wanted copulation. That it was perfect he proueth because the angel called her Iosephs wife. And S. Ambrose saith. That *not deflowring of virginity but coniugal couenant maketh wedlock.* And S. Austin writeth· That *we rightly vnderstand Ioseph to be maries husband, by very copulation of wedlock without commixtion of flesh.* Againe. *God forbid that the bond of wedloock (rumpatur) be broken betwixt them, who are content vpon mutual consent, to abstein for euer from vse of carnal concupiscence.* For it was not falsly said of the Angel vnto Ioseph, *Fear not to take thy wife mary.* Answer: Al these proofs conuince no more, then that contracted matrimony is true mariage, as we willingly confesse was betwixt Ioseph and our B. Lady, For the Angel calleth her not Iosephs perfect, wife, but absolutly his wife. Wherupon S. Hierom l. cont. Heluid. saith s. *Ioseph was rather a keeper, then a husband,* and in c. 1. Math. *when thou hearest an husband do not suspect mariage, but remember the custome of Scripture that spouses are called husbands, and spousesses wifes.* And S. Basil hom. de human. Chrif. gener. calleth that dispousation wherwith S. Ioseph,

and

Math. 1.

S. Ambros. de institut. virg. ca .6. tom. 1.
S. August. l. 2. de consens. Euang. c.1.tom.4, Lib. 1. de nupt. & concup. c, 11.to. 7.

S. Hierom, pr. fin.

S. Basil

and our Lady were maried, *beginning of Mariage* As for S. Ambrofe he denyeth not that deflowring perfecteth mariage, but that it maketh it. And S. Auftin in the firft place affirmeth that we truly vnderftand Iofeph to be Maries hufband without copulation, but addeth not that he is fo perfectly.

12. To the fecód place I anfwer that S. Auftin fpeaketh there only of cófummated mariage, both becaufe his intention in thofe books was as he profefteth in the beginning to shew againft the Pelagians. That though childté infected with original finne do proceed from mariage, it felfe is no finne, which difficulty hath no place but in cófummated mariage. As alfo becaufe after he had proued in the forfaid 11. chapter that the bond of wedlock is not broken by purpofe of abfteining from vfe (as he fpeaketh) of concupifcence, or exercife of marigeable acts, in the next chapter he concludeth thus. *VVherfore then may not they remain man and vvife, vvho of confent leaue of companying together, if Iofeph and mary remayned man, and vvife, vvho not fo much as began to company together.* By which Conclufion of his, it is euident that before he had fpoken only of confummated mariage, and only meant to proue that it is not broken by priuate determination, or purpofe of the parties to abfteine from exercife of co-

Lib. 1. c. 1.

Cap. 11.

of copulation. Which he proued by an argument *a fortiori*, becaufe vnconfummated
matrimony of our B. Lady, and Iofeph was
not broken by their purpofe of abfteining
from al carnal knowledge. But whither vnconfummated matrimony which is not
broken by fuch priuate purpofes of the parties maried, may vpon iuft and vrgent caufe
be diffolued by the Churches authority S.
Auftin there faith no word at al.

13. Finally Bel concludeth this Article
with an egregious flaunder of the Pope,
and falfe dealing with S. Antonin. For he
auoucheth that *P. Martin 5. difpenfed with one*   Bel pag. 40.
who had contracted, and confummated matri-
mony with his owne natural, and ful fifter of the   45. *vntruth*
fame father, and mother. This he proueth out
of S. Antonin: faying: *That P. Martin difpen-*   Antonin. 3.
fed with one who had contracted, and confumma-   part. tit. 1. c.
ted matrimony cum quadam eius germana. Here   11.
Bel maketh a ful point and addeth no more.
But S. Antonin addeth *quam cognouerat For-*
nicarie, with a fifter of hers, with whom he
had committed fornication. And before the
words cited by Bel he faith that *feeing affi-*
nity is contracted by fornication, as by coniugal act,
he that hath committed fornication with any wo-
man can not mary cum filia eius, vel germana eius,
with her daughter, or her fifter. And affirmeth
that Paludan thinketh the Pope can not
dif-

diſpenſe in this matter, yet (ſaith he) *Mar-*
tin 5. diſpenſed with one who had contracted,
and conſummated cum quadam eius germana
quam cognouerat fornicarie, with a certain ſiſter
of hers with whom he had committed fornication:
What now more euident then that S. Antonin ſpeaketh not of a man marying his
owne ſiſter, but his harlots ſiſter? wherin
though the Pope (as he ſaith) made great
difficulty, yet perhaps Proteſtants wold
make ſmale, or no ſcruple at al. Behould
therfore gentle Reader not the excellency
of holy Popery (as Bel ſcornfully excla-
meth) but excellency of wholy miniſtery

Iſai. c. 28.
v. 15.

which hath as Iſay ſaid of ſome *made lying*
their hope. Is this M. Bel your promiſe, pag.
22. of auouching no vntruth vpon any
man? Is this the ſincerity you make shew
of pag. 5. and 221? Is this your proteſtation

Bel bound
to recant
the 3 tyme

made in your preface *to yeeld if any can con-*
uince you to haue alleadged any writer corruptly,
quoted any place guilfully, or charged any author
falſly. Let now the Reader be iudge by this
your dealing with S. Antonin whether you
be not bound to recant the third tyme. *Be*

Apocalip.

mindful therfore (Bel) *from whence thou art*
fallen, and do penance: Apocal. 2.

THE

THE
FOVRTH ARTICLE
OF ORIGINAL CON-
CVPISCENCE IN THE
REGENERATE.

CHAP. I.

The Catholique doctrin touching concupis-
cence explicated and proued.

 ECAVSE Bel in this Article
doth after his accustomed manner, proceed confusedly, and
deceitfully, before I answer his
obiections I wil particulerly
by Conclusions set downe the Catholique
doctrin vpon this matter, wherby the Reader may clearly see, both what Catholiques
defend, and what Bel ought to impugne.
Supposing therfore a distinction of Concupiscence, which Bel him self vseth pag. 49.
into Habitual, which is the pronesse, and
inclination in the inferior portion, or powers of our corrupt nature vnto disorderly
actions, and Actual, which is the disordinate Acts them selfs.

2. The first conclusion, is: That habi-
                                        tual

tual côcupiſcence in men not yet regenerat
is materially original ſinne. This teacheth
S. Thomas 1. 2. q. 82. ar. 3. and Bellarmin l.
5. de amiſſ. grat c. 5 (whoſe teſtimony I
the oftener, & more willingly vſe, becauſe

Bel accounteth it *moſt ſufficient in al Popiſh af-*
faires) and the Proteſtants deny it not, and
I proue it. Becauſe as original iuſtice did
formally conſiſt in the conuerſion of the
wil to God , and did materially con-
notate the due ſubiection of the inferior
powers: So original ſinne doth formally cô-
ſiſt in the auerſion of the wil from God, &
materially connotateth the rebellion of the
ſayd powers. And becauſe concupiſcence is
thus materially original ſinne S. Auſt. ſomtymes calleth it original ſinne, and ſaith it is
remitted in baptiſme, when the guilt of A-
dams ſinne annexed vnto it (which maketh

it formally ſinne) is taken from it, as herafter ſhalbe ſhewed.

3. Second concluſion: Habitual concupiſcence euen in the regenerate is euil: This

teach S. Thomas 3. p q. 15. ar. 2. and q. 27.
ar. 3. Bellarmin l. de grat. primi. hom. c. 7.
and l. 5. de amiſſ grat. c. 10. and al Catholiques. And the contrary is Pelagianiſme, as

is euident out of S. Auſtin l 6. cont. Iulian.
c. 5. l. 5. c. 3. tom. 7. and l. 1 de nupt. & concupiſ. c. 35. And the Concluſion is manifeſt,
                                         becauſe

becauſe Habitual concupiſcence includeth Habitual
not only prones to euil, but alſo difficulty Concupiſ-
to do good, and want of habitual order in cence both
the inferior powers, and therfore is both poſitiue &
poſitiue, and priuatiue euil. Hereupon S. euil.
Paul Rom. v. 7. 18. calleth concupiſcence S. Paul.
in him ſelfe *not good.* And v. 21. *euil* : and v.
16. he ſaith that he hateth it. And S. Auſtin
lib. 6. cont. Iulian c. 15. ſaid : *Who is ſo impu-*
dent, or mad, as to graunt ſinne to be euil, and
to deny concupiſcence of ſinne to be euil. And becauſe concupiſcence allureth to euil, it is
ſomtyme called of the Apoſtle *ſinne, lavv of*
ſinne. Rom. 7. of Deuines *fomes peccati* : *the*
fomet of ſinne, and tyrant, of S. Auſtin *iniquity* S. Auſtin ſe-
ſerm. 12. de verb. Apoſt. c. 5. *Vice.* l. 2. cont. him lib 2.de
Iulian. c. 3. to. 7. *Vitions,* and *culpable.* l. de cup.c.9.
perfec. iuſtit. c. 6. S. Ambroſe de apolog, S. Ambroſe
Dauid c. 13. *Root and ſeminary of ſinne.* And
becauſe it cauſeth difficulty to do good, it is
otherwhile called of S. Auſtin. l. 6. contr. S. Auſtin,
Iulian. c. 19. 1. Retract. c. 15. ſerm. 12. de tom.7.
verb. Apoſt. l. de continent. c. 4. & others
languor, ſicknes, defect : infirmity. As becauſe it
is in our inferior portion it is called of the
Apoſtle. Rom. 7. v. 23. *lavv of our members,*
and of others, *lavv of the fleſh.* And finally
becauſe it is inflicted vpon vs for Adams
ſinne : S. Auſtin. 1. Retract. c. 15. calleth it
punishment of ſinne, and alſo *ſinne* becauſe it

is the

S. Auguftin.
to. 7.

is the eff ct therof l. 1. contr. duas epist.
Pelag. c. 13. and l de spirit. & lit. c. vltimo
tom. 3.

4, Third conclusion : Actual concupiscence though inuoluntary, is euil. This
teach al Catholiques with Bellarmin loc.
cit against the Pelagians, and it is manifest
by S. Paul Rom. 7. v. 19. *The euil which I wil*

S. Auguftin.
to. 7.
Tom. 8.

not, that I do : by S. Austin lib. 1. de nupt. &
concup. c. 27. and 29. and l. 6. cont. Iulian.
c. 16. l. 5. c. 3. in psal 118. conc. 8. and otherwhere often, and by the reason which he
giueth l. 5. cont. Iulian c. 3. because it is a
disordinate act contrary to the rule of reason: Hereupon men are ashamed of it, and
S. Austin lib. 2. cont. Iulian. c. 5. and lib. 6.
c. 15. calleth it *iniquity*: and lib. 1. de nupt.
& concupisc. cap. 27 *filthy and vnlawful.*

More requi-
red to for-
mal sinne
then to euil.

Hence Bel pag. 53. inferreth inuoluntary
concupiscence to be formal , and proper
sinne, but he is far deceaued . For formal
sinne beside euil, and vnlawfulnes requireth voluntarines, as I shal hereafter proue,
and is euident in fooles, and beasts , who
though they haue these inuoluntary acts
are no formal sinners.

5. Fourth Conclusion : whensoeuer it
is any way voluntary eiher in it self, or in
any needles cause therof , it is formally
sinne. This is euident: because then it hath
the

the whole essence or definition of sinne: for it is a voluntary act against Gods law, or right reason. I say needles cause, because if the cause be necessary, or honest, it excuseth the actual concupiscence following therof from fault.

6. Fift Conclusion: Habitual, and actual Concupiscence whatsoeuer, euen in the regenerate may be called sinne. This is manifest out of that which hath bene said in the 2 and 4. conclusion. For ether it is voluntary, and then it is formal sinne, & properly so called: or though it be vnvoluntary, it is the cause, effect, punishment, or material part of sinne: and any of these reasons suffice to make it figuratiuely be called sinne. And they al are taken out of S. Austin. For 1. de nupt. & concup. c. 23 he saith Concupiscence may be called sinne, because it is the effect of sinne, as writing is called a hand. And in the same place because it is the cause of sinne: as coldnes is called sluggish because it maketh sluggish. Likwise 1. Retract. c. 15. he calleth it sinne, because it is the punishment therof. So Zachar. vlt. v. 19. punishment of sinne is called sinne. And finally lib. 5. cont. Iulian. c. 3. he calleth actual concupiscence sinne, because it is a disorderly act; and it wanteth nothing of sinne, but voluntarines, and

Al Concupiscence may be called sinne & vvhy.

1.

2.

3.

4.

L 2 therfore

therfore may as wel be called finne as a
dead body is called a man. And who wel
remembreth what is faid in thefe fiue Conclufions, need no more to anfwer al Bels
arguments. For, as we fhal fee, he proueth
no more then they containe.

*Actual Con-
cupifcence
if inuolun-
tary is no
formal
finne.*

7. Sixt Conclufion : Actual concupifcence whenfoeuer it is inuoluntary is no
formal or proper finne, or offence to God.
This is againft Bel in this whole Article.
But I proue it. Firft becaufe fome acts of
Concupifcence be but temptatiõs to finne,
and are before finne be brought forth. Ergo
fuch are no formal finne. The confequence
is euident. For what is but tentation to
finne, and goeth before finne be, is no proper finne. The Antecedent I proue out of

*S. Iames c.
1.v.14.15.*
See S. Auftin
lib. 6. cont.
Iul. cap. 15.
to. 7.

S. Iames faying *Euery one is tempted by his Concupifcence,* behold an act, but a tempting of
vs to finne: *aftervvard vvhen concupifcence hath
conceaued it bringeth forth finne,* behold alfo
an act of Concupifcence going before finne

vvillet con-
trouerf. 17.
q.1.p.558.

be brought forth. Willet faith nothing to
the firft part of tentation, but to the fecond
of bringing forth he anfwereth. *That it fol-
lovveth not Concupifcence to be no finne, becaufe it
bringeeh forth finne, becaufe one viper may bring
forth an other.* But we infer not Concupifcence to be no finne, becaufe it bringeth
forth finne : for we wel know that one
finne

ſinne may bring forth an other: but we gather that that act of Cõcupiſcence, which S. Iames tearmeth *conceauing of ſinne*, is no ſinne, becauſe he affirmeth it to go before the bringing forth of ſinne, in ſaying *Aftervvard vvhen Concupiſcence hath conceaued it bringeth forth ſinne*, and this could not be, if it were ſinne, it ſelf. Caluin anſwereth this argument otherwaies, whom Bellarmin confuteth.

Caluin.lib.3, inſtit.c.3.paragr.13.
Bellarm.l.5. de amiſſ. grat. & ſtat. peccat.c.7.

8. Secondly becauſe whiles a man with the minde ſerueth the law of God he can not by ſinne ſerue the dyuel. But S. Paul euen when he had inuoluntary motions of concupiſcence, ſerued with the minde the law of God. Therfore then he ſinned not. The Propoſition is euident by the ſaying of Chriſt. *None can* (at once) *ſerue tvvo maiſters.* The aſſumption S. Paul teſtifieth Roman. 7. v. 25. ſaying, *I my ſelf vvith the minde ſerue the lavv of God, but vvith the fleſh the lavv of ſinne.*

S. Math. 6. v. 24.
S. Paul.

9. Thirdly nothing inuoluntary, or done againſt our wil is ſinne, diuers acts of Concupiſcence be ſuch. Ergo no ſinne. Bel wold gladly (as ſome of his fellowes do) deny the propoſition, and therfore ſtreight after he had propounded the argument, telleth vs (though falſly) that S. Auſtin proueth inuoluntary motions to be ſinne indeed,

Bel pag.50.
Perkins refor.Cath.tit. Of original ſinne.

L 3   deed,

deed, and towards the end of this **Article**
auoucheth *a man to be guilty of sinne in that*
vvhich he doth against his vvil, and can not auoid,
yet at last resolueth rather to deny the Af-
sumption: wherfore I proue them both:
The proposition I proue out of that very
place of S. Austin, which Bel citeth to the
contrary. *Sin* (saith he 1. Retract. c. 13.) *is so*
far forth voluntary euil, as it is no vvay sinne, if
it be not voluntary. And this (saith he lib. de
vera relig. c. 14.) *is so manifest, as nether the*
fevvnes, of learned, nor the multitude of vnlearned
doth deny it. And wil Bel now deny that
which in S. Austins tyme nether learned,
nor vnlearned would deny? Now let the
Reader iudge, with what face Bel affirmed
that S. Austin in the foresaid place 1. Retract. proueth inuoluntary Concupiscence
to be sinne, where he most manifestly affirmeth nothing to be any way sinne if it be
not voluntary, and therupon laboreth to
shew original sinne in infants to be some
way voluntary. And in an other place he
auoucheth it *to be high iniustice, and madnes,*
that a man shold be guilty of sinne, because he did
not that which he could not do And S Hierom.
epist. ad Damas. de exposit. fid. Accurseth
their blasphemy vvho say that God hath comman-
ded any impossible thing, as no doubt he hath,
if we sinne in that which we cannot auoid:

See

pag. 57.

pag. 58.

S. Augustin. *10. 1.*

46. vntruth

S. Augustin. lib. de duab. animab. c, *11.*tom. 6. & 1. Retract. c. 15.*to.*1.

6. Hierom.

See him dialog. cont. Pelag. S. Chrisostom
hom. 13 ad Rom. Prosper de vita contempl.
c. 4. S. Austin serm. 61. de temp. de nat. &
grat. c. 69. in psal 56. and others. By reason
also it is manifest. For if inuoluntary acts
done against our wil be true sins, much
more the acts of fooles, and mad men, yea
of beasts, which are not done against wil,
but only without wil, and they true malefactors, and sinners before God and men,
which I think none, but a madde man, wil
graunt. And I doubt not but Bel would
think him self vniustly executed, i. he were
put to death for a thing done against his
wil, and which he labored al he could to
hinder.

10. The Assumption I proue, because if
that be not inuoluntary, wherof we giue
no occasion, nor consent vnto, yea detest
and hinder al we can, (as it hapneth oftentymes in the motions of Concupiscence,)
I can not see what can be inuoluntary vnto
vs. And if they be Papists, (as Bel tearmeth
them pag. 51.) who cal such acts of Concupiscence inuoluntary. A Papist is S. Paul
saying, Rom. 7. v. 19. *I do the euil which I
wil not.* And S. Austin when he saith. *I wil
not that Cocupiscence couet. we wold ther were no
Cocupiscences, but wil we, nil we, we haue them.*
Yea Bel him self no les then they, thrice in

L 4   this

S. Chrysost.
tom. 4.
S. Prosper.
S. Augustin.
tom.10.
Tom. 7.

*If Concu-
piscence be
not some
tymes inuo-
luntary no-
thing is in-
uoluntary.*

S. Paul.
S. Augustin.
serm. 43. de
verb. Dom.
See serm 3.5.
and 12 de
verb. Apost.
*Bel a Papist
by his owne
iudgment.*

this Article pag. 50. 51. and 57. in plaine termes calleth these motions inuoluntary.

Bel pag. 51.

11. But to this argument he answereth,
That they be voluntary in their origin, and therto

S. Austin 1.
retract. c. 13.
tom. 1.

citeth S. Austin affirming original sinne of
infants to be voluntary in their origin, and
calleth this the Gordion knot which Papists can neuer vntie, and so clear and euident a solution of the argument, as euery
child may behold the weaknes, falshood,

VVhat is to
be volun-
tary in the
origen.

and absurditie therof. But Bel is ignorant
what it is to be voluntary in the origen.
For this is nothing els but to be willed of
him, from whom we took our origin, and
whose wil is accounted ours. As original
sinne is voluntary to infants in their origin,
because it was willed of Adam in the eating
of the forbidden Aple, and his wil was in
that fact accounted theirs. And this ment

1. Retract. c.
13.19.1.

S. Austin loc. cit. But as for actual motions
of concupiscence, he neuer said they were
voluntary to vs in their origin; nether can

VVhy in-
uoluntary
motions are
not volun-
tary in
their ori-
gen.
S. Gregory.

they both because Adam had no wil of có-
mitting these acts, as he had of leesing original iustice in eating the Aple; as also because his wil was not accounted ours in any
other act, then in his keeping, or first leesing
of original iustice. Besides as S. Gregory
writeth l. 15. moral. c. 22. *Original sinne being*
blotted out, children are not held by the iniquity of
parents,

parents, and therfore Adams wil, can not make thoſe acts in the regenerate to be ſinne, which of their nature are none.

11. And though the forſaid motiós were voluntary in their origen, yet could they be nether, original, nor actual ſinne. Not original, becauſe they are acts, and not common alike to al : Nor actual, becauſe they haue no actual wil of the doer, and as voluntary in general is eſſential to ſinne in general, ſo is actual voluntary, to actual ſinne. Yea for an act now done to be formal ſinne when it is done, ſufficeth not, that it was actually voluntary in the cauſe done long ago, if now it be againſt wil. For albeit when I gaue cauſe of an vnlawful effect, which I did ſee wold after enſue, I was guilty of the effect, when I did the cauſe : yet if after the cauſe done I repent & be ſory before the effect follow, I do not ſinne a new in the effect. As if by ſome thing yeſterday done, I gaue occaſió that diſordinate motiós riſe to day, though I was then guilty of theſe motions riſing, yet if I ſince repented I do not ſinne a new when they riſe now againſt my wil. Els I ſhould againſt my wil leeſe that grace which I got by repentance. Wherfore wel wrote S. Gregory to S. Auſtin our Apoſtle. *Oftentymes it is done without fault which cómeth of fault.* And much les ſhould inuoluntary

Inuoluntary motions though they were voluntary in their origen could be no ſinne.

S. Gregory epiſt. ad Auguſtin. Cant. c. 10.

luntary motions be sinnes in vs, though
they were originally voluntary vnto vs only
by the wil of an other. Thus is this Gordion
knot two waies vnryed. But him selfe hath

Bel dispro-
ueth him
selfe.

with his tong tyed so fast a knot for proofe
of my conclusion, as with his teeth he wil
not be able to loose. For pag. 48. he affir-

12. Contra-
dict.

meth S. *Paul to haue bene most free, and innocent*
touching actual sinne, and he proueth it, *be-*
cause he fought mightily against his raging concupis-
cence, and did in no wise yeeld therunto: which
is both to confesse that S. Paul had inuoluntary motions of the flesh, which him
selfe acknowledgeth Rom. 7. v. 15 17. 19. 23.
& yet to proue them to be no sinne in him,
because they were inuoluntary, which is
both my conclusion, and reason.

S. Augustin.
to. 2.
See S. Austin
lib. 2 cont.
Iul. c. 3. & 10.
l. 5. c. 3. 15.

13. As for S. Austin he is so far from
thinking that we sinne by inuoluntary motions of the flesh, as he saith epist: 200. ad
Asellicum: *That if we consent not to them we*
need not say: Forgiue vs our trespasses: which he

Tom. 3.

repeateth againe l. de spir. & lit. c. vlt. adding *that if we consented not to these acts we should*
disproue that saying of S. Ihon: If vve say vve haue
no sinne vve deceaue our selfs, and proueth it l.

Tom. 5.

1. de ciuit. c. 15. thus. *If concupiscential disobe-*
dience be vvithout fault in the body of one sleeping,
hovv much more in the body of one not consenting.
And l. 1. de nupt. & concupis. c. 23. explicateth

teth how it is called sinne vz: *as vvriting is called a hand , or cold sluggish vvhich is figuratiuely , & improperly.* Nay he not only excuseth vs from sinne, when we consent not vnto inuoluntary motions of the flesh, but auoucheth that then we do much good, *a great matter, for vvhich vve shal be crovvned:* lib. 1. de nupt. & concupisc. c. 29 *He doth much good vvho doth that vvhich is vvritten. Follovv not thy lusts.* And serm. 5. de verb. Apost. c. 6. *It is a great matter for me not to be ouercome* of concupiscence, and cap. 9. *who consenteth not doth much, it is a great matter he doth.* And lib. 2. de Gen. cont. Manich. c. 14. *Somtyme reason doth manfully refraine and bridle Concupiscence euen stirred vp vvhich vvhen it is done vve fal not into sinne* (mark Bel) *but vvith some striuing are crovvned.* Wherfore if they be Papists (as Bel saith pag. 46. and 49.) who say we merit when we resist Concupiscence , surely S. Austin is one. Yea Bel himselt if he account it a good deed (as I hope he wil) to resist lust: for art. 5. pag. 61. he graunteth *al good deeds to be meritorious* S. Gregory also epist. ad Augustt. c. 11. teacheth, *That pollution in sleep is not at al to be feared vvhen it proceedeth of superfluity, or vveaknes of nature,* And lib. 21. moral. c. 3. *Vnclean cogitation defy'eth not the mynde vvhen it beateth, but vvhen it subdueth the mind vnto it by delight.* More Fathers I might adde

but

Merit in resisting Concupiscence according to S Austin.
Tom. 7.
Tom. 10.

Tom. 1.

Contradict. 13.

S. Gregory.

Caluin. but it were needles, becaufe Caluin lib. 3.
inftit. c. 3. paragr. 10. confeffeth that *al the*
Fathers before S. Auftin are of the fame opinion
Vvith S. Auftin.

14. Seauenth Conclufion: habitual Concupifcéce in the regenerate is no proper, or
formal finne. This euidently followeth out
of the former. For if the acts be not formal
finne, but by confent of wil, much les the
proanes vnto them: but it may be proued
alfo otherwaies. Firft becaufe if it be any
finne, it is original (for actúal it can not be,
being no act) but original it is not, becaufe
by regeneration, *vve put of the old man.* Coloff. 3. v. 9. or lay away the old man Ephef.
4. verfic. 22. and *put on the nevv*: Coloff. 3.
v. 9. and Ephef. 4. v. 24. And by keeping
original finne we keep on the old man as
by firft contracting it we put him on. But it
is contradiction at the fame tyme to keep
on, and put of or lay away the old man.
Ergo in our regeneration we keep not original finne. And this is confirmed: becaufe
by finne we bear the image of the earthly
man, by regeneration the image of the heauenly according to that 1. Corinth. 15. v.
49. *As vve haue borne the image of the earthly*
(man) *let vs bear alfo the image of the heauely.* But
2. Cor.6.v. thefe two images be oppofit. For *vvhat*
15. *agreement Vvith Chrift and Belial,* Therfore we
 can

can not haue damnable sinne, as original sinne is, and be regenerate.

15. Secondly in regeneration either we remaine guilty of damnable sinne, or become guiltles of al such sinne. If we remaine guilty, then is not our sinne forgiuen: contrary to that article of our Creed. *Forgiuenes of sinnes.* For it is impossible to be guilty of sinne, and to haue sinne forgiuen. Then remaine we also guilty of damnation *the stypend of sinne,* Rom. 6. v. 23. For the guilt of punishment riseth of the guilt of sinne, as necessarily as fatherhood riseth of begetting a child. Wel may God chuse whether he wil punish a malefactor, or no, yet he can not make, that a malefactor remaining a malefactor, and guilty of sinne, shal not be guilty also of punishment. But a iustified or regenerate man can not be guilty of damnation; becaue *There is no damnation to them who are in Christ Iesus:* Rom. 8. v. 1. And Bel pag. 45. confesseth *That a man can not be iustly condemned for sinne remitted.* If in regeneration we become guiltles of al damnable sinne, then haue we no such sinne in vs. For as S. Austin saith, *To be not guilty of sinne is to haue no sinne:* And again: *Sinnes remaine but by their guilt.* As adultery once committed remaineth in the Committer, only becaue he is stil guilty of the adultery he did, vntil

it be

Symbol. Apost.

Vbicunque peccatum est illic se profert ira & vltio Dei. Caluin.3. instit.c. 11. parag.2.

S. Paul.

Bel.

S. Augustin. l. 1. de nupt. & concup. c. 16.to.7.

it be remitted.

Perkins re-
tor. C.tnol.
pag. 36.
See S. Austin
lib. 6. cont.
Julian. c. 6.

16. Protestants answer. *That by regenera-*
tion guilt is taken from vs, but not from the sinne
which is in vs. But this is contradiction : for
if the guilt be in the sinne, & the sinne stil in
vs the guilt is also stil in vs. Beside the guilt
of sinne (wherof we speak, and not of the
guilt of punishmēt) can not be in our sinne,
which can not be guilty of it selfe, but in vs
only, who are guilty of sinne, which we haue
cōmitted. And the remaining of sinne in vs
consisteth only in the remaining of this guilt

S. Augustin.
1. de nupt.

(as saith S. Austin) as the remaining of adultery cōsisteth only in this that a man is stil

VVhat it is
for sinne to
remayne.

guilty of the adulterous fact he did. And
therfore if this guilt of the fact be taken frō
him, it is impossible for adultery to remaine
in him. Beside it is manifest contradiction
to say one hath sinne in him, and yet is not
guilty of sinne, or a sinner, as it is to say
the ayer hath darknes in it, and yet is not
darke.

S. Ihon.
Micheas v.
19.
Psalm. v.
11.

17. Thirdly God in regeneration *taketh*
away sinnes : Ioan. 1. v. 29. Miche. 7. *casteth*
them into the depth of the sea : Seperateth *from*
vs as far as the East is from the vvest : psal. 101.
But concupiscence is not taken away, it is
not cast into the depth of the sea, nor separated from vs as far, as the East from the
west. Ergo it is no sinne. Againe : By iusti-
fica-

fication he maketh vs *more White then snoW:*
psal. 50. v. 9. but how can we be whiter
then snow, if the blacknes of sinne stil remaine in vs? Fourthly Adam by his sinne depriued of grace, and transfused sinne into al
them that are generate of him. Ergo: Christ
by his merit expelled sinne, and transfused
grace into al them that are regenerat of him.
The Antecedēt is euident. The consequéce
I proue. For els Christs merits had not bene
so potent and effectual to do good, as A-
dams sinne was to do euil, seeing Christs
merit can not as really, and truly take sinne
from vs, as Adams sinne transfused it into
vs. Which is both contrary to Christs honor, and to the Apostles doctrin Rom. 5. v.

S. Paul.
Bel dispro-
ued by him
self.

17. 18. 19. Fiftly *how shal one be iustly condem-*
ned for that Which is remitted in baptisme? it can
not be. Ergo after baptisme there remayneth
no damnable sinne. The Antecedent is the
very words of Bel pag. 44. and 45. and agreable to S Paul Rom. 8. v. 1. *There is no damna-*
tion to them, that are in Christ Iesus. The consequence is euident for one that hath damnable sinne may be iustly condemned.

18. I need not cite Fathers for proofe of
this Conclusion because as I said before
Caluin confesseth that *s. Austin had faith-*
fully, and very diligently gathered the sentences of
al holy Fathers, and yet disagreeth from him.

Caluin.lib.3.
instit.c.3. pa-
rag.10.

For

For S. Auſtin (ſaith he) *dare not cal concupiſcence ſinne, but is content to tearme it infirmity.*
Let now any indifferent Reader iudge whither we haue not reaſon to boaſt (to vſe
Bels tearms) that S. Auſtin is on our ſide.
And no maruel. For 1. de nupt. & concupiſ.
c. 23. he writeth thus : *Truly this ſame Concupiſcence is now no ſinne* (mark Bel) *in the regenerat when conſent is not giuen vnto it to vnlawful acts.* And ſoone after. *But in a certain
kind of ſpeech it is called ſinne : and* he giueth
there two reaſons of this figuratiue ſpeech,
becauſe (ſaith he) *it was made of ſinne, and
maketh ſinne if it ouercome.* Again : *So is* (Concupiſcence) *called ſinne, becauſe it was made by
ſinne, vvheras novv in the regenerate it ſelfe is no
ſinne* (mark again) *as ſpeech which the tong
maketh is called a tong, & writing a hand vvhich
a hand maketh. So alſo it is called a ſinne, becauſe
it maketh ſinne if it ouercome as cold is called
ſluggish, becauſe it maketh ſluggards.* Can any
Catholique now ſpeak more plainly. In
theſe few words al in one chapter, he twiſe
denyeth concupiſcence in the regenerate to
be ſinne, once affirmeth it to be improperly
ſo called, and giueth two reaſons, and two
examples of ſuch figuratiue ſpeech : The
ſame doctrin he teacheth l. 1. contr. duas
epiſt. Pelag. c. 13. and l. 2. cont. Iulian. & in
al his tomes as Bellarmin sheweth. So that
what-

S. Auguſtin.
to. 7.

S. Auguſtin.
to. 7.
Bellarm. l. 5.
de amiſſ.
Grat. & ſtat.
peccati c. 8.

whatfoeuer Bel hereafter shal obie&t out of
S. Paul: S. Auftin, or others calling concupifcence finne, I need not anfwer my felfe,
but referre the Reader to thefe words of S.
Auftin, wherin he explicateth both why,
and how, S. Paul, him felfe, and others
meane not properly, but improperly and figuratiuely, when they cal concupifcence
finne. Yet becaufe Bels arguments containe
diuers vntruths requifite to be taxed, I wil
anfwer them al in fuch order as he propofeth them.

s. Anftin hath pre-uented al Bels obie-ctions.

CHAP. II.

Diuers vntruthes of Bel difproued, his ar-
guments out of S. Paul againft the
doctrin in the former chapter
anfwered.

BEL beginneth this Article as he did
the reft with vntruths 1. *That S. Paul in*
the whole 7. chapter to the Romans proueth ori-
ginal concupifcence in the regenerate to be finne.
This is not fo: for he doth not proue it to
be any finne at al, but fuppofing it to prouoke to finne, calleth it finne. 2. *That Papifts*
can not abide the Apoftles doctrin. Forfooth
becaufe we can not abide Bels expofition.
3. *That the caufe of our denying Concupifcence to*
be finne is becaufe it ouerthroweth our holy fo fup-

Bel pag. 41.
vntruth 47

vntruth 48

vntruth 49

M   *pofed*

Bel blaspbe-
meth iuſti-
fication.

Bel art. 6. p.
81.

pag. 50.

vntruth 50
3. ſent. d.
19.

Bel pag. 42.

Ibid.

31. vntruth

poſed iuſtification (thus blaſphemouſly he denyeth iuſtification to be holy)*our inherent pu-*
rities, condigne merits, & works of ſupererogation.
This is vntrue: for it might be ſuch ſinne,
as Bel wold haue it (to wit venial) and deſtroy none of al theſe. But the true cauſes
are Scriptures, Fathers, & reaſon before alleadged, and Bel confeſſeth that the reaſon
which we euer haue in our mouth is the in-
uoluntarines of concupiſcence 4. *That the*
Maiſter of Sentences vtterly condemneth vs in cal-
ling concupiſcence culpam. But he meaneth improperly as is euident by his owne words
2. diſt. 31. *Concupiſcence after baptiſme* (ſaith he)
is only (mark Bel) *puniſhment of ſinne, but be-*
fore baptiſme both punishment, and fault.

2. Thus hauing made his way with vntruths, he proueth cōcupiſcence to be ſinne
out of S. Paul. Rom. 7. v. 25. ſaying. *I my ſelfe*
with the mynd ſerue the law of God, but with the
fleſh the law of ſinne. And hence noteth *that*
the regenerate do ſerue the law of ſinne. But he
forgot to note that it is but with the fleſh,
and that *with the mynd* (without which
there is no formal ſinne) *they ſerue the law of*
God. He alſo noteth. *That the beſt liuers can*
not merit grace, and glory ex condigno : becauſe by
ſinne they deſerue death. VVhich becauſe S. Auſtin
(ſaith he) *at the firſt could not diſgeſt, he vnder-*
ſtood S. Paul in the 7. chapter to the Romans, only
of the

of the wicked, not of the godly. But remitting *Bel forget-teth his matter.* the matter of merit, and defert of finne to their proper places art. 5. and 6. falfe it is that S. Auftin changed his opinion about the vnderftanding of thofe words of S. Paul Rom. 7. *I am a carnal man folde vnder finne:* and the like, becaufe he faw that iuft men finned. For as him felfe teftifyeth 1. Retract. *S. Auftin.* c. 23. (and Bel wrongly cited 22.) he reading other expofitors, found that the forefaid words might be vnderftood of the Apoftle him felfe, as the word *carnal* may be verifyed of him in refpect of his body, not yet fpiritual, and the word *finne* in refpect of concupifcence, which is finne vz: improperly, as the fame S. Auftin explicateth *Lib.1. de nupt. & concupif.c. 23. & l. 1. cont. duas epift. Pelag. c. 13.* in the books to which he referreth vs, and we cited them before. Wherby we fee, that S. Auftins error was in vnderftanding the forefaid words of formal, and proper finne (as Bel doth) and corrected it by vnderftanding them of improper finne. And yet euen when he was in that error, he was fo far from thinking (as Bel doth) that the beft liuers in rigor deferue eternel death, that then he wold in no wife thinke the Apoftle to fpeak of a mã in grace, affuring him felfe, that no fuch man is folde vnder finne that deferueth eternal death.

3. His fecond proofe is out of the 23. *Bel pag.42.* verfe

verſe of the ſame chapter where S. **Paul**
writeth *I ſee a lavv in my members ſubduing me*
to the lavv of ſinne. VVhat (ſaith Bel) *can he*
merit who is priſoner to the law of ſinne. But beſide that, Bel forgot what he was to proue :
vz. Concupiſcence in the iuſt to be ſinne,
not their merit to be none : S. Paul by the
word (*me*) vnderſtandeth only his fleſh, as
he had expounded him ſelfe before v. 18.
when he ſaid. *There dvvelleth not in me that is*
in my fleſh good. And S. Auſtin interpreteth
1. de nupt & concupiſ. c. 30. and 31. And v.
23. ſaith that *he Vvas priſoner to the lavv of ſinne*
in his fleſh, and in his mynd ſerued the lavv of God:
what maruel then , that one priſoner in
fleſh, but free in mynd (from which al our
merit, or ſinne proceedeth) may by ſeruing
Gods law, merit.

Bel pag. 43.　　4. His third proofe is out of the 19. verſe
where (as he citeth) S. Paul ſaith. *The euil*
vvhich I vvold not that I do. Omitting the falſe
tranſlating of *ou thelo* and *Nolo : I vvold not :*
as though S.Paul had not had a preſent, and
abſolute wil not to luſt, but an imperfect
velleity which euen the wicked haue, and
in engliſh we ſignify by *vvold, and Vvold not.*
I anſwer that S. Paul improperly ſaith ; He
doth that which he wil not, and therfore
in the very next verſe, as it were correcting
that ſpeech ſaith. *If I do that I vvil not, I vvorke*
it not

Bel forget-
teth vvhat
he is to
proue.

Falſe tranſ-
flat. 3.

v 20.

it not, wherin he both affirmeth & ptoueth that we do not what we wil not. And the reaſon is euident. For as the commonwelth is principally the Prince, Pieres, and Magiſtrats, which gouerne the reſt: ſo a man is principally his wil, which commandeth the reſt. And therfore as the cōmonwealth doth not that, which they do not, though ſome of the commonalty do it: ſo a man doth not, what his wil doth not, though ſome of his inferior powres do it. If therfore S. Paul did but improperly ſay, he doth what he wil not, Bel can therof inferre but improper ſinne. Beſides though it were a proper ſpeech, therof can be inferred no proper ſinne, for want of voluntarines. And here by the way Bel ſtraweth his flowers of leaſing, ſaying. *That the cauſe why* S. *Auſtin epiſt*: 105. *vvrote that God crovvned nothing but his ovvne gifts, vvhen he crovvneth our merits, is, becauſe the regenerate by inuoluntary aſts of Concupiſcence ſinne, and become guilty of damnation.* For nether doth S. Auſtin ſpeake there of inuoluntary acts, nether any where doth he ſay they exclude merit, or deſerue damnation, yea plainly auoucheth *that vve are crovvned vvhen vve haue them againſt our vvil.* And the true cauſe of his ſpeech ſhal be giuen in the next Article of merit, and his very words conuince that our merits

A man rather doth not then doth vvhat his vvil doth not. See S. Thomas 1. 2. q. 74. art. 3. ad 3.

Bel pag. 43.

52. *vntruth*

S. Auguſt. 2. de Geneſ. contr. Manich. c. 14. tom. 1,

M 3   are no

VVhy me-
rits are no
sinne, out of
S. Austin.

are no sinnes, and much les deserue damnation: for he calleth them Gods owne gifts
and saith he crowneth them: but God nether giueth nor crowneth sinne.

pag. 43.
Cap.1.parag.
3.4.6.13.18.

5. Fourthly Bel alleadged the Apostle
calling Concupiscence sinne: Rom. 7. v.14.
and 20. But this we answered before. Bel

53. *vntruth*

replyeth that *it wil not suffice to say with Bellar-*
min that it is called sinne only because it prouoketh

54. *vntruth*

to sinne, as a mans vvriting is called his hand, be-
cause it is vvritten vvith his hand. Here be two
vntruths fathered vpon Bellarmin. For nether doth he say Concupiscence is called
sinne only because it prouoketh to sinne:

Bellarm.

yea lib. 5. de amiss. grat. & stat. pec. c.8. he
giueth an other reason out of S. Austin, because it is the effect of sinne. Nether doth
he say that it may be called sinne, because it
prouoketh to sinne, as writing is called a
hand, because it is made by a hand; for so it
is a cause, and writing an effect; but as cold
is called sluggish, because it maketh slug-
gards. But let vs hear why S. Paul may not

Bel pag. 43.

be vnderstood of improper sinne. First *be-*
cause the Maister of Sentences graunted Concupis-
cence to be sinne. This is twise sod colworts
set again before his reader for want of other
meat, but reiected before. Secondly because

Sup.parag.1.

it maketh a man to serue the lavv of sinne, vvhich
seruice can neuer be but sinne. Here the question
it self

it selfis begged. For the question it self is, whither the seruice to the law of sinne done by the flesh not by the mynd (as S Paul speaketh Rom. 7. vers. 23.) be proper sinne, or no, and that Bel beggeth of vs to graunt But he must win it, ere he get it And though we did graūt it to him, yet could he no more infer therof that habitual Concupiscence, which causeth it, is sinne, then he can infer the powre of our wil, which is a gift of God, to be sinne, when it causeth sinne. Thirdly (saith Bel) *because the euil whereof S. Paul speaketh he hateth and wil not* (Bel hath wold not) *do it,* which must needs be meant of sinne. True, but of material, and improper sinne. For such also is to be hated, and not to be willed.

Bel assumeth what he vvas to proue, and yet concludeth nothing.

6. Bel hauing thus sillily proued his heresy out of S. Paul, endeuoreth to proue it out of our doctrin thus. *Al reprobates are reprobated both negatiuely, and positiuely for original sinne.* Ergo: *Concupiscence is sinne euen after baptisme.* The *Antecedent* (saith he) *is a maine point, and settled ground of Papists religion,* and *he vvillingly graunteth it.* The consequence he proueth because *some reprobates are baptized.* Answer. First I deny the Antecedent. For nether doth any Catholique affirme it to be any point at al of Popish faith, & much lesse a maine point, or ground therof : nether

Bel pag. 43. 44.

vntruth 55.

1. *Answer*

M 4　　(though

(though fome beleeue it as a fchool opinion)is it true,becaufe original finne being as
truly forgiuen in baptifme to many reprobates, as it is to predeftinates, they can be
no more pofitiuely fent to hel for it, then

S. Paul. predeftinates. For as S. Paul faith Rom. 11.
v. 29. *Gods gifts are without repentance*, fo that
what finne he truly forgiueth he neuer af-

S.Prosper in terward punifheth in hel. wherfore S. Pro-
reip. ad ob- fper writeth that *who goeth from Chrift , and*
iect. 2. Gal-
lor. *endeth this life out of grace , what goeth he but*
into perdition? yet he falleth not againe into that
which is forgiuen, nor fhalbe damned in original

How repro *finne.* Only as al finns are fayd to returne by
bats may be
fayd to be ingratitude, according to the parable of the
reprobated vngrateful feruant Math.18.becaufe a finne,
for original after others haue bene pardoned,becometh
finne.
greater by the ingratitude , then otherwife
it were: fo original finne pardoned to fome
reprobats in baptifme , may be faid to returne to them through their ingratitude in
finning after the faid pardon , and they
being pofitiuely damned for fuch finne ,
may in fome fort be faid to be pofitiuely

2. Anfwer damned for original finne. Secodly though
the Antecedent were true, it could not follow therof, that Concupifcence in reprobates is formal finne, but only that original
finne is not truly forgiuen in baptifme to
any reprobat,which though it be falfe, per •
teineth

teineth not to this queſtion. For as for habitual Concupiſcence, it nether before ba- Cap.1.parag. 2.&3.
ptiſme, nor after is formal ſinne, but be-
fore only materially ſinne, and after only
languor, and weaknes as is before explicated. But how Bel admitting al reprobates to
be reprobated poſitiuely for ſinne, agreeth
with his Maiſters Caluin, Beza, and others Caluin, Beza Rom. 9.
teaching that they are reprobated for Gods
pleaſure, and that he made them to damne,
and reprobate them, let his breethren in Bel contra-dicteth his fellovv Mi-niſters.
the lord enquire. Now to his places taken
out of S. Auſtin, whom he promiſeth to
ſhew to be ſo plaine for his doctrin, as none Bel pag. 45.
can ſtand in doubt therof. But who wel re-
membreth S. Auſtins words, and Caluins Chap. 1. pa-rag.13.&18.
confeſſion before cited, can neuer ſtand in
doubt but that Bel moſt braggeth wher he
hath leſt cauſe, and like a prating petty-
fogger cryeth lowdeſt, when he hath leſt
proofs.

CHAP. III.

Bels arguments out of S. Auſtin touching
Concupiſcence anſvvered.

THE firſt place he alleadgeth out of S. Bel pag. 45.
Auſtin is tom. 7. l. 6. contr. Iulian. c.
3. where he writeth. As blindnes of hart is
ſinne, puniſhment of ſinne, and cauſe of
ſinne. So cócupiſcence of the fleſh is ſinne,
puniſh-

punishment, and cause of sinne. Answer.
S. Austin compareth concupiscence with
blindnes of harr, in the material disorder of
sinne. For as sinne is against the rule of
reason, so disordinate lust, not in formality
of sinne. Nether say I this only, but can
proue it. And omitting that other where he
plainly auoucheth it to be no formal sinne,
as is before shewed, I proue it, first by his
reason, where with he proueth it to be
sinne: vz because *it is disobedient to the rule of*
reason, which conuinceth it to be material
sinne, and a disorderly and euil thing, but
not to be formally sinne, for want of voluntarines, which him selfe necessarily requireth to formal sinne as is before shewed.
Secondly because it sufficed to S. Austin to
proue concupiscence to be material sinne,
for to disproue Iulian the Pelagian against
whom he there disputed, who taught, as S.
Austin there and other where testifyeth,
that it was laudable & good, against whom
he there proueth by the example of blindnes of hart, that it was not only punishment and cause of sinne, but also sinne; that
is, naught, euil, and disorderly ; because it is
against the rule of reason, which is to be
sinne materially, though it want the forme
of sinne which is voluntarines.

2. Next he bringeth these words. *Some*
iniquity

Lib. de Spir.
& lit. c. vlt. l.
1. de nupt. &
concup. c. 23.
l. 1. con. duas
epist. Pelag.
c. 13.

Cap. 1. parag.
9.

Lib. de nupt.
& concup. c.
34. to. 7. & l.
6. cont. Iul.
c. 17.

Bel pag. 46.

iniquity is in man when the inferior parts do ftub-bernly ftriue againft the fuperior, albeit they be not fuffered to ouercome. And quoteth for them l.6. contr. Iulian c.8. as he found it through the Printers error, falfly quoted in Bellarm : but they are, l. 6. c. 19. which added to that, that almoft al he faith is found in Bellarmin, conuinceth that he made this boafting chal-lenge out of his obiections. As for S. Auftin his meaning when he calleth concupifcéce iniquity is fufficiently explicated before. And the very word, *Some,* argueth that he thinketh it not to be formal finne, but in fome fort vz : materially. Befides that him felfe l. 2. contr. Iulian c. 5. expoundeth the like words out of S. Ambrofe of no finful iniquity.

S. Auguftin tom. 7.

Bellarm. l. 5, de amiff. grat. & ftat. pec. c.9. Bels chaleg nothing but Bellarmins obiections. Sup. c. 1. par rag.3. & 4.

3. The third place cited by Bel is l. 1. de nupt. & concupif. c. 25. where S. Auftin writeth. *If* (concupifcence) *can both be in the baptized parent and be no finne, why is the felfe fame no finne in the child? To this I anfwer* (faith S. Auftin) *That concupifcence is not fo forgiuen in baptifme, that it is no more, but that it is no more imputed to finne.* Item. *There remaineth not any thing which is not remitted.* Wherupon Bel in-ferreth both that concupifcence is formal finne, els it need not be forgiuen, & that it is true finne, as wel after baptifme, as before though it be not imputed to finne after bap-tifme,

pag. 46.

S. Auguftin. tom. 7.

tifme, and biddeth vs mark that S. Auſtin
ſaid not: *Nothing is ſinne that remaineth*, or *no
ſinne remaineth* : but *not any thing remaineth
which is not remitted.* Anſwer. The forme, &
eſſence of habitual ſinne is the guilt of
actual ſinne before done, according to S.
Auſtin in the ſame book, and next chapter,
as the forme of habitual ſinne of adultery
is the guilt of actual adultery before committed : & the forme of that habitual ſinne
which we haue by origin, is the guilt of
Adams actual eating the Aple, which guilt
being annexed to Concupiſcence maketh
it formal ſinne, and to require forgiuenes,
but that guilt being taken away by Gods
forgiuing the ſinne (as the ſame holy Doctor teacheth in the ſame place, and lib. 6.
contr. Iulian. c. 17. and lib. 1. Retract. c. 13)
Concupiſcence need no more forgiuenes
(as the ſame B. Saint writeth. lib. de ſpirit.
& lit. c. vlt. and epiſt. 200.) Nor remaineth
any more true ſinne, more then the body
remaineth a man after the ſoule is departed.
And in this very place which Bel citeth,
when he asketh why Concupiſcence is
ſinne in the childe, if it be in the parent baptized, and be no ſinne in him, euidently
ſuppoſeth that it is no true ſinne in the
baptized.

4. As for that of not imputing ſinne,
what

---

*What is
the eſſ.nce
of habitual
ſinne.*
Cap. 26.

*How Con-
cupiſcence
needeth for-
giuenes.*

S. Auſtin.

To. 3. & 1. &
lib. 1. contr.
duas epiſt.
Pelag. c. 13.

what S. Austin meant therby we wil rather learne of himself then of Bel, he therfore in the very words which Bel citeth hauing asked *why Concupiscence is not sinne* (mark Bel) *in the parent baptized as wel as in the childe vnbaptized,* answered that *by baptifme non imputatur in peccatum* it is not imputed for sinne. In which answer vnles he did by not imputing for sinne, meane making no sinne, he had not answered the question, why Concupiscence was no sinne in the baptized parent. Therfore with him Concupiscence not to be imputed to, or for sinne, is to be made no sinne. And cap. 32. he saith that *Concupiscence to be imputed, is to haue the guilt* (vz of Adams actual sinne) *which it hath, with it* : and consequently to be not imputed is to haue this guilt taken away, but to haue no guilt is to haue no sinne, as him self saith c. 26. therfore with him Concupiscence to be not imputed is to be made no sinne. Nether indeed can God otherwise not impute sinne but by taking it away. For *his iudgment is according to truth.* Rom. 2. v. 2. and therfore if ther be sinne in vs, he must needs impute it to vs, and account vs sinners, els he shold not accout vs, as we are, and according to truth. And albeit S. Austin did not in this place say in plaine tearms. *Nothing is sinne that remaineth.*

or: *No*

VVhat not imputing of sinne is vvith S. Austin.

None but an infidel vvil say sinne is not tale avvay in baptifme S.August.l.1. cont. duas epift. Pelag. c.13.to.7.

S. Paul.

or : *No sinne remaineth* yet he manifestly sup-
posed the first, when he asked *why concupiscence is not sinne* (mark Bel) *as wel in parents
baptized as in the child,* & affirmed them both
in equiualent tearms when he answered
that by not imputation concupiscence became no sinne in the baptized, as is already
shewed. And otherwhere plainly affirmeth.

S.Austin.l.1.
contr. duas
epist. Pelag.
c. 13. In Psal.
72. l. 6. cont.
Iul. c. 16.17.
Tract. 41. in
Ioan. serm.
6. de verb.
Apost. lib.
20. de ciuit.
c. 26.

That al sinnes are forgiuen (in baptisme) *and
novv are no more at al.* What is this but to say
no sinne remaineth. And nothing more
vsual with him then to say. That *in baptisme
al sinnes are taken avvay, do dye, are vvholy forgiuen, al iniquity blotted out : the baptized haue
no sinne. Infants christened haue no filth.* Beside
in sense al is one to say. Nothing remaineth
which is sinne : and nothing is sinne that
remaineth. For God by remitting taketh
away the guilt of sinne, as S. Austin saith l.
1. de nupt. & concupis. c. 26. l. 6. contr.
Iulian. c. 17. and l. 1. Retract. c. 13. which
guilt is the very forme of sinne as is before
explicated out of S. Austin.

Bel pag.47.
S. Augustin.
to.7.

5. The fourth place is taken out of S.
Austin l. 1. de nupt. & concupis. c. 29. *He
doth much good who doth that which is written.
Follow not thy lust, but perfecteth it not because he
fulfilleth not that thou shalt not couet, or lust.*
Hence Bel inferreth. First *that the iust can do
no good, nor striue against lust so perfectly but it is
aunexed*

annexed to sinne. This is grounded vpon S.
Austins words of not perfecting good, and
not fulfilling the law of not coueting. But
the illation is quite contrary to his meaning
in this place and others before cited, where
he saith. *That as long as we consent not, we sinne
not, we need not aske forgiuenes, yea do much good
and are crowned.* And though he say we perfect not our good, yet not to perfect is not
to sinne, especially when it is against our
wil that we perfect it not, as it is in this
case. And S. Austin is so far from saying here
we sinne when we perfect not this worke,
as he affirmeth that we do much good. And
Bel can as wel combine good and sinne in
one act, as he can annex light and darknes,
heauen and hel, God and diuil. For as the
Philosopher saith *bonum ex integra causa,
malum ex quolibet defectu.* It is no good act
vnles it be good euery way, and it is sinne
if it be euil any way.

6. As for fulfilling the law: I answer
that who consenteth not to Concupiscence
fulfilleth it in al things which it commandeth to be performed vnder sinne as S. Austin expresly affirmeth in many places: as
lib. de spirit. & lit. c. vlt. epist. 200 lib. 1.
de napt. & concupisc. c. 29. lib. 2. de Genes.
contr. Manich. c. 14. whose words we cited before: though if he haue Concupiscence,

Epist. 200. l.
de Spir. &
lit. c. vlt. l. 1.
de nupt. &
concupis. c.
29. lib. 2. de
Gen. contr.
Manich. cap.
14.
Non est cul-
pæ deputan-
dum si non-
dum potest
esse tanta di-
lectio Dei
quanta ple-
næ perfectæ-
que cogni-
tioni debe-
tur.
Aug. de spir.
& lit. c. vlt.
tom. 3.
Aristotel,
Quæ parti-
cipatio iusti-
tiæ cum ini-
quitate. 2.
Cor. 6.

Sup. c. 1. pa-
rag. 13. & 18.

cence, he fulfil it not in a thing which the law, though it command not vnder sinne to be performed, yet it commandeth as the end to which we ought, al we can to endeuor and labor to attaine vnto. That to haue no Concupiscence at al, is commanded by the law, only as the end which we ought to endeuor vnto, is manifest both by S. Austins affirming that there is no sinne, when there is no consent, as also because in the very next words to those which Bel citeth he saith. *To this end the law said thou shalt not couet, that in this precept we mihgt know both what in this mortality we ought to endeuor vnto by profiting, and whither we ought to attaine vnto in that most happy immortality.* Behold how he saith in this life we ought to endeuor, and in the next we ought to attaine to haue no lust. And tract. 41. in Ioan he saith. *I can not fulfil that which is said thou shalt not couet, what therfore is it needful to fulfil? that. Goe not after thy concupiscences.* Behold he prescribeth this only as needful to attaine vnto. And in the same place, and serm. 12. de verb. Apost. he noteth that S. Paul said not *you shal haue no il desires, or let not sinne be in your members,* but *let not sinne raigne.* As if he said. We are not bidden vnder sinne to haue no lust at al: and the reason saith he, and S. Gregory after him, is, because it is impossible.

Hovv to haue no Cócupiscence is commanded by the lavv and hovv not.

see more herafter artic. 8. *chap.* 2 *paragr.* 3. *and chap.* 3. *parag.* 2.

S. Augustin. to. 9.

Item 10. de Gen. cap. 12. tom. 3. Cap. 5. to. 10.

S. Gregor. l. 21. Moral. c. 2.

7. The

7. The second thing which Bel inferreth and biddeth vs marke it wel is, That
the tenth commandement forbiddeth original lust
committed without consent, and habitual concupis-
cence. Did euer man read more markable
folly? 1. He maketh original lust to be committed, which is to make original actual,
because what is committed is actual, as
commission is action: 2. That habitual, &
original inclination to euil is forbidden by
the tenth commandement, and calleth the
contrary most abſurd. But nothing can be
more abſurd then to ſay that original, and
habitual inclination to euil is forbidden by
this commandement: *Thou shal not couet.* For
to couet is to doe, *ipsum agere concupiscere est.*
ſaith S. Auſtin ſerm. 5. de verb. Apoſt. c. 7.
and therfore to make habits and inclinations forbidden in theſe words, is to make
habits doings, inclinations actions. Or who
euer heard that new borne infants ſinne
againſt the tenth commandement, ſurely
if that be ſo, we muſt cal them no more In-
nocents.

8. But let vs hear him proue this abſurdity. *For although* (ſaith he) *S. Paul were most*
free, and innocent from actual ſinne, becauſe he
fought mightily againſt his raging concupiſcence,
and did in no wiſe yeeld vnto it, yet was he guilty
by reaſon of original concupiſcence. Behold Bel

N prouing

Bel pag. 48.

Original
luſt made
actual by
Bel.

S. Auguſtin.
to. 7.

Peccata pro-
pria non ha-
bent vnde
illos merito
Innocentes
nũcupamus.
Aug. 1. cont.
Iul. c. 6. to. 7.

pag. 48.

Bel proueth
idem per
idem.

prouing *idem per idem*, and withal ouerthro-
wing whatsoeuer he manteineth in this article. For the doubt is, whether original
Concupifcence be finne, and this he proueth becaufe S. Paul was guilty by reafon
of it. what is this but to proue original
Concupifcence to be finne, becaufe it is

Contradict.
14.

finne. And he affirmeth S. Paul to haue bene
moft free, and innocent from actual finne,

Bel ouer-
throvveth
at once
vvhat he
intended to
proue in al
this Arti-
cle.
Babilon is
yvonne, Bel
is confoun-
ded. Hiere.
50. v. 2.

and proueth it becaufe he fought mightily
againft his raging Concupifcence, and in no
wife confented vnto it. which is in plaine
tearms to confeffe that inuoluntary motions of the flesh are no finne, becaufe they
are not voluntary. O force of truth which
breakeft out of thy profeffed aduerfaries
mouth. Surely Proteftants may haue great
ioy of fuch a challenger. And no maruel if
he be defirous of an aduerfary to fight withal, who for want of one falleth thus to
fight with him felf, and maketh his aduerfaries fport to laugh, & moueth his friends
to compaffion and shame. But let vs fee
more of his paftime.

Bel pag. 49.
Rom. 7. v. 7.

9. *S. Paul had not known luft to be finne ex-*
cept the law had faid. Thou shalt not luft. But he
could not be ignorant that Concupifcence with con-
fent was finne, feeing the very heathens did know,

Math. 5. v.
22.

and confeffe it. Againe. *voluntary luft is forbid-*
den in the fixt, feuenth, and eighth comandement
                                        as Chrift

*as Chriſt him ſelfe expoundeth them. Therfore the
tenth forbiddeth the very habitual deſire, and inclination and fruits therof though not conſented
vnto: Anſvver.* S. Paul was ſo far from knowing by the law that natural inclination to
ſinne is formal ſinne, as nether he, nor any
man of iudgment could imagine it til Bel
with a new kinde of philoſophy taught vs
that habits are acts, and inclinations actiōs.
But to the argument I deny the aſſumption.
For he might be ignorant that luſt which
is only indirectly voluntary, and in the
cauſe, becauſe it is not preuented, is ſinne,
and this he might know by the law: nether
can Bel shew that euer any heathen knew
this. Yea he might be ignorant, that Concupiſcence directly voluntary, when it is
not put in execution, is true ſinne & learne
this by the law. For if Ioſephus, and Kimhi
though they had the law, and were great
Rabbins in it, yet thought ſuch concupiſcence no ſinne: and Ioſephus reprehended
Polybius for condemning it as a ſinne; why
might not the Apoſtle haue bene ignorant
of this, if the law had not taught it him.
Neither doth Bels reaſon cōuince the contrary. For though ſome Heathen by great
ſtudy in moral philoſophy came to know
this truth, yet perhaps S. Paul could not or
rather as he ſaieth did not. And Bel as we

*See S. Auſtin
ſerm. 4. de
verb. Apoſt.
c. 4. & 5. to.
10.*

*Concupiſ-
cence indi-
rectly vo-
luntary
I vovvne of
s Paul by
the lavv to
be ſinne.*

*Ioſephus l.
12. Antiquit.
c. 12.
Kimhi in
pſal. 66.*

shal fee hereafter citeth a place out of S. Am
bros where he writeth, that the Apostle
thought Concupifcence no finne *becaufe it*
delighted, and feemed a harmles thing to couet.
yet better it is to fay : (as I haue already)
that S. Paul meaneth, that by the law he
came to know al voluntary concupifcence,
though it be but indirectly voluntary, to be
finne, and this nether he nor any Heathen
could haue known, but by the law, or by
Gods reuelation.

10. Bels fecond reafon maketh againft
him felf. For if inuoluntary motions be as
true finnes as voluntary, why are not they
forbidden as wel in the fixt, feuenth, and
eighth cómandement as thefe ? And albeit
voluntary motions were implicitly forbidden, when the external acts were prohibited, yet it was neceffary to forbid them exprefly in the laft commandement for to in-
culcat it into the hard hartes of the Iewes:
nether yet with this expreffe forbiddance
wold fome of them beleeue voluntary concupifcence without the fact to be finne, as
appeareth by the example of Iofephus
Kimhi, and diuers Iewes, Math 5. v. 29.
After this Bel alleadgeth a place of S. Auftin wher he calleth defires of Concupifcence il, filthy, and not lawful, which haue
bene explicated before, and are verifyed of
inuo-

inuoluntary Concupiscence, becauſe it is materially ſinne, wanting nothing to be formally ſo but voluntarines, which Bel here goeth about to proue that they want not, but his proofe hath bene refuted before.

Chapt. 1. parag. 2. & 3.

Chapt. 1. parag. 11.

11. After the ſaid ptoofe he auoucheth Bellarmin to confeſſe that S. Auſtin acknowledgeth euen inuoluntary motions to be properly ſinne, and flatly condemned by the tenth Commandement, and in the margent biddeth vs ſee S. Auſtin lib. de ſpirit. & lit. c. vlt. becauſe Bellarmin writeth *that S. Auſtin teacheth al kind of motions of Concupiſcence to be aliquo modo in ſome ſort prohibited by that lavv. Thou ſhalt not couet.* Wheras Bellarmin profeſſeth. That *S. Auſtin not only no where in plaine words ſaith al Concupiſcence is properly ſinne, but alſo affirmeth the contrary in al the tomes of his works,* and in the words cited by Bel is ſo far from ſaying, that S. Auſtin thinketh al motions to be flatly condemned, as he wold not abſolutly ſay they were condemned but only with this limitation *in ſome ſort,* vz as far, as they lye in our poẁre, which limitation though Bel without proofe cal deceitful, and contrary to S. Auſtins meaning, yet haue we before ſhewed it out of S. Auſtin to be his true meaning. And I wold Bel had ſeene that place

Bel pag. 51.
Bellarm. lib. 5. de amiſſ. grat. & ſtat. pec. c. 10.
vntruth 56

Bellar. ſup. c. 8.

Sup. parag. 6.

N 3 of S.

of S. Auſtin to which he ſendeth vs: for
there ſhould he haue heard S. Auſtin teaching him that inuoluntary Concupiſcence
is ſo far from ſinne, as if we conſent not to
it we need not ſay in our lords prayer. Forgiue vs our treſpaſſes. And thus much of
his proofs out of S. Auſtin.

Chap. IIII.

Bels arguments out of S. Ambros, S. Bede,
S. Thomas touching Concupiſcence
anſwered.

Bel pag. 52.

AFTER his proofs out of S. Auſtin
Bel very methodically (forſooth) re-
turneth to Scripture citing a ſentence of S.
Ihon in greek, *pas ho poion hamartian cai ten*
ano mian poiei, cai he hamartia eſtin anomia: and
tranſlateth it thus. *Euery one that ſinneth tranſ-*
greſſeth the lavv; and ſinne is the tranſgreſſion of
the law. This place he citeth againe art. 6. to
proue al ſinne of it ſelfe to be mortal, and

Bel forget-
teth his
matter.

for that purpoſe it hath ſome ſhew of
proofe: but how it proueth al kind of Concupiſcence to be proper ſinne, paſſeth my
intelligence. For ſuppoſe that al ſinne were
tranſgreſſion of the law, (which he laboreth much to proue, & wil neuer performe)
what is this to proue. That al Concupiſcence is ſinne? And leſt of al it concerneth
habitual

habitual cōcupiscence. For S. Ihon speaketh
only of actual sinne, as appeareth by those
words *poiei amartian poiei anomian,* committeth
sinne committeth iniquity. And yet spendeth he
fowre leaues in nothing but in prouing *ano-*
mia to signify transgression of the law, and
euery sinne to be transgression of the law, &
saith that *Papists are put to a non plus. about the*　*pag. 58.*
doctrin of concupiscence in the regenerate : for both
anomia and adicia is truly, and fitly tearmed ini-
quity : But what shal a man say to such vanity? Be *anomia,* or *adicia* what you wil, be
al sinne transgression of the law : proue you
that al concupiscence is formal sinne? The
question is now, not what *anomia* or *adicia,*
or sinne is, but what concupiscence is, from
which Bel flying into an other question ,
sheweth him selfe to be at a non plus. Wherfore remitting this place of S. Ihon with
al which he bringeth to proue that euery
sinne is transgression, to the 6. article, to
which it belongeth and nothing concerneth this: I wil answer only foure authorities, which he abuseth to proue inuoluntary
concupiscence to be sinne.

2. The first is of S. Ambrose in c. 7.　*Bel pag. 56.*
Rom. where he saith that *a man is not free*　*S. Ambros.*
from cryme, because he sinneth inuitus ⁊nwillin-
gly or against his wil. Where Bel noteth that
he calleth concupiscence cryme, or mortal
sinne.

sinne. And, That a man sinneth in that
which he doth against his wil. But besides
that the Author of those commentaries is
not S. Ambrose: he meaneth not of concupiscence but of custome of sinning, which
begun in the sinner (saith he) *by his owne
fault, and sloath, and wherby he is laded and sooner
yeeldeth to sinne then to the law, and though he
wold do good, yet is he oppressed by custome.* And
therfore when he saith that such a one is
not free from cryme in sinning against his
wil, he meaneth not of absolute, and reso-
lute wil to the contrary (for custome can not
make a man to do a thing against his absolute wil, but of an imperfect wil which diuers cal velleity, which most sinners, though
neuer so accustomed to sinne, haue to do
good, and against which kind of wil they
sinne: but are not therfore (as that Author
saith truly free from cryme, because (notwithstanding this imperfect wil of doing
wel) they haue an absolute and perfect wil
to sinne. And so this place concerneth nothing acts of concupiscence altogether inuoluntary and against both perfect, and imperfect wil.

3. An other testimony he citeth out of
S. Ambrose in the same place where he
saith. *That S. Paul separated not this concupiscence from sinne, but mingled it.* But he mea-
                                            neth

neth only of voluntary acts, as is euident by the reason, wherwith he proueth that this concupiscence seemed no sinne, *because* (saith he) *it delighted, and seemed simplex causa, a harmles matter to couet a thing of our neighbour.*

4. The third authority is of S. Bede, whom he confesseth to haue bene renowned through out the christian world for learning, and vertue. And if he thinke as he writeth he thinketh Papistry to be true piety. For S. Bede was a notorious Papist approuing Masse, honoring of reliques, images, prayer for the dead, purgatory, and other such points of Papistry as is euident out of his Ecclesiastical history. Bel alleadgeth him because he saith. *They sinne who of frailty (lat: infirmitas) corrupt innocency.* What is here to the purpose ? who deny that sinne may be done as wel of frailty, as of malice ? For seeing none is so fraile, but he is assisted by Gods grace in which he may do al : Philip. 4. v. 13. and is not suffered to be tempted aboue his powre. 1. Corinth. 10. v. 13. if he sinne of frailty he sinneth voluntarily.

5. His fourth authority is out of S. Thomas saying. *That what a man doth without deliberation of reason he doth it not perfectly, because the principal thing in man doth it not, and therfore it is not perfectly a humaine act, and so perfectly ne-*
ther

Bel pag. 57.
S. Beda 1.
Io. 3.

S. Paul.

Bel pag. 59.
S.Thom. 1.2.
q.74. art. 3.

ther vertue, nor *sinne*, but *imperfectly.* VVherfore
such a motion of sensuality, preuenting reason is a
venial, & *imperfect sinne.* Out of these words
Bel noteth these important obseruations as
he calleth them 1. *That S. Thomas is a Popish*
Saint. 2. *That for his great learning* (and Bel to
his confusion confesseth him to haue bene
a great Cleark indeed) *he was surnamed the*
Angelical Doctor. 3. *That P. Vrban 4. and Inno-*
cent 5. confirmed his doctrin for authentical and
gaue it the first place after Canonical Scripture.
How wel these three notes are gathered out
of S. Thomas his foresaid words let euery
one be iudge. But Bel can gather quodlibet
ex quolibet, water out of a flint stone.

pag. 132.

6.   But I must note out of Bels important
obseruations diuers important vntruths. 1.
That P. Vrban 4. and P. Innocent 5. confirmed S. Thomas his doctrin for authentical. 2. That P. Vrban 4. gaue it the first
place after Canonical Scripture. Indeed. P.
Vrban 4. highly admired his doctrin, as i f
it were sent from heauen, & P. Innocét in a
sermon as a preacher by way of exaggeratió
n gaue it the first place after Scripture, but
neither did they confirme it as authentical,
nether did both of them giue it the next
place after Scripture. The 3. vntruth (which
he repeateth twise in thispage, & very often
in his booke) is. *That we are bound to defend,*
and

vntruth 57.
vntruth .58

Vrban. in
Confirmat.
doctrinæ S.
Thomæ.

Innocent. in
sermo. Ecce
plusquam
Salomo n
hic.

vntruth 59.

and beleeue S. *Thomas his doctrin, and may not in any case refuse or deny it.* This is a manifest vntruth. For albeit S. Thomas be, and that worthely of the greatest authority amongst schoolmen, yet his doctrin may and is often denyed in schools (as Bel hath heard many tymes) where it concerneth no matter of faith, yea Bel him selfe art. 7. pag. 133. affirmeth him to be commonly denyed about the conception of our Lady. And P. Vrban 4. commanded only the vniuersity of Tholouse to teach, and follow, *especially* (saith he) his doctrin. Wherby we see he commanded them not to follow his doctrin only, and none others, but chiefly his, nor as an infallible truth, but as most probable. Other vniuersities, and Catholiques are left to their liberty to follow (excepting matter of faith wherin al agree, or only erre of ignorance) what schoolmen they please.

Contradict. 15.

7. And this is so notorious as when we obiect to Protestants their dissention in matters of faith, they returne vpon vs the disagreement of schoolmen. But there is a great difference. For the disagreement of schoolmen is in things wherin S. Austin l. 1. contr. Iulian. c. 6. *The learnedest, and best defenders of Catholique verity, may salua fidei compage, disagree, and one say better and truer then an other.* And if of ignorance any of them

The disagreement of Schoolemen far different from that of Protestants.

S. Austin.

them erre it is alwaies with readines to
submit them selues to the iudgment of the
Catholique Church. Wheras Protestants
disagree about matters, which belong (as

Sup.

S. Austin speaketh) *ad ipsa fidei fundamenta.*
And omitting those notorious dissentions
amongst them, about the real presence, the
number of Canonical books, Christs suf-
fering the paines of hel, his discent into hel,

*Dissentions
of Prote-
stants tou-
ched in
their late
Conference.*

& the like I wil propose a few other points
of dissention amongst them, gathered out of
the conference at Hampton court. as 1: *Whether baptisme by vvoemen be allowable* : pag. 8. 14.
15. 17. 18. 2. *vvhether confirmation be lawful* pag.
10. 3. *vvhether baptisme be necessary* pag. 16. 4.
*vvhether after receauing the holy Ghost we may to-
tally depart from grace.* pag. 28. 5. *vvhether the
communion booke contradict the 15. article of their
faith.* pag. 25. 6. *vvhether there ought to be any
Bishops.* pag. 36. 7. *vvhether the intention of the
Minister be essential to the Sacrament.* pag. 38. 8.
*VVhether a man once iustifyed remaine truly iust
before God, whatsoeuer sinne he commit.* pag. 41.
and 14. 9. *vvhether a iustifyed man falling into
greeuous sinnes shal be saued without repentance
for them* 16. 10. *vvhether the English Byble be truly
translated.* pag. 45. 46. 11. *vvhether the communion booke corrupt the Byble in two places.* pag. 63.
12. *vvhether the Crosse be to be vsed in baptisme.*
pag. 65. 13. *VVhether the Church can institute, an
external*

1.
2.
3.
4.
5.
6.
7.
8.
9.
10.
11.
12.
13.

external significant signe. pag. 67. **14.** *vvhether the Churches institution can bynde in conscience.* pag. 70. **15.** *VVhether the communion booke containe errors repugnant to Scripture.* pag. 59.

8. Moreouer more then a thousand Ministers whom the whole vniuersity of Oxford calleth *their brethren and fellovv laborers in the Lords haruest* in the supplication to his Maiestie exhibited in April. 1603. professe. That *there is not in their Church an vniformity of doctrin.* This the Oxonians deny against their owne knowledge, and the knowlege of al England. For what vniformity is there, where a thousand Ministers their fellow laborers professe them selues to disagree in points of religion from the rest, yea his Maiestie witnesseth him selfe *to haue receaued many complaints through the dissentions in the Church, and purposeth* (as he saith) *to setle an vniforme order through the vvhole Church, and to plant vnity.* Wil now the Oxonians say there are no dissentions? wil they make his Maiestie actum agere in setling vniformity, and planting vnity where none wanteth. And in like sort of the Scottish Church he testifyeth. *That there is such dissention euen in the Catachisme doctrin, as vvhat vvas Catachisme doctrin in one congregation vvas scarsly accepted as sound and orthodox in an other.* And this dissention amongst Protestants about matters

14.

15.

In their Supplicatio exhibited in April 1603. Ansvver to the Supplication.

Conference p. 5. 22.

Conference p. 44.

ters

ters of religion is with such obstinacy, as
notwithstanding proclamations, disputations, conferences, and decrees, or Canons
of their Church it remaineth stil amongst
them, and wil as long as heresy remayneth
in them, which teacheth them to expound
Scriptures according to their priuate spirits
and to recant nothing, *because* (as his Maiestie saith of the Scottish Ministers) *it stan-
deth not vvith their credits.*

Conference
p. 102.

9. The fourth note, which Bel gathereth
out of S. Thomas his words, is more to the
purpose vz. *That motions of concupiscence preuenting reason are venial sinnes.* But if Bel had
amongst his important obseruations obserued also that S. Thomas spake immediatly
before of deliberate reason, he might haue
noted that he meant only of such motions
as preuent perfect but not imperfect deli-
beration, and *therfore are* (as he saith) *imperfect or venial sinnes : VVherfore be myndful* (Bel)
from vvhence thou art falne and do penance. Apocalip. 2.

THE

THE
FIFT ARTICLE OF
THE MERIT OF GOOD
WORKES.

CHAP. I.

*Of the Proteſtants enmity to good vvorks
and friendſhip vvith euil.*

E L beginneth this Article *Bel pag. 60.* with a greeuous complaint a-gainſt Papiſts *who* (ſaith he) *moſt vnchriſtianly ſlander the pro-feſſors of Chriſts Ghoſpel, as though they vvere enemies to good vvorks, of vvhich they thinke, ſpeak, teach, and vvrite more chriſtianly, and more religiouſly then Papiſts do.* Both theſe points he proueth no otherwiſe then with an (*I ſay*) *I ſay* (ſaith he) *that good vvorks though they can not go before, yet do euer follovv iuſtification ; are neceſſary to ſaluation, and true effects of predeſtination.* As if Bel were al the new Ghoſpellers, or they al agreed with him concerning good works: We alleadge their words, produce their deeds, ſhew the fruits, and effects of their enmity to good works, and Bel thinketh to anſwer al this with

with an (I say) Surely he presumeth of be-
neuolous, and partial iudges, or he wold
neuer answer thus. He with an (*I say*) may
slåder Popes, Princes & Papists whatsoeuer,
and an I say, yea manifest proofe to the contrary, wil not suffice him. Such force his I
sayes haue : *Dixit & facta sunt* : But Syr I
both say, & wil proue by words, and deeds
that both you, and your Ghospellers are not
only enemies to good works, but great
frends to euil works. And as for enmity to
good works.

2. First they bid vs beware of good
works. *Let vs bevvare* (saith Luther) *of sinne,
but much more of lawes, and good works.* And
some of his schollers in the conference of
Altenbnrg teach vs *to pray that we perseuer
vnto the end in faith vvithout good vvorks* : 2.
they teach good works to be harmful: *Good
vvorks* (said the forsaid Lutherans) *are per-
nitious to saluation.* Againe. *Christians vvith
good vvorks belong to Sathan* : And as Surius,
Staphilus and others report a Minister was
not allowed in Saxony because he beleeued
not this : 3. because they say al good works
are sinne, and vnclean so Luther art. 23. Caluin 3. instit. c. 14. parag. 9. & 11.c. 15. parag.
3. and 4. Whitaker contr. Duræ. l. 1. p. 49.
Bucley answer to 8. reasons p. 111. and 109.
Perkins tit of merit. and Bel art. 4. pag. 48.
tea-

Luther. ser-
mon. de no-
uo testamé-
to seu de
Missa.
Colloquiũ
Attenburg.

Surius com-
ment. Ann.
1564.
Staphil. in
Apolog.

teacheth that sinne is alwaies annexed to
good workes: 4. They teach that good
workes of their nature deserue damnation:
There was neuer (saith Caluin lib. 3. instit. c.
14. parag. 11.) *any work of a godly man which
if it were examined by Gods seuere iudgment
were not damnable.* How can Protestants
now be friēds to good workes which they
bid beware of, account hurtful, sinne, and
damnable? Surely their friendship can be no
better then Ioabs was to Amasa when he
kissed him, but withal thrust his dagger
into his body. 2. Reg. 20.

Epicure vvold seeme to loue vertue though he made pleasure his end.

Habentes speciem pietatis virtutem autem eius abnegantes. 2. Timoth. 4. v. 5.

3. And on the contrary side their friendship to euil workes is manifest. 1. because
they teach that euil workes make not an
euil man, nor any can damne a man but incredulity: this Luther teacheth in plaine
tearms: lib. de libert. Christian. and lib. de
capt. Babil. c. de baptis. 2. because they
make God author of sinne: Zuinglius saith.
*Numen ipsum author est eius quod in nobis est
iniustitia:* God him self is author of that
which in vs is iniustice. And Caluin lib. 1.
instit. c. 18. parag. 3. After he had brought
diuers proofs hereof concludeth thus: *Iam
satis apertè ostendi Deum vocari eorum omnium
authorem quæ isti Censores volunt otiosè tantum
eius permissu contingere.* Now haue I plainely
enough shewed that God is called the Au-

Frendship of Protestants to euil vvorks.

Luther.

Zvvinglius sermon. de Prouidentia ad Principem Cattorum 1530. c. 5.

Caluin in playne termes maketh God author of sinne.

O   thor

thor (heare Bel, & Blush) of al thefe things which thefe Cenfurers wil haue to fal out only through his idle permiffion. And Melanchton wrote, *That the adultery of Dauid, and treafon of Iudas was the work of God like as the Vocation of S. Paul.* 3. Beza teacheth that our fpirit muft wraftle againft finne, but fo as it ouercome not: Are not thefe (Bel) particuler fauors to euil works to fay they make no man euil, that none but one of them damne men, that God is their author, that we muft let them ouercome, or were not thefe whom I named profeffors of your Ghofpel.

4. But if we look into their deeds, and fruits, therin we fhal clearly fee how mortal foes they are to good, and great frends to euil works. For there is nether man nor nation, which of a Catholike becommeth a Proteftant, but he doth fewer goodworks, les faft, and pray, feldomer giue almes, do fewer works of charity then before, and more euil then before, as in ryot pride auarice, iniuftice, & the like. For proofe hereof I propofe only England for example, whither there be not now les fafting, praying, almes giuing, building of Churches, Hofpitals, Colledges, Schools, then there was in Catholique tyme. And on the contrary fide whither prifons be not fuller of malefactors

Melanchton in cap. 8. ad Rom.

Beza Rom. 6.v.12.

Fox Confiderat. 3. faith Englifh Proteftants are foe il as he thinketh they could not be vvorfe if they vvould. Read confiderat. 4. before his Martyral.

factors, more endited of thefts, murders, rapes, and other villanies, and far more executed then in former tymes. And whether it be not growne almost into a common prouerbe that a mans obligatió now, is not so good as his word was in former tymes. And in these 46. yeares of Protestantisme, when more then so many thousands of Protestants haue bene executed for murders, theft, robberies, rapes, coyning, purse-cutting, and like villanies; let Bel name how many Catholiques haue bene so much as called in question for such offences: yea this encrease of sinne, and euil works by Protestantisme is so notorious as Protestants confesse it. Luther said his followers were become *ten tymes worse then Sodomits:* a Bullinger testifyeth that in his church *euery where encreaseth haughtines, pride, auarice, vsury, blasphemy, slander, ribauldry, drunkenes, gluttony ryotousnes, lechery, incest, wrath, murder, contention, and enuy.* Wigand confesseth that *youth growe worse, & les tractable, & dare commit those vices to which men of ripe years in tymes past were not subiect.* Erasmus writeth of Protestants that he hath *seene many of them become worse but none better.* Let these different fruits shew the difference of these trees, let the effects testify, whither Protestants or Catholiques think more religiously of good works,

Luther. apud Sur. 1566.

Bullinger. in Coron. A-polog. cont. Brent.

VVigand de malis Ger-maniæ. See Sur. 1566.

Ex fructibus eorum cognoscetis eos. Math.7. v.16.

whither

Psalm. 36.

whether ministers or Priests teach the people more *to eschew euil, and do good.* Now let vs come to Bels positions of good works, whereby he hopeth to wipe away this deserued name which Protestants haue of being enemies to good works.

CHAP. II.
Of Bels positions touching good vvorks.

Bel pag. 60.

BELS first position containeth two partes the first is *that good works nether do, nor can go before iustification.* Behold Bel euen where he wold proue him self to be a fried to good works, shewing him self to be an enemy, & excluding them from any going before, or any way concurring to iustification, to which they so concurred in S. Mary Magdalen as our Sauiour said *many sins are forgiuen her, because she loued much,* making her loue a kinde of cause, vz disponent of her iustification. But because Bel proueth his position not at al, I wil stand no longer to disproue it. The second part of his position is: *That good works euer follow (as fruits the tree) the persons that are freely iustifyed.* This is most manifestly false in infants wherof many iustifyed in baptisme, dye before they do any goodworke. And if his comparison

Luc. 7. v. 47.

rifon of the tree be good, fome iuftifyed, neuer do good worke, and al want them long tyme, fome giue ouer doing good, as fome trees are barren, fome ceafe to beare fruit, and none beare alwaies. And I wold know of Bel, whither Dauid were iuftifyed when he committed adultery, and murder. If then he were not iuft? then loft he his fruits, if iuft? I wold know of Bel what good worke he did in tyme of his adultery, and murder. Likwife whither Proteftants be euer doing good works, or fome tymes be not iuft, and become infidels.

2. His fecond pofitió is: *That good workes goe fo neceßarily before faluatió, that no man without them can attaine eternal life', when poßibility is graunted to do them,* and afterwarde calleth them the *vfual ordinary means by which God bringeth men to faluation.* This is true doctrin, if it be meant of good works commanded, but how it agreeth with Proteftants doctrin before cited, paffeth my capacity, yea how it agreeth with his owne doctrin that *there is no good worke which wanteth finne;* is thinke we finne neceffary to faluation, or an vfual, & vndoubted meane to come to heauen? moreouer if Proteftants thinke their works to be the meane to faluation, they wil no more charge Papifts with trufting to be faued by their works.

Bel pag. 60 72.

Sup. c. 1. parag. 1.

pag. 48.

3. His

Belpag. 61.

3. His third position is: *That good works are the true effects of Predestination.* This if it be so meant, that al, and only predestinate do good works, is most false: for many infants are predestinat, and yet dye before they do good works, and many reprobate men do good works, as appeareth by Simon Magus who beleeued, and cleued to S. Philip act. 8. v. 13. But most absurd it is which he addeth *that the children of God by good works make their saluation sure vnto them selfs, and manifest to the world,* if he meane as Protestants do of such security, as is void of al doubt, or feare of the contrary. Because none can be so assured of Gods wil touching their saluation, but by manifest reuelation from God him self; but good works are no such reuelation ether to our selfs, or to others. Ergo by them nether we, nor others can be assured of our saluation. The proposition is manifest. The assumption I proue: 1. because reprobats may somtymes do good works, as did Simon Magus. Ergo: good works are no reuelation of saluation, 2. because euen the worker is not assured that his work is good, wanting no condition requisit to goodnes: for as Iob saith c. 9. *although I be simple, this same my soul shal not know,* and much les others can be assured of the goodnes of the work: for they not knowing

Act.

In omnibus actionibus in quibus tibi es bene conscia nunquam audeas esse securus. Ambros. epist. 84.

Iob v. 21.

knowing the purpose and intention for which the worke is done (according to that of Ieremy. *Mans hart is inscrutable, vvho shal knovv it*? and that of S. Paul *vvhat man knovveth the things of man, but the spirit of man that is in him*) can neuer be assured that the worke is fully good. 3. though I and others were assured that I do good works this day, yet nether I nor others can be assured, that hereafter I shal do good works, whensoeuer I shal haue possibility, or tyme, and yet Bel auoucheth that vnles we do good works when we haue tyme, or possibility therto we can not be saued. Ergo: good works make no vndoubted assurance of saluation. 4. good works are sinful and offensiue to God (as Protestants affirme) Ergo: according to their doctrin, they can be no euident signe of Gods fauor, and of our saluation : but rather of his wrath, and our damnation. And if Bel be so wel skilled in mens fortunes, as by their works he can euidently foretel their saluation, let him play the Aegiptian and tel Protestants whether they shal be saued, or damned. For if he can assure them of their saluation he wil get more in one day then his fifty pound pension, wherewith he is hyred to preach and write against Catholiques: and I can send him to one Protestant noble man, who wold giue

Hierem.17. v. 9. 1. Corinth. 2.v.11.

pag 61.72.

O 4   him

him ten thowsand pownd to be assured of his saluation. Finally this doctrin of his is not only against Catholiques, but also against his Maister Caluin who saith *labascit fides &c. faith quaileth if it respect good works: for none of the holiest men shal finde there wheron to trust:* And good reason for if good works be sinne (as Caluin and Protestants teach) what assurance or confidence can sinne giue vs of saluation.

Caluin. 3. institut. c. 11. parag. 11.

4. His fourth position is: *That good works are nether cause of predestination, nor of iustification, nether do, nor can merit ex condigno eternal life.* Touching the first point of predestination, there is no controuersy. For al Catholiques do with S. Austin against the Pelagians deny predestination to grace, to proceed of our merits, and the same do Deuines commonly affirme of predestination to glory, though this be no matter of faith. Nether is there any difficulty about the second point concerning iustification. For though faith and repentance dispose to iustificatiõ: yet Catholiques thinke them not to be proper cause and merit therof. as Caluin, Perkins, and Willet confesse. But the third point of meriting *de condigno* is that *about which I* (saith Bel) *contend with the Papists at this present, and namely with the Councel of Trent.* But because he proceedeth in this article

Bel pag. 61.

Auguft. l. de bono perfeueran. epift. 105. & alibi.

See Bellar. l. 2. de Grat. & lib. arb. c. 15.

Conc. Trid. feff. 6. c. 8.

Caluin. 3. institut. c. 14. parag. 11.
Perkins refor. Cathol. p. 64.
VVillet contract. 17. q. 5. part. 3. p. 588.

article confusedly enough confounding *Bel impug-* many questions together, and in stead of a *neth a Schole* point of Catholique faith impugneth a *point for* schoole point, I wil particulerly by Conclu- *a point of* sions set downe the Catholiques opinions *faithe.* concerning this matter.

CHAP. III.

The Catholiques doctrine touching merit particulerly set dovvne and proued.

AS about any matter, the first kinde of question is about the existence, whether it be or no? the second about the nature, or quality, what a one it is? and the last about the causes thereof, why it is such or such? So about merit of eternal life the first kinde of question is, whether there be any, or none. The second about the nature of this merit, whether it be *ex condigno*, and worthely deserue the reward, or *de congruo*, & only haue a certaine cōgruity, & agreeablenes therto. And if it be *de condigno*: whether it be absolute, and suppose or require no condition of Gods promise to reward it: or conditional, supposing the said promise: Likewise whether it be perfect hauing iust, and arithemetical equality to the reward, as a penny hath to a pennyworth; or imperfect hauing only due proportion, and

vertual

vertual equality to the reward, as accidents
be a proportionat difpofition to fubftance,
and great labors for Gods Church a proportionat defert of a Bishoprik, and feed
vertually equal to the tree: The third kinde
of queftion is about the caufes of this nature of merit, to wit, whether this condignity of merit rife, partly of any proportion
or fufficiency which is in the merit vnto the
the reward, or wholy and entirely of Gods
free acceptation, who feeing vs do the beft
we can to deferue heauen, accepteth it as a
condigne, and fufficient merit therof,
though of it felfe it be not. And to thefe
queftions I wil anfwer by the Conclufions
enfuing.

   2. Firft Conclufion: There is merit of
eternal life, and our fupernatural works
done by Gods grace (wherof only we
fpeak in this matter) are meritorious of
eternal life, and glory. This is a point of
faith with Catholiques, defyned in the
Council of Trent. feff. 6. can 32. and denyed by no Catholique though Bel falfly
affirme the contrary of fome, and taught
of holy Fathers, and antient writers, as Bel
confeffeth, and therfore graunted by him
felfe in words, though he expound merit by
Impetration. This he calleth a godly fenfe,
which is indeed his vfual vngodly shift
vfed

Concil. Tri-
dent.

Bel pag. 75.

pag. 61.

vſed of him hereafter art. 6. & 8. & of Proteſtants commonly, when they dare not
deny an Authors words, to deny his mea-
ning. For who ſeeth not that merit is a quite *Merit quite*
different thing from Impetration; for to *different*
merit is to deſerue, to impetrate is to obtain *from impe-*
by requeſt, beggars may be ſaid to impetrat *tration.*
1.
but not to merit their almes, and an hyred 2.
ſeruát meriteth, not impetrateth his wages. 3.
Merit ſuppoſeth ſome iuſtice, Impetration 4.
only prayers, in the obteiner, and liberality 5.
6.
in the giuer, merit may be, though the re- 7.
ward be not giuen : Impetration ſuppoſeth
the graunt therof. Merit anſwereth to reward : Impetration to gift. Merit requireth
at leſt ſome proportion in the worke to the
reward : Impetration none at al.

3. And euident it is that Fathers by me-
rit vnderſtád not impetration. For S. Auſtin S. Auguſtin.
tom. 2.
epiſt. 105. writeth that. *As death is rendred as* Deus pro-
a ſtipend to the merit of ſinne, ſo is euerlaſting life poſuit re-
gnum cælo-
as a ſtipend to the merit of iuſtice. S. Ireney l. 4. rum vænale
c. 72. ſaith. *By good works we conquer heauen* : in ep. 93.
S. Ireney.
S. Baſil. orat. in init prouerb : *By good works* S. Baſil. pro-
we buy heauen S. Gregory Nazian : *For good* pe ſin.
S. Greg. Naz.
works we may exact reward, not as grace but as orat. 3. in
bapt.
playne debt. S. Hierom epiſt. ad Celant. God S. Hierom.
hath cauſe to reward vs. S. Chriſoſtom hom. S. Chryſoſt.
to. 4.
7. in epiſt. Rom. calleth vs. *Gods creditors,*
and vſurers and him *our debtor.* and hom. 3. Tom. 2.
de La-

de Laʒaro : that by good workes we deſerue
heauen, as by euil hel. Yea Bel him ſelfe admitteth more then impetration, when hereafter he côfeſſeth heauen to be due to good
workes; for where duty is there is not meere
impetration, & that works are to heauen as
the loane of a cloake in a ſhower of rayne
vpon promiſe of an hundred pownds, for
here is ſome iuſtice. And profeſſeth to defend Durands opinion who vndoubtedly
admitteth more then ſimple impetration.
But if Bel had remembred his owne, and
the common doctrin of Proteſtants before
rehearſed that al good works whatſoeuer
are ſinne, he wold neuer haue graunted that
they are impetratorious of Gods fauor, and
reward. For how câ ſinne impetrate fauour,
or reward, and not rather offence, and puniſhment ? Wherupon Perkins in plaine
tearms affirmeth that our righteouſnes is
not capable of merit, and vtterly renoun-
ceth al merit of man. And Caluin not only
abhorreth the name of merit, affirming it
to be proude , and to obſcure Gods grace,
and to make men proude , but profeſſeth
that *our good vvorks are euer ſprinkled vvith many
filthineſſes for vvhich God may be iuſtly offended,
and angry vvith vs : ſo far* (ſaith he) *are they from
purchaſing his fauour , or procuring his liberality
towards vs.* Thus we ſee how conformably
                                        Bel

Bel pag. 77.

Contradict. 16.

pag. 79.
Durand. 2. d.
27. quæſt. 2.
expreſly ad-
mitteth con
digne me-
rit.
Cap. 1. parag.
2.

Perkins re-
fot. Cathol.
Of merits.
p. 112. 104.
Caluin. 3. in-
ſtit. c. 15. pa-
rag. 4. & 2.

Bel speaketh to his owne, and his fellow Ministers doctrine.

Bel against his fellovv Ministers.

4. Second Conclusion. Good workes done in Gods grace are condignely meritorious of eternal life. This is that which Bel impugneth in this Article as a point of our faith and auoucheth it to be defyned by the Councel of Trent but falsly. For the Councel hath no word of condigne merit but only of true merit which in plaine tearms Bel him self dare not impugne or deny. *If any shal say* (saith the Councel) *that a iustified man by good works which he doth by the grace of God and merit of Iesus Christ, whose liuely member he is, doth not truly deserue increase of grace, eternal life, and consecution therof, if he departe in grace, and also increase of glory, be he accursed.* Here are good works defyned to be true merit of glory, without determining whither they be cōdigne merit therof or no. Wherupon vega who was one of the Deuines of the coūcel writeth de fid. & ope. q. 4. That some noble schoole diuines being moued (saith he) with no light arguments and vsing a certaine sober and prudent moderation, haue denyed that there is any condigne merit of eternal happines. And againe. It is certaine (saith he) that there is merit in our works and some of them be meritorious, but of what reward and how they

Tridento.sess. 6.can.32.

Vega.

they are meritorious, it is in controuersy, &
there are diuers opiniós amõgst the schoole
divines. And q. 5. he affirmeth Gregory,
Durand, Marsil, Walden, Burgensis and
Eckins to deny condigne merit. Satus also
an other diuine of the sayd Councel l. 3. de
Nat. & Grat. c. 7. saith that there is some
difference amongst Catholiques about condigne merit, and c. 8. after he had proued
condigne merit out of the Councel and
otherwaies, yet concludeth not that it is a
point of faith but only calleth it *conclusionem
probatißimam* a most approued Conclusion.
And Bellarmin whome Bel tearmeth the
mouth of Papists, lib. 5. de iustific. cap. 16.
after he had rehearsed twoe opinions of
Catholiques, wherof the one seemeth
plainly to deny condigne merit, the other
admitteth it only in a large sense, proposeth and defendeth the third opinion which
defendeth condigne merit absolutly, only
as *Verißimam & communem sententiam Theolo-
gorum*, most true and the common opinion
of Diuines as indeed it is and we shal proue
it anone againſt Bel. Hereby appeareth Bels
shameful proceeding in this Article, in impugning condigne merit as a point of faith
defyned by the Councel of Trent, which
hath no word of condigne merit, and omitting the queſtion of true merit which the
Councel

Gregor. 1. d.
17. q. 1. Du-
rand. q. 2.
Marsil. in 2.
VValden. de
sacra. c. 7.
Burgens. in
psal m. 35.
Eckins in
centur. de
predest.

Councel defyned & Catholiques defend as
a point of their faith against Protestants.

5. The third Conclusion is : that This *This see-*
condigne merit is not absolute, but suppo- *meth defy-*
ned.
seth the condition of Gods promise made Conc. Trid.
to reward it. This is held of the best Diuines fess.6. c. vlt.
& in Bulla
and proued at large by Bellarmin. l. 5 de iu- Pij 5. & Gre-
stifi. c. 14. The fourth Conclusion is that gor. 13.
This condigne merit in our works, is not
perfect, hauing actual, and perfect arithme-
tical equality before explicated: This mani- S. August. in
psal.93.to.8.
festly the Fathers teach with al Catholiques, S. Chrysost.
and Bels arguments hereafter brought con- 1. Cor. 9.
S. Bernard.
uince it, and no more. The fifte Conclusion serm 1. de
is that the imperfect codigne merit which Annuntiat.
is in our works to heauen, riseth not meerly
of Gods acceptation, but partly of the due
proportion, and sufficiency before explicated, in them to the reward. This likewise is
no matter of faith, yet truth taught by S.
Thomas 1. 2. 4. 114. ar. 1. & 3. Bonauent. S, Thomas.
S.Bonauent.
2. d.17. and Deuines in that place comonly :
Bellar : l. 5. de Iustif. c. 17. though Scot. 1. Bellarm.
Scotus.
d. 17. and some others deny it with whom
Bel also falleth in league towards the end *Bel pag 79.*
of this Article. The sixt Conclusion is : that
the said condignity riseth not of any due
proportion, which is in the substance of our
worke if it be considered in it selfe, but as it
is the fruit of the holy Ghost mouing vs to
do it,

do it, and the effect of Gods grace helping vs in doing it : which grace *making vs parta-* *kers* (as S. Peter speaketh) *of deuine nature,* so dignifyeth our works, as (according to S. Paul) *we walke vvorthely of God, and become* *vvorthy of Godskingdome.* And becaufe Bel denyeth none of thefe Conclufions but the fecond and fieft, them only wil I proue.

1. Pet. 1. v. 4.

Coloff. 1. v. 10.

2. Theffal. 1. v. 5.

6. That good works are a condigne, or worthy merit of heauen in the fenfe before explicated, followeth of that they are a true merit therof, becaufe as I thinke only condigne merit is true merit. For congrual merit hath no iuftice in it (as appeareth in good works difpofing to iuftification, which fome cal congrual merits) and therfore no true merit, which can not be without fome title of iuftice. But I proue it other waies : Firft becaufe the Theffalonians fuffered to be made or accounted worthy of Gods kingdom 2. Theff. 1. v. 5. Ergo : fufferances make men worthy or (which commeth to one purpofe) to be truly accounted worthy of Gods kingdom. Secondly. Apocalip. 3. v. 4 : *They haue not defyled their garments, and* *they shal vvalke vvith me in vvhite, becaufe they be* *vvorthy* Ergo : Saints are worthy to walke with God in glory. Thefe places make Proteftanrs confeffe that Sainćts are worthy of heauen, but haue a shift of faying *They are* *vvorthy*

S. Paul. Eis to cata-Ziothenai bumas.

Apocal.

vvorthy for Chrifts merits, not for their ovvne. But
as plainly as S. Paule affirmeth the Theffalonians to be worthy of Gods kingdome,
fo plainly he affirmeth their worthines to
come of their owne fufferances. And likewife S. Ihon afcribeth the worthines of
Saints, to their not defyling their garments,
which is their owne merit. Moreouer
Chrift fpeaking of mans labours, faith. *The
worker is worthy of his hyer* Luc. 10. v. 7.
And we worke our faluation. Philip. 2. v.
12. And S. Auftin epift. 105. faith that *Eternal life is giuen to the merit of our iuftice, as
death is to the debt of our finne, and that God
crowneth our merits.* And in pfal. 93. that *we
buy heauen with labour*. Therfore the worthines of Saints proceedeth from their
owne merits, though it proceed alfo from
the merits of Chrift. For we are *branches, he
the vyne,* & therfore as grapes, which fpring
out of the branches, proceed from the
vyne, which giueth them their vertue: foe
al worthines, which proceedeth from
Saints, rifeth from Chrift as the roote and
fountaine thereof.

7. Thirdly: condigne merit requireth
not perfect, and arithemetical equality in
the worke to the rewarde, but only proportion: but good workes haue proportion to
glory. Therfore they are condigne merits

Perkins re-
fot. Cathol.
of merits.
p. 113.

S. Luke.
S. Paul.
S. Auftin.

Ioan. 15. 7.
5.

P   thereof:

thereof: The Proposition Bel him selfe pag. 77. alleadgeth, and approueth out of Ihon de Combis, and it is euident in mens deserts of a Bishopricke, which being a spiritual dignity passeth al price, and yet may be worthely deserued of men: The assumption shal be proued a none. Nether is our condigne meriting of heauen either blasphemous against Gods free mercy, or iniurious to Chrifts merits, as Bel bableth, but rather honourable. For though eternal life, as it is giuen to good workes, be mercy, or grace, (as S. Paul calleth it) yet neuer shal Bel proue, that it is meere mercy, or grace. Our Sauiour calleth it a *rewarde,* and saith we *get it by violence.* S. Ihon according to S. Austins exposition calleth it grace for grace, that is, grace of glory not absolutly, but for grace of merits, or grace mixt with iustice. S. Paul calleth it a goale, a crowne of iustice. The Fathers cal it a stipend, a debt. And by whose authority then doth Bel cal it a meere grace, or mercy. Harken to S. Paul. 1. Timoth.6. Bel, and leaue these same nouelties of wordes.

8. Likewise it is not iniurious to Chrifts merits but rather honourable to them. For as it is not iniurious to Gods doing good, that we by his grace do good for our selfs, but rather honourable according to our

Sauiours

Infra parag. 9.

Bel pag 61.
Rom. 6. v. 23.
Math. 5. v. 12.
Math. 11. v. 11.
Ioan. 1. v. 16.
S. Austin. epist. 105.
Philip. 3. v. 14.
2. Timoth. 4. v. 8.
S. Austin ep. 105.
S. Ambros. in c.6. Rom.
S. Chrysost. hom. 7. Rom.
S. Gregor. Nazianz. orat. 3. in S. lauacrum.
Our merits honourable to Chrift.

Sauiours saying. *In hoc clarificatus est pater* Ioan. 15. v. 8. *&c.* In this my father is glorifyed: Nor to Chrifts prayer, or impetration, that we alfo through him pray and impetrate for our Our merits no more iniurious to Chrifts merits then our prayer to his prayer. felfs: So likewife it is not iniurious to Chrifts meriting, but rather honourable therto, that we alfo through him, and as his liuely members do in fome fort merit for our felfs. What iniury is it to the tree that the branch thereof bringeth forth fruit: nether are we therfore more partners with Chrift in merit, then we are by prayers partners with him in impetration.

9. That our merits haue proportion, Merits haue proportion to glory. and vertual equality to their reward followeth alfo out of the former. For condigne merit requireth at left due proportion to the reward, but efpecially I proue it. Firft becaufe the reward confifteth in the cleare fight of God face to face, and in perfect loue of him, and our merit confifteth principally in faith which is a fight, or knowledge of God in a glaffe, and in louing him aboue al things. But there is due proportion between the fight of a thinge in a glaffe, and the cleare fight thereof, and betwixt perfect loue, and the loue aboue al things: Ergo: Secondly good workes are fruits of the holy Ghoft. Galat. 5. v. 22. and of Chrifts paffion: for by it we do thefe

good

good workes. Ergo it is iniury to the holy
Ghoſt, and to Chriſt to ſay that their ſuper-
natural fruits haue no proportion to a ſu-
pernatural rewarde. Thirdly glory is grace:
Rom. 6. Ioan. 1. and our merits are grace,
but there is proportion between two graces: 4. Grace is the ſeed of glory according to that 1. Ioan. 3. *The ſeed of God remai-*
neth in him, therfore in vertue it conteineth
glory as the ſeed doth the tree: 5. Glory is a
floode making glad the citty of God pſal.
45. and grace is a fountaine of water lea-
ping into eternal life. Ioan. 4. but there is
proportion between a floode and a fountaine which ſpringeth into the place of the
floode. Now let vs come to Bels arguments, which beſide that they impugne
no matter of faith as is before ſaid, they
diſproue no ſuch condignity of merit as
Catholiques teach, and is already explicated, but ſuch as is both abſolute, and perfectly equal to the rewarde. And at laſt
after he had runne him ſelfe out of breath,
confeſſeth that he can not impugne condigne merit as it is defended by Bellarmin,
who in truth teacheth no other herein then
is the common doctrine of the Church.

CHAP.

Chap. IIII.
Bels arguments out of Scripture against condigne merit answered.

His firſt argument is taken out of S. *Bel pag. 62.* Paul Rom. 6. v. 23. *To de Chariſma tou theou Zoe aionios en Chriſto Ieſou to curio hemon:* which he citeth in greeke perhaps to make the Reader beleeue he hath great skil in that tongue though the wordes be in his booke neither accented nor printed right; but remitting this fault to the printer, the text he englisheth thus: *But the gift of God is life euerlaſting in Chriſt Ieſus our lorde* and then argueth in this manner. Eternal life is the free gift of God, therfore it can be no way due to the merit of mans workes.

2. Anſwer: Firſt the conſequent ſee-meth oppoſite to this other propoſition of his: pag. 77. *Eternal life is due to the workes of Gods elect.* Secondly the Antecedent is falſe, *Foure rea-ſons why eternal life is grace.* and neither here, nor any where els taught by S. Paul. He calleth here eternal life grace, as it may be called for diuers cauſes: 1. becauſe God gratiouſly couenanted with 1. vs to giue it as a rewarde of our good wor-kes, which (we being his ſlaues by creation) he might haue exacted of vs without any rewarde at al. This is S. Thomas his reaſon: S. Thomas.

 I. 2.

2.

1. 2. q. 114. art. 2. 2. becaufe the workes them felues for which God giueth vs life eternal, were freely giuen vnto vs by Gods grace. This is S. Auftins reafon epift. 105.

S. Auftin.

3.

3. becaufe the workes haue no perfect a-ctual equality to eternal life, but only vir-tual, and proportionate, and this reafon gi-

Theodoret.

ueth Theodoret. in cap. 6. Rom. where he faith that temporal paines, and eternal ioyes

Bel pag. 63. Fals tran-flation. 4.

in æquilibrio non refpondent, and Bel falfly tran-flateth, *are nothing anfwerable.*   4. becaufe as

4.

workes are rewarded euen aboue their vir-tual and proportionate equality as Deuines fay *vltra condignum.* No maruel if S. Paul called eternal life rather grace, or gift, then a ftipend, feeing it hath much more of grace then it hath of iuftice: yet notwithftanding he no where called it meere grace, yea in

1. Cor. 3. Philip 3. v. 14. 2. Timoth. 4. v. 8.

calling it *a rewarde, a goale, and crowne of iuftice* he clearly declareth that it is no meere grace, nor free gift: befide that as S. Auftin writeth epift. 105. he might haue called it

S. Paul might haue called glory a ftipend. S. Auftin.

a ftipende as he calleth death in refpect of finne, but forbore left we should thinke it were fo iuftly deferued by good workes, as death is by euil. And perhaps he called it fo in the next verfe before, where he calleth

Beza Rom. 6.

eternal life in greeke *telos,* which as Beza confeffeth may there fignify *vectigal* or *mer-cedem,* and is equiualent to ftipend.

3. Not-

3. Notwithstanding this, Bel exclaimeth against the Rhemists that *they translated Charisma grace in steed of gift, for to extenuate the clearnes of this text* : wherin he sheweth his malice, and folly. For malice it is to accuse men to corrupt Scriptures of set purpose, and to bring no proofe therof, yea to confesse (as he doth) that *they follow the auncient Vulgar edition,* of which S. Hierom was either Author, or amender. And folly it is, to condemne that translation as done for to extenuate the clearnes of Scripture , and withal to confesse (as he doth) that it is according to the olde vulgar edition, and that it may be here admitted, and to approue an other translation of Donation or Gift (which maketh no more for his purpose then Grace, which him selfe in the next page englisheth Free grace,) and finally to alleadge in his owne behalfe Theodoret. S. Chrisostom, Origen , Ambros, Theophilact and Paul of Burges, whoe al in the very places which he citeth for him selfe, read as the Rhemists translate grace, though some of them explicate it by Gift, as it is indeed, though no free gift.

4. But let vs heare why the Rhemists did not wel translate the worde *Charisma* by Grace. *Because* (saith he) *it signifieth a gift freely bestowed.* If so Syr, why did not you, your

P 4　　　mates,

pag. 62.

In cap. 6. ad Rom.

Bel sup.
Perkins refor Cathol. p. 107.

Bibles printed by Barker. 1584.

mates, and your Bibles so translate it, but absolutly by gift. So you condemne other, and commit your selfe the like fault. Remember what S. Paul saith to such Rom. 2.

But how proueth he *Charisma* to signify a Gift freely giuen. Forsooth *autos ephe* This great Grecian hath said it contrary to the Lexicons made and printed by Protestants, who make *Charisma* al one with *Charis*, and to signify Grace, or gift without mention of Free gift; contrary to the old vulgar translation, contrary to the vniforme reading of Fathers, contrary to his owne, and his fellows translations. Are these your cleare and euident demonstracions, which shal be able to put al Papists (as you promise) to silence for euer in this behalfe?

Lexicon Grӕci Basilӕ. 1539. vvho citeth Budӕus. Lexicon Gesneri auctū per Arlemium, Iunium, Hartengum, Basilӕ.

pag. 61.

5. *Novv* (saith he) *let vs vievve the iudgement of holy Fathers vpon this text.* With a good wil Syr; But marke good Readers how the Fathers are holy, their wordes are golden, their mouthes golden, and them selfes glistering beames and strong pillers of Gods Church, when they seeme to make for Bel, who otherwise amongst Protestants are but plaine Austin, and Hierom, and their doctrine stubble, errors, (spottes, & blemishes: Likewise when Popish writers seeme to fauour Bel, they are with him famous, renow-

See Bel p. 61. 64. 65. 71. 75. 67. 59. 104. 132.

nowned, zealous, great fchoole doctors, great Clerks indeed, whoe other whiles are but parafites, and dunces.

6. Firft he produceth out of Theodoret in c. 6. Rom. that *S. Paul did not cal here eternal life a revvarde, but grace, becaufe it is the gift of God, and al our labours are not of equal poife vnto it.* This is nothing againft vs who neither fay that S. Paul did in this verfe cal eternal life a rewarde, nor deny that it is the gift of God, nor affirme, that our labours are of equal poife vnto it. Next he produceth S. Chrifoftom in c. 6. Rom. writing, that *The Apoftle called not eternal life a revvarde, but grace* (as Brixius tranflateth) or *gift,* (as Bel hath) *to shevv that they vvere deliuered not by their ovvne ftrength, nor that there is debt, revvarde, or retribution of labour, but that al thofe things came by Gods grace,* or (as Bel hath) *they receaued them freely by Gods gift.* Here S. Chrifoftom at the firft fight feemeth to deny eternal life to be a rewarde or retribution of good workes, which is not only contrary to Scripture Gen. 15. 2. paralip 15. prouerb. 11. pfal. 118. Sapient 5. Ecclef. 18. Ifai. 40. Math. 5. 1. Corinth. 3. Apoca. vlt. v. 12. but euen to him felfe hom. 43. in 1.Corinth. faying, that *VVe shal haue perfect revvarde, and moft ful retribution not only for the good vve do, but alfo for the euil vve fuffer.* And hom. 1. de Refur.

pag. 62. Theodoret.

S. Chryfoft. p. 63.

Genef. v 1. Prouerb. v. 18. 2. Paralip. v. 7. Sap. v. 16. Eccl. v. 22. Ifai. v. 10. Math. v. 12. 1. Corinth. v. 8. S. Chryfoft.

Resur. tom 3. *VVhat care* (saith he) *vvil he haue of vertue, vvho expects no retribution of labours*: And hom. 15. in Math. that we haue God our debtor, when we do any good, and may exact vsury of him. And the like speeches he hath hom. 3. and 36. in Math. and 42. in Gen. and in Philog. and other where, which alone might assure vs, that he meaneth not to deny eternal life to be a true reward of our supernatural labors. But ether by labors he vnderstandeth natural labors done (as he speaketh there) *by our ovvne strēgth*, of which labors doubtles eternal life is is no reward, debt, or retribution. Or rather, by eternal life he there vnderstood not heauenly glory, but only iustificatiō, which he may cal eternal life, because it causeth eternal life, as our Sauiour for the same

S. Ihon. cause calleth faith so, Iohn 17. v. 3. and for the contrary sinne is called death, and this doubtles is no reward, debt, or retribution of any labour at al of ours. That this is his meaning I proue it: 1. because he saith eternal life was called grace to shew that they were not deliuered &c. Therfore by eternal life he vnderstandeth some thing, which had deliuered the Romans already from some thing vz. from sinne 2. because he saith that they, to whom S. Paul wrote had receaued that eternal life, wherof he speaketh

but

but they being yet aliue had not receaued eternal glory, but only iuſtification. And S. Chriſoſtom being thus expounded ſpeaketh not againſt him ſelfe other where, nor a-gainſt Scripture, and truth.

7. Thirdly he cyteth Origen ſaying. *Deum vero non erat dignum militibus ſuis ſtipendium quaſi debitum aliquod dare, ſed donum, & gratiam, quæ eſt vita æterna*: which Bel thus engliſheth. But it was not a thing worthy beſeeming God to giue ſtipends to his ſol-diers, as a due debt or wage, but to beſtow on them a gift, or free grace, which is eternal life. Here Bel tranſlateth *donum* a gift, and *gratiam* free grace, albeit before he prefer-red the word *donatio* which is al one in this matter with *donum*, before *gratia*, be-cauſe it better inſinuateth the freenes of the gift. But if you aske him wherfore he tran-ſlateth *gratia*, free grace, he can giue no bet-ter reaſon then his Grandſier Luther did when he tranſlated *fides iuſtificat*, faith alone iuſtifyeth vz: *Sic volo, ſic iubeo, ſtat pro ratione voluntas*. As for Origen he meaneth nothing els, but that it beſeemed not God to giue a ſtipend ſo due to good works, *as* (ſaith he) *the king of ſinne payeth ſtipends due to them, that obey his tyranny, which is moſt true*. For al-though the iuſt by good works deſerue life, yet not ſo iuſtly, as the wicked by ſinne de-

ſerue

Bel *pag. 63.* Origen.in *o. 6. ad Rom.*

Falſe tran-ſlat. A. 5.

Surius *Anno 1530.*

S. Auſtin *ep. 105. to. 2.* S. Anſelm. Rom. *6.*

serue death, nether is life so due to them, as death to these, as is euident by what hath

VVillet controu.17. q. 3. art.3.p.587.

bene said before, and Willet in affirming vs to teach the contrary sheweth a trick of his Ministery.

pag. 63. S. Ambros. Rom. 6.

8. S. Ambrose he also alleadgeth, but his words are rather against him, for he saith. *As the followers of sinne get death, so the followers of Gods grace, that is the faith of Christ, which forgiueth sinnes shal haue eternal life.* What is here for Bel, or rather not against

S. Ambros.

him. But most clearly doth S. Ambrose confound Bel immediatly before the words cyted. *VVho from hence forth (saith he) absteine from sinne receaue a stipend eternal life.* And serm. 7. in psal. 118. affirmeth that Dauid could say to God *I am a souldier, I exact a stipend of my captaine.*

Theophilact.Rom.6.

9. He citeth also Theophilact because he saith, *S. Paul called eternal life grace, and not a revvard, as if he should say, for ye receaue not revvards of labours, but al these things are done by grace in Christ Iesus, who worketh, and doth them.* But this is nothing against vs, who willingly acknowledge eternal life to be grace, and not to proceed of our owne labours done by our selfs, but done and wrought also by the grace of Christ: After this he citeth Anselme, and Photius but alleadgeth not their words; yet confesseth that in effect

feɛt they are the same with others, and
therfore seeing S. Anselme vpon this place
of S. Paul teacheth plainly that eternal life
is a stipend of iustice, and that S. Paul might
haue called it so, we may be assured that in
effeɛt other Fathers do cal it so, as he after
S. Ambros and S. Austin doth in expresse
words. Wherfore vainly doth Bel boast *that*
it is manifest by the foresaid testimonies of holy
Fathers that eternal life is the free gift of God, for
rather the quite contrary is manifest, because none of them say it is a free gift, or
any thing whereof it may be iustly inferred, and some of them expresly say it is a
stipend, and such a one as a souldier may
exaɛt of his captaine, such as death is to
sinne, which are euidently no free gifts.
Wherfore to helpe vp this matter he addeth
these wordes of Paulus Burgens. *He would*
not therfore say eternal life is the stipend of iustice,
because the same merits, to which it is rendred are
not of our selfs, but wrought in vs by God through
grace. These words, make not any thing for
him, but rather against him. For in that he
saith, eternal life is rendred to merits, he
insinuateth it to be no free grace, and in
saying S. Paul chose rather to cal it grace,
then stipend, insinuateth that he might
haue called it a stipend, and in saying it is
grace, because it is repaid to merits, which

we do

S. Anselme.

S. Austin ep.
105.
S. Ambros.
Rom. 6.
Bel pag. 64.
vntruth 60

Vt Retribu-
tionem non
vt gratiam
sed plane
debitum
occupas.
S. Greg. Na-
zianz. orat. 3.
in sanɛtum
lauacrum.
Burgens. ad-
dit. 2. in c. 6.
Rom.

we do by grace, he affirmeth it to be partly grace, which no Catholique denyeth.

10. The second text of Scripture Bel *False tranſlat. 6.* bringeth out of Rom. 8. v. 18. and tranſlateth thus: *I account that the afflictions of this preſent tyme are not worthy of the future glory:* Anſwer. Here is euil tranſlation: for where the Apoſtle ſaith afflictions, are *Non condigne ad futuram gloriam ouc axia pros ten mellouſan doxan,* are not condigne to the future glory Bel tranſlateth : are not worthy of the future glory. And the Apoſtles meaning is not to tel there whether ſufferances of this life be condignely meritorious , of future glory or no, but intendeth to ſay that they are not comparable to future glory ether in greatnes, or in continuance which hindereth not their condigne merit, *v. 17.* as is euident in Chriſts ſufferances. For hauing immediatly before ſaid , that we ſhal be coheirs with Chriſt, if we ſuffer with him, leſt we ſhould be vnwilling to attaine to ſuch glory by ſufferance he addeth in the verſe cited , *that ſufferances are not condigne,* (that is , not comparable in greatnes, or continuance) *to future glory.* Which meaning of his he vttereth in plaincr tearms : 2. Co-*S. Paul.* rinth. 4. v. 17. ſaying *our tribulation which preſently is momentary, and light, worketh aboue meaſure exceedingly an eternal weight of glory in*

ys.

vs. Where he ſaith our tribulations are momentary, and light, and the glory is eternal, and weighty, which he meant when he ſaid here, they are not condigne to future glory. And hereby are explicated the words both of Theodoret, and S. Anſelme vpon this place. For Theodoret ſaying the *Crovvns exceed the conflicts, and the labour is not comparable to the revvard* compareth them not in the reſpect of deſert, and reward, but in greatnes of paine, and pleaſure: *for* (ſaith he) *the labour is litle, and the gaine great.* And the ſame compariſon in bitternes of paine and greatnes of pleaſure made S. Anſelm when he ſaid. *Al the bitterneſſes of al the paines of this life should not be a digne merit to future glory:* For doubtles the bitternes of al the paines of this life is not ſo great, as the pleaſure of heauély ioyes. But this worthy Champion who challengeth al Papiſts to combat, sheweth him ſelfe ignorāt in tranſlating Theodorets words. *Superant certamina coronæ* : thus: *The conflicts of the crovvne remaine* ; taking the nominatiue caſe for the accuſatiue, and the genitiue for the nominatiue, and perhaps *ſuperant*, for *ſuperſunt* both contrary to the latine, and to ſenſe. For who heard of conflicts of a crowne, or that conflicts remaine in heauen. Surely this challenger should rather be ſet to ſchoole to learne latine then to chal-

S. Anſelm. Rom. 8.

Bel vvanteth latin.

to challenge Deuines to difputation, rather taught to conftrue the Fathers, then to difpute out of them. But as S. Hierome wrote epift. ad Euagr. *Imperitia confidentiam parit.* None fo bold as blinde Bayard.

S. Hieron.

Bel pag. 65.

11. The third text he cyteth is out of S. Paul Tit. 3. v. 5. *Not by vvorks of iuftice, which we haue done, but according to his mercy he hath faued vs by the lauer of regeneration, and renouation of the holy Ghoft. By* which vvords (faith Bel) *it is moft cleare that* we *are not only iuftifyed, but alfo faued by meere mercy, and confequently eternal life hath no merit vpon the behalfe of man.* Omitting that before our good works were merit in a godly fenfe, & now there is no merit on mans behalfe: I anfwer, that the Apoftle meaneth only of fauing from finne. vz iuftification. Firft becaufe fpeaking of him felfe, and others then aliue he faith *God hath faued vs*: Secondly becaufe hauing faid in the third verfe. *VVe vvere fomtymes vnwife incredulous &c.* he addeth v. 5. and *God according to his mercy hath faued vs,* vz. from the forefaid finnes. Thirdly becaufe explicating by what means God had faued them, he faith it was *by the lauer of regeneration, and renouation of the holy Ghoft,* which moft plainly expreffeth iuftification. And no doubt but faluation from finne proceedeth of Gods meere mercy but this is not to the purpofe. And of this

faluаfaluation fpeaketh S. Anfelme vpon this place, whofe words Bel curtailed leauing out thefe words, *By the lauer of regeneration, and renouation of the holy Ghoft, that is, by baptifme,* becaufe they clearly shew of what faluation this holy Saint did meane. And of the fame meant Dionif. Carthuf. vpon this *Carthuf.* place as is plaine by his explicating what the faluation was, vz. *from povvre of the Dyuel, and guilt of eternal torment.* And thus much of Bels firft reafon out of Scripture now to his arguments out of Fathers.

Chap. V.
Bels arguments out of holy Fathers againft condigne merit anfvvered.

S. Auftin he alleadgeth epift. 29. ad Hieron, whofe words I wil fet downe at
large that the Reader thereby may fee how
falfly Bel auoucheth him to confirme his
doctrine. *Charity* (faith he) *is a vertue, with which we loue that, which is to be loued. This is great in fome, in others les, in others none at al, but moftful charity, which can be no more encreafed, is in none, whiles a mã lyueth here, but whiles it may be encreafed furely that vvhich is les then it should be, is ex vitio, of vice.* (Bel tranflateth finne) *by reafon of vvhich vice there is no iuft on earth, which doth good, and finneth not: by reafon of*

Q   *which*

Which Vice no liuing man shal be iustifyed in Gods sight. For vvhich Vice if vve say we haue no sinne we seduce our selfes, and there is no truth in Vs. For which also though vve haue profited neuer so much, we must of neceßity say Forgiue Vs our trespasses, euen when our vvords, deeds, & thoughts are already forgiuen in baptisme.

pag. 67.
vntruth 61

2. Hence Bel gathereth 1. *That S. Austin saith that no man can haue charity in that perfect degree Which the lavv requireth.* This is vntrue: for he only saith, that no man hath in this life that most ful charity, which can not be encreased. 2. *That the Want therof proceedeth of Vice.* This is true, but of what kinde of vice he meant, him selfe had explicated a litle before in the same place: saying: *VVho therfore is Without some Vice, that is Without some fomite, or as a roote of sinne.* Wherfore he meant not that the want of most ful charity proceedeth of formal sinne, but of that which is cause, and roote of sinne, to wit, concupiscence. And by this are answered al the rest of Bels notes out of this place. As that by reason of this vice euery man is a sinner, none iustified before God, if we say we haue no sinne we be lyers, we haue need to aske God forgiuenes euen after baptisme. For al these things are verifyed of Concupiscence, not formally but effectiuely, that is, Concupiscence (which S. Austin calleth vice, becauſe

becaufe it is the roote, and caufe of formal vice) caufeth finne in vs, which finne maketh **vs** formally finners, not iuftifyed before God, and to neede forgiuenes euen after baptifme. And hereby are explicated the like words of S. Ambrofe which hereafter he citeth: *That by reafon of the rebellion of the flesh that is vnderftood of euery one, which s. Ihon faith. If we fay we haue no finne we feduce our felfs.*

Bel pag. 68.

S. Ambrof. e-pift. 84. to. 4. prope finem

3. But fuppofe that S. Auftin had faid al that Bel inferreth, though it would proue Concupifcence to be formal finne, yet would it not proue that our workes are no condigne merit, which is the queftion now in hand. For though Concupifcence were as Bel rhinketh venial finne, which he art. 9. calleth finne not regnant, yet might other fupernatural works of ours, as faith, hope, and charity be condigne merit. But Bel careth not how he fpeaketh to the purpofe fo he fay fomwhat: Euen fo in the former Article when he should proue Concupifcence to be finne, he proued our merits to be none, and now when he should proue our merit to be none he proueth Concupifcence to be finne: After this he citeth S. Auftin faying tract. 4. in 1. Ioan. that *Our iuftice of faith is imperfect.* Ergo faith Bel there is no condigne merit. wheras he should

Bel forget-teth his matter.

pag. 67.

S. Auguftin. to. 9.

haue

haue inferred the quite contrary. For if in
vs there be imperfect iustice, there is iustice, and if there be iustice, there is condigne merit to that whereto we haue iustice.
And the most that Bel could inferre for
him selfe, is that there is no perfect condigne merit, which I willingly graunt: Albeit
indeed S. Austin in that place calleth not
our iustice imperfect, because there is any
thing wanting to it selfe, which is requisit
to iustice, for epist. 105. he calleth it true

S. Augustin.
to. 2.

Tract. 4. cit.

iustice, but because we, who haue it, *delight
in other things, and haue rebellion,* which things
being seperated from it, *our iustice* (saith he)
shal be perfected vz. not by any addition but
by seperating our iniustice from the company of it.

Bel pag. 68.
S. Chrysost.
l 2. de com-
punction.
cordis.

4. He citeth also S. Chrisostom affirming that *Though we dye a thousand tymes, and
accomplish al vertues of the mynde, yet do we nothing worthy to those things, which ipsi percepi-
mus, we haue receaued of God :* But besides that
S. Chrisostome speaketh not of eternal glory, but of benefits of this life, which we

False tran-
slat. 7.

(saith he) *haue receaued,* and Bel falsly englis-
hed, *we receaue.* He is to be vnderstood of
perfect equality, or of works considered in
their owne nature not as they proceed of

pag. 69.

grace, and are fruit of the holy Ghost. Next
he alleadgeth Theophilacts words in c. 3.
　　　　　　　　　　　　　　　　　Tit.

Tit. *He hath saued vs for euer, not of works which we did, that is, nether did we works of iustice, nether by them are we saued, but al our saluation his goodnes, and clemency hath wrought.* But besides that these words I found not in that place, they may be vnderstood of saluation from sinne, vz. of iustification: as appeareth because the text which they expound, doth so meane, as is before proued, as also speaking of men aliue he saith *we are saued,* which he calleth saluation for euer, because iustification is such in hope, according to that Rom. 8. v. 24. *Spe salui facti sumus.*

5. Bel finding so few Fathers to speake any thing, to his purpose, thought best to supply the rest of this chapter with the words, of S. Bernard, and Angles, whom he confesseth to be Papists, though his Maister Caluin accounted S. Bernard a holy man, and his brother Perkins citeth him as a Father of the auncient Church such *rara est concordia fratrum Protestanticorum.* Angles he tearmeth a famous, and one of our best Doctors, though he be a very late, and meane writer, and of purpose impugned the Protestants. But let his handling of Angles be to the Reader an example and taste of his foule vsage of Fathers, and other writers.

6. *And other holy Doctors also* (saith Angles

Theophilast.

Cap. 4. parag. 11.

Bel pag. 69. 70.

Caluin lib.4. instit.cap. 7. parag 22. Perkins refor. Cathol. Of merits. p. 109. pag. 70. Bel promise: y̆ to yaeld if he haue charged any Author faisly. Preface of his chalēg. Angles 2. sent.p. 103.

Q 3 accor-

according to Bels translation) *considering*
after the same manner, the natural valew only of
good works, and perceauing that it is exceeding far
distant from the valew, and iust estimation of
eternal life said wisely. That our works, are not
meritorious of eternal life. Yet for the couenant
and promise made vnto vs, the good works of man
with the helpe of Gods grace are worthy of eternal
life, and equal with it, which for al that, that
promise of God (which is frequent in the Scripture)
set aside, were altogether vnworthy of so great re-
vvard. Hereupon Bel auoucheth Angles to

pag. 70.

graunt that *al holy Fathers with one assent af-*

vntruth 62

firme (a testimony (saith he) almost incredible to
proceed from the mouth of a Papist so deare to the
Pope) That good works nether are meritorious, nor
worthy of eternal life. And in the margent addeth this note: *Loe this fryer graunteth that al*
holy Fathers are against Papists.

A taste of
Bels false
changing
Authors.

7. But better may I say this is a slaunder almost incredible to proceed from the mouth
of a Minister, if his ministery were not in
lying. Angles said that *al holy Fathers affirme*
our good works not to be meritorious of eternal life,
according to their natural valew, & the same al
Catholiques now affirme? Is this absolutly
to say, that al holy Fathers affirme good
works are not meritorious? So thê, because
one may say, that Bel according to his natural valew is no better then an infidel, an
other

other may abſolutly ſay,he is no better then
an infidel,or rather worſe, becauſe *qui fidem*
negauit eſt infideli deterior : This ſlaunder is ſo
euident , as him ſelfe ſoone after is faine to
côfeſſe that Angles ſaith *The Fathers ſpeake of*
good works only in reſpect of their natural valevv.
So il hath he learnt that firſt leſſon of his oc-
cupation *mendacê oportet eſſe memorem.* His ſecond note out of Angles is: that he grâuteth
good works côſidered in their owne nature
to be vnworthy of eternal life. This is true,
& taught by vs before, & confirmed by S.
Auſtin epiſt. 105. ſaying.*Nothing but grace ma-*
keth al our good works. Thirdly he noteth in
Angles that he graunteth *good works euen as*
they proceed of grace are vtterly vnworthy of eter-
nal life if Gods free promiſe, & acceptation be ſet
a part. True it is, that Angles, as a follower
of Scotus, ſeemeth to thinke that the condignity of good works to eternal life, riſeth
not of any equality which is in them vnto
glory:but of Gods promiſe to reward them,
which is a far different queſtion from this,
as is before explicated : yet withal in the
very words cited he profeſſeth them *to be,*
(ſuppoſing the ſaid promiſe, which is euery
where founde in Scripture) *vvorthy of eter-*
nal life and equal vnto it. Let now any indifferent Reader iudge what face Bel had when
vpon theſe words of Angles he wrote that

1. *Timoth.*
5.v.8.

Contradict.
17.

*pag.*70.

S. Auguſtin.
to.2.

Hæretico-
rum frons
nô eſt frons
ſi non mem-
brum quod
fecit Deus
ſed pudo-
rem intelli-
gas. Aug. 4.
cont.Iul. c.3.
to. 7.
vntruth 63.

vntruth 64 *Papifts graunt as much as* vve (Proteftants) *de-fire, and that* vve (Proteftants) *defend nothing herein, but euen that* vvhich *their ovvne beft Do-ctors in their printed books do teach.*

Belpag. 71.   8. Out of S Bernard he alleadgeth thefe
S. Bernard.   words ferm. 1. de annunt. *The fuffering of this time are not condigne to future glory, no, not if one fuffer al*; *For the merits of men are not fuch as eter-nal life is due to them ex iure,* (of iuftice) *that God should do any iniury if he gaue it not.* Here-upon Bel inferreth diuers things, but al depend of his falfe vnderftanding the words iuftice, and iniury. For S. Bernards mea-ning is only to deny, that al the fufferings of this life can be abfolute, and perfect e-qual merit of glory, depending of no grace, or promife of God to reward them: but that God of his meere iuftice, without al refpect of mercy should be bound to repay them with eternal life, and otherwife should do abfolute iniury. And meaneth not to deny that fuppofing Gods gratious promife of re-warding works, and affiftance in doing them, heauen is due to them of fome iu-ftice , and that he should do fome iniury if
S.Augustin,   he did not giue heaue. For as S. Auftin faith
to. 7.   l. 4. con. Iulian, c. 3. *God him felfe shal be vn-iuft if the true iuft be not admitted to his kingdome.*
S.Paul.Heb.   And the fame infinuateth S. Paul, when
6, v. 10,   writing to the Hebrews he faith God is not
vniuft

vniuſt to forget their worke, as if he should
do ſome iniuſtice, if he should forget it.

9. Next he citeth his words ſerm. 67. in *pag.* 71.
Canti: *It wanteth to grace whatſoeuer thou aſ-*
cribeſt to merits. I wil no merit which excludeth
grace. I abhorre whatſoeuer is of myne, vnles per-
haps that is more myne which maketh me myne
owne, Grace reſtoreth me to my ſelfe freely iuſti-
fyed, and ſo deliuered from ſlauery of ſinne. Here
Bel noteth diuers things againſt al merit & *pag.* 72.
auoucheth moſt falſly *S. Bernard to renounce al* *vntruth* 65.
merit of man whatſoeuer. Wheras the B. Saint
ſpeaketh only againſt meere humaine merit,
done by our owne powre without aſſiſtance of grace, ſuch ſaith he excludeth grace,
and is of our owne. And ſuch indeed he and
al Catholiques renounce, and leaue to the
Pelagians, but willingly he accepteth ſuch
merit as proceedeth from grace, and (as he
ſpeaketh) maketh me myne owne.

10. Laſtly he alleadgeth his words ſerm. *pag.* 71.
68. in Cant. *So there is no cauſe, why thou ſhoul-*
deſt now aske by what merits we hope for goods,
eſpecially ſeeing thou hearest the Prophet ſaying.
Not for you, but for me I wil do it ſaith our Lord.
It ſufficeth to merit, to know that merits ſuffice not.
But as it ſufficeth to merit not to preſume of merits,
ſo to want merits is enough to iudgement. Bel in- *pag.* 72.
ferreth that *the moſt ſufficiet merit in man is to* *vntruth* 66
know and confeſſe, that our merits are no merits
indeed.

indeed. Did euer honeſt man deale thus. S.
Bernard ſpeaketh not of the moſt ſufficient
merit, but only telleth what ſufficeth to a
merit : vz. not to preſume of merits which
no doubt is an act of humility, and a meritorious act. And leſt of al dreamed that our
merits are no merits (yea plainly affirmeth
that to want merits ſufficeth to be damned)
but only telleth vs that our merits ſuffice
not vz: without Gods mercy of pardoning
our ſinnes, and gratious promiſe of rewarding them, which is only to deny abſolute,
& perfect equal merit, which we alſo with
him deny. But marke good Reader how

pag. 61.

Bel, who before admitted our merits in a
godly ſenſe, now plainly auoucheth them to
be no merits, which plainly diſcryeth his
godly ſenſe of expounding merit by Impetration, to be an vngodly ſhift of his for to
delude the authorities of Fathers, expreſly
auouching merit. And thus much of his
proofs out of Fathers. Now let vs view his
proofs out of Popiſh writers.

CHAP. VI.
Bels arguments out of late Catholique
vvriters againſt condigne merit
anſvvered.

THE firſt Papiſt which Bel citeth is S.
Thomas 1. 2. 4. 114. ar. 1. *It is manifeſt*
that

that betvveene God, and man, there is moſt great inequality, for there is infinit diſtance betvveene them, al the good Vvhich *is mans is from God.* VVherfore *mans iuſtice receaued of God can not be according to abſolute equality, but according to a certaine proportion, to* vvit, *in as much as ether* vvorketh *according to his manner. But the manner, and meaſure of humaine povvre in man is from God, and therfore mans merit before God can not bee but according to the ſuppoſal of Gods ordinance, to* vvit, *ſo that man obtaine of God by his vvorke that as a revvard, to* Vvhich *God hath deſigned him povvre to* Vvorke. Hence Bel infer- *pag. 73.* reth diuers things. ι. *That* S. Thomas telleth vs *vntruth 67 that vvhere there is not perfeɛt equality, there is no merit properly.* This is an vntruth properly, for Aquinas denyeth only merit or iuſtice according to abſolute equality, yea affirmeth that proportionate merit may be betwixt them that infinitly differ. 2. *That there is infinit inequality betvvixt God and man* : This is a needles note made only to fil roome, and make number. 3. *That mans iuſtice is not abſolute, but imperfeɛt.* This is true, and we teach the ſame. But marke how he noteth this to be the doɛtrine of Aquinas, which a none he wil ſay is Proteſtantiſme.

2. That *Aquinas graunteth* vvillingly *that* vntruth 68 *man doth merit nothing in Gods ſight ſaue only by* vvay *of his free acceptation.* This is an vn- truth

truth willingly tolde. For Aquinas only
faith. *That man can not merit any thing of God,*
but only according to the presupposal of his ordi-
nance, that is, vnles God had promised, and
ordeined to reward our merit, and graunteth (as is said) that we haue proportionate
merit, and therfore only denyeth absolute
merit: 5. *That Aquinas confesseth that eternal*
life is not properly hyre. This is vntrue: For he
only faith that it is *quasi merces* as a hyre, or
reward, vnles Bel wil make S. Ihon to haue
denyed Christ to be properly the sonne of
his Father, when he said, *vve savv his glory as*
it vvere of the only begotten of his Father. And
though S. Thomas had said it were not properly hyre, his other words would enforce
vs to vnderstãd him not of al kinde of hyre,
but only of such as is betweene equals,
when one free man hyreth an other, for
such doubtles can not be betwixt God, and
man; nay it is not so perfect hyre, or iustice
as may be betwixt a man, & his bondslaue,
if he should liberally giue his slaue his labours, and promise to reward them as wel
as if he were a free man: For though such a
maister of liberality, both giue his slaue his
labours, and promise to reward them, in
which he is like to Gods dealing with vs,
yet neither doth he giue his slaue powre to
labour, nor assists him in his labour, nor rewardeth

vntruth 69

Ioan. 1. *v.*
14.

Note this
example.

1.
2.
3.

wardeth him aboue defert of his labour, as
God of his liberality doth with vs. And
therfore our reward hath leſſe the nature
of hyre then the wages of ſuch a ſlaue
ſhould haue. And yet notwithſtanding it is
not a free gift, as almes is to a beggar, or a
benefit ſhould be to a ſlaue, if his Lord had
not beſtowed his labours vpon him, & promiſed to reward them as if he were not his
ſlaue. And hereby is reproued an other vntruth which Bel afterward auoucheth vpon   *Bel pag.76.*
S. Thomas : vz. *That he affirmeth that God is*   S.Thomas 1.
not ſaid ſimply and truly to be debtor vnto vs.   2.q.114.aft.1.
For the worde (*truly*) is by Bel vntruly ad-   *vntruth 70*
ded: And S. Thomas meaneth that he is not
ſimply and abſolutly our debtor, but vpon
preſuppoſal of his promiſe, and ordinance.

3. Many lines he citeth out of Durand to   *Bel pag.73.*
proue that he denyed códigne merit, but o-   Durand.1.d.
mitted other immediatly before where Du-   27.q.2.
rand diſtinguiſheth two kinds of merits *de*
condigno, largely & ſtrictly ſo called. *Códigne*
merit largely called (ſaith he) *is a certaine wor-*
thines, vvhich God requireth in the worke for to
revvard it vvith eternal life, and this (ſaith he)
vve haue. and in theſe words which Bel citeth denyeth only that condigne merits
vvhich is (ſaith he twiſe) *ſtrictly* (and this   *Falſe tranſ-*
word Bel left twiſe out in his tranſlation)   *ſlat. 8.*
                                             and

and properly so called, and is found betwene man,
and man, & he defyneth it to be *a voluntary*
action, vvherby revvard is so due to the vvorke, as he
to vvhom it apperteineth to giue it, is simply, and
properly vniust if he do not: which kinde of
condigne merit I also deny to be in our
works. For nether is it strictly condigne,
nor such as is betwixt man and man, nether
should God be simply coniust if he did not
reward it, as appeareth by what hath bene
said before. But suppose that Durand had
absolutly denyed al condigne merit in our
works. What hath Bel gotten more then
that one schooleman who hath many other
singuler opinions, did in this matter, which
is no point of faith, dissent from the common doctrine of Schools?

Bel pag. 175.

4. After this Bel auoucheth *Gregory of*
Arimino: Marsil: Thomas of VValden, Paul of
Burges, and Eckins, to affirme *very constantly,*
That mans works are not meritorious of eternal
vntruths
71. *life.* But this he affirmeth very vntruly, and
lest he should be tript would neither cite
their words, nor quote the place. For no
Catholique denyeth our supernatural works
to be meritorious of eternal life, though
Paul of Burges, in psalm. 35. deny them to
be meritorious *de condigno* and Walden. tom.
3. de sacramentalibus c. 7. counselleth to
absteine from the name *de condigno*, & con-
                                          gruo,

gruo, yet he exprefly auoucheth our works
to be meritorious. Gregory alfo confeffeth Gregor. 2.d.
them to be fo meritorious as in refpeſt of 17.
merit *de congruo* they may be faid to be meritorious *de condigno*: Marfilius, and Eckins
books I had not at hand to perufe, yet
doubtles they denyed not our fupernatural
works to be meritorious, but either only to
be meritorious *de condigno*, which (as I
faid) is no point of faith, or els perhaps
only to be abfolutly and perfeſtly meritorious *de condigno*, which I alfo do not deny.
But I maruel why Bel would make mention of Eckins, whofe very name bringeth
to memory that he foyled Luther fo in dif- Sur. 1519.
putation, as being admonifhed by the
Counfellors of George Duke of Saxony to
behaue him felfe modeftly he cryed out.
This matter was nether begun for God, nor fhal Luthers ab-
be ended for him. hominable
vvords.

5. Next he produceth Sotus writing Sotus lib. 3.
that perfeſt fatisfaſtion requireth that the de nat. &
whole valew proceed from the debter with- Grat.c. 6.
out any fauour at al of the Creditor, and
that there be a reftoring of an equiualent
thinge otherwife vndue. Whereupon Bel Bel pag. 75.
auoucheth him to teach, that *euery fatisfa-* vntruth 72
ſtion requireth the like conditions. This is ma-
nifeftly falfe: for he fpeaketh only of perfeſt fatisfaſtion as was the fatisfaſtion of
Chrift.

Chrift. But to Bels argument framed hereupon. *None can fatisfy for finne, therfore none
can condignely merit heauen:* I anfwer by di-
ftinguifhing the Antecedent. If it be meant
of finne it felfe I graunt it, but deny the
Confequence. And the difference is, becaufe there can be no fatisfaction at al, vnles the fatisfyer be in Gods fauour, which
can not be, vnles the finne be already pardoned, and therfore al fatisfaction fuppofeth finne to bee forgiuen freely, but merit
doth not fo fuppofe eternal life to be already giuen. But if it be meant of temporal
punifhment, which is called finne according to the Scriptures phrafe Zachar. vlt.
and oftentymes remayneth after the finne
it felfe is pardoned, as appeareth in Dauid
Moyfes, and others: I deny the Antecedent. For as Daniel faid c. 4. we may redeeme our finnes by almes, and by mercy
prouerb. 16. And albeit this fatisfaction be
not fo perfect, as it hath al the conditions
which the perfection of fatisfaction requireth, yet hath it al which the effence thereof
exacteth. Nether doth Ariftotle alleadged
by Bel teach the contrary.

6. After this becaufe Angles (as I faid
before) feemeth to fay that the condignity
of our merit rifeth only vpon the promife
of God made to reward it Bel here a new
auou-

Zachar.

*2. Reg. 12.
v. 14.
Deuter. 32.
v. 51.
Daniel. v.
24.
Prouerb. v.
6.*

Bel pag. 76.

vntruth 73.

auoucheth him *to confeſſe plainly the ſelfe ſame doctrin which he intendeth to proue,* which how true it is hath bene already shewed, and withal addeth that *this is the maine point, and only foundation to which al Papiſts do, and muſt appeale in this queſtion.* And he reproueth this by the example of the loane of a cloake in a shower of raine vpon promiſe of an hundred pownds, notwithſtanding which promiſe (ſaith he) that loane can not be condigne merit of that price. But moſt ſalſe it is that Angles his reaſon is the maine or only foundation, to which al Papiſts doe and muſt appeale in this queſtion. For to it appeale only ſuch as follow Scotus. And S. Thomas 1. 2. q. 114. ar 3. Bonauent: 2. diſt: 17. Bellarm. l. 5. de iuſtif. c. 17. and Iohn: de Combis (as Bel him ſelfe teſtifyeth) with the beſt Deuines appeale to the vertual, and proportionate equality before explicated, which is already proued to be in our merits: And account that foundation of Angles vnſure, and inpugne it better then Bel doth with his example of the loane of a cloake which maketh nothing againſt vs. For it hath not ſuch vertual, and proportionate equality to an hundred pownds, as our merits haue to glory. I omit Bels fonde inferring, that we do not condignly deſerue eternal life if (as Deuines ſay) *God re-*

Cap. 5. parag. 7.

vntruth 74

Bel pag. 77. Bel diſproueth him ſelf.

R   *ward*

ward *vs vltra condignum* aboue our deſerts.

Deuines in
4.ſent.d.46. For it only proueth that we doe not condignly deſerue that exceſſe of glory, which
S. Luke. God wil giue vs, when as Chriſt ſaith Luc.
6. v. 38. He wil giue *good meaſure, and preſſed
doẃne, and shaken together. and running ouer.*
And rather proueth that we doe condignly
deſerue ſome degree of glory. Fot if God
rewarde vs *vltra condignum,* beyond our deſerts he rewardeth vs according to our deſerts, and more two.

*pag.*77.
Lyra in c. 3.
Tit. 7. Likewiſe he citeth Lyra ſaying that
*Eternal ſaluation wholy exceedeth the power of
mans nature: Therfore he can not attaine vnto it
but by liberality of gods mercy.* True: But what?
becauſe it exceedeth the power of mans nature, wil Bel haue it alſo to exceede the power of Gods grace in which according to
Philip. 4.*v.*
13. S. Paul we cã doe al thinges: Or becauſe we
need Gods liberality vz. for to haue his promiſe of reward; his grace, and to haue the
good works, therfore can we not haue his
2. *Timoth.*
4.*v.* 8. iuſtice to giue (as S. Paul ſpeaketh) a crowne of iuſtice for our works, and conſummation of our race? Are Gods liberality and
iuſtice ſo oppoſite, as they can not concurre
to one worke? Why then did the Pſalmiſt
*Pſalm.*100.
v. 1.
9. *Falſe
tranſlat.* ſing pſal: 100. *Iudgment and mercy* to God?
This Bel would; & therfore when lyra ſaid
niſi ex largitate diuina miſericordiæ Bel engli-
shed

shed him, *But only by the liberality of Gods mercy.* adding, *only,* of his owne ſtore. And albeit Carthuſianus profeſſe that merits are not excluded, yet Bel beggeth his fauour, becauſe he writeth that *Eternal life is ſaid to be giuen as revvarde by grace, and principally attributed to grace, becauſe God revvardeth vs vltra condignum.* Who pittieth not this poore beggar, who is faine to goe to his enemyes dores a begging that, which wil doe him no good, and now and then is faine to ſteale. I haue giuen him more before, let him take that, and be thankful, and try what thereof he can gather againſt ſuch códigne merit as Catholiques defend.

8. But wil you ſee this braue champion challenger, who hitherto hath ſownded Alarme, and fought furiouſly againſt condigne merit, now at the end of this Article ſounding a Retreit, and confeſſing that, that condigne merit which Catholiques defend is too good for him to deale withal. After he had cited out of Bellarmin, that our merits are not condigne of iuſtice abſolutly, but *poſita liberali Dei promiſſione* ſuppoſing Gods liberal promiſe, (which Bel falſly tranſlateth in reſpect of Gods liberal promiſe.) And that abſolutly a man cannot exact any thinge of God, ſeeing al are his, but only ſuppoſing his wil, and couenant,

Carthuſ. in c.6.Rom.

Bel left out this. For the Elect by Grace deſerue eternal life.

Bel recanting p.79.

Bellarm.lib. 5. de iuſtific. c.16.

10. Falſe tranſlat.

nant, that he wil not exact our works of vs
for nothing, but giue vs reward according
to the proportion of our works. As a slaue
(saith he) can not absolutly demaund any
thing of his maister, seeing al the slaue getteth he getteth to his maister, yet if it please
his maister to bestow his works vpon him,
and to promise reward for them, as if they
were not due to him, the slaue may iustly
demaud reward for them, Bel I say, after he
had cited these words out of Bellarmin, and
affirmed that Bellarmin taught this after
mature consultation with the best learned
Iesuits, and the Pope him selfe telleth vs
that *Bellarmin maketh good his doctrine in them,
and that if he, and his fellowes, and followers
vvould stand constantly to their ovvne doctrine,
vvhich they publish in printed books,* vve (Protestants) *and they should soone agree, and these
controuersies vvould haue an end.*

The Triden-
tin Councel
defyned
only that
vve truly
deserue
heauen, and
Bel impug-
neth it.

9. What is this but in plaine tearms to
confesse, that he can not impugne Bellarmins printed doctrine of condigne merit,
which is the very same which al Catholiques commonly print, preach, and beleeue.
For Bellarmin in the very words cited saith.
A man may *ex iure iustly demaund revvard at
Gods hands for his vvorks:* that *our merits are ex
iustitia supposing Gods promise:* and that *God
revvardeth them secundum proportionem* according

ding to their proportion. And affirmeth
in the next chapter to thefe words that *good* Sup.cap.17.
*vvorkes are condignely meritorious of eternal life
by reafon of the couenant, and vvorke together,
not that a good vvorke should not haue proportion to eternal life vvithout the couenant, but becaufe God is not bound to recompence the vvorke
vvith that revvard, albeit it be iuft, and equal to
the revvard, vnles he before had couenanted.* Doe
you holde Syr this printed doctrine of Bellarmin, doth it like you? fpeake plainly and
renounce your meere acceptation, and
bare impetration, and be not ashamed to
fay *deuterai phrontides fophotatai*: for your fecond faith was beft.

10. But he meaneth nothing les, then
to holde Bellarmins printed doctrine, *vvhich*
(faith he other where) *is approued by the* pag. 26.
Pope, vvho hath faid al that can be faid for Po- 125. 87.
pery, and vvhofe teftimony alone is moft fufficient And p.29.
in al Popish affairs. But only by occafion of The Iefuits
his owne forefaid falfe tranflation he ho- (Bellar-
ped to make his Reader beleeue that Bel- min) do-
larmin helde condignity of merit to arife Erin is the
Popes
meerly of Gods promife, which though he ovvne do-
did (as fome Catholiques doe) belonged Erin.
not to this queftion as is before declared,
and rather fuppofeth, then denyeth condigne merit. Yet is it defended of the fame
Catholiques in a farre different fenfe as
R 3 Bellar-

Sup. c. 17. Bellarmin him selfe sheweth then of Protestants. For they thinke our supernatural
workes to be truly good, and condignely
to deserue some reward, though not so
great as eternal life is, vnles God had promised it to them: But Protestants thinke
them to be truly naught, and sinne, and to
deserue no reward, but punishment, and
that God in accepting, and rewarding them

Prouerb. 6.
v. 16.
Psal 5. v 7
Sapient. 14.
v. 9.
Apocal. 2.
v. 6.
Iudith 5. v.
21.

accepteth, and rewardeth sinne, which is
a horrible blasphemy contrary to Scripture, auouching that he hateth sinne, contrary to his goodnes, that can not accept
naughtines, and sinne, more then fyer can
water, and contrary to his iustice, which
can not reward it.

Psalm. 44.
v 8
Bel pag. 80.
S. Augustin.
lib. 9. Con-
fess. c. 13.
L. 2. de Gen.
côt. Manich.
c. 14.
L. 1. de nupt.
& concupis.
c. 29.
Serm. 5. de
verb. Apost.

11. After al this Bel alleadgeth a saying
of S. Austin *VVoe euen to the laudable life of
man, if thou discusse it setting thy mercy aside:*
which maketh litle to the purpose. For S,
Austin denounceth not woe to good mens
merits, which otherwhere he saith are
great matters, and to be crowned, but to
the men them selfs, because as they haue
merits to be crowned, so they haue deme-
rits to be punished, which if they were punished without mercy, woe should be to
them: Not because they should be sent to
hel, but to purgatory, or (as he calleth it

S. Austin. sermon. in psalm. 37.) *Emendatory fyer*, and
there

there punished without mercy, which fyer (faith he) *is more greeuous then any thing, which man can suffer in this life.* And to procure Gods mercy in this behalfe to his mothers soule he both prayed him felfe, and requested others to pray for her. Be myndful therfore (Bel) from whence thou art fallen, and do penance. Apocal. 2.

Confeff. lib. 9.c.13.eix.

R 4　　THE

THE
SIXT ARTICLE OF
THE DISTINCTION
OF MORTAL AND VE-
NIAL SINNES

CHAP. I.

The true Distinction proued, and Bels obiection ansvvered.

BE l perceauing that Catholiques do euidently proue that there is a difference betweene mortal, and venial sinnes durst not deny it, but proceedeth as

Bel pag. 81. he did in the former Article, allowing in words the distinction of mortal, and venial sinnes in a godly sense, which though he be

Bel admit- ashamed to expresse, yet doth he insinuate *teth venial* in other tearms of regnant, & not regnant, *sinnes.* and meaneth (as I suppose) that voluntary euil acts are mortal , & inuoluntary venial, which doctrine is already disproued in the fourth article. Wherfore here he vnderta-keth to proue that euery sinne is mortal of it owne nature, and some become venial only for free acceptation, & mercy of God.

2. Sup-

2. Suppoſing therfore that ſome ſinnes are mortal, and others venial, I intend to proue by Scripture, Fathers, and reaſon, that they are ſuch of their owne nature. The Scripture compareth ſuch ſinnes as are mortal, and venial to things, which of their owne nature are different as Math. 23. to a Camel, and a gnat. Luc. 6. to a ſtrawe, and a beame: Ergo: theſe kinde of ſinnes are different of their owne nature. Likewiſe our Sauiour Luc. 12. 58. compareth ſome ſinnes to mites or farthings, which of their nature are ſmal debts. Moreouer God hath no where reuealed that ſome kinde of ſins become venial only by his mercy. Therfore we ought not to ſay ſo. The Conſequence is euident. for none knoweth the pleaſure of God but by his reuelation. The Antecedent I proue: for Proteſtants can neither name the ſinnes, which God hath made venial, nor the place, where God hath reuealed any ſuch making of his. Bel citeth Math. 12. v. 3. where it is ſaid, that *VVe ſhal giue account of euery idle word.* And 1. Iohn. 3. v. 4. where ſinne is called iniquity. But in neither place it is ſaid that Gods mercy maketh any ſinne venial, and other like places cited by other Proteſtants rather proue that al ſinnes notwithſtāding Gods mercy are now mortal, then that any, which of them ſelfe were

mortal,

Mortal and venial ſinnes are ſuch of their owne nature.

Math.23.v.24.

Luc.6.v.41.

Math. 5. v. 27.

mortal, became venial by his mercy. Likewise for venial sinne he nameth sinne not
regnant, wherby he vnderstandeth inuoluntary motions of concupiscence. But for such

Bels beleefe
of venial
sinnes be-
sydes Gods
booke.

inuoluntary motiõs (which Bel rightly calleth not regnant sinne, but wrongly venial)
nether are they any true sinne as venial sinne
is; nor is it any where reuealed, that they
being of their nature mortal sins, are made
venial only through Gods mercy. Therfore
Bels beleefe of some sinnes made venial by
Gods mercy is wholy besides Gods booke.

Fathers.

3. Holy Fathers also in calling some sinnes
litle sinnes light, short, least, & daily offen-

S. Hierom.
prope fin.
S. Austin. to.
10. & 3.
S. Chrysost.
tom. 1. &
Conc. 3. in
Lazar. 10. 2.

ces: as S. Hierom in c. 5. Math. & l. 2. in Iouinian: S. Austin serm. 41. de sanctis. and
in Enchir. c. 71. and S. Chrisostom. hom.
24. in Math. insinnuate that venial sinnes
are such of their owne nature, for they were
neuer litle, nor light, if of their nature they
were mortal, and damnable: as a wounde,
which of it nature is mortal, and deadly,
could neuer be called a litle or light wounde,
though God of his mercy did cure it: Like-

S. Hierom.
dial. 2. cont.
Pelag.
S. Gregor. 21.
moral. c. 9.
S. Austin.
hom. 19. de
tempore.

wise S. Hierom putteth a difference betweene cacia, and hamartia: and S. Gregory, and S. Austin betwixt crimen and peccatum yea S. Hierom epist. ad Celant. accounteth it a paradox of the Stoiks to put no
difference betwixt scelus, and erratum.

4. By

Reason.

4. By reason alſo this is euident. For who ſeeth not that to ſteale a pinne is of it nature a ſmal offence. And I would aske of Bel whither a ſinne after it is by Gods mercy made venial, reteineth the ſelfe ſame nature of offending God, deſeruing Hel, and the like, which it had before, or it changeth it nature? If it change it nature, then after Gods mercy, of it nature it is venial, and Gods mercy is only the cauſe of changing the nature of it. If it retaine the ſelfe ſame nature, how is it poſſible, but God if he account of it truly, according ro truth (as al his iudgements are. Rom. 2. v. 2.) ſhould not account of it as a mortal ſinne, and deſeruing hel. Wherfore what Proteſtants talke of ſome ſinnes becomming venial, or no ſinnes at al, by Gods meere not imputing them for ſinnes, without any alteration in the ſinnes them ſelfs, is meere contradiction, and contrary to S. Auſtin, and reaſon as is ſhewed in the fourth Article, c. 3. parag. 4.

5. Againe: infidels haue venial ſinnes. Ergo venial ſins become not ſuch only by Gods meere not imputing them for mortal. The conſequence is cleare out of the Proteſtants doctrine, who put that *not imputing* only towards the faithful & regenerate. The Antecedent I proue becauſe they can doe al the

VVillet contrac. 17. part 3. p. 560.

ſinnes

finnes which the faithful doe. If one fay
that finnes which in the faithful, be but
venial are in Infidels mortal. This is contrary to reafon, becaufe knowledge of Gods
precept in the faithful rather encreafeth
his fault : *for the feruant which knovveth the*
vvil of his maifter, and doth it not, fhal be beaten
vvith many ftripes, and ignorance in infidels
diminifheth their fault : wherupon S. Paul
faid *I haue gotten mercy becaufe I did it ignorāt-*
ly in incredulity. And I aske of Bel why God
maketh finne not regnant, venial, rather
then regnant, and either he muft fay that
God doth it without any caufe, or becaufe
they are inuoluntary and thefe voluntary,
which is to fay, that by their different nature they are made mortal, and venial.

6. Finally fome finnes of their nature
breake frendfhip with God, and deferue his
eternal hatred, and punifhment. others do
not. Ergo : fome of their nature are mortal
others venial. The confequence is euident :
The Antecedent I proue : becaufe he is no
wife perfon, who wil fal out, and be offended for euer with his friend for euery trifle,
as the taking vp of a ftraw : nor he is a iuft
Prince, who fhould inflict death for ftea-
ling a pinne : & I beleeue Bel would thinke
him felfe vniuftly hādled if he were fo dealt
withal. Wherfore if God fhould do this we
should

Luc. 12. 7.
48.

1. *Timoth.*
1. 7. 13.

should neither account him a wise friend,
nor a iust Prince. Now let vs heare what
Bel obiecteth against this so manifest truth.

7. Al his proofs may be reduced to this *Bel pag.* 81. 82.
syllogisme, what is against Gods law is mor-
tal sinne: al sinne is against Gods law: Ergo al
sinne is mortal. Behould Bel here absolutly
cōcludeth al sinne to be mortal, & after calleth our venial sinnes cursed, & deformed,
which argueth that he thinketh al sinne to
be indeed mortal notwithstanding Gods
mercy. The Proposition he supposeth. The
Assumption he proueth out of Scripture:
Fathers, and Schoolmen. Out of Scripture
because Christ said Math. 12. v. 5. that we
shal giue account for euery idle worde: and
S. Ihon 1. c. 3. v. 4. *telleth vs that Euery sinne is
anomia that is, transgression of the lavv* : S. Ambrose also defineth sinne in general to be
transgression of Gods law: And S. Austin
describeth it to be *Euery worde, deed, or desire
against Gods law.* Bellarmin affirmeth *euery* Bellarm. lib.
sinne to be against Gods law . Rhemists also 4. de Rom.
Pont. c. 21.
confesse, *Euery sinne to be a swaruing from the* Rhemist. 1.
Law : and doubtles (saith he) what swar- Io. 3. v. 4.
Angles 4.
ueth from the law, is truly against the law. sent. p. 215.
Likewise Angles, and Durand teach venial Durand. 2. d.
42. q. 6.
sinnes to be against the law.

8. To this argument Catholiques answer differently, some by denyal of the Pro-
posi-

position, others by denial of the Assumption. Some say that euery sinne which is against the Law is not mortal, but only that which is perfectly against it, so that it destroieth the end of the law, which is Charity & this venial sinnes do not. And if I should answer thus, Bel were by and by at a Non plus. Others say that venial sinnes are not against the law, because they are not against the end of the law, but beside the law. But this difference is rather in words then in matter, al agreeing that venial sinne destroieth not Charity nor breaketh friendship with God, which is the end for which the law was made. Yet better it is to say, that venial sinnes are beside the law, then against the law: because what is not contrary to the end, but may stand with out breach of it, is not contrary to the meanes, but may stand without breach of them, but venial sinnes are not contrary to Charity the end of the law: but may be without breach of it. Ergo neither are they contrary to the law, but may be without breach of it. And as a man trauailing, though he steppe out of his way is not said to goe contrary to his iourneys end: so a man walking to heaue, though by venial sin he steppe out, or besides the way, yet doth he not goe the cotrary way to hel: The Proposition of myne argument is euident :

1.Timoth.1.
y. 5.

VVhy ve-
nial sinnes
are not
against the
law.

dent: for what can stand with the end, can
not be contrary to the meanes necessary to
that end. The Assumption both Catholicks
graunt, and Hereticks can not deny if they
admit that there are indeed any venial sins.
For venial sins (whence soeuer they come
to be such) breake not friendship with God.
And therfore if Bel graunt in deed (as he
doth in words) that by Gods mercy some
sins are made venial, he must also confesse
that by Gods mercy, they are not against
his Charity, and friendship: and so must
answer his owne argument, which indifferently proueth that there are no venial sins
at al, whither they be said to be such by their
owne nature, or by Gods mercy: for the argument assumeth not that al which is sinne
of it owne nature is against Gods law, but
absolutly, al which is sinne is against Gods
law. And therfore if Bel thinke venial sinne
notwithstanding Gods mercy to be true
sinne, he must as wel answer his owne argument as I.

Bels arguments as much against himself as against Catholiques.

9. Admitting therfore his Proposition
I deny his Assumption: and to his proofe
out of S. Mathew. I answer that we must
giue account for euery idle worde, not because they be a against Gods law, but because they be beside it: And Bel wil beate
his horse not only when he turneth backe,

but

but alſo when he ſtarteth out of the way.
As for the text of S. Ihon, he telleth vs not
(as Bel auoucheth) that euery ſinne is *anomia*
but abſolutly Sinne is *anomia*, and may wel
be vnderſtoode of only mortal ſinne which
antonomaſtice is ſo called. This anſwere
might ſuffice to what he bringeth about
this text in this Article, yet becauſe art. 4.
he brought out of their due place many
things about the greeke words *anomia* and
adicia vſed by S. Ihon, which we remitted
to this place, we wil here anſwer them at
large, and afterward the reſt of his proofs
concerning this Article.

Chap. II.
A text of S. Ihon epiſt. 1. ex-
plicated.

Bel pag. 52.

1. Ioan. 3.
v. 4.

S. Ihons words he citeth in Greeke *pas
ho poion ten hamartian, cai ten anomian
poiei, cai he hamartia eſtin he anomia* and tranſlateth them thus. *Euery one that ſinneth tranſ-
greſſeth the law, and ſinne is the tranſgreſſion of
the law,* And hereupon inferreth that Euery
ſinne is tranſgreſſion of the law, and conſequently mortal. Catholiques anſwer twoe
waies. Firſt that S. Ihon in this place by
ſinne vnderſtandeth only ſuch ſinne as c. 5.
v. 16. he calleth *ſinne to death* vz. mortal
ſinne.

sinne. And this I proue: First becauſe in the next verſe but one vz. v. 6. he ſpeaketh only of mortal sinne, when he ſaith. *Euery one that remaineth in him* (Chriſt) *ſinneth not*, and v. 8. *who doth ſinne is of the Diuel*, and v. 9. *Euery one that is borne of God committeth not ſinne, becauſe his ſeede remaineth in him.* In theſe verſes it is euident S. Ihon ſpake only of *ſome certeine kinde of ſinne which* (as S. Auſtin S. Auſtin. tract: 5. in 1. Iohn tom.9. ſaith) *one borne of God can not commit*, vz. of mortal sinne: wherfore of the ſame did he meane. v. 4. when he in ſome ſorte deſcribed sinne by iniquity. Both becauſe els it should ſeeme a kinde of equiuocation, as alſo becauſe if he had deſcribed sinne in general, it is likely he would haue afterward diſcourſed of the ſame, and not of one only kind of sinne. Secondly becauſe when a worde principally ſignifyeth one thing, it is not to be extended to an other, which ſecondarily it ſignifieth, vnles ſuch extention be gathered by ſome circumſtances of the ſpeech, ſeeing therfore the worde Sinne doth principally ſignify only mortal sinne, and ſecondarily venial sinne, according to S. Thomas. 1. 2. S. Thomas. 4. 88. ar. 1. & there is no circumſtance here conuincing it to be extended to ſignify venial sinne, but rather to the contrarie as hath bene shewed, it is not to be extended

S   to ve-

to venial finne. And this is confirmed becaufe Scriptures Fathers, and Catholicke
writers by Sinne vnderftād ordinarily only
mortal finne, as appeareth by their attributing of death, loffe of grace, and heauen,
guilt of hel, feperation from God, and the
like to Sinne, and by defyning it to be
againft Gods law, or tráfgreffion of the law:
which agree only to mortal finne.

S. Beda 1.
Io. 3.

2. Thirdly becaufe S. Bede vnderftandeth it of fuch finne, as either is of contépt
of the written law, or corrupteth the innocency of the law of nature. And the glof.
ord. followeth his very words: alfo glof.
interlin. vnderftandeth it of finne contrary
to equity of Gods law: which he tooke of

Lyra 1. Io. 3.

S. Bede loc. cit. Lyra expreffly expowndeth
it of mortal finne, and defyneth it to be
tranfgreffion of the law. and the fame doth
Carthufia: and to this purpofe ferue al Bels
proofs, that *anomia* fignifyeth tranfgreffion
of the law: for if that be fo, then finne is taken for mortal finne. Nether againft this
expofition fee I any obiection, more then
that the worde Sinne may fignify venial
finne, and that alfo it is taken for it c. 1. v. 8.
where he faith *If we fay we haue no finne we
deceaue our felfs.* But we may anfwer that,
though it may fignify venial finne yet ordinarily it doth not, and therfore it is not wel
infer-

inferred, that here it doth, especially seeing
that there are diuers circumstances to the
contrary. And though it signify sinne in general c. 1. v. 8 yet seeing it doth signify only
mortal in this same chapter. v. 6. 8. and 9.
better it is to gather the signification of a
worde out of the next vse therof, then out
of the further of. And if one wil thus expownd the place of S. Ihon (as to me it seemeth best) Bel were straight at a Non plus.
For he supposeth that the worde sinne is
taken for al kinde of sinne, and only proueth that the worde *anomia iniquity* is taken
for perfect sinne, and transgression. yet because I wil giue him al the scoape he can
aske, I admit that by Sinne S. Ihon vnderstood al kinde of actual sinne, and deny (as
many Catholicks do) that *anomia Iniquity* is
taken for wickednes, and perfect transgression of the law: but generally as it is common to perfect transgression, and only
swaruing frō the law. Now let vs see how
Bel improueth this.

*s. Ihon mea-
neth onely
of mortal
sinne.*

3. His first proofe is because Arias Montanus saith, that *anomia* is transgression of
the law. But this is not against vs, because
we graunt that it may signify so, only we
deny that to be the proper signification of
the worde, as is euident by the etimology
therof, which is as much as *sine lege* without

*pag. 52.
Arias Mon-
tan.1.lo.3.*

S 2   the

the law, and not *contra legem*: against the
law, yet becaufe al acts againft law are alfo
without law, the worde may be vfed for
acts againft law, and fo fignify tranfgreffion
of the law. It fufficeth vs that the propriety
of the worde is for vs not for Bel, and therfore we better expownd it of fwaruing
from the law, then Bel or any other doth of
tranfgreffion of the law.

Bel pag. 53.
S. Ambrof.
S. Auftin.

4. His fecond proofe is that S. Ambros
de Parad. c. 8. and S. Auftin l. 2. de confen.
euang. c. 4. and l. 22. cont. Fauft. c. 27. defyne finne to be preuarication, or tranfgreffion of the law, or to be a thought, worde
or deede againft the eternal law, which
(faith S. Auftin) is deuine reafon, or the
wil of God commáding the order of nature
to be kept, and forbidding it to be broken.
But thefe, Fathers define only mortal finne;
becaufe Catholicks ordinarily vnderftand
only that finne, when they abfolutly fpeake
of finne, as men, when they fpeake of a
thinge meane of fubftance. As alfo becaufe
S. Ambros had before fpoken only of mortal finne vz. of Adam, and Iudas his finne.
And S. Auftin in the firft place fpeaketh of
finne againft the tenne commandements,
which no doubt is of it nature mortal, and
in the fecond place he plainly defineth fuch
finne, as breaketh the order of nature, which
also

alfo is mortal finne not venial; for who wil
fay that a litle fuperfluous laughterbreaketh
the ordet of nature. Befides it followeth
not that if S. Ambros, and S. Auftin defined
finne to be tranfgreffion of the law, therfore S. Ihon did fo cal it in this place.

5. His third proofe is out of S. Bede. But
he is rather againft him. For. he faith that
anomia fignifieth *quafi contra legem vel fine lege
factum*: as it were againft law or without
law. He faith not againft, but as .it were
againft, which more plainly he explicateth
faying. *Or without the law.* Lyra, and Carthufia: whom he citeth feeme by *anomia,* and
iniquity to vnderftand wickednes, but then
by finne they vnderftand only mortal finne,
and fo fauour Bel nothing. But becaufe the
Rhemifts as preuenting an obiection write,
that *The worde iniquity is otherwife taken* 1 *.Io.*
3.v.4. where finne is faid to be iniquity then *c.5.*
ver. 17. where iniquity is faid to be finne, which
they proue becaufe though the latine worde
be al one, yet the greeke is differēt vz *adicia*
which fignifyeth iniuftice: Bel replyeth very wifely forfooth out of S. Auftins words
trac. 4.in 1, Io.to.9. *Let none fay finne is one thing
and iniquity an other; Euery one that finneth committeth iniquity.* As if the queftion now betwixt the Rhemifts, and him had bene, whither finne and iniquity were al one, and

S.Bed. 1.10.
3.

Bel pag. 56.
Rhemift..1.
10.3.

S. Auguftin.
to. 9.

not whether *anomia*, and *adicia* be al one.
Better therfore he replieth afterward pag,
58. where he proueth *anomia*. and *adicia* to
be al one, becaufe the vulgar latine tranflateth them both *Iniquitas*. But the Rhemifts
anfwere, That the worde *Iniquitas* is vfed in
a different fignification, and proue it by the
different greeke words, for which it is vfed;
And againft this Bel faith nothing, But being at a non plus him felfe, and not able to
reply againft this anfwer, and reafon, he
cryeth out that *his anfwerer is at a non plus, &*
impudently denyeth euery iniquity to be finne.

6.   But as for the Rhemifts, euident it is
that herein they are neither impudent, nor
at a *Non plus*, feeing they giue a reafon of
what they fay, againft which Bel can not
reply; And as for iniquity and finne, though
they be oftentymes confounded both by
Scriptures, & Fathers, yet if we wil fpeake
exactly and properly, more is requited
to formal, and proper finne, then to formal
iniquity. For iniquity requireth only want
of equity, and conformity to Gods law. formal finne befides this requireth voluntarines, & fo al formal finne is formal iniquity
but not contrarywife. As adultery or murder committed by a foole or mad man is ini.
quity, but no more finne then it is in beafts.
Hereupon S. Auftin l. 2. contr. Iulian. c. 5.
diftin-

Pfalm. 50.
118. & alibi
fup.

Difference
betvvixt
formal
finne and
iniquity.

S. Auftin.

diftinguished two iniquityes, one which is
finne and blotted out in baptifme, an other
which is the law of finne & infirmity,& remaineth, & is yet iniquity: *becaufe* (faith he)
*iniquum eft that the flesh should rebel againft the
spirit* & l.6. c. 19. calleth luft againft wil *fome
iniquity*, & yet oftentymes denyeth it to be
true finne. nether doth he fay in the place
which Bel citeth, that iniquity & finne is al
one, but that finne is, not a different thing
from iniquity, but that who comitteth finne
committeth iniquity, which how it is true
is euident by that which is faid. Albeit
when he faith, that al iniquity is blotted
out in baptifme, he confounde iniquity
with finne, as before is cited out of Scripture, which argueth that wel may the
worde iniquity be taken in a different fenfe
Iohn. 5. and 3. as Iohn 5. for voluntary iniquity, and proper finne, as appeareth by the
greeke worde *adicia*, and c.3. for iniquity in
general, as appeareth by the worde *anomia*,
which is comon to voluntary, or inuoluntary.

7. The places of S. Ambros and S. Auftin are already anfwered for they define
only mortal finne. And of the fame vnderftandeth Bellarmin, when he faith al finne
is againft the law: for venial finnes he proueth not to be againft the law: tom. 3. lib.1.
de amiff. grat. & ftat. pecc. cap. 11. Nether

followeth it as Bel thincketh that some
sinnes, are no sinnes, but only that Some
sinnes are not perfectly sinnes, as Bellarmin
proueth loc. cit. As for the Rhemists. doubtles it is false which Bel addeth, that what
swarueth from the law is against it, as I
haue proued against his bare assertion of the
contrary. Durand and Angles I confesse
did thincke venial sinnes to be against the
law, but neither is this a matter of faith,
neither do they intend to fauour Bel any
thing, but answer his argument an other-
way as hath bene shewed before.

Sup. c. 2. pa-
rag. 8.

8. But pretty it is to see, how that because Angles writeth, that *it seemeth now to
be the commoner opinion in schooles, that venial
sinnes are against the law.* Bel noteth the Romish religion of mutability, confessing that
the olde Romane religion was Catholique,
sownde, and pure, with which he wil not
contend. Beholde the ytch which this fellow hath to calumniate the Romane religion. Angles insinuateth Schoole opinions
to be mutable. Bel applieth it to Romane
religion. as if it consisted of schoole opinions, which may be helde *pro & contra,
salua fidei compage* with vnity in faith, as S.
Austin speaketh. But seeing you haue graū-
ted the olde Romane religion to haue bene
Catholique and pure, & slaunder the late,
I bring

Bel pag. 82.
Angles 2.
Sent. p. 275.

Olde Ro-
man religiō
Catholique
sound and
pure.

S. Augustin.
l. 1. cont. Iul.
c. 6. to. 7.

I bring an action of slaunder against you, and charge you that you doe not like *dolo-sus, versari in generalibus,* but to bringe good witnesses, when, wherin, and by whome the late Romane religion corrupted the purity of the olde, knowing that otherwise (to vse your phrase) al the world wil cry with open mouth Fye vpon you, and your slaunderous Ministery. But in the meane tyme let vs proceed with him here.

9 . *Their canonized Martyr Bishop Fisher* (saith he) *and Popish Bishop Gerson wrote, that venial sinnes were such only by the mercy of God.* Here Bel for one truth vttereth twoe vntruths. True it is that B. Fisher and Gerson were in that errour, but that was both before it was condemned in the Church, as it was since by Pius 5. and Gregorius 13. neither did they account inuoluntary motions of Concupiscence for venial sinnes , as Bel doth, but such as Catholiques account venial. But vntrue it is that either B. Fisher is canonized, or Gerson was a bishoppe who was only Chauncellor of the vniuersity of Paris.

10. Finally he concludeth this Article with this goodly reason. *one stealeth iust so many egges as are necessary to make a mortal sinne, an other stealeth one les, but there can be no reason why God may iustly condemne the one to hel, and*

not

Bel *pag.* 83.
Ruffens. art, 32. cont. Luther.
Gerson de vit. spirit. lect. 1. part. 1.

75. *vntruth*

76. *vntruth*

Trithem. in Gersone.

pag. 85.

A reason not vvorth a rotten egge.

not the other. therfore both sinne mortally alike.
To this I anſwer by demanding a reaſon.
why the iudge may condemne him to death
that ſtealeth thirteene pence halfe penny,
and not him that ſtealeth one penny les . If
he anſwer, becauſe the law condemneth
one, and not the other. I aske againe, what
reaſon was there, that the lawe was made
againſt the one, and not againſt the other?
And if Bel can finde a reaſon in this, he wil
finde one in his owne queſtion. The reaſon
of both is. becauſe ſuch a quantity is a notable iniury to our neighbour. and conſequently is againſt charity , & ſo breaketh
Apocalip. the law,and a les quantity is not; *Be myndful*
therfore (Bel) *from whence thou art fallen and*
do penance. Apocal. 2.

THE

THE
SEVENTH ARTICLE
OF VNVVRITTEN TRA-
DITIONS.

Bel intituleth this seuenth article of traditions, though therein he handleth diuerse other matters, as of the sufficiencie and perspicuity of Scriptures, and of the readinge them in vulgar tongues, and by the common people, of the authoritie of Councels and oathes of Bishops. But these he handleth so confusedly & so tediously, being almost as longe in this one article as in al the rest, as I founde much more difficultie to gather togither, what he saied of euery point in different places, and to bringe them to some methodical order for the healpe of the readers memory, then I had to frame an answere. first therefore I wil entreate of Scriptures next of Tradition, then of Councels, and lastly of Bisshops oathes.

Chap. I.
The Catholique doctrine touching sufficiency of Scriptures propounded and proued, certayne vntruthes of Bel disproued.

ALBEIT euery one be forbidden to deny any point of the Christian faith, yet are not al cōmaunded to know actually
euery

euery point thereof, but to fome it fufficeth, that they beleeue the fundamental pointes conteyned in the Apoftles Creede, and fuch like: and to be fo defpofed in minde, as they woulde beleeue the reft, if they knewe them: which is to be beleeue them implicitely or virtually. Moreouer one thinge may conteyne an other, either actually, as fyer doth conteyne heate, and the funne light, or virtually, as a flynte conteyneth fyer and euery caufe his effecte. Thefe things fuppofed.

2. Firft Conclufion is. Al fuch pointes of Chriftian faith, as are neceffarie to be actually beleeued of euery one, that hath vfe of reafon, though he be neuer fo fimple, are actually conteyned in Scripture , either clearely, or obfcurely. This is nothing againft traditions, becaufe wel may they be, and are, pointes of Chriftian faith, though they be not fuch, as the actual and explicite beleefe of them be fo neceffarie , as none whatfoeuer can be faued without it. For it fufficeth that they be fuch as the implecite and virtual beleefe of them is neceffary to euery ones faluation , and may be denyed of none vnder payne of damnation. And the conclufion is taught of Bellarmin lib. 4. *de verbo non fcripto, cap.* 11. Where expounding thefe wordes of S. Auftine . *In thefe*

S. Auguftin. lib. de doct. Chriftian. c. 9. to. 3.

which

Which are plainely set dovvne in scripture, are al
those thinges founde, vvhich conteyne faith and
maner of life : he answereth that S. Austine
speaketh of those pointes of doctrine which are necessary simply to al, as they (saith he) are which
are conteyned in the Apostles Creed and
tenne cõmaundements. Likewise Stapleton
affirmeth, that the Apostles wrote al, or almost al that parte of faith, which is necessary to be explicitely beleeued of al and
euery one. And it seemeth euident, because
such pointes of faith, as are precisely necessary to be actually knowen of euery one
what so euer, be both fewe and are the fundamental, and most notorious pointes of
Christianity, as the mysterie of the Trinity,
the incarnation and passion of Christ, and
such like, which are al actually (at least obscurely) conteined in scripture. For surely
the prophets and Euangelists writinge their
doctrine, for our better remembrance,
would omitte no one point, which was necessary to be actually knowen of euery one,
especially seeinge they haue writen many
things with are not so necessary. And this
cõclusion teacheth S. Austin when he saith,
that *those thinges are written which seemed suffi-*
cient for the saluation of the faithful. Where I
note that he sayd not, *vvhich seemed sufficient*
to Christian faith, but *which seemed sufficient to*
saluа-

Staplet. Re-
lect. Con-
tract.5.q.5.in
explic. Ar-
tic.

S. Augustin.
tract.49. in
Ioan.to.9.

saluation, becaufe fewer pointes fuffice to faluation then the Chriftian faith conteineth, againe *In thefe* (things) *which are plainly sett downe in scripture, al thofe thinges are founde which conteine faith and maner of life.* Where I alfo obferue, that he faied not abfolutely al things (as Bel tranflateth him) but al thofe things, infinuatinge, that he fpeaketh not of al things belonging to Chriftian faith, but onely of thofe which are neceffary to be beleeued and done of euery one, which he calleth precepts of life, and rules of faith. And yet more plainely, *I beleeue alfo that herein there would be moft cleere authority diuinorum eloquiorum of Gods word, if man could not be ignorant of it, without loffe of his promifed faluation.* Where if by *diuina eloquia* we vnderftand holy writte (as Bel tranflateth pag. 95. and S. Auguftin feemeth to meane , becaufe immediatly before he fpake of fcriptures) me thinks he plainely auoucheth, that God hath procured euery thinge to be clearely written, which to knowe is neceffary to euery mans faluation. The fame teacheth S. Cyril faying. *Not al things which our Lord did are written, but what the writers deemed fufficient, as wel for manners as for doctrin, that by right faith, and works we may attayne to the kingdome of heauen.* And S. Chrifoftome 2. Theff. hom. 3. *what things foeuer are ne-*

L.2.de doct. l.cit.fup.

Bel pag. 94. 110.
11. *Falfe tranflation.*

S. Auguftin. lib.2 de pec. mer. & remif. cap.vlt. to.7.

S. Cyril. lib. 12. in Ioan. cap. 68.

S.Chryfoft.

are neceßary are manifeſt out of Scripture.

3. Here by the way I muſt aduertiſe the
Reader of Bels euil dealing with his maiſter
Bellarmin and other Catholiques. For becauſe Bellarmin affirmeth. *That the Apoſtles*
wrote al things which are neceſſary for al men,
and which they commonly vttered to al, but not
al the reſt, Bel inferreth: *That al things written*
are neceſſary for al. As if it were al one to ſay;
Al things neceſſary for al are written, and
al things written are neceſſary. Perhaps he
thinks to turne propoſicions, as eaſely as he
did his coate. And if al things written be
neceſſary for al, as Bel gathereth, ſurely (as
S. Hierom ſayd to the Pelagians teaching
as Bel doth, that none can be without ſinne,
but they that are skilful in the law) a great
part of Chriſtendome muſt needs be damned, yea Luther and Caluin who profeſſe
their ignorance in diuers points of Scripture. I omit that the vttering of ſome things
to ſome fewe, who were perfect, ſpiritual,
and fit to teach others, and capable of ſtróg
meate, as is manifeſt S. Paule did 1. cor. c.
2. v. 6. c. 3. v. 1. 2. Heb. 5. 14. 2. Timoth. 2. v.
2. Bel ſcornfully calleth *preaching in corners,*
and ſuch hearers *Ieſuited Popelings.*

4. And Catholicks he falſly chargeth
with denying, that baptiſme of infants
conſubſtantiality of God the Sonne with
his

Bellarm. lib.
4. de verbo
Dei c. 11.

Bel p. 114.

S. Hierom.
dial. 1. cont.
Pelagian.

Luther. præ-
fat. in pſalm.
Caluin. 3. in-
ſtit. c. 2. pa-
rag. 4.

Bel p. 114.

Bel p. 139.
141.

his Father, and the miftery of the B. Trinity
are in Scripture, or can be proued thence.
For Bellarmin proueth baptifme of Infants
by as many arguments out of Scripture, as
Bel doth vz. by three, out of the figure of
circumcifion gen. 17. out of Chrifts words
Ioan 3. and out of the practife of the Apoftles act. 16. and 1. cor. 1. wherof Bel bor-
rowed the firft and laft. The miftery of the
Trinitie Bellarmin proueth by fix arguments out of Scripture, and and the confubftantiality of Chrift he proueth lib. 1.
de chrifto. c. 4. out of eleuen places of the
olde teftament, to which he addeth c. 5.
nyne more, and c. 6. fifteene places out of
the new teftament.

5. Better he might haue charged his good
maifters Luther and Caluin with this matter. For Luther faid, *his foule hated the vvorde
omoufion,* or confubftantial, and Caluin expoundeth thefe places, which make moft
for the confubftantiality, as the olde Arrians did. Likewife Luther lib. cont. Coch-
leum an. 1523. faid *Infants are not at al to be bap-
tiʒed, if they do not beleeue.* And lib. de capt.
Babil. c. de bapt. *Sacraments profit no body but
faith alone.* And Caluin wil not haue the
words Ioan 3. v. 5. (which made the very
Pelagians to graunt neceffity of baptizing
Infants) to be meant of baptifme. Hereupon

(marginal notes:)
Bellarm.lib. 1. de baptif. c. 8. to. 2.

Bellarm.lib. 1.de Chrifto c.6.to.1.

Luther. lib. cont. Iacob. latomum. Caluin. in Ioan.10. See Staplet. Antidat. Euangel. in Io.10.v.30.

Caluin.Io.3.

Ex Auguft.l. 1. de pecc. mer. & re-miff.c .30.

upon the Anabaptiſts who deny baptiſme of children, profeſſe that they learnt their doctrine from Luther, and the new Arrians in Tranſiluania who deny the Trinity and conſubſtantiality of Chriſt in their diſputation with Proteſtants, appealed to Caluins iudgement, & profeſſed they receaued their doctrine from him. And Smidelin a great Proteſtant writeth. *That it is no maruel that very many Caluiniſts in Tranſiluany, Poleland, and Hungary became Arrians, and of Arrians ſoone after Mahometans.*

6. But ſport it is to heare Bel anſwer an obiection, which is the groūde of the Anabaptiſts. Infants haue no faith. Ergo they are not to be baptized. Firſt he ſaith they haue faith, & that their faith & profeſſion is to be baptiſed of faithful parents in vnity of the Catholique Church. After he denyeth them to haue faith in act, but to haue faith fundamentally, and by inclination. How theſe anſwers agree let the Reader iudge. I would know of him. Firſt whence he hath this new point of faith, that baptized infants haue to be borne of faithful parents. Are none borne of heretiks, or Infidels? Secondly. How they make profeſſion of it by words or deeds, and whether Bel by their profeſſion could diſcerne a baptiſed infant from one vnbaptized. Thirdly: how infants

T can be

Balthaſar Pacimontan. apud Cocleum in oſtis Lutheri.
See Poſſeuin de atheiſmis Hæreticorum.
Smidelin in refutat. blaſphemæ apolog. Danzi 1583.
Bel p. 140.

Inclination to faith iustifyeth Infants according to Bel.

Scripture containeth virtually al points of Christian faith.

See Staplet. Relect. controu. 5. q. 5. art. 1.

S. Austin l. 1. cont. Crescon. c. 33. Nullum mihi sacramétum aut sermo aliquis admodum obscurior de sacris literis aperitur vbi non eadem præcepta reperio. August. epist. 119.

Propter duo præcepta charitatis fensisse Maist. quicquid in illis libris sensit nisi credideriinus mendacem facinnus Deum. Auguit. 12. confeff. c. 25. tom. 1.

can be iustified by faith alone, and haue no faith in act, but only an inclination therto. Surely they can haue iustification no otherwise then they haue faith, and therfore if they haue not faith in act, they can haue no iustification in act, but only be inclined to it, as they are inclined to faith.

7. Second conclusion. Al points of Christian faith are vertually conteyned in Scripture. First because it teacheth vs to belieue the Church, which teacheth actually al points of Christian faith, and therfore Scripture vertually teacheth vs al. Hereupon wrote S. Austin *That in doing what the Church teacheth, we holde the truth of Scriptures, albeit they afforde no example thereof, because we therin follow the Church, which the Scripture vndoubtedly sheweth.* Secondly because the end of al Gods worde, whether written or vnwritten, is loue of him selfe aboue al things, and of our neighbour as our selfe, as appeareth by that 1. Timoth. 1. v. 5. *The end of the precept is charity,* and Rom. 13. v. 8. *who loueth his neighbour hath fulfilled the law,* and to the better comprehending and obtayning of this end, he referreth al whatsoeuer he reuealed, and this end being contayned in Scripture it followeth, that the Scripture doth vertually contayne (as a cause doth the effect) al points of faith.

8. And

8. And hereupon alſo it followeth that al the reſt of Gods worde whether written, or vnwritten may be called an explication of the foreſaid cómandements, becauſe it contayneth nothing, but which is vertually contayned in theſe commandements, & thereto referred by God, as to their end, which our Sauiour meant when he ſaid. *In theſe tvvo commandements, al the lavv and Prophets hange,* becauſe of them depend, as of their end, al the reſt, which the law and Prophets contayne. And hereupon ſaid S. Epiphan. hær. 65. *That vve may tel the inuention of euery queſtion, out of the conſequéce of Scriptures.* He ſaid not out of ſcripture. For al can not be taken thence, as him ſelfe writeth hær. 61. but *of the conſequence of them,* becauſe al queſtions are reſolued out of the Scriptures, or out of that which followeth of them, as the effect of the cauſe. And according to theſe two concluſions, we may expound other Fathers, when they ſay al things are contained in Scripture. For either they meane not abſolutely of al points of Chriſtian faith, nor of actual containing (as appeareth by that other where they manifeſtly defend Traditions) but either only of points neceſſary to be knowne of euery Chriſtian, or of vertual containing.

9. Third concluſion: Al points of Chri

Matth. 22. v. 40.

S. Epiphan.

ſtian

Al points of Christian faith are not actually in the scripture.

Article 6.

1.

stian faith are not actually cōtained in scripture, neither clearly nor obscurely, neither
in plaine words, nor in meaning. This con-
clusiō Bel seemeth to graunt, pag. 118. where
he admitteth of a thing although not expresly written, yet *vertually* (saith he) *and effectu-
ally contained in Scripture.* And the whole English Cleargy defyne. *That what may be proued out of Scripture is necessary to be beleeued,
though it be not read.* But what can be proued,
what not, they alone wil be iudges. But
whatsoeuer Protestants say. I proue the
conclusion. For no where in Scripture it is
sayd, either in plaine words or in meaning.
That al the books, chapters, verses, and
sentences, which in the Bible are admitted
for Canonical, are truly Canonical, and
Gods pure worde, without the mixture of
mans worde. If Bel can finde any such place
from the first of Genesis to the last of the
Apocal: let him name it. And yet this is a
point of Christian faith, yea thereupon de-
pende al the Articles we gather out of Scripture. For as S. Austin said epist. 9. and 19.
*If any vntruth be founde in Scriptures what au-
thority can they haue?* So if any part or parcel
of the Bible be doubtful, what certainty
can the rest haue? Secondly the perpetual
virginity of our B. Lady is a matter of faith,
as appeareth by S. Hierom, and S. Austin,

S. Austin.
2.
S. Hierom.
con. Heluid.
S. Augustin.
hæres. 84. 82.
S. Epiphan.
hær. 78.
S. Hilar. in
1. Math. Can.
1.

who

who accounted Heluidius, and Iouinian
heretiks for denying it, and Proteftants
confeffe it. And yet it is no where teftifyed
in Scripture. Thirdly that the feauenth day
cōmanded by God to be kepte holy,is tranf-
ferred lawfully from Saterday to Sunday is
a matter of faith, and yet no where actually
warranted by Scripture. For albeit S. Ihon
Apoc. 1. 10. fpeake of our lords day, yet he
no where warranteth the faid transferring.
See more in Bellarmin. tom. 1. lio. 4. de
verbo Dei.

VVillet Te-
tract, 2. pil-
ler.part.3. p.
76.77.
3.

10. Fourth Conclufion: Al points of
Chriftian faith can not be fufficiently , and
immediatly proued out of Scripture. In this
conclufion I fay not. That no points of
Chriftian faith, nor that al can not by fome
way or other be proued, by fome fimili-
tude, congruity, or probable illation; nor
that immediatly by teftimony of the
Church whofe teftimony in al doctrine of
faith can be immediatly proued out of Scripture. But only deny, that al can be immediatly proued out of fcripture by the very
words of Scripture , and fo fufficiently
as it fufficeth to captiuate our vnderftanding into obedience of faith. This is directly againft the fixt Article of Proteftants faith, and againft Bel in this whole
Article: But I prooue it as I did the former

*Al points
of Chriftiañ
faith can
not be pro-
ued fuffi-
ciently and
immediatly
out of Scri-
pture.*

*Articles 39
decreed by
Bifhops and
Minifters
1562. and
1571.*

T 3   conclu-

*Al thinges
can not be
taken out of
Scripture.*
Epiphan.
hær. 61.

See Concl
art. 4. p. 31.
*& Hooper
vvith him*
Bel p. 134.
135.

Luther.
See Roffens.
con. Luther.
verit. 4. &
Bellarm. lib.
4. de verb.
Dei c. 4. col.
164.
*Luther cer-
taine of
Purgatory.*

conclusion. For there is no place of al the
Scripture, which sufficiently proueth al the
rest to be Canonical, our B. Lady to be a
perpetual virgin, and the Sabbath to be
lawfully translated from Saterday to Sunday. And it shal be more euident out of
that, which we shal say of Traditions, and
in answer to Bels arguments. For the present it sufficeth, that it is so cleare, as our
very aduersaries do somtime confesse it. As
Bel pag. 134. and 135. art. 7. admitteth one
point of faith, which is not in the Bible, &
professeth that they meane not of it, when
they say al things necessary to saluation are
contained in Scriptures. And Luther art.
37. said *That purgatory can not be proued out of
Scripture,* and yet in the assertion of the same
he said. *That he was certaine there was Purgatory,* nor *cared much what Hereticks babled to
the contrary.* Now let vs come to Bels obiections, which albeit for the most part be
against Traditions, yet because the matters
of sufficiency of Scripture, and of Traditions are connexed, and because we wil
keepe his order, as much as we can, we wil
here answer them in that order; as they are
propunded by him.

CHAP.

CHAP. II.

Bels arguments out of the oulde Testament
concerning the sufficiency of Scri-
pture answered.

B el citeth dyuers places which make
nothing for absolute sufficiency of
Scriptures, or against Traditions, but only
bid vs obey, and follow the law, as Iosue 1.
v. 7. and 23. v.6. & Malach. 4. v. 4. omitting
therfore these places I answer to other as
Deuter. 4. v. 2. and Prouerb. 30. v. 6. where
God forbiddeth vs *to adde to his worde,* and
Deuter. 11. v. 32. where we are bidden to
doe to the lorde onely that which he commandeth
without adding, or taking avvay First that these
places make as much against Protestants
as Catholicks. For they admit one vnwritten Tradition, as Bel confesseth and appeareth by Brentius, Kempnitius,& the Deane
of the chappel, and the places cyted by Bel
forbid as wel the adding of one thing, as of
many to Gods worde.

2. Secondly. I answer that they make
nothing against these Traditions , which
Bel impugneth vz. such as are necessary, to
mans saluation for such are indeed Gods
worde though vnwritten. For the two first
places only forbid adding to Gods worde

Bel pag. 86.
87.88.89.

Bel p. 134.
135.
Brent. in
prolegom.
Kemnit. in
examin.
Conc.Trid.

Bel pag 86.
in præfat.
Articuli.

T 4   any

any thing of our owne head, or which is
mans worde as may be proued. Firſt by the
reaſon of the forbiddance prouerb. 30. cit.
vz. *leaſt we be diſproued, and ſo wnde lyers:* as
no doubt we might , by adding mans
worde which is ſubiect to lye, but not by
addingGods Worde,which can neuer proue
vntrue , though it be not written. Secondly , becauſe the Iewes did euer adde one
thing to Gods written worde , as Bel confeſſeth pag. 134. and the Deane of the chappel affirmed *they added both ſignes, and words
vnto the inſtitution of the Paſſouer preſcribed vnto
them by Moyſes: which addition and Tradition of
theirs* (ſaith he) *was approued by our Sauiour at
his laſt ſupper.* And this doctrine was exceeding wel liked in the conference at Hampton Court. Thirdly becauſe the Prophets,
and Euangeliſts, did adde to Moyſes law
without breaking of the commãdement in
the aforeſaid places .

3. Bel anſwereth. *That the doctrine of the
Prophets, is nothing els but an explication of the
law.* But if by the worde *explication,* he vnderſtand only ſuch as adde nothing to the
ſenſe, or meaning of the law , but only explicate in other words, types or figures,the
bare meaning of the law, he ſpeaketh moſt
abſurdly. For beſide that it is ſpoken without any reaſon at al,it is againſt reaſon, and
ſenſe,

*Conference
at Hamp-
ton Court.*
p. 68.

*Ievves ad-
ded ſignes
and vvords
to Gods
vvord and
their addi-
tion confir-
med by
Chriſt.*

Bel pag. 89.

ſenſe, to ſay that al the books of Ioſue, Iudges, Kings, and Prophets adde no ſenſe to
the law of Moyſes. For where doth the
law of Moyſes tel vs of euery worde, or
action of euery particuler man, or woeman
recorded in the books of the oulde Teſtament, written ſince the law was giuen?
Where is euery worde or deede of euery
perticuler perſon in the new Teſtament?
And although dyuers actions of Chriſt eſpecially his death, and paſſion was preſigu-
red in the law, yet the like can not be
thought of euery action, or ſpeech of euery
perticuler perſon, ſo that the words or
figures of Moyſes law, actually tolde whatſoeuer perticuler things ether Prophets, or
Euangeliſts euer wrote. Wherfore S Auſtin   S. Auſtin.
lib. 1. retract. c. 22. recalled what he had
ſaid lib. cont. Adimant. c. 3. *That al the pre-*
cepts, and promiſes in the new Teſtament, are in
the oulde. For certaine precepts there be (ſaith he)
not figured, but proper, which are not found in
the oulde Teſtament, but in the new. And for
this cauſe. Tertullian. lib. cont. Hermog.   Tertullian.
called the Ghoſpel a *ſupply of the oulde Te-*
ſtament.

4. But if Bel by the word (explication)   *How tra-*
comprehend al ſuch additions, as though   *ditions are*
they adde to the ſenſe and meaning of the   *explicatiõs*
law, yet are ether of their nature, or of the   *of the law.*
inten-

intention of the adder referred to the better, vnderstanding, comprehension, and fulfilling of the law, as al the reasons, similitudes, comparisons, examples, and sentences in an oration, are explications of the theame therof, because though they adde sense to the sense of the theam, yet they al tend to the perfect comprehension of the theame, I graunt al the writings of Prophets, and Apostles to be explications of the law, as

Chapt. 1. parag. 7. & 8.

hath bene explicated in the second conclusion, but withal adde, that the Traditions of the Church are such like explications. For what they containe, is in like sort referred (as a meane to the end) to the perfect vnderstanding, and fulfilling of the said law, and so they are no other additions to Moyses law, nor no otherwise prohibited therby then the rest of Scripture is.

5. What hath bene said to the place of Deut. 4. may be applyed to the other place Deut. 12. if it be vnderstood of the moral law, which God gaue to the Iewes. But rather I thinke it is to be vnderstood of the Ceremonial law. Both because it is not said absolutly what I command that only do, as it would, if it had bene meant of the Moral law: but *That only doe thou to the lord*, which words (*to the lorde*) insinuate the meaning to be only of the Ceremonial law, & manner of

ner of sacrifice to be done to God. As also immediatly before, God had forbidden the Iewes in their manner of worshipping him to imitate the ceremonyes of Gentils in worshipping their Gods, becaufe they had many abhominable vfes, as of facrifizing their children, and ftreight after concludeth *what I command, thee that only do thou to the lorde, nether adde any thing, nor deminish.* Wherby we fee that the worde (*Command*) he extended only to facrifices, and ceremonyes, which before he had prefcribed to be done to him felfe, and would haue therin no alteration at al.

6. Nether hindereth this that which Reinolds obiecteth. *That mention here is made of facrificing children, which is forbidden by the morall law.* For mention is made therof, not as of a thing forbidden there, but as of a reason of forbidding the Iewes, in worshipping God to imitate Gentils, becaufe (faith God) *they facrifice children,* And of this Ceremonial law very likely it is. that God abfolutly would haue no addition, or alteration at al to be made, vntil it were quite abrogated by Chrift. And the like reafon is not of Gods law concerning faith, and manners. For there being no fuch difference in the Ceremonies of the law, but what fome Iewes obferued al might alike, expedient it

was

Reinolds apol. thef. p. 207.

Ceremonial lavv perfectly prefcribed to the Iewes and why.

was that al the Ceremonies should be prescribed at once, to the end al might worship God after the same manner, especially seeing the Iewes were as S. Paul writeth, *S. Paul.* Gal. 4. v. 1. 2. 3. *litle ones nothing differing from seruants vnder tutours, and gouernours, and seruing vnder elements of the worlde.* And therfore had al the rudiments, and ceremonies of religion most exactly prescribed vnto them by God, with commandement to abstayne from any alteration.

VVhy the lavv touching faith and manners not prescribed al at once.

7. But seeing in matters of faith, and precepts of manners there is great difference, because euen the same men are not capable at once of vnderstãding al misteries, as appeareth by our Sauiours words to his Apostles. Ihon 16. v. 12. *I haue many things to say vnto you, but you can not carry* (them) *novv.* And much lesse are al men a like capable of the same misteryes. And in like manner al men were not a like capable of the same precepts of life. And therfore as S. Austin *S. Augustin. de sermon. Domini in monte.* saith: *God gaue by Prophets the lesse precepts to that people, vvhich vvas yet to be tyed vvith feare, and greater precepts by his Sonne to a people, vvhome he had agreed to free vvith loue.* Therfore it was not expedient, that God should at once prescribe vnto men al that they were to beleeue, or doe: but at such tymes, as seemed fit to his dyuine wisdome to adde therunto

by his

by his Prophets, and Euangelifts.

8. Moreouer Bel alleadgeth Efay. 8. *Bel pag.* 88.
v. 20. *Ad legem magis & ad teſtimonium.*
Quod ſi non dixerint iuxta ver um hoc non erit
eis matutina lux. Rather to the law, and to the teſtimony. If they ſpeake not according to this worde
ther ſhal not be morning light to them. This place
helpeth him nothing. Firſt becauſe the
Prophet nameth not only the law, but teſtimony alſo, which comprehendeth Gods vn-
written worde: as appeareth: Ioan. 3. v. 11. *Ioan.* 1.7.8.
Rom. 8, v. 16. Hebr. 11. v. 39. Act. 4. v, 33. 1. 15. 18.
Ioan. 5. v. 33. and other where and therfore 1. *Timoth.* 6.
maketh more for vs then againſt vs. Se- *Apoc.* 12.
condly becauſe Efay doth not abſolutly
bid vs recurre to the law, & teſtimony, but
magis, rather to them then to witches, of
whom he had immediatly forbidden vs to
enquire. Wherfore Bel in not engliſhing
the worde *magis* as he did the reſt, corrupted
of ſet purpoſe the Scripture, to make it
ſeeme *magis* more for his purpoſe Thirdly *Corrupt. of Scripture.*
though by the law, and teſtimony we vn-
derſtood only Gods writtē worde, the place
maketh nothing againſt vs. For then Efay
indeed ſhould bid vs goe to Gods written worde, which we refuſe not to doe in al
doubts, wherin it reſolueth vs, but forbiddeth vs not to goe to any other, which is as
he ſaith *iuxta verbum hoc,* agreable to this
worde

worde. yea God him selfe commanded vs
Deutr. 32. v. 7. *to aske our Fathers, and elders,*
and. Iob. 8, v. 8. *to aske the ancient generation,*
& seeke out the memory of the Fathers. Wherfore
ether must Bel proue, that the Churches
Traditions are not *iuxta verbum hoc* agreable
to Gods written worde (which he shal
neuer doe:) or he must know, that God not
only forbiddeth vs, but rather commandeth vs to seeke after, and follow them.

9. S. Hierome alleadged by Bel only
saith absolutly. *That doubts may be resolued out*
of Scripture, and who wil not seeke Gods worde
shal abide in errour, which is vndoubted
truth, but nothing against vs. But affirmeth
not. That al doubts may be determined out
of Scripture, and that we ought to seeke
nothing els whatsoeuer. Yea him selfe epist.
ad Marcel. resolueth lent to be keapt only
by Apostolical tradition: And l. cont. Heluid. bringeth not one place of Scripture to
proue our B. Ladyes perpetual virginity
against that hereticke, though he bring
many to shew that the places, which the
hereticke alledged conuince not the contrary. And thus much touching Bels places
out of the oulde Testament.

Deuter.
Iob.

Bel pag. 89.
S. Hierom.
in c. 8. Esaiz.

S. Hierom.

CHAP.

Chap. III.

Bels arguments out of the newv Testament touching sufficiency of Scripture ansvvered.

His first place out of the new Testa- Bel pag. 90. ment is Ioan. 20. v. 30. *These are written that you may beleeue, that Iesus is Christ the sonne of God.* & *that in beleeuing, you might haue life through his name.* And biddeth vs obserue that S. Ihons *Ghospel was written after al other Scriptures, euen when the Canon of Scripture was compleat, perfect, and fully accomplished:. Vz. about the 14. yeare of Domitian almost an 100. years after Christs ascension:* and thereby thinketh to auoyde al our sottish cauils (as he tearmeth them.) Meaning forsooth that S. Ihon meant these words: (*These are vvritten*) of the whole Canon of the Scripture.

2. Omitting Bels manifest error, where *Tvvo grosse errors in Chronographie.* Baron. An. 97. Onuphrius chron. 96. Euseb. chronic. 97. he maketh the 14. yeare of Domitian to be about 100. years after Christs ascension, which was but about the 97. yeare after Christs natiuity, as is euident by al Chronicles, or supputators of tymes, and so wanted almost 40. of an 100. after his ascension. Omitting also an other manifest error, in affirming S. Ihon to haue written his Ghospel almost an 100. years after Christs ascension

See Baron.
An. 101.
Eufebius in
chron.
S.Hieron.in
Scriptur. Ec-
clefiaft. in
Ioanne & in
chron.

sion, who dyed the 68. yeare after his paf-
sion, as Eufebius and S. Hierom teftify, and
therfore could not write almoft an 110.
years after Chrifts afcenfion, vnles he wrote
many years after his owne death.

3. But omitting thefe errors, as teftimo-
nies of Bels ignorance in hiftories, which I
regard not. To his argument I anfwer. That
thofe words (*Thefe are written*) are meant
only of (*figna*) miracles done by Chrift,
and written by S. Ihon, to moue vs to beleeue that Chrift was God. Reinold. thef. 1.
pag. 60. confeffeth. *That they are referred pro-*
perly to (figna) myracles, yet wil haue them
alfo meant of precepts, & doctrine written
by S. Ihon, becaufe *myracles are to confirme,*
and perfvvade doctrine and precepts. But I proue
that they are meant only of miracles. Becaufe S Ihon hauing recorded diuers miracles of Chrift, afterward (immediatly before thofe fayd words) faith, *Many other mi-*
racles did Iefus in the fight of his difciples, vvhich
are not vvritten in this booke. And then addeth.
but *Thefe are written that you may beeleue that Ie-*
fus is Chrift the fonne of God. &c. Who feeth not
here, that the demonftratiue pronowne
(*Thefe*) is referred only to miracles. For S.
Ihon hauing faid that many miracles were
vnwritten, ftreight after with the aduer-
fatiue, or exceptiue particle (*But*) which
                                                    Bel

See S. Cyril.
l.12. in Ioan.
c. 61.

Reinolds.

v. 30.

v. 31.

Bel guilefully leaft out) excepteth thefe
which he had written from the condition
of others, which he had not written faying
But thefe are written: &c? And Reinolds reafon is fo far from prouing his purpofe, as it
proueth the quite contrary. For becaufe *Reinolds
proof a-
gainft him
felf.*
Chrifts doctrine, and faith was the end of
S. Ihons writing, and myracles the meanes,
and motiues to bring men to Chrifts faith,
as him felfe profeffeth in the forfaid words,
euidēt it is that he meaneth both of Chrifts
doctrine, and miracles, in the forefaid verfe,
but differently, and vnder different words.
For of myracles he meaneth as motiues, and
meanes, vnder the words. (*Thefe are written
&c.*) And of doctrine he meaneth as the
end of his writing the myracles, vnder the
other words (*That you may beleeue;* &c.)

4. But fuppofe that S. Ihon by (*Thefe*)
vnderftood both myracles, & doctrine, can
Bel therfore infer that S. Ihon meant of the
whole canon of Scriptures? Surely no: becaufe he hauing before faid. That many
other myracles of Chrift were not written
in this booke, and immediatly adding. *But
thefe are written:* &c. can not be vnderftood
but of his owne writing, and in his owne.
Ghofpel. wheruppon if Bel infetre any
thing, he muft inferre that S Ihons Ghofpel alone is abfolutly fufficient, and contei-

V neth

conteineth al things necessary. Which I
hope he wil not doe. Reinolds graunteth
that S. Ihons Ghospel is sufficient, supposing that we heare of no other. But this is
nothing to the purpose. For they out of this
place inferre the Scripture to be absolutly
sufficiēt, so as we may reiect al other things
though we heare of them: And therfore
seeing S. Ihon in this place can not be vnderstood, but of his owne Ghospel, if hence
they proue absolute sufficiency of Scripture against Traditions, they must inferre
absolute sufficiency of S. Ihons Ghospel
against al other what soeuer: I omit a place
Bel alleadgeth out of S. Cyril, with an other
out of S. Austin, which I cited in the first
conclusion. For they proue no more then is
there affirmed.

5. His second place out of the new testament is act. 20. v. 27. *I haue not spared to
shew vnto you the whole counsel of God.* Therfore (saith he) the whole counsel of God
touching our saluation, is conteined in holy
Scripture. Omitting his needles proofs out
of Lira, and Carthu: that S. Paul meaneth
of al counsel touching our saluation. I answer that this place ether maketh directly
against Protestants, or not at al against Catholiques: For seeing S Paul speaketh of his
owne shewing vnto the Ephesians, if he be
vnder-

vnderstood of shewing only by writing, it followeth, that his epistle to the Ephesians conteineth al Gods counsel, and is absolutly sufficient, which is against Protestants. But if he be vnderstood (as he should be) of shewing in general, ether by worde, or writing, nothing followeth to Bels purpose or against Catholiques.

6. But (saith Bel) *it wil not suffice to an-* *svver That al Gods counsel was preached, but not* *written, because S. Paul was an Apostle of that* *Ghospel, which was promised by the Prophets, &* *taught no other thing, then that the Prophets had* *foretolde.* But this proueth no more of S. Paul, then of al the Apostles. For they were al Apostles of the same Gospel, and taught the same doctrine, which he did, and yet some of them wrote neuer a worde. Some shew it hath to proue, that al which S. Paul preached was written by the Prophets which how it is to be vnderstood hath bene before explicated.

pag. 91.

Rom. 1.
Act. 26.

Sup. e. 1. pa-
rag. 7. &8.

7. And because Bellarmin saith. *That the* *Scripture is an infallible, and most secure rule of* *faith.* And *That he is mad who reiecting Scrip-* *ture followeth inward inspirations.* Bel char-geth him *to contradict him selfe teaching els* *where the contrary,* but cyteth no place, be-cause none is to be found) and *to confound* *him selfe because he wil not rely vpon Gods writ-*
V 2 *ten test-*

Bellarm.lib.
1. de verbo
Dei. cap. 1.
& 2.

Bel pag. 93.
vntruth 77

vntruth 78

ten *testimonies, but seeke after vnvvritten vanities,
and ground his faith vpon them.* Here Bel slan-
dereth Bellarmin. For when did euer he or
any Catholique refuse to rely vpon Gods
written testimony ? when did they not account it a most infallible rule of faith ? vpon what vanities do they ground their
faith ? we confesse Scripture to be an infal-

Bellarmin.

lible rule but not the total rule, but as Bellarmin saith lib. 4. de verb. dei c. 12. *the partial rule.* Let Bel improue this *Hic Rhodus,
hic saltus.*

Bel pag. 93.
S. Augustin.
cont. Adi-
mant. cap. 3.
to. 6.

S. Augustin.
lib. 1. Retrac.
c. 22. to. 1.

S. Paul.

Hovv Scri-
ptures are
able to
make men
vvise to sal:
vation.
    1.
    2.

8. Moreouer he alleadgeth S. Austin
writing. *That there are no precepts, or promises
in the doctrine of the Ghospel, and Apostles,
which are not in the old Testament.* True. But as
S. Austin afterward in expresse words recalled, and corrected this error: so I would
wish Bel to do: His third place is 2. Timoth
3. v. 15. *Holy scriptures are able to make thee vvise
to saluation.* This maketh not against vs. both
because we deny not that Scripturs are able
to make men wise to saluation : but only
deny that they alone do it. As also because
we graunt, they actually conteine whatsoeuer is necessary to euery mans saluation, and
vertually whatsoeuer els. And lastly because
the forsaid words are meant only of the
old Testament, which S. Timothy (saith S.
Paul there) *Had learned from his infancy,*
                                                which

which alone being not (as Proteſtants confeſſe) abſolutly ſufficient, ſo as we may re-
ieĉt the new teſtament, they can not therof
inferre Scripture to be ſo abſolutly ſufficient, as that we may reiect Traditions. Now
let vs come to his proofs out of Fathers,
which particulerly proceed againſt Traditions.

Chap. IIII.

*Bels arguments out of Fathers touching
ſufficiency of Scripture, and Traditions anſvvered.*

Vincentius lyrin : who lyued in S. Auſtins tyme writeth . *That he enquiring
of many holy and learned men . How he ſhould
eſcape hereſy: they al anſwered him by ſticking to
Scripture and the Churches Traditions.* And. S.
Ireney writeth of him ſelfe , that *by traditions of the Church of Rome, he confounded al thoſe
that teach otherwiſe then they ſhould.* No maruel therfore if Bel being deſyrous not to eſcape, but to ſpread hereſy, and loth to be
confownded , do with the olde hereticks
Marcionits, and Valentinians: ex Iren: l. 3.
c, 2. and Tertul. de præſcrip with the Ari
ans ex Hilario l. cont. Conſtant. Auguſt. l,
1. contr. Maximin. with the Aerians ex
Epipha, her. 75. with the Ennomians ex
V 3   Baſil.

(marginal notes:)
Vincent. Lyrin. con. hæreſes.

S. Ireney lib. 3. c. 3.

Ould heretiks deteſt traditions.
S. Iren.
Tertullian.
S. Hilarie.
S. Auguſtin, c. 1. to. 6.
S. Epiphan.

S. Bafil.
7. Synod.

Bafil. l. de fpir. fanct. c. 27. 29. with the
Neftorians, and Eutichians ex. 7. Synod.
act. 1. impugne Traditions. And let not the
Reader maruel that Bel bringeth the words
of dyuers Fathers againft Traditions, which

Bellarm. lib.
4. de verbo
Dei c. 11.

almoft al are obiections taken out of Bellarmin. For they make no more for his purpofe, then the words of Scripture did for the

Math. 4. v.
6.
Ioan. 12. v.
34.

Diuel. or Iewes, when they alleadged them
againft Chrift. And we wil bring fuch expreffe words of the fame Fathers for Traditions, as fhal cleare al fufpition, and can
admit no folution.

Bel pag. 94.
S. Dionyf. de
diu. nom.
c. 1.

2. Firft he cyteth Dionif. Areopag. fai-
ing *vve muft nether fpeake nor thinke any thing of
the Deity (præter ea) befide thofe things, vvhich
Scriptures haue reuealed.* I might except, that

Centur. Cét.
1. lib. 1. c. 10.
Luther. &
Caluin. ex
Bellarm. l. 2.
de Mona-
chis c. 5.

Proteftants deny Dionif. Areopag. to be
author of thofe bookes, but I neede not. For
the words make nothing to the purpofe;
both becaufe they forbid only fpeaking
or thincking of the Deity befide that which
Scripture reuealeth: as alfo becaufe by (*præter*) he vnderftãdeth not euery thing out of
Scripture, els we fhould not vfe the words
Trinity, and Confubftantiality but only
fuch as are quite befide, and neither actually
nor vertually are conteined in Scripture.
But let S. Dionif. tel plainly his owne minde
concerning Traditions, *Thofe firft Captai-*

nes

bes (faith he) *and Princes of our Hierarchy haue deliuered vnto vs diuine, and immaterial matters partly by written, partly by their vnwritten institutions.* How could Apostolical Traditions be more plainly auouched.

n 3 Two places Bel bringeth out of S. Austin, which becauſe we alleadged them in cap. i. concluſ. 2. and proue no more then is there taught I omit. And as for S. Auſtin, he not only auoucheth Apoſtolical Traditions, epiſt. 118. but de Geneſ. ad litt. l. 10. c. 23. tom. 3. profeſſeth, that *baptiſme of infants were not to be beleeued, if it were not an Apoſtolical tradition*, and obiecteth them againſt the Pelagians in lib. cont. Iulian. amoni, and giueth vs this rule to knowe them. *If the whole Church obſerue them and no Councel appoynted them:* l. 2. de bapt. c. 7. 6. 23. 24. S. Ireney he cyteth, becauſe he writeth *That the Ghoſpel which the Apoſtles preached, they afterward deliuered vnto vs in Scriptures, and it is the foundation of our faith.* Theſe words proue no more then that the Apoſtles preached not one Ghoſpel, & writ an other, but one and the ſelfe ſame. But that euery one of them, or any one of them writ euery whit they al preached S. Ireney affirmeth not. And his affection to Traditions is euident, both out of his words before rehearſed, as alſo lib. 3. c. 4. where he ſaith *we ought to*

V 4 *keepe*

S. Dionyſ. l. de eccleſiaſtic. Hierarch. c. i.

S. Auguſtin. 2. de doct. Chriſtian. c. 6. & 2. de peccat. mer. & remiſſ. c. vlt.

s. Auſtins rule to knavv Apoſtolical traditions. S. Ireney lib. 3. c. i.

S. Ireney.

keepe Traditions, though the Apostles had written nothing. And affirmeth *many barbarous nations of his tyme, to haue beleeued in Christ, keapt the doctrine of saluation, and antient Tradition without Scripture.*

Bel pag. 95.
Tertul. con.
Hermogen.

4.   The next he produceth is Tertullian writing thus, *I reuerence the fulnes of Scripture, which sheweth to me the Maker, and the things made.* And soone after. *But whither al things were made of subiacent matter. I haue no where readde, let Hermogenes shoppe shew it written. If it be not written, let him feare that wee prouided for them, that adde or take away.* Answer. Tertullian speaketh of one perticuler matter, which the hereticke Hermogenes of his owne head, not only without Tradition, or Scripture, both contrary to both, taught of creating the worlde of subiacent matter, & not of nothing. And no maruel if Tertullian said the Scripture was ful in this poynt, and required Scripture of Hermogenes, for proofe of his heresy; being sure he could alleadge no Tradition. But for true Traditions, Tertullian is so great a manteiner of them, as lib. de prescrip. he thincketh hereticks ought to be confuted rather by them,

Tertull. lib.
de Corona
milit. lib. 1.
cont. Mar-
cionem l. 2.
ed vxorem.

then by Scripture, and other where affirmeth diuers things to *be practised in the Church as the ceremonies in baptisme, signe of the Croße, and such like, only by authority of Tradition without al*

vvithout al proofe of scripture. vvhere of (saith
he) *Tradition is the beginner, custome conseruer,
and faith the obseruer.*

5. Of S. Cyprian Bel much triumpheth,
because writing against one particuler Tradition, of not rebaptizing the baptized by
hereticks, which he thought had bene a
meere humane and mistaken tradition, he
saith *Cometh it from our Lord, or the Gospels authority? Cometh it from the Apostles precepts,
or epistles? For God witnesseth that the things are
to be done, which are written, and proposeth to
Iesu Name saying. Let not the booke of this law
depart from thy mouth, but thou shalt meditate
therin day, and night, that thou mayst obserue to
doe al things that are written in it. If therfore it
be commanded in the Ghospel, or contayned in
epistles of Apostles, or acts, that who came from
any heresy be not baptized, but hands imposed vpon them for pennance, let this diuine, and holy
Tradition be kept.*

6. These words at the first view seeme
to make for Bel, but if the cause and circumstances of S. Cyprians writing be considered, they make rather against him. S.
Cyprian neuer reiected al Traditions (yea
by it l. 2. epist. 3. he proued water to be mingled with wyne in the sacrifice, and in the
epistle cited by Bel, biddeth vs recurre to
Apostolical Tradition) but only the foresaid

Bel *pag.* 96.

Primo imi-
tare pieta-
tem humili-
tatemque
Cipriani &
tunc profer
consilium
Cipriani.
Auguft. lib.
2. cont. Cref-
con. cap. 31.
to. 7.
S. Cyprian. e-
pift. ad Pom
peium.

S. Cyprian.

said Tradition, becaufe he thought as he
faith epift. ad Iubaian. that it *was neuer before commanded or written*, but (as he writeth
epift, ad Quint:) *miftaken for an other Tradition of not rebaptizing fuch as fal into herefy.*
Wherfore Bel pag.118. moft falfly affirmeth
*that he sharply reproued P. Steeuen for leaning to
Tradition.* For he reproued h'm only for leaning to a miftaken (as he fuppofed Tradition) And as it is euidét out of his epiftles,
and the hiftories of that tyme, the queftion
betwixt him and S. Steeuen pope, was not
whether Tradition were to be obferued, or
no, but whether this were a true Tradition
or no. Wherin, S. Cyprian erronioufly thincking it to be a miftaken tradition, argued
againft it as he did, demanding Scripture
for proofe therof, which he would neuer
haue done, if he had not thought it to haue
bene miftaken. The moft therfore that Bel
hath out of S. Cyprian for him felfe, is, that
what is no true tradition, muft be proued
by Scripture, which I willingly graunt, but
it maketh nothing for his purpofe, as is
euident.

7. But many things I obferue in S. Cyprian which make againft Bel. 1 He admitteth dyuers Traditions: Bel reiecteth al. 2,
He impugneth one only Tradition: Bel impugneth al. 3. He erred in impugning one,
and

and much more Bel in impugning al .4. He
recanted his error before his death as S.
Auſtin thincketh, and of his fellow biſhops S. Hierom teſtifyeth: Bel perſiſteth
obſtinatly. 5. He erred in a new queſtion,
and not determined in a ful Councel ſaith
S. Auſtin: Bel erreth in antient matters de-
cyded by many general Councels. 6. He although he thought the Pope did erre, yet ſe-
perated not him ſelfe (as Bel doth) from
his communion as him ſelfe and S. Hierom
teſtifyeth. 7. He condemned none that followed the Popes opinion againſt his, as Bel
doth. 8. He thought the Pope to erre in a
cōmandment onely of a thing to be done:
Bel condemneth him of errors in his iudicial ſentences of faith, where as S. Cyprian
profeſſeth, *that falſe faith can haue no acceſſe to*
S. Peters chayre: 9. He diſobeyed for a tyme
the Popes commandement concerning a
new, and difficult queſtion: Bel diſobeyeth
obſtinatly his definatiue ſentence.

8. Hereby we ſee how litle S. Cyprian maketh for Bel, and though he had made more
for him, let him know from S. Auſtin: lib.
de vnic. bapt. c. 13. and lib 1. de bapt. cont.
Donatiſt. c. 18. and epiſt. 18. that this error
was in S. Cyprian. *an humane and venial error*
and like a blemiſh in a moſt white breaſt, becauſe
it was not then perfectly defyned by the Church.

But

S. Auguſtin.
l. 6 de bapt
c. 2.
S. Hieron.
dial. contr.
Luciferian.

S. Auguſt. l.
de vnic. ba-
ptiſm. c. 13.
& lib. 5. de
bapt. c. 17.
S. Cyprian. e-
piſt. ad Iu-
baian.
S. Hieron.
contr. Luci-
fer. Auguſt.
ſup.
S. Cyprian.
epiſtol. ad
Pompei.
Euſeb. lib. 7.
c 3.
Vincen. cōt.
hæreſ.
S. Cyprian. l.
1. epiſt. 3.

See S. Auſtin
lib. 2. contr.
Creſcon c.
31.32. to .7.
S. Auſtin.

But in his folloẘers (saith he: lib. 1. cit. c. 19.
it is smoake of hellish filthines, and as Vincent

Vincent. Ly-rin.

Lyrin writeth *The author ẘas Catholicque, his
folloẘers are iudged heretiks, he absolued, they
condemned, he a child of heauen, they of hel.* And

Example of the force of tradition and the Popes iudgements.

let the Reader gather by this example, the
authority of Tradition and Pope. For if
one Tradition preuailed then againſt S. Cyprian, and a whole Councel of Bishops, alleadging dyuers places of Scripture, much
more it wil preuaile againſt Proteſtanrs.
And if the Popes iudgement euen then,
when it seemed to many holy, and learned
Bishops, to be againſt Scripture, & was ſup-
ported only by Tradition, did preuaile, and
they at laſt condemned as Heretickes, who
resiſted: much more it wil præuaile againſt
Proteſtants, being vpholden not only by
Tradition, but by manifeſt Scripture alſo.

80 vntruth

And Bel in blaming S. Steeuē Pope, for pre-
tēding (as he saith) falſe authority shěweth
him selfe to bee a malepert miniſter, seeing

S. Cyprian.

S. Cyprian neuer reprehended him for any
ſuch matter: yea lib. 1. epiſt. 3. acknowledgeth in the Church one Prieſt, and iudge,
who is Chriſts Vicar, meaning the Pope as
is euident: becauſe lib. 2. epiſt. 10. he saith
that the Nouatiās in making a falſe Bishop
of Rome, made a falſe head of the Church
and l. 1. epiſt. 8. aud epiſt. ad Iubaian: that
Chriſt

Vincent.Ly-
rin.con. hæ-
reses.
S.Auguftin.
lib. de vnic.
bapt. cont.
Petil. c. 14.
Bel pag 97.
S.Athanaf.

Chrift builded his Church vppon S. Peter.
And as for S. Steeuen, Vincent Lirin: highly
commendeth him, and the very Donatifts
as S. Auftin writeth, confeffed, that *he incorruptly gouerned his Bifhoprike.*

9. Next he cyteth S. Athanafius cont.
Idol: faying *That Scriptures fuffice to fhew the
truth.*. True. But that truth wherof S. Athanafius there difputed againft Gentils, to wit
that Chrift was God, as he him felf explicateth in thefe words: *I fpeake of our beleefe in
Chrift.* But (faith Bel.) *He had made a foolifh
argument, and concluded nothing at al, if any neceffary truth had not bene fully contained in Scripture,* As though S Athanafius had in thefe
words argued againft Gentils, in which he
only gaue a caufe why he wrote that trea-
tife. Becaufe (faith he) *Though Scriptures fuffice to fhevv the truth, and dyuers haue written of
the fame matter* (which argueth that he fpake
of fome determinate truth) *yet becaufe their
writings are not at hand, I thought good to vvrite.*
But fuppofe he had argued, what folly is in
this argument? Al contained in Scripture
is truth: Chrifts godhead is there contained.
Ergo it is truth. But perhaps Bels dul head
thought it al one to fay. Al conteined in
Scripture is truth (wherupon the faid Syl-
logifme dependeth) & Scripture côteineth
al truth. As for S. Athanafius his reuerence
of Tra-

S.Athanaf. l
de Nicen.
Synod. &e-
pift ad Afri-
can. apud
Theodoret.
lib.1.c.8.

of Traditions, it is euident by his prouing the Godhead of Chrift, and name of confubftantiality by Tradition, & by his words lib. de incarn. verbi; *who ſticketh to Traditions is out of danger.*

Bel pag.98.
S. Epiphan.
hær. 6t.
Chapt.1. pa-
rag.8.
S. Epiphan.

10. S. Epiphan he alleadgeth writing: *That VVe can tel the finding of euery queſtion by conſequence of Scripture.* But thefe words haue bene explicated before. As for Tradition, he faith hære. 61. *VVe muſt vſe it, for althings can not be taken out of Scripture, For the Apoſtles haue deliuered ſome things by writing, ſome things by Tradition:* The like he faith hære. 55. and 75.

S.Cyrill. lib.
2. de recta
fid. ad Re-
gin.

S. Cyril he citeth where he faith. *That VVe muſt follovv Scriptures, & in nothing depart from their preſcript:* This maketh not againſt vs, who profeffe fo to doe, and yet withal fol-

S. Cyril.

low Traditions. And what account S. Cyril made of Traditions appeareth by his obſeruing lent. lib. 10. in leuit. and vſe of the Croffe. lib. 6. in Iulian. which are Tradi-

S. Ambrof.
Tertullian.

tions Apoſtolical as witnes S. Ambrof. ſer. 25. 34. 36. Tertul. de corona mil. and others.

Bel pag.98.
Chryfoft. in
pſalm. 95.

11. He citeth S. Chrifoftome writing *That if any thing be ſpoken without Scripture the hearers mynde wauereth ſomtymes doubting, ſomtymes aſſenting, otherwhile denying.* But maruel

S. Chryfoft.

it is that Bel would touch S. Chrifoftome, who hom. 42. Theſal. vpon thefe words: (Holde Traditions) faith. *Hence it appeereth, that*

that (the Apostles) *deliuered not althings by letters. And the one as vvel as the other are worthy of the same credit. Wherfore we thincke the Churches Traditions to deserue beleefe. It is a Tradition* (marke Bel) *aske no more.* And if Bel had cyted the words immediatly before, he had explicated of what kinde of speaking without Scripture S. Chrisoftom meant, namely (*fine testibus solaque animi cogitatione*) *vvithout vvitnesses, and of his ovvne head.* But Churches Traditions haue her for witnes, & descend from the Apostles. An other place he bringeth out of the same S. Chrisoftom (as he saith) but it is out of the Author imperfect, who was a flat Arian, and therfore his testimony is worth nothing, otherwise then he agreeth with holy fathers: though his saying cyted by Bel : *That al is fulfilled in Scripture vvhich is sought to saluation, may be explicated by the first, or second conclusion* :

Author imperf. hom. 41. in Math.

11. Next he bringeth S. Ambrose *bidding vs not to beleeue argument, and disputations, but aske the Scriptures, Apostles, Prophets and Christ.* This maketh rather for vs; because it alloweth enquiring, of others besides Scriptures, namely of Apostles from whom the Churches Traditions came. And nothing against Traditions, because they be no arguments, or disputations. And indeed S. Ambrose meaneth of humane arguments, and reasons

Bel pag. 98. S. Ambros. de fide ad Gratian. c. 4.

such

such as in the Chapter before he said the A-
rians vsed; to proue Christ to be vnlike to
his Father. Besides he speaketh only concerning one point vz. the consubstantiality
of Christ. And therfore though he had bidden vs therin seeke only Scripture he had
nothing preiudicated Traditions, which

S. Ambros. plainly he maintaineth ser. 25. 34, 36. 38 epist
81. and other where. Only I maruel wher-

Corrupt. of fore Bel corrupted S. Ambrose his words.
Fathers. For where he saith *vve deny,* yea *abborre* Bel
maketh him say, *vve deny not, but abborre,* Making S. Ambros teach heresy in graunting
Christ to be vnlike his Father, which was
the matter he spake of, and to speake ab-
surdly in abhorring a speech which he doth
not deny.

Bel pag. 99. 13. S. Basil he citeth saying *vvhat soeuer is (*
S. Basil. in *extra scripturam) out of the Scripture seeing it is not*
Ethic. defin. *of faith is sinne.* And in an other place. *Let vs*
vlt & ad Eu- *stand to the iudgment of Scripture, and let the truth*
stachium *be iudged on their side, whose doctrine is agreeable*
medicum. *to Gods oracles.* Answer. In the first place by
extra scripturam he vnderstandeth things contrary to Scripture, as in the same place he
vnderstandeth with the Apostle by *non ex*
fide things contrary to faith, as appeareth.
both because he saith such things are sinne,
which is not true of things which are barely
beside Scripture, as also because he proueth
such

ſuch things to be ſinne, becauſe they be *non
ex fide* contrary to faith, as the Apoſtle ſpeaketh Rom. 14. v. 23. Beſide, by Scripture he
vnderſtandeth al Gods words, as vſually we
vnderſtand the whole by the cheefeſt part.
Wich may be proued, becauſe before he
defined faith *to be certaine perſuaſion of Gods
vvorde,*& affirmed it to a riſe of hearingGods
worde,and therupon inferreth, what is beſide Scripture is not of faith. In which illation, if he tooke not Scripture for Gods
whole worde, as he did in the Antecedent,
he did manifeſtly paralogize. And th.us vnderſtood, he ſpeaketh nothing againſt Traditions, which are part of Gods worde, and
as him ſelfe ſaieth otherwhere *of as equal
force as the written worde is.*

S. Baſil. lib.
de Spir.c.27.
& 29.

14. The ſecond place maketh nothing to
the purpoſe. For he biddeth not vs be iudged by only Scripture,yea in allowing thoſe
opiniós for true,which are agreable to Scripture , he inſinuateth that to diſcerne the
truth of opiniós, it is not neceſſary to proue
them out of Scripture, ſo they be conſonát
thereto. How earneſt a defender of Traditions S. Baſil was, appeareth lib. de ſpir. c.
29. *I thincke* (quoth he) *it an Apoſtolical thing
to ſticke vnto Traditions not* written and c. 27.
*Some doctrine vve haue by writing, ſome vve re-
ceaued of the Apoſtles Tradition, and both haue*

S. Baſil.

X   *equal*

equal force to piety. Nor any contradicteth these (marke Bel) vvho neuer so slenderly haue experienced the rights of the Church And c. 10. he

A Trick of Heretiks to reiect tradttion.

writeth. *That Hereticks abolish Apostolical Tradition, and reiect vvritten testimonyes of Fathers as of no account.*

*Bel pag 99.
S.* Hierom.

15. The last Father he citeth is S. Hierom, out of whom he alleadgeth three places. The first is in math. 23. *This because it hath no authority from Scripture is as easely reiected, as it is affirmed.* The second is in psal. 86. where vpon that verse *Dominus narrabit in scripturis populorum.* he saith. *God vvil shew not by vvorde, but by Scripture, that excepting the Apostles, what is said afterward shal haue no authority.* The third place is in Hierem. c. 4. *That we must not follow the error of our Auncestors or parents, but authority of Scriptures, and command of God teaching.* Answer : In the first place S. Hierom speaketh of a perticuler opinion vz: That Zacharias who was slaine betwene the Temple and the Altar was S Ihon Baptists father : which he supposeth to haue bene no Apostolical Tradition, and therfore of it saith, because it is not proued out of Scripture, it is as easely reiected as affirmed. But what S. Hierom writeth of a particuler opinion helde without tradition, Bel can uot iustly extend to certaine Traditions . The second place maketh nothing

against

againſt vs. Becauſe the Traditions of the
Church were taught by the Apoſtles, and
not by any other afterward. And S.Hieroms
meaning is to deny, that any man may teach
of his owne worde, and authority any new
doctrine, as Montanus, and ſuch like Hereticks did, but only that, which they receaued from the Apoſtles, who were as S. Paul
ſaith, Eph. 2. v. 20. *our foundation.* The thirde
place maketh les to the purpoſe. For tradition is no error of Anceſtors. And Scripture we graunt to be followed, but not it
alone, but (as S. Hierom ſaith) *the command-*
ment of God teaching whether it be by writing
or tradition. As for traditions S. Hierom
plainly alloweth them, Dialog. cont. Lucif.
where he confeſſeth it *to be the cuſtome of the*   S. Hierome.
Church, to obſerue many things by tradition, as
if they were written laws. And epiſt. ad Marcel. receaueth lent. and lib. cont. Heluid:
defendeth our Ladies perpetual virginity
only by tradition.

16. Many more Fathers I might alleadge
for traditions. But I content my ſelfe with
the teſtimonies of them, whom Bel brought
for the contrary. Let the indifferent Reader
weigh the places cited by him, and me, and
vprightly iudge as he tendreth his ſaluation;
Whether the holy Fathers reiected, or im-
braced eccleſiaſtical traditions. Perhaps Bel

wil anſwer. That the Fathers contradict
them ſelfes, and ſay as the falſe mother did.

3. Reg. 3. v.
26.

Let them be neither myne nor thine, but be deuided.
But who remembreth Salomons iudgment,
wil by this alone perceaue to whom of right
the Fathers belong. I haue anſwered al that
Bel hath brought out of them, and moſt of
the authorities alleadged by me (eſpecially
thoſe of S. Dioniſ. S. Epipha: S. Chriſoſt.
S. Baſil) admit no anſwer at al: Now let vs
come to Bels arguments out of Catholique
writers.

CHAP. V.

Bels arguments out of late Catholique vvri-
ters touching ſufficiency of Scrip-
tures and Traditions an-
ſvvered.

Bel p. 100.
Roffenſis
artic. 37. Lu-
ther.

THE firſt he alleadgeth is the learned
and holy Biſhop Fiſher (whom he
vntruly tearmeth a canonized Saint with
vs) Becauſe in one place he calleth Scripture
the ſtorehouſe of al truthes neceſſary to be known

Veritate 4.
cont. art. Lu-
theri.

of Chriſtians. And in an other ſaith *when here-*
tiks contend with vs we ought to defend our cauſe
with other help then Scripture. Becauſe (ſaith Bel)

vntruth 81.

Popery can not be defended by Scripture, and auou-
cheth Papiſts to confeſſe, That they can not manteine
their faith by Gods written word. *Anſwer.* How
Scri-

Scripture may be called a Store-house of al truths necessary to Christians, appeareth out of the first, and second Conclusion. And in the said place B. Fisher writeth of Purgatory. *That though it could not be proued out of Scripture, yet it ought to be beleeued for Tradition.* And in the secōd place he nether saith absolutly; That we ought not to proue our faith, out of Scripture at al, nether to Catholiks, nor to Heretiks : Nor that we ought not to proue it out of Scripture euen against Heretiks : For him selfe so proueth it against Luther, And much lesse saith. That we can not proue it out of Scripture (as Bel falsly forgeth)But his meaning is, That when we dispute with Heretiks, we ought to haue *aliud subsidium quam scripturæ* : other proofs beside Scripture, & hereof he geueth foure reasons.

Sup. c. 1. parag. 2. & 7.

2. First because Luther professed to beleeue Purgatory though it were not in Scripture : 2. Because Scripturs in some points at the first sight, and in words seeme to fauor Heretiks more then Catholiques, as appeareth in the controuersy between S. Hierom, & Heluidius about our Ladies perpetual virginity 3. Because Heretiks deny many parts of Scripture. 4. Because though they admit the words, yet they peruert the sense and meaning of Scripture, which is as

X 3 much

much (faith Tertullian) as if they denied
the words. And oftentimes the true fenfe
is not fo euident that it alone fufficeth to
conuince an Heretik, when to contend a-
bout it *wearyeth*(as the fame Tertullian writeth) *the conſtant, ouer turneth the weak, and*

Eſp.cap. 19. *ſcandaliʒeth the midle ſort.* Wherupon he adui-
feth vs wifely *That in diſputing with Heretiks*
before we come to proofs out of Scripture, we try
whoſe the Scriptures are, & to whoſe poſſeſſion of,
right they belonge. For that being cleared it wil
ſoone appeare (faith he) *who hath the true Chri-*
ſtian faith the true vnderſtanding of Scripture, and
al Chriſtian Traditions. And the fame meant B.
Fiſher who alfo citeth Tertul. & his words
make rather forTraditiõs then againſt them.
And if this courfe were taken with Proteſtants, they wold be quickly confounded.

Doue of Re-
cuſancy. p.
23. For they (as Doue confeſſeth and it is euident) *had the Scripturs from vs,* not by gift, or
loan ; For we nether gaue nor lent them to
Proteſtants ; but by theaft, and ſtealth, as
Turks and Infidels may haue them, and
therfore are wrong vſurpers of our goods
and poſſeſſions, and iuſtly may we fay to

Supra c. 57. them with Tertullian. *VVhen & whence came*
you ? What do you in my poſſeſſion being none of
myne? By what right Marcion (Luther) *doeſt*
thou ſel my vvood? With what lycence Valentine
(Caluin)*doeſt thou turne a vvay my fovvntains;*
                                                    VVith

VVith VVhat authoryty Apelles (Beza *) doest thou moue my limits? It is my possession VVhat do you others sovve, and feed at your pleasure? It is my possession, I possesse it of ould, I possesse it first, I haue strong originals from the Authors VVhose the thing vvas.* Thus Tertullian. And here I omit that Bel citeth an apocriphal sentence out of Esdr. 3. 4. vnder the name of the wise man as if it were Salomons.

3. Next he alleadgeth Canus his words. *Seeing the Canon of Scripture is perfect, and most sufficient to al things, VVhat need the Vnderstanding, and authority of Saints be adioined therto.* But Bel forgot to tel that Canus proposeth this only as an obiection; which he answereth by denying the illatiō therin included. *Because (*saith he*) the Fathers, are needful to right Vnderstand the Scripture,* Nether denying nor graunting the Antecedent concerning the perfection and sufficiency of Scripture. But how sufficient he thought Scripture to be: appeareth l. 3. c. 6. where (after S. Ignatius epist. ad Heronem) he calleth them wolues & Heretiks, which refuse the Churches Traditions and c. 7. solueth the best arguments Protestans bring against them.

4 Out of S. Thomas he citeth *That we must speak nothing of God which is not in Scripture, by vvords, or sense,* But this is nothing against Tradition of other things An other place

Bel p. 101.
Canus de locis lib. 7, c. 3.

Canus.

Bel p. 102.
S. Thom. 1, part. q. 36, art. 2.

place he citeth out of 5.p. q. 42. ar. 4. *VVhat-*
soeuer Christ vvold haue vs read of his doings, and
sayings, he commanded the Apostles to vvrite. as
vvith his ovvne hands. This also maketh nothing against vs. Both because S. Thomas
saith not what Christ wold haue vs beleeue,
but what he wold haue vs read, and Traditions be such as Christ wold haue vs beleeue, though we read them not, as appeareth by his Apostle 2. Thess. 2. v. 15. *Ho'd*
the Traditions vvhich you haue learnt, ether by
speech or by my epistle. As also because S. Thomas speaketh not of al points of beleefe, but
only of Christs sayings, and doings, besids
which the very sayings, and doings of the
Apostles recorded in their acts, & epistles,
or testifyed by Tradition, are to be belee-
vntruth 82   ued. I omit a pettie vntruth, which Bel
often repeateth. *That vve nether vvil nor can*
S. Thomas.   *deny S. Thomas doctrin.* But S. Thomas his
mynd concerning Traditions appeareth by
his words. 2. Thess. 2. *It is euident that there*
are things vnvvritten in the Church, taught by the
Apostles, and therfore to be kept: For as S. Dionis.
saith. The Apostles thought it better to conceale
many things.

Bel p. 103.   5. He citeth also Victoria saying. *I am*
Victoria de   *not certaine of it, though al say it, vvhich is not*
sacrament.   *conteined in scripture.* But Victoria meaneth
of things spoken not by Tradition, but by
proba-

probable opinion , as the conception of
our lady without original sinne, and such
like: or he meaneth of things nether actually nor vertually conteined in Scripture, as
Traditions be according to our 2. Conclusion cap. 1. An other place he alleadgeth
out of Victoria writing, *That for opinions*
we ought no way to depart from the rule of Scri-
ptures. What is this to the purpose ? Let Bel
proue that we ether for opinions , or any
thing els depart from Scripture, and let
him not slander vs as he doth , *That we be-*
leeue whatsoeuer the Pope telleth vs, though it be
neuer so repugnant to Scripture. For who shal
be innocent if it suffice to accuse.

Victor. de
augmento
charitatis,
relect. 8.

Bel p. 103.
83. vntruth.

6· Lastly he quoteth S. Anselme 2. Timoth. 3. and Lyra Math. 19. but omitteth
their words , becaufe they make litle for
him. S. Anselm faith that Scripture , (and
meaneth the old Teftament) can make one
fufficiently learned to get faluatió, to keape
the commandements, and what is more is
not of neceffity but of fupererogation .
Which how litle it maketh againft the beleefe of Traditions were fupererogation to
declare. And thus much touching the fufficiency of Scriptures : now let vs entreat
of their hardnes , or difficulty.

CHAP.

CHAP. VI.
Of the Difficulty or easynes of Scriptures.

Scriptures.

S. Peter.

Bel p. 107.

S. Chrysost.
& Concion.
3. de Lazaro.

S. Austin.

Lex partim
in aperto est
partim etiã
inuelatis
tegitur. Na-
zianz. orat.
1. de Theo-
log.

SCRIPTVRES are difficult, and hard to vnderstand. This is against Bel pag. 107. but expresly taught by S. Peter, 2. Pet. 3. v. 16. where speaking of S. Pauls epistles he saith. *In which are some things hard to be vnderstood.* To this Bel frameth three answers. First *that S. Peter saith not the whole Scripture is hard to vnderstand, but some things in S. Pauls epistles.* This is not to the purpose; because we say not that the whole Scripture, that is euery part thereof, is hard to vnderstand: But graunt with S. Chrysostom. 2. Thessal. hom. 3. *Whatsoeuer is necessary* (to euery mans saluation) *is manifest out of Scripture.* And with S. Austin lib. 2 doct. Christ. c. 9. *Al those things which concerne faith and manners are plainly set dovvne in Scripture.* And lib. 2. de pec. mer. & remiss. c. vlt. tom. 7. *I beleeue euen in this point we shold haue most cleare testimony of Gods word, if man could not be ignorant of it without losse of saluation.* Yet withal affirme with the same holy Doctor in psal. 140. *If Scripture were no where obscure it wold not exercise vs.* And the like he saith serm. 13. de verb. Apost. Only we affirme
that

that abſolutly the Scripture is hard, and to this it ſufficeth that ſome places are hard. As for away to be dangerous, it ſufficeth that ſome places be perilous, though others be ſecure.

The Scripture abſolutely hard though not euery place thereof.

2. His ſecond anſwer is: *That S. Peter only ſaith ſome places are hard to the vnlearned, vvhich are vnſtable.* And like is his third anſwer. *That they are hard to the vvicked, vvhich depraue them.* But to anſwer thus is in deed to depraue Scriptures, and to ſhew him ſelfe to be one of the vnlearned, and vnſtable, wherof S. Peter ſpeaketh. For S. Peter abſolutly ſaith ſome things in S. Pauls epiſtles are hard, not reſpectiuely to theſe or other kind of men. *In vvhich* (epiſtles) ſaith S. Peter) *ſome things are hard to be vnderſtood, vvhich the vnlearned, and vnſtable depraue to their owne perditiō.* Behold he ſaith not ſome things are hard to the vnlearned, and vnſtable, but abſolutly ſome things are hard, which hard things the vnlearned, and vnſtable depraue. And as S. Auſtin ſaith lib. de fid. & oper. c, 14. one ſpecial hardnes meant by S. Peter in S. Pauls epiſtles is his difficult ſpeech, and high commendation of iuſtifying faith, which now Proteſtants depraue to their owne perdition, in gathering therof that faith alone doth iuſtify, as ſome gathered in the Apoſtles tyme, againſt which opinion eſpecial-

S. Peter.

S. Auguſtin. tom. 4.

especially (as the same holy Doctor witnesseth) S. Peter, S Ihon S. Iames, and S. Iude writ their epistles: An other special difficulty meant by S. Peter (saith S. Austin ib. c. 16) are his words 1. corinth. 3. *If any build Vpon the foundation.* &c.

3. Againe if Scripturs be not hard, what meant S. Philip to ask the Eunuch (who was as holy & studious a man as S Hierom, ae he him selfe testifyeth epist. ad Paulin:) If he vnderstood them? What meant the Eunuch to answere. 6 *How can I if some do not shew me?* Could not an holy man so wise as he was, being Treasurer to the Q: of Ethiopia vnderstand easy matters? If Scripturs be

so easy what need had K. Dauid to pray for vnderstanding to search Gods law: for opening his eyes to consider the wonders of it? what hapned to the Apostles that they could not vnderstãd Christs parables? what

needed the gift of interpretation giuen to some: 1. corinth. 12. v. 10. Nay al are interpreters if the Scripture be cleare to al.

4. Origen saith that *Scripture is reuera multis in locis obscura,* in *very deed obscure in many places.* And that they take away the key of science, who say the Scripture is manifest:

hom. 20. in Math. S. Chrysostom noteth, *That Christ bid not read, but search Scriptures, because summa indigent diligentia they need great study.*

ftudy. S. Hierom writeth that al the epistle
to the Romans *is nimys obscuritatibus inuoluta*
wrapped in excessiue obscurities. That the Apo-
calips *hath as many misteries as words.* S. Auftin noteth, That to tame our pride some
things are so obscurely said *as densissimam*
caliginem obducunt they bring ouer a most thick
darknes. And wil Bel account that cleare
which the glistering beam of Gods Church
(for so Bel tearmeth S. Auftin) accounted
so dark and obscure. And epist. 119. c. 21.
professeth to be ignorant of many more
things in Scripture then he knoweth: If
Bel after our holy Fathers, please to heare
his owne vnholy syers. Luther telleth him
that he is most impudently rash who professeth to
know one book of Scripture in al points. By daily
reading (of Scripture saith Caluin. 3. instit.
c. 2. parag. 4.) *we fal vpon many obscure places*
which conuince vs of ignorance. Nay to what
purpose doth Bel require the commentaries of Fathers for better vnderstanding
of Scriptures, if there be no difficulty in
them.

5. Finally if our common lawes handling
nothing but buying, selling, bargaining,
and such common, and vsual matters, as are
daily practized of men, be so hard and difficult, as they require great study to be wel
vnderstood, and Clients wil giue great fees
for

S. Hierom.
epist. ad Al-
gosiam. q. 8.
Epistol. ad
Paulin.
S. Augustin.
l. 2. de doct.
Christ. c. 6.
See 12. Conf.
c. 14 serm. 4.
5. 13. de verb.
Apost. Iren.
lib. 2. cap. 47.
Cyrill. præ-
fat. lib. the-
saur.
S. Augustin.
tom. 2.

Luther. præ-
fat. in psal.

Caluin.
Quotidie
legendo in
multos ob-
scuros lo-
cos incidi-
mus, qui
nos igno-
rantiæ coar-
guunt.
Bel p. 102.
Reason.

for Lawyers counsel in them, what shal we thinke of Gods laws, which entreat of deuine, and supernatural things, far aboue mans reach, and capacity. Or if as S. Austin saith lib. de vtil. cred. *c.* 7. *He that hath no skil in poetry, dare not medle with Terentian Maurus without a maister, Asper, Cornutus, Donatus and infinit others are requisit to vnderstand any Poet, and doest thou without a guide rush vpon holy books ful of deuine matters?* O exceeding boldnes or rather madnes. And againe: *If euery art though base and easy require a teacher, or maister to get it, VVhat is more foolish heady pride, then not to learne the booke of deuine sacraments of their interpreters?* Now let vs heare Bels reasons to the contrary.

6. *Salomon* (saith he) *Prouerb.* 8. v 8. 9. *teacheth That the Words of Wisdom are easy and open to euery one of Vnderstanding.* But let vs heare Salomon him self. *Al my speeches are iust, there is not in them any thing wicked or peruerse. They are right to such as Vnderstand, and euen to such as find knowledge.* What word is here of easynes, or manifestnes of Gods words? but only of their vprightnes, and equity. And let Bel learne of S. Austin in psal. 146. to. 8. *That in Scripture there is nothing peruers, but some thing obscure.* But perhaps Bels english Byble deceaued him, which to deceaue the Reader vsed the ambiguity of the english **word**

S. Augustin. tom. 6.

Ib. cap. vlt.

Bels Arguments. p. 108.

Ansvver.

S. Austin.

Bible printed 1584.

word (plaine) which may ſignify ether manifeſt or euen) for the latin word (*æqui.*)

7. After this Bel cyteth dyuers places of
Scripture to proue That *God reuealeth his wil*
to al that fear him, to litle ones : That the *doers*
of his wil know his doctrin and truth. But ſeeing
it is no where ſaid That God reuealeth his
wil, or the good know it, by bare reading
his word, but rather the contrary ; becauſe
faith commeth of hearing, and how ſhal they heare
without a preacher Rom. 10. v. 17. 15. Theſe
places make nothing for eaſines of Scripture. Beſids that they may be expownded,
not of Gods wil in al points, but in ſuch as
are neceſſary to euery mans ſaluation, which
we graunt to be plainly reuealed in Scripture. I omit his other places. That the Scripture *is a lanthern, light or candle* : and That *the*
ſpiritual man iudgeth, or (as he expowndeth)
vnderſtandeth al things : for they are anſwered
hereafter.

8. He alleageth S. Chriſoſtom ſaying.
What need we a preacher ? our *negligence hath*
brought this neceſſity. For to what end is a ſermon
needful. Al things are clear and plaine out of
Scripturs: What things ſoeuer are neceſſary are ma-
nifeſt : But S. Chriſoſtom ſpeaketh not of al
things in Scripture, but only of ſuch as are
neceſſary to euery ones ſaluation, as is euident by his laſt words And ſuch need no
preacher

pag. 108.
Pſal. 25. v.
9.
Ioan. 7. v.
17.
Ioan. 8. v.
31. 32.
Math. 11.
v. 25.
S Paul.

Pſalm. 119.
al. 118. v.
105.
2. *Pet.* 1. v.
19.
1. *Cor.* 2. v.
15.
Cap. 9. pa-
rag. 17.
Bel p. 108.

S. Chryſoſt.
hom 3. in 2.
Theſſalon.

preacher for to be vnderstood, though they need to be beleeued as S. Paule testifyeth

S. Paul.

Roman. 10. 17. But besides these there are things obscure as the same holy Doctor witnesseth in the same place in these words. *Thou knowest which are cleare, what askest thou the obscure?* And hom. 10. in Ioan. he biddeth men note *which is cleare which obscure in Scripture, and to harken the exposition of them in the Church.* And for such points, preachers, and preaching is as necessary now to vs, as wel for vnderstanding as for beleeuing them, as they were to the Eunuch. act. 8. to the two disciples Luc. 24 Other places he cyteth out of S. Chrysostome concerning reading of Scripture which shal be answered in his proper place.

S. Chrysost. item Concion. 3. de Lazaro.

Homil. 9. Coloss. and Concion. 3. de Lazaro.

9. What hath bene answered to the words of S. Chrysostom is to be applyed to the like in S. Austin lib. 2. de doct. Christ. c. 9. *In these things which are plainly set down in Scripture are found, al those things which concerne faith and manners.* For he saith not absolutly. Al things: but al those things: therby insinuating that he meaneth only of things necessary to be beleeued, and done of euery one: which Bel perceauing in englishing his words leaft out the word. *Those.* But I maruel what he meant to cite S. Aust. writing: *The holy Ghost hath so tempered Scriptures*

S. Augustin. tom.

False translat.

S. Augustin. l. 2. de doct. Christ. c. 6.

ptures that locis apertioribus by manifester places
(Bel tranflateth manifold places) *he might*
prouide for hunger (defire of knowledge) *and*
by obfcurer wipe away loathfomnes. For here he
plainly teacneth Scripture to be obfcure in
fome places. But perhaps it is becaufe S.
Auftin addeth. *Almoft nothing is in the obfcure*
places., which is not moft plainly vttered other-
where. But this helpeth Bel nothing. For nether faith he that al obfcurities are plainly
other where explicated. Nor that it is plaine
in what places they are explicated. And fo
S. Auftin admitting fome obfcure places of
Scripture to be no where explicated in Scripture, and fuppofing it not to be plaine in
what places fuch obfcure places as are explicated, be explicated, admitteth Scripture
to be obfcure . An other place he citeth *Bel p.* 111.
out of S. Auftin, as alfo S . Hierom and 112.113.
Theodoret concerning reading of Scripturs, which fhal be anfwered in the next
chapter.

Chap. VII.
Of the vulgar peoples reading
Scripture.

FIRST conclufion, it is not neceffary to
al forts of people, that defire to attaine
to eternal life to read Scripturs. The contrary

trary auoucheth Bel pag.103. & 109. wherin he exceedeth the heretike Pelagius who required not reading, but only knowledge of Scripture for to be without sinne,& therby condemned a great part of Christians as S.

S. Hierom. Hierom writeth dialog. 1. cont. Pelag. But it is so manifest as it needeth no proofe. For how should they doe that can not read? Doth Bel thinke Scripture to be like a neck verse, that who can not read it, shal be hanged? where doth God command euery one vpon paine of death to read Scripturs? whence came this new law which Bel proclaimeth? But marke Reader, Protestants taught at first that no works were necessary to saluation. And now Bel auoucheth one more (vz. reading of Scripturs) then euer Catholiques dreamed on.

See S. Gre-gor. Nazian-zen. in Apo-loget. & o-rat. 1. de Theolog.

2. Second conclusion, It is not expedient for euery one of the vulgar sort to read Scripturs. This I proue becaufe vnlearned, and vnstable persons depraue the Scripture to their owne perdition. Many of the vulgar sort are vnlearned, and vnstable. Therfore many of them ought not to read Scripture. The Minor is euident. The Maior is auer-

Hacket. Mo-re. Ket Ham mont. See Stovv Ann. 1561. 1579. red by S. Peter 2. c. 3. v. 16. and proued by daily experience of new Chrifts, new Iewes, new herefyes daily gathered out of Scripture. And in truth the Protestants counsel-

ling

ling of common people to read Scripturs, is
much like to the Diuels perſwading of Eue
to eat the Apple. He asked Eue why God
forbad her to eat?they aske:why the Church
forbiddeth vs to read? And both anſwering
alike : He replyeth you shal not die but become like Gods. They ſay you shal not fal
into errors, but become like Deuines. And
the euent is like in both. Eue by eating fel
out of Paradiſe, and incurred death : ſimple
people by reading dye in ſoule, & fal out of
the Church.

3. But ſaith Bel. A good should not be
taken wholy from the godly for fault of the
bad. Anſwere. The godly are not debarred
from reading Scripture if they be deſyrous,
and iudged by their Paſtors to be ſuch as
wil reape good therby. Neuertheles they
ought not without lycence, leſt as S. Auſtin
writeth in the like caſe. *Though they hurt not*
them ſelfs by reading, they may hurt others by ex-
ample. As he that could fly be made to go leſt his
example prouoke others to ſo perilous attempt. This
(ſaith he) *is the prouidence of true religion,* and
deliuered from our Auncestors, and to alter this
courſe were nothing els then to ſeeke a ſacriledgious
way to true religion. Moreouer though a thing
be good in it ſelfe, yet it is not good but to
ſuch as know how to vſe it ; But euery one
of the common people knoweth not how

Bel p.107.

S. Auſtin.
lib.de vtilit.
credend. c.
10.tom.6.

Y 2 to vſe

S. Nazianz.
orat. Quod
non liceat
semper &
publice de
Deo conté-
dere.
In Apologe-
tico.
S. Hierom.
epiſtol. ad
Paulin.

See Theo-
doret.lib. 4.
c. 17.

to vſe Scripture. For as Gregory Nazianzen
writeth *The vvord of holy vvritt is not ſo baſe,
that it is open to the Ʋnlearned common ſort, and
ſeely men creeping as yet Ʋpon the ground.* And
againe *To ſome it is better to be taught by others.*
And S. Hierom complaineth that euery one
challengeth the knowledge of Scripture,
and *that the chatting old vvife, the doating old
men, and the prating Sophiſter take it in hand.*
What wold he ſay now if he ſaw Proteſtants
children reading Scripture, and taught to
read engliſh by the Bybe? Now let vs ſee
Bels obiections.

Bel p. 103.
104.
S. Chryſoſt.
proœm. ep.
ad Rom.

4. Bel alleadgeth S. Chriſoſtom as affirming 1. *That if we read Scripture ſeriouſly vve
ſhal need no other thing.* 2. That it is a great
shame for men charged with wife and children only to heare ſermons, and not withal
to ſtudy Scripturs. 3. *That many euils come of
ignorance of ſcripture, as hereſies, and diſſolute
life.* Anſwer. The firſt point is not againſt
vs, who graunt that in reading Scripture
we may find al things neceſſary. But the
queſtion now is whither it be better for
euery one to find ſuch things him ſelfe out
of Scripture or no. As for the ſecond point
S. Chriſoſtom only ſaith that it is a ſhame
not to exact more diligence of men in hearing ſermons, then in gathering mony. *At
leſt* (ſaith he) *be ready to heare what others haue
gathered,*

gathered, and bestovv so much diligence in hearing vvhat is said as in gathering mony. For though it be a shame to exact but so much of you, yet wil we be content if you performe so much. The third point is easely answered: because he saith not: That much mischeef commeth of not reading (as Bel falsly affirmeth pag. 105.) but of not knowing the Scripture: vz if men wil nether read it them selfs, nor heare it readd and expounded by preachers. Nether could he thinke that much mischeef can come of not reading Scripture, if so be it be heard, seeing he promiseth to be content if men wil heare it.

Innumera mala nata sunt quod scripturæ ignorantur. Chrisf. sup. *vatruth* 84

5. An other place he citeth out of S. Chrisostom where he exhorteth men *auscultare lectionem scripturæ* to harken to the reading of Scripture. And againe : *At home to apply them selfes to read Scripturs.* Answer. The first part maketh nothing for reading, but only for hearing Scripture as is euident. The second exhorteth to reading but 1. not euery man woman, & child as Protestants do, but men, and namely such who (as he saith proem. epist. ad Rom.) *haue wiues, charge of children, and family.* And hom. 9. Colos. *Hear you* (saith he) *who liue in the vvorld, haue care of vvines and children: who* (as he writeth conc. 3. de Lazaro) *haue publicke offices, mantein wiues, and children.* And yet Bel wil haue

Bel p. 105. S. Chrysost. hom. 29. in 9. c. Genes. tom. 1.

Differences betvvixt S. Chrysost and Protestants. 1.

Bel p. 110.

Y 3   him

him to speake to both sexes as if both sexes

Hom. 9. ad
Coloss. &
hom. 37. 1.
Cor.
had wiues. As for woemen and children he affirmeth *That they ought to be instructed of men.*

2.
6. Secondly he exhorteth not (as Protestants do) al kind of secular men, to wit

S. Peter. 2. c.
3. v. 16.
vnstable (as S. Peter calleth them) and inconstant in their faith. For such are like rather to depraue Scripturs to their perdition (as S. Peter testifyeth) then to reape good

5.
by reading them. Thirdly the secular men whom he exhorteth, he exhorteth not (as Protestants do) to the reading equally of al parts of Scripture, but especially such as are plaine, and easy, namely histories, as appea-

S. Chrysost.
reth by these his words 2. Thess. hom. 3. *But thou vvilt say they are obscure, What obscurity is this? I pray thee are there not Histories? Thou knowest which are cleare, what askest thou of the obscure places? There are a thousand Histories in Scripture tel me one of them.*

4.
7. Fourthly he exhorteth them not absolutly (as Protestants do) in al tymes, without regard of any occasion or circumstance : but seeing the people of Constan-

Proæm. ep.
ad Rom.
tinople (to whom he preached) giuen (as he saith) to dissolute life, to idlenes, to haunting after dishonest shewes, and riot, for to withdraw them from such vice, and to imploy their tyme better, he exhorted them
to buy

to buy **Bybles**, and to read the Scripture;
and vpon this occasion he said. *That the A-*
postle commanded to read the Scriptures diligently.
And in like sort seeing their children to
haue learnt diuelish songs and dances (as
he tearmeth them) for to take such from
them he biddeth men *to teach them to sing*
psalmes. But how things ought absolutly to
proceed, he vttereth in these words vnto
men. *Vos oportebat duntaxat à nobis instituí,*
Vxores vero à vobis, à vobis & liberos: you
ought only to be instructed of vs, but your
wiues, & children of you. And 1. Corinth.
hom. 37. he saith: That S. Paul appointed
men to teach their wiues, as indeed he did
in these words. *If they (woemen) list learne*
any thing let them aske their owne husbands at
home. 1. Corinth. 14. v. 35. And the like he
hath 1. Tit. 2. Behould S. Paul bids woemen learne of their husbands. Bel bids them
read, and learne of Scripture, let woemen
chuse whether they wil follow.

8. Fiftly: he exhorteth not secular men
to read Scriptures with that mynd, and
purpose, which Protestants doe, to wit
vpon curiosity, and to become their owne
interpreters following their owne priuate
spirits, and thereby to iudge of the doctrine
of the Church, and their Pastors, whome
Christ hath giuen to expound Scripturs, *lest*

Marginal notes:
Homil. 9,
Coloss. cit.

Ibid.

Ibid.

S Paul.

5.
A mayne
difference
betwixt S.
Chrysost.
and Prote-
stants.

Ephef. 4. v. 14.

they fhold be carryed away with al wind of doctrine. But S. Chryfoftoms meaning was,
that reading Scriptures for their confort
(as he writeth hom. 9. cit.) in aduerfity, for
auoyding of vice, and fuch like holy purpofes, they fhould expound them accor-

*See S. Chry-
foft. homil.
10. in Ioan.
& 3. de La-
zaro.
Origen. 4. in
Leuit.
Autor im-
perfecti.*

ding to their Paftors inftruction: *you* (faith
he) *ought to be inftructed of vs*, and the Author
imperfect. hom. 43. in Math. amongft other
means, which he prefcribeth to lay men to
know the truth of Scripture, one is to aske
the Priefts whome he calleth *clauicularios
fcripturarum*, key keepers of Scripturs. which
is the right order prefcribed by God him

*Deuter.
Agge.
Malach.*

felfe Deutr. 17. v. 9. Agg. 2. v. 12. and Malach. 2. v. 7. And the contrary courfe obferued by Proteftants, maketh Chrift to haue

*Ephef. 4. v.
11.
1. Cor. 12.
v. 28.
Luc. 10. v.
16.*

giuen vs needles Paftors, and Doctors, bidding vs heare them as him felfe, maketh
euery one his owne Paftor, and to haue the
gift of interpretation contrary to S. Paul 1.
Corinth. 11. v. 10. 30. And by this which
hath bene faid is anfwered, whatfoeuer Bel
alleadgeth out of S. Chryfof. pag. 108. 109.
111. and he found to be quite againft Proteftants, and nothing againft Catholiques
proceedings. And though S. Chryfoftom

Note this.

had giuen far more lyberty to common
people to read Scriptures, then now the
Church doth, as not hauing then experience

rience of the harme redounding thereof,
what maruel if the Church, finding by the
experience of more then a thowsand years
since S. Chrysostoms tyme , that more
harme then good commeth therby , hath
abridged that lycence? For as S. Austin saith
Epist. 50 Experience of many euils maketh
many medicins to be found.

   9. Now let vs heare what Bel replyeth
against this kind of answering to S. Chrysostoms authority. First he saith , *That the*
doctrine in the pulpit ought to be as true as in the
schoole. This is true, but not to the purpose,
because we reproue not S. Chrysostom of
vttering vntruths in the pulpit . Next he
saith, *That the doctrin in the pulpit ought to be as*
exact, and absolute as in the schoole, and the only
difference is, that in the pulpit it hath the pricke of
exhortation, which is wanting in schools. What
Syr? Are these speeches of S. Chrysostom
cited by your selfe. *VVhat need a sermon? What*
need a preacher? as exact , and absolute as can
be deliuered in schools ? Surely then your
preaching is needles, and consequently the
fifty pound pension giuen to you for it,
may be wel spared . Yea if the doctrin of
pulpit, and schools be of like exactnes, cer-
tes the auditors in both places are of like
capacity, and so Bels deuines be no better
schollers then his common people.

                     10. But

Margin notes:
S. Augustin. tom. 2.

Bel p. 116.

1.

2.

S. Chrysost. hom. 3. in 2. Thessalon. Bel p. 108.

Bel knovv-
eth not
vvhat be-
longeth to
a sermon.

10. But little knoweth he what belongeth to sermons, who thinketh them to
differ from schoole doctrine in nothing but
in exhortation. Are amplifications, hyper-
boles, and like figures excluded as wel from
pulpits, as from schools? Are the same parts
prescribed to be in a lecture by school men,
which are by Orators to be in a sermon or
oration. Doth Bel exact as strong proofs,
and like propriety of words of an orator, or
preacher persuading probably, and accom-
modating him selfe to the capacity of his
hearers, as he doth of a Philosopher, or Deuine teaching dogmatically. Sure I am that
Aristotel. 1.
Ethic.
both Aristotle, and common sense teach
contrary. But Bel euery where sheweth
him selfe to be one of them, *who* (as S. Paul
1. Timoth. 1.
v. 7.
saith) *vnderstand not what they say* , *or of what
they talke.*

11. Againe suppose that S. Chrysostom
had spoken of this point, as exactly in the
pulpit as any Dyuine can in schools: what
pag. 103.
followeth thereof? Forsooth that Bels proposition vz. *That al persons of what sexe, state,
calling, or condition soeuer, may , and ought to
read Scriptures, and can not othervvise attaine to
eternal life* , passeth exact speech , and al-
bounds of truth . Because S. Chrysostom
hath no such exact words : yea the words
which Bel wresteth to his purpose S. Chrysostom

foſtom him ſelfe otherwiſe expoundeth as
hath bene ſhewed. And thus much of Beis
ſecond replv to the foreſaid anſwer.

12. *Thirdly* (ſaith he) *Dauid, and the Ber-* 3.
heans, had no regard of this popish diſtinction of pag.116.
more exact ſpeech vttered in ſchools, then in pul-
pit. Becauſe Dauid Pſalm. 119. v. 9. affirmeth.
That a yong man ſhal cleanſe his waies by ſtudy,
meditation, and keeping of Gods law. The Ber- Corrupt. of
rheans ſearched the Scriptures, and examined the Script.
Apoſtles doctrine by them. Anſwer. Dauid Pſalm.118.
ſaith: A yong man ſhal correct his waies by al. 119. v.
keeping Gods lawes. But *ſtudy, and medita-* 9.
tion are added by Bel, I wonder he added
not alſo *reading.* But ſuppoſe Dauid had
ſaid. That a yong man amendeth his life by
reading Scripture, ſhal we infer that he
thought preachers ſpeake as exactly as
Schoolmen? The like reaſon is the other.
The Berheans examined the Apoſtles doctrine by Scripture. Ergo they thought
the doctrine of the pulpit as exact as the
ſchoole: O wit whither wilt thou? But Chapt.11.pa-
of the Berheans fact we ſhal ſpeake more rag. 4.
hereafter.

13. After this Bel falleth to entreat in *Of woe-*
perticuler of woemens teaching, and rea- *mens tea-*
ding Scriptures, propounding vnto him *ching and reading*
ſelfe this obiection of Catholiques. *s. Paul* *scripture.*
wil haue woemen to learne in ſilence, and per-
mitteth

Bel *p.* 116. *mitteth them not to teach.* 1. *Timoth.* 2. ϒ. 12. &
anſwereth, *That though S. Paul permit them not*
to teach publikly before men , yet he forbiddeth
Prouerb. 31.
ϒ. 1.
Act. 18. ϒ.
26.
2. *Timoth.*
1. ϒ. 5. & *c.*
3. ϒ. 15. *them not to read Scripture, nor to teach priuatly*
where due circumſtances occurre, becauſe Bethſabe
taught Salomon, Priſcilla expounded Scriptures to
Apollo, Eunice , aud Lois inſtructed Timothy in
Scriptures. Here Bel is aſhamed to lycence
woemen to teach publikly before men ,
though he was not to make one of them
head of the Church, which is a far greater
matter, and neceſſarily includeth authority
*Heretical
ϒϒoemen
hoϒϒ male-
pert. ϒϒho
dare tea-
che?*
Tertull. l. de
præſcript.
*Some prea-
ched pu-
blikly in
Germany.*
Sur. An. 1522. to teach the Church publikly : but whether they may teach publikly before woe-
men, or priuatly before men, and what the
due circumſtances are , when they may
teach priuatly, he ſetteth not downe. Nether do I thinke his Proteſtant ſiſters wold
regard them, who publikly before men at
table, and in their aſſemblies in houſes, take
vpon them to expound Scriptures . Surely
he ſhould do wel to informe his ſiſters of
his circumſtances. But as for S. Paul he giueth them no lycence at al to read, or to
teach Scriptures , (excepting the caſe of
perticuler inſpiration, or of neceſſity, when
they are permitted alſo to baptize.) For he
in the foreſaid words not only forbiddeth
them abſolutly to teach , but withal ap-
pointeth them to learne , as if this alone
were

were their duety, and belonged to them.
And left we should thinke they might
learne of them felfs by reading Scriptures,
he explicateth 1. Corinth. 14. v. 35. both of
whome, and where they muft learne: vz.
of their husbands, and priuatly at home.
If they lift to learne (faith he) *any thing, let them*
(not read Scriptures) *aske their husbands at*
home. Behold woemen appointed not to
teach ether publikly, or priuatly, but to
learne, and that priuatly at home, and of
their husbands. And the fame faith S. Chrifoftom. hom. 9. in epift. ad Coloff. S. Hierom dialog. 1. contr. Pelag. where he reprehendeth the Pelagians for licenfing
their woemen to fing with them, (as Proteftants do now, and Bel paffeth in filence)
and faying they ought to be skilful in Scripture. But no maruel if Proteftants being
fo womanish, as they profeffe they can no
more liue without them, then without
meat, or drinke, and herefies haue bene
euer fpred by fauour, and helpe of woemen
(as S. Hierom faith epift. ad Ctefiphontem)
be more liberal to woemen, then the Apoftle, who faid *it was good not to touch them.* 1.
Cor. 7. v. 1.

14. The examples alleadged by Bel for
woemens teaching are partly falfe, partly
not to the purpofe. For Bethfabees words
came

Marginal notes:
S. Paul.

S. Chryfoft.
S. Hierom.

Luther. de
vo. coiug.
Affert. attic.
16. vid. ferm.
de matri-
mon. edit.
VVitember-
bergenf. fol.
116.
S. Paul.

came ether from Gods perticuler inspiration, and so her teaching maketh not to the purpose, or from her owne head, and so she taught not Gods word, though what she said being after recorded by Salomon, became Gods worde. Priscilla is not said act. 18. v. 16. (as Bel affirmeth) to haue expounded Scriptures, but the way of the Lord, to Apollo: which she might do with-out expounding Scripture, as S. Ihon prepared the way of the Lord, without preparing Scripture. That of Eunice, and Lois is vncertaine. For albeit it be said. 2. Timoth. 1. v. 5. *That they were faithful woemen*, and c. 3. v. 15. that *Timothy was instructed from his infancy in scripture.* Yet it is not said he was instructed of them; but might wel be instructed of some other at their procuremēt (as it is vsual for to hyre maisters to teach children) wherfore fondly doth Bel auouch it to be cleare, and euident by their example, that mothers must teach, and yong babes learne Scripture.

Luc. 1. v. 76
Math. 3. v. 3.

15. But suppose that they taught their childe, or grandchild for want of sufficient men to teach, (as may be presumed, be-cause his father was a Gentil. Act. 16. v. 1;) what is this to woemen teaching without al necessity priuatly whome soeuer, euen their husbands, contrary to the prescript,

and

and otder sette down by S. Paul: yea suppose that Bethsabe, Priscilla, Eunice, and
Lois had without perticuler inspiration, or
necessity (which Bel can not proue) taught
men priuatly Scriptures, who seeth not,
but that S. Paul knew better woemens
duety then they, and that we ought rather
to follow his prescript, and order, then the
example of two or three woemen, not the
learnedest, nor greatest Clerks.

16. After this Bel alleadgeth Origen for
proofe of common peoples reading Scripture, and affirmeth him to exhort the people to read Scriptures, because he writeth.
*If we can not al things, let vs at lest remember
that we are now taught, or is rehearsed in the
Church.* But Origen here exhorteth the people only to remembring, *at lest* (saith he)
*those things which are taught and rehearsed this
day in the Church,* to wit by ecclesiastical persons. He bringeth likewise S. Austin ex-
horting his people *not only to heare diuine les-
sons in the Church, but also at home to read them
selfs, or to heare others.* Wherupon Bel noteth.
*That we must read Scriptures at home in our hou-
ses, and not heare them read in the Churches,*
which note is more absurd then I need re-
fel, yet let the Reader remember it. But S.
Austins speech was not to al kind of men,
nor at al tymes, but to his owne people,

whome

*Bel p.*107.

Origen. ho-
mil. 4. in Le-
uit.

*Bel p.*111.

S. Augustin.
serm. 55. de
tempore.

*Grosse ab-
surdity of
Bel.*

whome he knew were like to encreafe
their deuotion in the holy tyme of lent
(whereof he fpake) by reading Scripture.
And the like exhortation may any Catholique Bishop make to his flocke, whome

2. Timoth.
4. v. 4.

he knoweth not to haue, *itching ears, and
not to be foone conuerted to fables,* & yet withal
condemne the promifcual licence graunted by Bel to al forts of people, of what
fexe, ftate, calling, or condition foeuer. For
fo the vnlearned, and vnftable be licenced,

pag. 103.
S. Pet. 2. c. 3.
v. 16.

yea *neceffarily ought* (faith Bel) *to read Scripture,* though (as S. Peter teftifyeth) *they wil
depraue it to their owne perdition.*

17. And fuch conftant Catholiques were

S. Hierom.
in pfalm. 133.
Epiftol. ad
Gaudent. &
epift. ad Ce-
lantiam.

thofe men, and woemen, which (as S. Hierom writeth) *did ftriue, who should learne
moft Scriptures, and whome he exhorted to learne
the Scripture without booke, and to haue it alwaies in their hands, and to teach it their children.* For as him felfe writeth epift. ad Gaudent. cit. *what we fpeake we fpeake not in general, but in part, nor fay of al, but of fome.* And
epift. ad Paulin. reprehendeth greatly. That
euery one should take Scripture in hand.
Wherfore if Bel apply S. Hieroms words

Bel like a
foolish Phi-
fition.

to al forts of perfons of what condition
foeuer, he doth not only againft the holy
Doctors meaning, but sheweth him felfe
to be a foolish Phifition prefcribing the
like

ke diet to al kinde of perſons: not knowing who *can eat milk*, but *not ſolid meat* (as
the Apoſtle ſpeaketh 1. Corinth 3. v. 2.
Hebr. 5. v. 12. For ſome (as he ſaith Hebr.
5. v. 11.) *are weake to heare ſome part of Gods
word*, and much weaker wold be to read it
al. Wherfore the Catholique Church (like
a prudent nurſe) permitteth ſuch children,
as ſhe ſeeth ſtrong, and able, to read Scripturs, to feed them ſelfs, and cut their owne
meat, but to ſuch as ſhe perceaueth to be
weake, and not ſo able, ſhe wil not graunt
the like liberty, but cheweth their meat, or
cutteth it her ſelfe by preaching, & expoū-
ding Scripturs to them, leſt if they were
their owne caruers, they ſhould hurt them
ſelfs. And Proteſtants like careles nurſes,
let al alike carue them ſelfs, and therby cut
their owne fingers, yea throats, & kil them
ſelfs by taking oftentymes poiſon inſteed
of meat.

18. And hereupon I muſt aduettiſe the *Bel p. 112.*
Reader of two vntruths, which Bel fathe-
reth vpon Catholiques vz. *That they deeme,* *vntruth 85*
them moſt holy, who can by hart no Scripture at *vntruth 86*
al, but abſteine from reading therof, as from poiſon
of their ſouls. For ignorance of Scripture in *Ignorance*
it ſelfe we account no holyneſſe at al, and *of it ſelf no*
much leſſe deeme them moſt holy who *holynes.*
know leſt of Scripture. But great holines

we efteeme it, to chufe rather harmles ignorance, then curious, and difobedient

Bonum ip-
fum vtiliter
aliquando
ignoratur.
S. Auguftin.
l.6.cont.Iul.
c. 16.

skil. As great holines it had bene in Eue, to
haue made choife rather of ignorance of
good, and euil, then of knowledge therof.
And the like ignorance of Scripture in Catholiques we preferre before Proteftants
knowledge. For to be thus ignorant (faith

Tertuil.l. de
præfcript.

Tertullian)*is better, left we know that we should
not. Faith* (faith he) *shal faue* vs, *not exercife
in Scripture. Faith is commanded, exercife in Scripture confifting in curiofity hath glory only in
ftudy of knowledge. Let curiofity giue place to faith,
let glory yeeld to faluation.* Thus Tertullian a
moft antient writer, whofe counfel I wold
to God Proteftants did follow. And as for
Scripture we account it no poifon, but the
food of life, and the reading therof good
and holfome, if it be done as it should, not
vpon curiofity, and difobedience to the
Churches precept, as the Aple was good in
it felfe, and the eating therof had not bene
hurtful, if it had not bene againft Gods
commandement.

Bel p. 113.
Theodoret.
lib.5.de Græ-
can. affe-
ction.

19. Bel citeth alfo Theodoret writing.
*That the Hebrew books are turned into al langua-
ges.* Againe, *That we may find ditchers, and
neatheards, and planters reafoning of the Trinity,
and creation of al things.* Anfwer. That of the
Scripturs tranflation shal be anfwered in
the

the next chapter. The other proueth no
more then that simple people knew the said
misteries, whereof, he saith not, they read,
but reasoned. And S. Gregory Nazianzen.
greatly discommendeth such for it. And by
the like reason, might Bel proue euery Catholique to read Scripture. Because (as Bellarmin saith truly:) *Catholique rusticks , and*
woemen, though they vnderstand not the sentences
of Scripture, yet they vnderstand the misteries of
our redemption, and can reason of them, yea better then many Protestants, who dayly read
Scripture. *But* (saith Bel) *why are not al per-*
mitted to read Scripture , if al can vnderstand
therein the misteries of our redemption. And like
to one that hath no thing to doe , proueth
a needles matter , that the knowledge of
the misteries of our redemption , is necessary, and sufficient to saluation , though in
the next page before he noted *that al things*
conteined in the written worde, (which no
doubt are more then the misteries of our
redemption) *are necessary for al people.* But o-
mitting Bels contradiction: To his argument out of Bellarmin : I answer that Bellarmin affirmeth not (as Bel imposeth.)
That al can vnderstand the misteries in the
Scripture, but rather the contrary , when
he saith. *That many vnderstand not the sentences*
of Scripture. And though al could vnderstand

S. Greg. Na-
zianz. orat.1.
de Theol.

Bellarm.lib.
2. de verbo
Dei. c. 4.

Bel p.115.

Contradict.
18.

vntruth 87

Z 2 the

the misteries in Scriptures, yet al were not
to be permitted to read them, becaufe al
haue not (as S. Paul writeth) *their fenfes exer-*
cifed to the difcerning of good and euil: al are not
perfe&t to haue wifdome fpoken amongft
them: al are not to be inftru&ed as fpiritual, but fome as carnal : Al wil *not be wife*
to fobriety, but fome more wife then behooueth
them. Rom. 12. v. 3. Finally al are *not capable*
of folid meat, but fome of mikle only.

Hebr. 5. v.
14.
1.Cor.2.v.
5.
1. Cor.3. v.
1.
Rom. 12.v.
3.
1.Cor.3. v.
2.
Hebr. 5. v.
12.

Chap. VIII.
Of the tranflation of Scripture into vulgar tongues.

Scripture
not to be v-
fed com-
monly in
vulgar ton-
gues.

I T is not expedient to haue or vfe commonly Scriptures in vulgar languages.
This is againft Bel p. 106. but it followeth
of that which hath bene proued in the former Chapter. For if it be not expedient abfolutly for the vulgar fort to read Scripture,
it is not expedient that it be common in
vulgar tongues; left fome like foolifh Eue
be tempted by the fight thereof, curioufly
and againft command to read it . Secondly
becaufe nether the Iewes , after their language was corrupted by their captiuity,
tranflated the Scripture into their vulgar
language. Nor the Church euer commanded the Scriptures to be tranflated into
euery

euery vulgar tongue , but generally vſed
them in Hebrew , greeke, and latine, in
which tongs they were written. As for the
English Bybles tranſlated by Proteſtants , *See Confe-*
they al hitherto haue bene naught, as them *rence at*
ſelfs confeſſe , and are now about a new *Hampton*
tranſlation , which hereafter perhaps wil *Court. pag.*
be found as faulty as the former . Whereby *45.46.47.*
we ſee that the English faith hitherto hath
bene falſe , as builded vpon the English
Bible, which was falſe , and conſequently *The good*
who dyed in it, dyed in a falſe faith, and re- *vvhich*
lyed vpon mans worde in ſteed of Gods. *Proteſtants*
And this is the true death which common *haue gotten*
people haue incurred, and al the good they *by Engliſh*
haue reaped by reading Scriptures in En- *Bibles.*
glish, according to the ſerpentine counſel
of Miniſters. For where before they knew
ſo much of Gods worde, as was ſufficient
to ſaluation, by reading English Bibles they
haue read a lying worde, as now after 46.
years experience they both ſee, and confeſſe, and becauſe they would not content
them ſelfs with knowledge ſufficient to ſo-
briety , and ſaluation, but as the Apoſtle *S. Paul.*
writeth Rom. 12. v. 3.) *be more wiſe then be-*
booued them, God hath ſent them (as the ſame
Apoſtle ſaith) 2. Theſſ. 2. v. 11. *the operation*
of error to beleeue lying.

2. Againſt this Bel obiecteth : *That the* *Bel p. 106.*

Apoſtle

1. Cor. 14.
v. 24.

Apostle calleth them madde who read the Ghospel to people in a language vnknovvne to them, and the people also that listen therto as Catholiques doe. Anſwer. The Apoſtle is ſo far from condemning ſeruice of God in a tongue vnknowne to the hearers, as he ſaith to ſuch a one. *Thou doeſt vvel.* 1. Corinth.14. v. 17. But indeed he ſaith, That if Ideots and infidels hard vs ſo doing they wold ſay we were madde. *If al the Church meet together* (ſaith he) *and al ſpeake vvith tongues, and Ideots or infidels enter, vvil they not ſay that you are madde?* 1. Corinth. 14. v. 23. Wherfore not S. Paul, but onely Ideots or infidels cõdemne theChurches ſeruice in an vnknowne tongue.

Only Idiots
and infidels
condène ſer-
uice in an
vnknovvne
tonge.

Luc.1.v.10.
& 11.

3. And if the ſacrifice and prayer of Zachary (which the people did not ſo much as heare or ſee) did greatly profit them, why may not the ſacrifice, and prayers of Prieſts, which the people both ſee, and heare, greatly profit them, though they vnderſtand them not. And if Bel wil excuſe Zachary, and the Iewes, (yea God who commanded it Leuit. 16.) from madnes though they ſtood without dores, and could nether heare, nor ſee, and much les vnderſtand the ſacrifice, and prayers. Much better (if he pleaſe) may he excuſe Catholiques who both ſee, and heare, and partly vnderſtand the Catholique ſeruice. And
though

though Bel fcoffe at Catholiques, liftening
to the Ghofpel redde in latine. Yet Origen Origen.
hom. 20. in Iofue writeth, *That with only*
hearing fcripture, though we doe not vnderftand *The Diuels*
vvords not
it, the poifon of naughty fpirits, which befiege vs, *vnderftood*
is driuen away as it were with a prayer, and holy *vvorke euil*
fpirits are inuited to helpe vs. For (faith he) *If* *Ergo Gods*
vvords not
words of coniuration pronounced, though not vn- *vnderftood*
derftood, worke inchantments, how much more *do good.*
vertue thinke we haue the words of holy Scrip-
ture. And if S. Chryfoftom hom. 3. de La- S. Chryfoft.
zar. might fay, *That though we vnderftand not*
Scripture, yet ex ipfa lectione multa nafcitur fan-
ctimonia, much holines rifeth by very reading.
Why may we not fay the like of very hearing? And becaufe Bel vrgeth this obiection no farther, I anfwer it no fuller, who
lift fee more of it, let him read Rhemift. 1.
Corinth. 14. D. Stapleton vpon the fame
place, and Bellar. l. 2. de verb. Dei c. 16.

4. Bel obiecteth out of Theodoret, *That* *pag.* 111.
the Hebrew books were tranflated into al langua- Theodoret.
lib.5.de Græ-
ges. This is nothing againft vs, who deny can. affe-
not but Scripture hath bene, and may be, ction.
vpon iuft and vrgent caufes tranflated into
vulgar languages, fo it be not vulgarly vfed,
and common to al kinde of vulgar people: *Bel p.*106.
And here by the way, I muft aduertife the *vntruth* 88
Reader of dyuers vntruths vttered by Bel, Vid. Indic.
concerning this matter. 1. *That the Pope bur-* libror. pro-
hibit.

neth Scriptures in vulgar tongue. This is not fo:
For he burneth only heretical tranflations,
and al England knoweth, how currant the
Rhemifts teftament is amongft Catholiques. 2. *That the Pope excommunicateth al lay*
men, that reafon of matter of faith, or difpute of
his power. & citeth 6. decret. lib. 5. cap. *Qui-*
cunque. Here be two vntruths. For nether is
there any worde of reafoning of the Popes
power, but only of difputing of the Catholique faith; without touching whereof,
we may reafon of the Popes power in diuers waies, as is shewed art. 1. cap. 1. Nether forbiddeth he lay men to reafon, or
difpute of faith with whom-foeuer, or in
what cafe foeuer, but only with Heretiks
(as is euident out of the whole chapter,
which inftructeth Catholiques, how they
ought to behaue them felfs towards Heretiks) and when Cleargy men may difpute,
as when that Canon was made they might
in al Chriftendome. And in this cafe it is
vnlawful for lay men to difpute of faith,
both becaufe generally they are not fufficiently learned to defend the faith againft
Heretiks, as alfo becaufe difputing of faith
is proper them, to whome preaching belongeth, who are not lay but Cleargy men.
Whereupon faid S. Gregory Nazianz. *It is*
not euery ones part to difpute of God.This is not fo
bafe

vntruth 89
vntruth 90

At vvhat
tyme lay
men are for
bidden to
difpute of
faith.

S. Greg. Na-
zianz.orat.1.
de Theol. in
Apologet.&
orat. Quod
non liceat
femper &
publice de
Deo contre-
dere.

baſe matter, or pertaining to them, vvho as yet creeping on the ground, are buſyed vvith earthly ſtudy. Euery one may thinke of God, but not diſpute of God. Thus S. Gregory for his great knowledge ſurnamed the Deuine, whoſe counſel I ſuppoſe euery wiſe man wil ſooner follow then Babling Bel. And the ciuil law puniſheth al lay men, that publikly diſpute of faith. *3. That Prieſts oftentymes vnderſtand not the latin vvords of abſolution.* This he might better obiect to his fellow miniſters, made oftentymes of coblers, tinkers, and taylers, who may thanke the Lord (as one of them did) that they know nothing of the Romiſh tongue. *4. That in the Churches vve read vnto the common people latin ſermons.* In deed we read ſuch in our ſeruice, but read them to the common people no more, then we read the Maſſe to them. But read both in honour, and ſeruice to God, who vnderſtandeth as wel latin as engliſh. And thus much touching Scripture: now let vs come to Traditions.

Cod. de Sum. Trin.

vutruth 91

See Bels lacke of latin art. 5. c. 4. paragr. 10. & art. 2. c. 4. parag. 13. and ar. 7. c. 9. parag. 19. vntruth 92

Chap. IX.

Of Apoſtolical Traditions vvhether there be any or none.

OF the Traditions which the Church manteineth, ſome were inſtituted by Chriſt,

Chrift, some by his Apoftles by the infpiration of the holy Ghoft, and others by the Chnrch it felfe. The queftion is whether there by any of the two former kinds of Traditions inftituted, or deliuered by the Apoftles, and therupon called Apoftolical without writing, *which concerne things* (as Bel faith in the beginning of this article pag. 86.) *neceffary to mans faluation.* For though (as I faid before) the Scripture conteine al things, which are neceffary to be knowne actually of euery one, yet becaufe euery one is bound to deny no point of chriftian faith, but at left vertually, and implicitly to beleeue al, fuch traditions, as concerne matters of faith, or manners, may (as Bel fpeaketh) be faid to concerne things neceffary to mans faluation. This fuppofed, I affirme with the vniforme confent of al holy Fathers, that there are fuch traditions, and it followeth of that which we proued in the firft chapter, that the Scripture conteineth not actually al points of chriftian faith, and otherwife I proue it : becaufe S. Paul 2. Theff. 2. v. 15. faith *Hold the Traditions Which you haue learned, whether it be by worde, or by our epiftle,* therfore he deliuered fome Traditions only by worde as S. Bafil. S. Chrifoftom. S. Epiphanius S. Damafcen out of this place do gather.

2. Se-

what kind of traditiōs Bel impugnēth.

Chapt. 1.

S. Paul.
S. Bafi. de Spirit. c. 29.
S. Chrfoft. 2. Thefalon. hom.—
S. Epiphan. hær. 61.
S. Damafcenus 4. æ fid. c. 17.

2. Secondly S. Ihon the laſt writer of Scripture ſaid. *Hauing many things to vvrite to you, I vvould not by paper, and inke.* Ergo many things which were to be told to chriſtians, S. Shon left vnwritten, yea thought it not expedient to write them. Bel anſwereth *That the Apoſtles taught no needful doctrin, which they did not after commit to vvriting.* This anſwer inſinuateth, that the Apoſtles taught ſome needles matter, contrary to S. Paul 2. Timoth. 2, Tit. 3. and that, which S. Paul commanded the Theſſalonicenſes to hold, & S. Ihon ſaid he had to write, were needles things, which is but to blaſpheme the Apoſtles. Thirdly in the law of nature there were traditions as is euident, and teſtifyed Gen. 18. v. 19. Likewiſe in tyme of the law written as English Proteſtants confeſſe: why not therefore in tyme of the Ghoſpel?

3. Fourthly I wil propoſe to the Reader a choiſe ſomwhat like to that which a Roman made to his Citizens, when being accuſed of his aduerſary in a long oration, he ſtept vp and ſaid, my aduerſary affirmeth & I deny it, whether beleeue you citizens. And ſo in few words reiected his aduerſaries long accuſation. For S. Dioniſius Areopag. S. Ignatius, both ſchollers of the Apoſtles, S. Ireney, S. Cyprian, S. Baſil. S.

Chri-

3. Ioan. v. 13.

Bel p. 117.

Conference at Hampton Court. p. 68.
Valer. Max. lib. 3. c. 319.
de ſcauro & vario ſeuero,
S. Dioniſ. l. 1. eccleſ. hier. c. 1.
S. Ignat. ep. ad Heron.
S. Iren. lib. 3. c. 3.
S. Ciprian. l. 2. epiſt. 3.
S. Baſil. lib. de Spirit. c. 27. 29.

S. Chrysost.
2. Thessal.
hom.4.
S. Epiphan.
hær.61.
S. Hierom.
dial. contr.
Lucif.
S. Augustin.
epist. 118. &
l. 10. de Ge-
nen. ad lit.
c. 23.

Chrisostom S. Epiphanius S. Hierom. S. Austin and others affirme, that there are Apostolical Traditions: Bel & some few new start vp Heretiks deny it. Whether beleeue you Christians? This choise is far aboue that of the Roman. For there was but one against one, yea ones bare denyal against the others proofs. But here are many against few: Saints against (to say the lest) ordinary fellows: Doctors of Gods Church, against vnlearned Ministers: Catholiques against Heretiks: yea manifest proofs against bare denyals. And shal we not especially in a matter of fact (as is whether the Apostles left any vnwritten Traditions or no) beleeue many, most holy, most learned, most incorrupt, most antient witnesses, yea wherof some were eye witnesses of the matter, before a few, vnlearned, vnconstant, iangling, new fellowes?

S. Hierom.
epist 61.c.9.
S. Augustin.
de Symbolo
ad Catechu-
men.
Ruffin. in
Symbol.
S. Hierom.
con.Heluid.
S. Augustin.
hær. 55.
S. Epiphan.
hær. 78.
Locis supra
cit. & c.3.

4. Moreouer whence haue we the Apostles Creed, but by Tradition, as testify S. Hierom, S. Austin, and Ruffinus: whence the perpetual virginity of our B. Lady, as appeareth by S. Hierom, S. Austin, S. Epiphanius: whence the lawful transferring the Sabbath day from Saterday to Sonday, but by Tradition. Whence many other things, as testify S. Hierom S. Dionis. S. Iren. S. Cyprian, Tertull. Origen, S. Basil S. Epiphan.

Epiphan, S. Chrifoft, S. Hierom, S. Auſtin,
S. Ambroſe, and others, but by Tradition.
But eſpecially, whence haue we the Bible
it ſelfe ? Whence haue we that euery booke
chapter, and verſe of it is Gods worde, and
no one ſentence therin corrupted in al theſe
16 0 0. years ? where haue we that the Goſ-
pel bearing the name of S. Thomas, who
was an Apoſtle, and eye witnes of Chriſts
actions, is not as wel, or better Chriſts
Ghoſpel, then that which carrieth the name
of S. Luke, and was written only by heare- *Luc. 1. v. 2.*
ſay as is profeſſed in the very beginning, but *S. Hierom.*
by Tradition ? This reaſon ſo courſeth Bel *de Scriptur.*
vp and downe, as like fox many tymes vn- *ecclef. in*
earthed, euen for wearines he runneth into *Luca.*
the hunters toyle, graunting what the ar- *geth ſix*
gument would. *anſwers.*

5. His firſt anſwer is *That there is great dif-* *Bel p. 134.*
ference betwixt the primatiue Church, and the
Church of late daies. For the Apoſtles heard
Chriſts doctrine, ſavv his myracles, and were re-
plenished with the holy Ghoſt, and conſequently
muſt needs be fit vvitneſſes of al that Chriſt did,
and taught, vvhich adiuncts the Church of Rome
hath not. Here Bel blaſphemeth Chriſts
Church of late daies, auouching her to be
nether replenished with the holy Ghoſt, *Symbol. A-*
contrary to our Creed, profeſſing her to be *poſtol.*
holy, and Chriſts promiſe, *that the holy Ghoſt*
should

Ioan. 14. v. 16.

should remaine *with her for euer.* Nor to be a fit witnes of his truth, contrary to S. Paul,

1. Timoth. 3. v. 15.

affirming her to be *the piller, and ſtrength of truth* ; and to Gods, ſending her to preach, and teſtify his truth to infidels, to whom if ſhe be no fit witnes , the fault is in God to ſend ſuch inſufficient witneſſes, as infidels are not bound to beleeue.

6. And Bel is far deceaued in thinking, that ſeeing, or hearing make men ſufficient

VVhat maketh ſufficient vvitneſſes of Goas truth.

witneſſes of deuine, and infallible truth, or the want of them maketh inſufficient. For not humane ſenſe, which is ſubiect to error, and deceit, but Gods deuine aſſiſtance, maketh men infallible, and ſufficient witneſſes of his truth, and the want of this, inſufficient. Wherfore S. Mathew was as ſufficient a witnes of Chriſts natiuity, which he ſaw not, as of other things he ſaw, and S. Luke as ſufficient a witnes of the things he wrote by hear-ſay, as S. Ihon who ſaw, and heard almoſt al he wrote becauſe they were equally aſſiſted by God in their writing. And in like ſort the Church of what tyme ſoeuer is equally a ſufficient, and infallible witnes of Chriſts truth, though ſhe be not an eye, or eare witnes of his ſpeeches, and actions, as the primatiue Church was. Be-

Math. 28. v. 20. Ioan. 14. Math. 16.

cauſe Chriſts promiſes of his preſence , and the holy Ghoſts aſſiſtance , and that the

gates

gates of Hel should not preuaile againſt
her, appertaine equally to the Church of al
tymes:

7. But ſuppoſe that the preſent Church
could not be a fit witnes as the primatiue *Bel anſwe-*
was, what is this to the argument, that pro- *reth not to*
ueth neceſſity of Tradition, becauſe with- *the purpoſe.*
out teſtimony of the Church, we can not
diſcerne true Scripture from falſe. This Bel
ſhould ether graunt, or deny, if he meant
to anſwer to the purpoſe, and not tel vs
of an other matter, vz. That the preſent
Church can be no fit witnes, whereof (if it
were true) wold follow, that we can beleeue no Scripture at al, ſeeing we haue
no other infallible external witnes of Scripture.

8. His ſecond anſwer is: *That as Papiſts* *Belp. 134.*
admit the Iewes Tradition of the old Teſtament,
to be Gods word, and withal refuſe many other
Traditions of theirs: So Proteſtants admit this Tra- *Bel admit-*
dition (of the Bible to be Gods worde) *and* *teth tradi-*
reiect al other. And pag. 128. He dareth not *tion.*
deny Traditions abſolutly, yea admitteth
them, when they be conſonant to Scripture. Behold the ſilly fox in the toyle. We
contend againſt Proteſtants, That Scripture is not ſufficient to proue al points of
Chriſtian faith, but that Tradition is neceſſary for ſome, and Bel here confeſſeth it,
where

where is now the *downeful of Popery*? Me
thinks. it is become the down-fal of Prote-
stantry. Where is now Bels first proposition? *That Scripture conteineth in it euery doctrine*
necessary to mans saluation. Where is now that
vve must not adde to Gods vvritten vvorde, if
this Tradition must needs be added therto?
where is now, that *the present Church can be*
no fit vvitnes, if by her testimony, we come
to know Gods truth? Where is *now the curse,*
vvhich S. Paul (as thou saist pag. 117.) *pronoun-*
ceth against him, that preacheth any doctrine not
conteined in Scripture? where is now. *That Scri-*
pture is the sole, and only rule of faith?

9. But seeing the fox is in the toyle, we
must needs haue him preach, and tel vs of
whome he first had this Tradition. Perhaps
he wil confesse with his brother Doue, that
Protestants had the Bible as Gods worde
from Papists. Sure I am, he can name no
other of whome he first had it. Likewise
he must tel vs. How he beleeueth this Tradition. Whether as fallible and humane
truth, or as infallible and deuine. If as fallible, and humane, surely he can beleeue nothing in the Bible as deuine truth. If as infallible, and deuine truth, surely the Papists
Church for whose only testimony (speaking of outward testimonies) Protestants
first beleeue: as an infallible truth that the
Bible

pag. 86. &
88.

pag. 87.

pag. 134.

Bel cursed
of S. Paul
by his ovv-
ne iudge-
ment·
pag. 128.

Doue of Re-
cusancy.
pag. 13.

Bible was Gods worde) hath infallible authority.

10. Nether is Bels comparison true. For we beleeue not the old testamēt to be Gods worde, for any Tradition, which the Iewes haue, but which the Catholique Church hath from the Apostles, & their successors, *enen* (as S. Austin writeth) *from the very seat of Peter, to whom our Lord commanded his sheepe to feed, to this present Bishop,* who deliuered vnto the Church, and she to vs, as wel the olde as the new testament for Gods worde. Let Bel if he list beleeue the old testament, for the tradition of Iewes, and if he can not finde the like vninterrupted tradition for the new testament, but in the Papists Church, let him confesse, that for her authoriry he beleeueth this tradition as infallible truth, and I aske no more.

Cont. epist. fundam.c. to. 6.

11. But what shift findeth he for this notorious contradiction, in admitting one tradition, and before impugning traditions in general. Forsooth because as he saith (and it is his fourth solution) *VVhen Protestants say Scriptures conteine al things necessary to saluation, they speake of Scriptures already agreed vpon to be such, and so exclude not this tradition, but vertually include it in their assertion :* Behold the fox againe in the toile, admitting one tradition ful sore against his wil. O violence

Bel p. 135.

Protestants admit tradition.

Aa   *of truth*

of truth (faith S. Auſtin l. cont. Donatiſt.
poſt Collat. c. 24.) *ſtronger then any racke, or
torment for to ʒring out confeſſion.* For here

*Proteſtants
ouerthrovv
their ovvne
arguments
againſt tra-
ditions.*

Bel in name of Proteſtants confeſſeth, that
they muſt needs admit one tradition, which
not only ouerthroweth al their arguments
againſt other traditions, For why may they
adde one tradition to Gods written worde,
rather then more? why may they beleeue
any thing out of Scripture, and no more?
why is one tradition equal to Gods written
worde, and no more? How is one tradition
certaine and no more: But alſo sheweth
that ether they receaue this tradition for no
authority at al, but only becauſe it pleaſeth
them, or that they beleeue it as infallible
verity, for the authority which they account but fallible. For I aske why they beleeue this tradition? If they anſwer, becauſe it commeth from God. I demand how
they know that? Not by the Bible as is euident. If by the Church; then I aske why
they beleeue the Church, rather in this tradition, then in other, and whether they beleeue her teſtimony to be infallible in this
point or no: And whatſoeuer they anſwer,
they muſt needs fal into the toile.

Bel p. 135.

12. His third ſolution is. *That the nevv
Teſtement is but an expoſition of the olde, and
therfore may be tryed and diſcerned by the ſame.*
                                                    But

But Syr? wil you indeed try the new testa- *Bel wil ex-*
ment? wil you take vpon you to iudge Gods *amin Scri-*
worde? Surely this pride exceedeth Luci- *ptures.*
fers, this is to make your selfe iudge aboue
the highest. And if you wil try Gods word,
by what wil you try the old testament? Surely by tradition, or by nothing. Thus we
haue heard Bel twise plainly confessing some
tradition to be necessary, & now the third
tyme supposing it. For *magna est vis veritatis
& preualet.*

13. Yet because his stomacke could not *pag* 135 *al.*
disgest any one tradition at al, he flyeth to a 117.
Fift solution, commonly giuen by Protest-
ants. vz. *That Canonical Scripture may be discer-* *Psalm.* 119.
ned from not Canonical by themselues, as light is v.105.
from darknes. This he proueth *because Gods* 1. Pet. 1. v.
worde is called a light, and a lantherne, sayd to 19.
shyne to men. spiritual men sayd to iudge al things, 2. Cor. 5.
v. 3.
the vnction to teach al things, and Chrifts sheepe 1. Cor. 2. v.
sayd to heare, and know his voyce. But this is 15.
easely refelled. Firft because though Sa- 1. Ioan. 2.
muel were a faithful, & holy man, and God v. 27.
Ioan. 10. v.
spake thrise to him, yet he tooke his worde 3. 4.
for mans worde, vntil Hely the high Prieft 1. Reg. 3.
tolde him it was Gods worde 1. Reg. 3. Ge-
deon was faithful, and yet knew not at firft
that it was God that spake vnto him by an Iudic. 6.
Angel, and therfore demanded a miracle in
confirmation of it Iudic. 6. The like may
A a 2   be said

be said of Manues wife Iud. 13. and perhaps
of Manue him selfe. For though in his
prayer he proiesse that God had sent the
Angel, whom he tooke to be a man, yet
doth he not professe that God had sent him
especially, and perticulerly to do that mes-
sage, and seeing he knew not, that it was an
Angel, vntil he ascended in the flame of the
sacrifice, yea seemed to doubt whether his
words would proue true, when he sayd. *If
thy speech be fulfilled*, likely it is that he was
not certaine that it was Gods worde, before he was certaine, that it was his Angel.
Likewise S. Peter was faithful, and yet at
first he knew not, that it was an Angel that
spake, and deliuered him act. 12.

Act. 12.

14. Secondly the true sense, and meaning of Gods worde, is not so euident to the
faithful, for to discerne it from the false
sense, as light is discerned from darknes.
Ergo, nether Gods true worde is so euidently discerned by them from the false worde.
The consequence I proue, because Gods
worde consisteth more in his meaning then
in letters. *Let vs not thincke* (saith S. Hierom)
*that the Ghospel is in the words of Scripturs, but
in the sence.* Againe: *Scripturs consist not in reading but in vnderstäding.* And therfore if it be
discerned by it selfe, it is rather discerned
by the sense, then by the letters or words.

S. Hierom.
in Calat.1.&
dialog. con.
Lucif.

The

The antecedent I shal proue hereafter, and it is euident by the example of the Apoftles, who though they were faithful oftentymes vnderftood not Chrifts meaning, efpecially when he fpake in parables, or of his paffion by the example of the faithful Eunuch, and by the teftimony of S. Peter 2. Pet. 3. v. 16.

15. Thirdly the diftinction of Scripturs from not Scriptures, is not fo euident, as the diftinction of light from darknes is. Ergo, they are not fo eafely difcerned. The confequence is euident. The Antecedent I proue, becaufe then no man could erre in it, as none can erre in the diftinction of light from darknes. Bel faith. *That only faith-ful can difcerne Scriptures.* But this conuinceth that their diftinction is not fo euident as that of light from darknes: for this al men, yea beafts of fight can difcerne. Nether can faith be needful to difcerne light, or any thing which is fo euident, becaufe as S. Paul faith Hebr. 11. v. 1. *It is an argument of things not appearing,* and it breadeth certain-ty, not euidency in the beleeuer.

Faith can not difcerne any thing clearly.

16. Befide if faithful could as clearly dif-cerne Scriptures, as they can light, they should no fooner here a fentence of Scrip-ture, then they should difcerne it to be Scripture, as they no fooner fee light, then

they difcerne it from darknes, which experience teacheth to be falfe: yea Luther a
faithful man (in Bels opinion) could not

Luther.edit.
Iennen.
Surius Ann.
1522.

VVhitaker.
lib.1. contr.
Duræum p.
11.

difcerne, yea could not beleeue S. Iames e-
piftle to be canonical, but called it ablolut-
ly a ftrawish thing, as his books firft printed, and diuers others teftify, and Whitaker
dare not deny, yea confeffeth that he calleth *it ftrawifh in refpeƈt of other epiftles*, which
is more then to deny it to be Gods worde.
Wherfore let Bel make his choyfe, whether
Luther was not faithful, or S. Iames epiftle
not fo euidently difcerned by the faithful
to be Gods worde as light is. Finally Proteftants admit one Tradition, as neceffary to
difcerne Scriptures, or Bel lyeth pag. 135.
Ergo: Scriptures are not fo euidently difcerned by them felues as light is. For what
neede is there of an other thing to difcerne
light, or any thing fo euident.

17. Nether haue Bels arguments any difficulty to anfwer. For Gods worde is called
a lantherne, or light, not becaufe it is fo
euident, as light is; but becaufe, being once
beleeued to be Gods worde, it sheweth vs
the way to heauen, as light doth to earthly
places, and thereupon it is called of the

Pfalm. 118.

Pfalmift a *lantherne to our feete*. And for the
fame caufe faith is called light, though it be
an obfcure knowledge. Hebr. 11. v. 1. and
by it

by it we fee God only *in ænigmate*: 1. Cor. 13.
v. 12. and not clearly. And in like fort S.
Paul 2. Corinth. 4. v. 4. (where Bel citeth 2. *Corinth.*
amiſſe. c. 5.) faith the Ghofpel shineth, not 4. *v.* 4.
becaufe it is euident, and cleare, but becaufe it expelleth the ignorance of infidelity, which metaphorically is called darknes. That of the fpiritual man 1. Corinth. 1.
v. 15. is nothing to the purpofe, both becaufe al faithful are not fpiritual, but fome
carnal 1. Corinth. 3. v. 1. 2. 3. and Galath. 6.
v. 1. and therfore may we better infer that
the Ghofpel is not euident to al faithful: As
alfo becaufe S. Paul explicateth, not by
what means the fpiritual man iudgeth al
things, whether by the euidency of the
things (as Bel wold haue him to iudge Scripture) or by fome outward teftimony. Mo-
reouer S. Ihon faith the vnction teacheth 3. *Ioan.* 2. 7.
vs al things, which we deny not, but no 27.
where, that it alone teacheth vs without
the teftimony of the Church, which is that
we deny, & Bel should proue. Finally Chrifts
sheep heare, and know his voice Ioan. 10. *Ioan.* 10. *v.*
v. 3 4 which no man doubteth of, but the 3. 4.
queftion is whether they heare it of him
felfe alone, or of the Church, and whether
they know it by it felfe, or by teftimony of
the Church, to which purpofe this place
ferueth nothing.

Aa 4   18. Bels

Bel p. 136.

18. Bels sixt solution is, *That we beleeue not the Scripture to be Gods worde, becaufe the Church teacheth vs fo, but becaufe it is of it felfe axiopiftos worthy of credit, and God inwardly moueth vs to beleeue it.* That we beleeue it not for the Churches authority he proueth. Becaufe els the formal obiect of our beleefe, and laft refolution therein, fhould not be the firft verity, God him felfe, but man, which is contrary to S. Dionif. and S. Thomas Aqninas, who teach. That the formal obiect of our faith is the firft verity, and S. Thom. addeth, That faith beleeueth nothing, but becaufe it is reuealed of God: Alfo becaufe *s. Auftin faith, That man learneth not of man, that outward teachings are fome helps, and admonitions, but who teacheth the hart hath his chayre in heauen.* That the Scripture is of it felfe *axiopiftos,* or worthy of credit, we deny not, only we deny, that by it felfe without teftimony of the Church, we can knowe that it is fo worthy. Nether deny we, that God inwardly moueth our harts to beleeue it, only we fay that therto he vfeth alfo the teftimony of the holy Church, nor ordinarily moueth any therto, without the external teftimony of the Church. wherfore albeit it be moft true that we beleeue the Scripture to be Gods worde, becaufe God moueth vs therto: yet

false

S. Dionif. de diuin. nom. c. 7.
S. Thom. 2. 2. q. 1. art. 1.

S. Auguftin. tractat. 3. in Ioan. to. 9.

falſe it is to deny, that we beleeue it not alſo, becauſe the Church doth teach it. Becauſe Gods inward motion, and the Churches outward teſtimony, are no oppoſit cauſes, and impoſſible to concurre to one, and the ſame effect; but the ſecond is ſubordinate to the firſt, and can not worke without it, as the firſt (though it can) doth not worke this effect without the ſecond. Wherfore wel ſaid S. Auſtin *Non crederem Euangelio niſi* Cont. epiſt. fundam. c.4. *me Eccleſiæ authoritas commoueret.* I wold not to. 6. beleeue the Ghoſpel, vnles the authority of the Church did commoue me therto.

19. This place of S. Auſtin ſo ſtingeth *pag.* 137. Bel, as he wyndeth euery way to auoid it. Firſt he telleth vs *that there is a great difference* Bels lacke *betweene* mouere *and* commouere : *becauſe* mouere of latin. *is to moue apart by it ſelfe,* commouere *to moue to-gether with an other.* This difference is falſe. For nether is *mouere* to moue apart, but ab-ſolutly, as it is cōmon to mouing apart, or with an other. Nether, though *commouere* do more properly ſignify mouing with an other, is it alwaies ſo taken, as infinit pla-ces both of holy and prophane writers can teſtify : yea Bel him ſelfe with in 8. lynes *pag.* 138. after engliſheth it abſolutly *mouing*. But ſuppoſe it were : what inferreth Bel there-upon. Forſooth *that* S. *Auſtins meaning is no-thing els, but that the authority of the Church did*

out-

outwardly concurre with _the inward motion of_
God, to bring him to beleeue the Ghofpel. That
the Church did ioyntly concurre to S. Auftins faith of the Ghofpel is certaine, and fo
Bel tranflating _commouere_ for ioyntly mouing I refufe not. But falfe it is that the
Church did iointly concurre with God,
only to the bringing of S. Auftin to the
faith of the Ghofpel, and not to the confer-
uing him in the fame faith. Becaufe c. 4. he
S. Auftin. faith, _That if thou percafe canft finde any mani-_
feft thing in the Ghofpel of Maniches Apoftlefhip,
thou fhalt weaken the authority of Catholiques
with me, who bid me beleeue not thee, which au-
thority being weakned, now nether can I beleeue
the Ghofpel. Behold the authority of Catholiques conferued S. Auftin in the faith of
the Ghofpel, without which he profeffeth
that he could beleeue the Ghofpel no longer. And againe, Amongft other things,
which moft iuftly as he faith holde him in
the Church he reckoneth authority, and
fucceffion in the Church.

20. But do you thinke that Bel wil ftand
to his expounding of _commouere,_ and graunting the Church to concurre with the inward motion of the holy Ghoft to bring a
man to beleeue the Ghofpel? No furely:
[_pag._ 138. For in the next page he telleth vs. _That the_
authority of the Church, did moue (beholde
iointly

iointly mouing forgotten) *S. Auſtin to heare
the Ghoſpel preached, and to giue ſome humane
credit ʸnto it. For deuine faith proceedeth not from
the outward teachings of man, as I haue proued*
(ſaith he) *already out of S. Auſtin.* This denyal of deuine faith to proceed from outward teaching of man, is directly againſt
Scripture, and S. Auſtin. For Rom. 10. v. *S Paul. Ro-*
17. *Faith commeth of hearing* (the preacher.) *man. 10.*
The Coloſſians learnt the grace of Chriſt
of Epaphoras. Coloſſ. 1. v. 7. The Theſſa- *Coloß. 1.*
lonians learnt the Traditions, which they
ſhould keep by ſpeech and letter: 2. Theſſ. *2. Theßa-*
2. v. 15 S. Paul begate the Corinthians in *lon. 2.*
the Ghoſpel. 1. Corinth. 4. v. 15. He begate *1. Corinth.*
Oneſimus: Philem. v. 11. He and Apollo *4.*
were Gods helpers in bringing the Corin- *Philemon.*
thians to Chriſts faith. 1. Corinth. 3. v. 9.
They that ſuccour preachers are called *coo-*
perators of the truth. 3. Ioan. v. 8. and therfore *3. Ioan. 8.*
much more the preachers them ſelfs. And
if deuine faith proceede not at al from out-
warde teaching of men, why did Chriſt
ſend his Apoſtles to *teach al nations?* Math. *Math. 28.*
28. v. 19. why appointed he in his Church
ſome *teachers for conſummating of ſaints* Epheſ. *Epheſ. 4.*
4. v. 11, Why was S. Paul a *teacher of Gentils?*
1. Timoth. 2. v. 7. others? act. 13. v. 4. How *2. Timoth.*
could S. Paul *beſtovv ſome ſpiritual grace ʸpon
the Romans.* Rom. 1. v. 11. Did Chriſt ſend *Act. 13.*

theſe

Rom. 1. thefe Apoftles to teach humaine faith? was
S. Ihon Baptift fent before Chrift to giue
humane knowledge of faluation to his peo-
Luc. 1. ple? Luc. 1. v. 77. Laftly nothing is more
frequent in Scripture then that one man
teacheth an other, and furely it meaneth
not of humane learning, or beleefe. For
what careth the Scripture for that, but of
deuine, and fuch as bringeth to heauen &
faluation, fuch as made Iewes compunct in
Act. 2. *&* hart. act. 2. v. 37. fuch as difpofed Gentils
10. to receaue the holy Ghoft. act. 10. v. 44.

21. Likewife it is againft S. Auftin : Firft
he thinketh (as Bel confeffeth) the Church
to concurre, with the inward motion of the
holy Ghoft to the faith of the Ghofpel :
But faith of the Ghofpel, to which the holy
Ghoft inwardly concurreth is deuine. Ergo
to this the Church concurreth : Befids S.
Cont. epift. Auftin affirmeth, that authority holdeth
fundam. c.4. him in the Catholique Church. And that if
tom. 6. the authority of Catholiques were weakned, he wold not beleeue the Ghofpel,
which he would neuer fay, if his deuine
faith did not depend vpon the Catholiques
authority. Moreouer what more euident
then the holy Fathers, when they fpeake of
beleeuing the Ghofpel, they meane of deuine, and Chriftian faith. And what faith
fhould S. Auftin meane of, but of fuch faith
as he

as he exhorted the Maniches vnto, which was deuine. And in the place alleadged by Bel, he calleth outward teaching helpe to faith, and only meaneth, that a man can not learne faith of man alone, without al inward teaching of God. And therfore addeth. *That if he be not within, who teacheth the hart, in vayne is our sound, and where Gods inspiration is not, there in vaine words sound outwardly.* which is most true, and nothing against vs. Lastly it is against reason. For the authority of Gods Church is not meere humane, but in some sort deuine, as a witnes by God him selfe appointed to testify his truth. And therfore he said, *Who heareth you heareth me:* therfore the faith that proceedeth from such authority is not humane.

Tract.3.in I. Ioan.10.9.

Luc. 10.y. 16.

22. Wherfore Bel not trusting much to this shift flyeth to an other: vz. *That S. Austin said not these words of him selfe, as he was then a christian, but as he had bene in tymes past a Maniche.* This he proueth: Because in the same chapter he saith. *That the authority of the Ghospel is aboue the authority of the Churche,* & in the chapter before. *That the truth of Scriptures must be preferred before authority, consent of nations, and the name of Catholique, and promiseth to yeeld to Maniches doctrine, if he shal be able to proue it out of Scripture.* But both this

vntruth 93 1.

vntruth 94 2.

vntruth 95 3.

answer,

anſwer, and proofs are moſt falſly auouched vpon S Auſtin. For if he had meant the foreſaid words of him ſelfe only, as when he was a Manichiſt, he wold not haue ſaid, *Non crederem niſi commoueret* &c. I wold not beleeue, vnles the Church did commoue me: But *non credidiſſem, niſi commoniſſet*: I had not or wold not haue beleeued, vnleſſe the Church had commoued me. Which Bel wel marking, made him ſay ſo in engliſh, though he had not ſaid it in latine. Beſides in the ſame chapter he addeth. *Qua (autho-ritate Catholicorum) infirmata iam nec potero E-uangelio credere.* which (authority of Catho-liques) being diſcredited, I ſhal not be able now (marke Bel) to beleeue the Ghoſpel. Moreouer cap. 4. he ſaid, *That beſides other motiues, the authority of Catholiques (*tenet*) doth holde me in the lap of the Church.*

Falſe tran-
ſlat. 12.

23. Bels proofs are nothing but his owne vntruths. For though it be true· That the Scripture is of greater authority then the Church, yet nether doth S. Auſtin ſay it in that place, nether maketh it any thing a-gainſt vs. For albeit the Scripturs be in it ſelfe of greater authority, yet the authority of the Church is both infallible, and more euident to me. And what maruel if for an infallible authority more euident, I beleeue an other though greater, yet not ſo mani-feſt.

fest. As S. Ihon was sent to giue testimony
of Christ Ioan. 1 v. 8. and yet far inferior to
Christ. Nether saith S. Austin. That truth
of Scripture is to be preferred before authority and consent of Catholiques. But
Bel added the worde *Scripturs* as though S.
Austin meant, that their truth could be
knowne, without the authority of Catholiques, or be opposit vnto it, which he manifestly denyeth. Nether meaneth he of the
truth of Scripturs (which the Manichist
against whom he wrote reiected almost
wholy, and he him selfe professeth he could
not take for truth, if it were contrary to
Catholiques) but of any knowne truth in
general, which he saith (and truly) is to be
preferred before al authority opposit vnto
it, becaufe fuch authority is not infallible,
but falfe, and deceitful. And therfore he
speaketh vppon suppofition, that if it were
true (which other where he auoucheth to
be impoffible)that Manichists taught truth,
and Catholiques error, *then their truth vvere*
to be preferred before the name of Catholiques, con-
fent of nations, and authority begun with miracles,
nourished vvith hope, encreafed vvith charity, efta-
blished vvith antiquity, and fuccefsion of Priests,
euen from the feat of Peter,to vvhom our Lord after
his resurrection commanded his sheep to be fed
Ynto this prefent Bishop. But faith the glorious
Saint

S. Austin
fpeaketh of
moft mani-
fest and eui-
dent truth
and fuch is
not the Scri
ptures.

Saint vnto maniches, & I after him to Protestants. *Amongst you only soundeth the promise
of truth, vvhich if it vvere so manifest, as it could
not be doubted of, it vvere to be preferred before al
things, that hold me in the Catholique Church.*

24. His third vntruth of S. Austins promise, is directly contrary to S. Austin in the
same place. *If* (saith he) *thou shalt read any
manifest thing for Manichey out of the Ghospel, I vvil beleeue nether them nor thee. Not them
because they lyed to me of thee. Not thee, because
thou bringest me that Scripture, Vvhich I beleeued
through them vvho haue lyed:* As for Bels reasons to proue, that we beleeue nothing with
deuine faith for authority of the Church,
they are easely answered. For though the
formal obiect of faith be the first verity, yet
not simply as it is in it selfe, but as it is proposed vnto vs by the Church. And therfore
though we beleeue nothing, but because
it is spoken, and reuealed by God, yet because he speaketh not immediatly to vs by
him selfe, but by the mouth of his Church,
whome who so heareth, heareth God, and
whose worde is *not mans vvorde, but truly
Gods worde.* therfore faith is not without
the testimony of the Church. As for S.
Austins authority it hath bene answered
before: as also his arguments. which Bel
bringeth against Traditions.

CHAP.

*S. Austin
vvold not
beleeue Ma-
niche
though he
had mani-
fest Scrip-
ture.
Sup. paragr.
18.*

*Lue. 10. v.
16.
1. Thess. c. 2.
v. 13.*

Chap. X.
Of the certainty of Apostolical Traditions.

THERE are certaine and vndoubted
Apostolical traditions. This is against
Bel pag. 128 129. &c. But I proue it, becaufe
the traditions of the Byble to be Gods
worde, of the perpetual virginity of our
B. Lady, of the transferring of the Sabbath, and fuch like, are certaine and vndoubted. Befids if in the law of nature,
and Moyfes, traditions were keapt certaine,
why not in the law of grace. But more euident wil the conclufion be, if we defcend
to perticuler traditions, which Bel endeuoreth to proue vncertaine. Firft he fetteth-
downe this Propofition. *Vnwritten traditions
are fo vncertaine as the beft learned papifts are at
great contention about them* This he proueth in
the tradition of Eafter, about which contended *s. Victor P. & the Bishops of Afia about* 1400
*years agoe both earnestly alleadging Apoftolical
traditions. Likewife s. Anicetus, and s Policarpe
who liued al within* 200. *years after Chrift, when
the Church was in good eftate, and ftayned with
fevv, or no corruptions.*

2. Marke good Reader his conclufion,
and proofs therof, and thou wilt neede no

Bb   more

*Bel p. 128.
129.*

more to aſſure thy ſelfe of the truth of Romane religion : His concluſion is : That traditions are ſo vncertaine as the learnedeſt Papiſts contend about them. This he proueth : becauſe S. Victor P. contended with the Biſhops of Aſia. S. Policarpe with S. Anicetus P. Surely he meaneth that theſe men were Papiſts, or els his concluſion is vnproued. And conſequently Papiſts, and Popery were 1400. years agoe within 200. years after Chriſt, when the Church (as he ſaith) was in good eſtate. And if P. Victor were a Papiſt, then was alſo his immediat predeceſſor S. Eleutherius, who ſent S. Fugatius and Damian to conuert Britany, and conſequently this Iland was firſt conuerted from Paganiſme to Popery. Moreouer both ſides earneſtly alleadged Apoſtolical tradition, and ſtowtly defended the ſame ſaith Bel, Ergo : nether ſide was Proteſtant, and both agreed againſt him, that there are Apoſtolical traditiõs,& that they are of great weight , ſeeing ſuch great Saints ſo long agoe did ſo ſtowtly defend them, on what ſide now is Bel, who ſtowtly oppugneth, what Saints with al Gods Church ſo long agoe defended? what need more proofe of traditions or of Papiſtry ? Surely Bel *quaſi ſorex ſuo iudicio periit.* Here he hath bewraied him ſelfe to be againſt al Saints, that were

within

Popery confeſſed to be vvuth in 200. years after Chriſt.

Great Britany conuerted firſt to Popery.

Bel againſt al Gods Church vvhich liued vvuthin 200. years after Chriſt ;

within 200. years after Chrift, aud againft the Church, when she was in good eftate.

3. But now to Bels argument. The tradition of keeping Eafter was vncertaine 200 years after Chrift. Ergo it is now. Anfwer. This tradition was then vncertaine only in Afia, and certaine in the reft of Chriftendome, as is euident by the Councels then helde in Rome, Paleftine, Pontus, France, Achaia, who al accepted this tradition, as did after the firft general Councel in Nice. And though it had bene then vncertaine, Bel could no more infer it to be fo now, then he can infer the fame of many parts of the Bible, which both then, and long after were doubted of, and yet accepted now of Proteftants. But wel may I infer, if S Policarpe and his fellowes erred in not accepting one popish tradition, much more Bel in accepting none.

Eufeb. lib. f. c.23,25.& l.3. de vit Conftan. c.18 19. Nicephor. l. 4. c.36. Theodoret. l.2. hift. c.9. Epiphan. hær. 70. Tripart. lib. 9. c.38. Epift.2. Petri 2 & 3. Ioan. Epift. Iudæ & ad Hebræos. Apocalipfis See S. Hierom. in Script. ecclefiafticis. Et Eufeb. l.5. c.3.

4. *But (faith Bel)* S. *Policarpe Policrates, and other Bishops did in thofe daies make no more account of the Popes opinion, then of an other mans, did thinke them felfs his equals in gouernment, & that he defended an error, and withftood his proceedings.* Here is falfe conueiance to ioyne S. Policarp, who liued, and dyed in vnion, and communion of the Pope, and before this controuerfy was defyned, with Policrates, and his fellows. who were excom-

pag. 129.

Eufeb. lib. 5. c.24. & Iren. apud ipfum.

muni-

Loc. cit.

municated, *as declining* (saith Eusebius) *into heresy* for their obstinacy in error, after the whole Church had defyned the contrary. These indeed (as heretiks vse to do) made no account of the Popes opinion, or iudgement, but condemned him of error, and withstood his proceedings, though they neuer thought them selfs his equals, as Bel without al truth, or proofe affirmeth, yea

S. Hierom. de script.ec-clei. in Pa-pia. Nicephor. l. 4. c. 37.

Polecrates when he saith, *I wil not feare them, who threaten me, and I must obey God more then men,* sheweth him selfe to be vnder the Popes obedience, but supposing him selfe to defend truth, feared not his excommunication. But how much al Christendom at that tyme, and euer since made account of the Popes sentence, appeareth by that (as

Euseb. sup.

Eusebius, and others write) they al followed it, and condemned them as Heretiks

Euseb. lib. 5. cap. 24. & 5. Ireney apud ipsum. Nicephor. l. 3. c. 30.

who withstood it. And S. Policarp so esteemed it, as that he came to Rome to confer with the Pope about that matter, & doubtles wold haue subscribed to his sentence, if it had ben pronounced in his daies, as his scholler S. Ireney did, by whom we may gather his maisters account of the

S. Iren.

Church of Rome He therfore lib. 3. cap. 3. calleth Rome the *greatest and antientest Church founded by S. Peter, and Paul,* and that *by Tradition which it hath from the Apostles,* and alwaies

waies keapeth, by fucceßion of Bishops we confound (faith he) *al them that gather otherwise then they should,* and that *al Churches mußt recur to Rome for her more potent principality.*

5. The fecond Tradition is that of keeping lent *which* (faith Bel) *is not Apoftolical:* becaufe S. Chrifoftom writeth. *That Chrißt bid vs not imitat his faßt,* but *be humble:* Nor certain becaufe *Eufebius out of Ireney writeth That in his tyme fome thought we ought to faßt one day, others two, others more and nonnulli forty, which variety of fasting began not now firßt, or in our daies, but long before, I thinke by them, who keeping not fimply what was (traditum) deliuered from the beginning, did afterward fal into an other cußtome either of negligence, or of ignorance.* Here Bel sheweth his lacke of iudgement in citing a place clearly againft him felfe. For here S Ireney, and Eufebius after him clearly affirme. That at the beginning there was one manner of fafting lent appointed, though fome afterward ether of ignorance or negligence did breake it, which proueth not the faid Tradition to be vncertain in the whole Church, vnles Bel wil impute the fault of fome few to the whole. And of the Roman Church, *she* (faith Ireney lib. 3. cap. 3.) *alwaies keapt the Apoßtles Tradition.* And by this is anfwered what he bringeth out of Socrates touching

Bel p. 130.

S. Chryfoft. hom. 47. in Math. to. 2. Eufeb. lib. 5. c. 24.

S. Ireney. Ex hiftor. tripart. lib. 9. c. 38.

Bb 3   the

the diuerfity of tyme, and meat vfed in fafting lent. Albeit what Socrates faith of
the Roman Church fafting but three weeks
before Eafter, and not on Saterday is an vntruth. For they fafted 40. daies, as witnes
S. Leo. ferm. 12. de Quadrag. and S. Gregory hom. 16. in Euang. And likewife Sa·
terdaies as teftify S. Innocent. epift. ad De-
cent. and S. Auftin epift. 86. and 118. where
alfo he alleadgeth S. Ambrofe.

6. And that lent is an Apoftolical Tradition, not only S. Hierom epift. ad Marcel. witnefleth, and S. Ambrofe ferm. 25.
34. and 36. faith it was cōmanded by Chrift:
and S Auftin hær. 53 accounted the Aërians
heretiks for *denying the fet-faft* (of lent, and
others) *to be folemnely kept*. But it is euident
alfo becaufe euermore it hath bene obferued, as appeareth by S. Ignatius epiftol. ad
Philip. S. Ireney loc. cit. Origen. hom. 10.
Leuit. Bafil. orat. 2. de ieiunio: Chryfoftom
hom. 1 in Gen. and 11. hom. 16. and 73. ad
populum. S. Auftin epift. 118. and 119. and
ferm. de quadrag. Leo and Gregor. loc. cit.
And what S. Chryfoftom meant in the
words cited by Bel, he him felf explicateth
in thefe words. *Becaufe I am forry* (faith he)
*if neglecting the reft, you thinke fafting fufficient
to faue you, which is the meaneft of the vertues.*
So that he meant that Chrift bid vs not
only

S. Leo.
S. Gregory.
S Innocent.
S. Auguftin.

S. Hierom.
S. Ambros.

S. Auguftin.
S. Epiphan.
hær. 75.

S. Ignatius.
S. Ireney.
Origen.
S. Bafil.
S. Chryfo·
ftom.
S. Auguftin.
S. Leo.
S. Gregory.
S. Grego. Na-
zianzen. in
fanct. laua-
crum.
Concil. Lao-
dicen. Can.
50.

only faſt lent, but more eſpecially be humble, and milde. The like ſpeech vſed Chriſt
when he ſaid: *I wil haue mercy, and not ſacri-*
fice vz. only, and rather then mercy. And ſo
we may ſay with S. Chryſoſtom he commanded not faſting, but humility. And Bel
vſeth his old trade in auouching vs to *think*
it greater ſinne to eat fleſh in lent, then to commit
adultery, murder, or periury. Whereas euery
Catholique knoweth theſe ſinnes to be a-
gainſt the law of nature, and lawful in no
caſe whatſoeuer, and the other againſt a poſitiue precept, which according to the general cuſtome of the Church, bindeth none
vnder 21. or aboue 60. years old, no ſicke
body, no laboring man, no woeman bearing, or nurſing children, beſides many
other perticuler caſes wherein faſting in
lent is diſpenſed withal.

7. Eight Traditions more Bel reckoneth
as of celebrating in vnleauened bread, of
Chriſts age, when he dyed, of his raigne on
earth after iudgement, of Zacharias that
was ſlayne betwixt the Temple, and the altar, of the Popes teaching ſucceſſiuely the
ſelf ſome doctrin with S. Peter, of our ladies conception without original ſinne,
of Conſtantins baptiſme at Rome, and laſtly
of honoring Saints: But theſe are ether
falſly alleadged for traditions. or litle, or

Bb 4 nothing

See S. Hie-
rom. ep. ad
Celantiam.
Math. 9. *v.*
13.
Oſe. c. 6. *v.*
6.
vntruth 96
Bel p. 150.

Bel p. 131.
132. 133.

Leo 9. ep. ad
Michaelem
Patriarchã.
c. 29.
Eugen. 4. in
decreto v-
nionis.
*These two
were no
traditions
but errone-
ous opiniõs.
See S. Hie-
rom. de scri
ptur. in Pa-
dia.
*Bel impug-
neth histo-
ries in steed
of Tradi-
tions.
Origen. in
25. Math.
Basil. homil.
de human.
Christi Ge-
neral.
Nissen. orat.
de Christ.
natiu.
Cyrill. cont.
Anthropo.
*This is no
Tradition
but if it be
ment of the
Popes tea-
ching as he
is Pope it is
in Scripture
if as a pri-
uat mã, it is
as opinion.

nothing to the purpose. For that of celebrating in vnleauened bread, concernes no
thing necessary to mans saluation, as testify
P Leo 9. and P. Eugenius 4. and therfore
is none of these which Bel vndertooke in
the beginning of this article to impugne.
And though S. Ireney were deceaued about
Christs age when he suffered, and Papias
about his reigne after iudgement, that maketh not much to the purpose. For wel
may the Church be certain of Traditions,
though one Father were mistaken about
one Tradition, and an other about an o-
ther. That of Zachary that he was S. Ihon
Baptists father who was so slain S. Basil reporteth not as an Apostolical, but an histo-
rical Tradition, and though S Hierom deny it, yet Origen, S. Greg. Nissen, S. Cyril
and Valentinian affirme it.

8. As for the Popes successiuely teaching
the self same doctrin with S. Peter, the
truth thereof vnto S Victor P. tyme about
the year 187. is testifyed by S. Ireney lib. 3.
c. 3. vntil S Cornelius P. about the yeare
251. by S. Cyprian lib. 1. epist 3 vnto S. Lucius 1 P. about 257. by him self epist. ad E-
pisc. Hispan. & Gall. vntil S. Dammasus P.
about the year 380 by S. Hierom epist. ad
Damas. vntil S Leo 1. Pope about 450 by
Theodoret epistol. ad Renatum: vntil S.
Gelasius

Gelaſius 1. P. about 496. by him ſelf epiſt. ad
Anaſt. vntil S. Ihon 2. Pope about the year
533. by him ſelf epiſt. ad Iuſtin. vntil S Gregory the great about the year 600. by him
ſelf lib. 6 epiſt 37 vntil Pope Agatho about
the yeare 681. by him ſelf in his epiſtle approued 6. Synod. act 8. and 18. vntil P. Nicolas about the year 860. by him ſelf ep:ſt
ad Michael. Imperat. vntil P. Leo 9 about
the yeare 1050. by him ſelf epiſtol. ad Petr.
Antioch: vntil Pope Innocent. 2. about the
year 1140 is inſinuated by S. Bernard epiſt.
190. And the ſame may be proued of the
reſt of the Popes ſince . Now let vs ſee
whome Bel oppoſeth to theſe ſo many , ſo
holy, ſo antient witneſſes.

9 Forſooth Nicolas de Lyra a late fryer.
O truly ſaid of S. Paule, that Heretiks are
condemned by their owne iudgements. For who
condemneth not him ſelf if he wil beleeue
one late writer, before ſo many, ſo holy, ſo
antient. And much more, if that Author
be found to affirme nothing to the contrary For he only ſaith, That *ſummi Ponti-
fices inueniuntur apoſtataſſe à fide*. Popes haue
apoſtated from the faith. which is a far different thing. For wel may one be an Apo-
ſtata, and yet teach the doctrin of his Predeceſſor. As S Peter denyed his maiſter, &
yet taught no contrary doctrin. S. Mar-
cellin

margin notes:

S. Ireney.
S. Cyprian.
S Lucius.
S. Hierom.
S. Theodo-
ret.
S. Gelaſius 1.
S. Ihon. 2.
S. Gregory.
Agatho.
Nicolas 1.

Leo 9.

S. Bernard.

Bel b. 132.
Lyra in cap.
16. Math.
Tit. 3. v. 11.

Math. 26.
v. 70.
Concil. Si-
nueſſan.
Damaſus in
Marcelline.

cellin offered facrifice to Idols, and yet
taught no Idolatry. Caïphas murdered
Chrift, and yet prophecyed. For as S. Auftin faid of fome Bishops that they durft
not teach herefy, left they should leefe their
Bishopriks. So we might fay of Popes, that
though fome of them had apoftated from
Chrift, yet they durft not teach herefy, or
apoftafy, left they shold be depofed, but
might *with a wicked, and deceitful hart* (to vfe
S. Auftins words) *preach things, which are
right, and true*, or (as S. Paul fpeaketh) *preach
Chrift vpon occafion not vpon truth.* But indeed
neuer did any Pope in his hart apoftatat
from Chrift.

10. That point of our ladies conception
without finne is no Tradition, but a pious,
and probable opinion of many, and denyed
of diuers Catholiques, as of S. Thomas, &
S Bernard whome Bel him felf citeth and
others. And as for Conftantins baptifme at
Rome it concerneth no matter of faluation, but is a meere hiftorical Tradition, fufficiently proued by Card. Baronius Annal.
Ann. 3 4. and vnawares contefted by Bel
him felf when he faith, that *he hath feen at
Rome the font, and that Conftantin is worthely
called great.* For why shold that font be conferued fo long, but as a monument of fo
memorable a chriftning. How can Conſtantin

Ioan. 11. v. 51.
S. Auguftin. L. 4. de doctr. Chriftian. c. 27. 10. 3.

Philip. 1. v. 18.

*Bel impug-
neth an opi-
nion for
tradition.*

*Bel impug-
neth a Hi-
ſtory in
ſteed of tra-
dition.*

pag. 133.

See Nice-
phor. lib. 7. c. 35.

ſtantin be worthely ſurnamed great of
Chriſtians. if at his death he communicated with Arians, and was baptized of them
at Nicomedia, as their fellow heretik Euſebius firſt reported to purchaſe credit to his
hereſy. If this had bene ſo, he ſhold rather
haue bene ſyrnamed of Catholiques the A-
poſtata, or Heretike.

11. The laſt tradition of honoring Saints
(Bel ſaith) made ſome to honor Heretiks
for Saints *as Platina* (ſaith he) *writeth of the
corps of Herman an heretike honored as Saints reliques at Ferrara for* 20. *years together* : Anſwer
How Apoſtolical a thing the honoring of
Saints is, Bellarmin ſheweth lib. de Sanct.
beatit. c. 19. Where beſids Scripturs, and
Councels he proueth it by the teſtimony of
30. Fathers, wherof 25 liued aboue a thowſand years ago. But is not this a ſtrange me-
tamorphoſis, to make the error of common
people a popiſh Tradition. Beſide Platina
affirmeth no ſuch thing him ſelfe, but only,
that ſome others write ſo. But nether he
nor any other write, that it roſe of popiſh
Tradition. That is Bels accuſtomed vſe of
addition. And therfore where he noteth
danger in beleeuing Tradition, he might
haue noted danger in crediting his owne relation. Yea what danger is in not beleeuing
Roman Tradition, appeareth both by the
teſti-

Bel p. 133.

Platina in
Bonif. 8.

vntruth 97

teſtimony of Fathers before cited, and by the example of Policrates and his fellows the Quartadecimans, and by S. Cyprian, and his followers the Donatiſts reproued only by Roman Tradition. As teſtifyeth Tripartit lib. 9. c. 38. and Vincent Lyrinen: But ſuppoſe that they of Ferrara had vpon Tradition taken occaſion to commit Idolatry. Shal we reiect al things wherof men take occaſion to offend? So we might reiect Chriſt who was ſet vnto the ruine of many Luc 2. v.34. and by whom the Iewes took occaſion of ſcandal: So we might reiect Scripturs, by which heretiks haue taken occaſion he hereſy: Sunne and Moone becauſe Gentils haue by them fallen into Idolatry. Cannot Bel diſtinguiſh between vſe, & abuſe of Traditions, betwixt ſcandal giuen & taken. Thus much of the certainty of Tradtions: Now let vs come to the examination of them.

Quartadecimans are Heretiks ex Epiphan. hær. 50. & 70.
Nicephor. l. 4. c. 39.
Auguſt. hær. 29.
Socrates lib. 5. c. 22.
Tripartita hiſt.
Vincent. Lyxin.

Chap. XI.
Of the examination of Traditions.

APoſtolical Traditions are not to be examined by Scripture. This is againſt Bel pag. 117. but euident. Becauſe Apoſtolical Tradition is the Apoſtles word, their word, is Gods word 1. Theſſ. 2. v. 16. But
Gods

Bel p. 117

S. Paul.
S. Luke.

Gods word is not to be examined at al:
Ergo: nether is Apostolical Tradition. Wel
might the Church at first examine a Tradition, whether it were Apostolical or no (as
she did examine diuers parts of the Bible
whither they were Scripture or no) but
finding it to be Apostolical, she could no
more examine it by the Bible, then she can
examin one part of the Bible by an other.
And Bel in saying *That the new testament may* *Bel p. 135.*
be examined by the old sheweth him selfe ra- *al. 117.*
ther to be a Iew then a Christian. For how
dare he examin that which is certaine to be
deuine truth? Or how can he examin the
new testament by the old, if he be not more
certain of the old then of the new. But how
Traditions ought to be proued heare Ter- *Tertullian.*
tullian. *It can not seeme none, or a doubtful fault* *lib. de Co-*
against Custome, which is to be defended for it *rona.*
name sake, and is sufficiently authorized by pro-
tection of consent. Plainly reason is to be enquired,
but so as the Custome be reteined, not to destroy it
but to vphold it That thou maist obserue it more,
when thou art sure of the reason of it. But what a
thing is it that one shal cal Custome in question,
when he hath fallen from it.

  2. But (saith Bel) *Scriptures are called cano-* *Bel p. 117.*
nical because they be the rule of faith. Therfore al
things are to be examined by them. And for *this*
cause (saith he) *Esay sent vs to the Law and testi-* *Esaie 8.*
mony

Malach. 4.
Psalm. 119.
2. Pet. 1.
Ioan. 5.
Math. 22.
Act. 17.
1. Ioan. 4.
Gal. 1.

mony to try the truth. *Malachias bid vs be myndful of Moises lavv: Dauid said Gods word is a lathern: S. Peter a shyning light. For this cause Christ exhorted the Iewes to read Scripturs, and said the Pharises erred, because they knew not the Scripturs. The Berheans examined S. Paules doctrin, S. Ihon bid try the spirits: S. Paul pronounced him accursed That preached any doctrin not conteined in Scripture as S. Austin and S. Basil expound him.*

S. August. l.
3. cont. Peril.
c. 6.
S. Basil. sum.
72 c.1.
*Bible onely
Canonical
Scripture,
but not it
alone Canonical.*
Sup. c. 2. parag. 1. & 7. &
c. 9. paragr.
17.

3. **Answer.** The Bible alone is called Canonical Scripture, because it alone of al Scripturs the Church followeth as an infallible rule in beleeuing, or defyning any thing. But it nether is, nor is called the only Canon of faith. In the rest Bel affirmeth, but proueth not that that was the cause why the Scripture said so. As for the places of Esay. Malachy, Dauid and S. Peter they haue bene answered before. As for exhortation of Christ, I might deny that he there exhorted the Iewes to read Scripture, but affirmed that they did read them, because they thought they conteined life. But suppose he did exhort them to read Scripturs for to finde whether he were the Messias or no, wherof as he saith there, they giue testimony, what is this for trying of al matters by them. Can Bel inferre an vniuersal propositiō of one singuler? That of the Pharises conteineth two corruptions of Scripturs.

Scrutamini
Scripturas.
See S. Gyrill.
l. 3. in Ioan.
c. 4.

*Corrupt. of
Script.*

For

For neither did Chriſt ſay, The Pharaſes, 1.
but the Saduces erred about the reſurrection, nether doth he ſay the cauſe of their 2.
error therin was only ignorance of Scripture (as Bel inſinuateth leauing out the
words, *povvre of God*,) but ignorance both *Math. 22.*
of Scripture, and of Gods powre : *you erre* *v. 29.*
(ſaith he) *knovving nether Scripturs, nor the
powre of God*. So if they had known Gods
powre, though it had not bene by Scripture
but by Tradition, or reuelation (as Iob and *Iob 19. v.*
the faithful vncircumciſed did) they had *25.*
not erred about the reſurrection. Beſide ,
the reſurrection is a perticuler matter, and
euidently teſtifyed in Scripture, what proueth this concerning al points of faith ?

4. As for the Berhæans whom Bel wil
haue to haue examined the truth of S. Pauls *Act. 17.*
doctrin : I ask of him whither they were
faithful whilſt they examined it, or faithles?
If faithles, why propoſeth he them to vs as
an example to imitat? If he wil follow them
let him confeſſe him ſelfe to want faith, &
none wil diſcommend him for examining
ether Traditions, or Scripture ; For in infidels ſuch examination is ſome diſpoſition
to faith, but in the faithful an argument of
doubt, and diſtruſt. If faithful ? how could
they examin, whither that were true or no,
which they aſſuredly beleeued to be deuine
truth ?

truth? Wherfore they examined not the truth of S. Pauls doctrin. For *they receaued it* (saith S. Luke) *with al greedines, and beleeued* : but did for confirmation and encrease of their faith, *search the Scriptures whether these things were so or no*, vz in Scripturs, that is fortold in Scripturs; And this kind of examining Traditions we disalow not.

Hovv the Berhaans examined S. Pauls doctrin.

5. As for S. Ihon: He bid vs try doubtful spirits, but not Apostolical spirits, or Traditions. Besids he bid vs not try them only by Scripture, and therfore he maketh nothing for Bels purpose. Finally as for S. Paul he accursed not (as S Austin noteth tract 98. in Ioan) him that should preach more then he had done. For so he should preiudice him selfe, who coueted to returne to the Thessalonians to preach more then he had done, and to supply (as he writeth the points which wanted to their faith. But only such as preach things *beside* (vz quite) *that Ghospel which he had preached*, which things v. 6 and 7. he calleth an other Ghospel inuerting Christs Ghospel. Such were the cirrumcision, & obseruation of Iewish ceremonies, against which he disputeth in the whole epistle. But what is this against Apostolical Traditions, are they a second Ghospel? do they inuert Christs Ghospel? are they Iewish ceremonies.

What S. Ihon bid vs trye.
1 Ioan. 4.

S. Augustin. 10. 9.

1. Theß. 3. v. 10.

Hovv S. Paul vnderstood the vvord besyde Gal. 1. v. 2.

6. Be-

6. Befide S. Paul nether fpeaketh of Scripture, nor can be vnderftood of it alone.
For when he faith (*befids that vvhich vve haue*
euangeliʒed to you) he nether had written any
thing before to the Galathians; Nor then,
nor after writ to them al points of Chriftian
faith. And therfore when he fpeaketh
ofhis owne euangelizing both in tyme before
the writing of that epiftle, and vnto
the Galathians, euident it is he meant not
of euangelizing by only writing, but rather
of euangelizing by word of mouth, becaufe
before the writing of that epiftle, he had e-
uangelized to the Galathians only by word
of mouth, and of that euangelizing he fpeaketh,
which before tymes he had vfed to
them. And fo this place maketh more for
vs then for Bel.

S. Paul
fpeaketh
not of Scri-
pture but of
his ovvne
preaching.

The like
faieth S. Ig-
nat. epift.
ad Heron.
of thofe
that teach
præter ea
quæ tradita
funt.

7. As for S. Auftin, and S. Bafil they fay
not That S. Paul meant of euangelizing by
only Scripture, but out of this place infer,
that nothing is to be preached which is befide
Scripture, in that fenfe wherin S. Paul
vfed the word (*Befide*) vz: fo befide as it is
an other Ghofpel, inuerting Chrifts Ghofpel,
which they rightly inferred. For what
is fo befide Scripture, as it is a new Ghofpel,
and inuerteth Chrifts Ghofpel, is in like
fort befide that which S. Paul had euangelized
to the Galathians, and no Apoftolical

Tradition, but a cursed doctrin. And thus much of Bels proofs out of Scripture touching examination of Traditions; Now let vs see his proofs out of Fathers.

CHAP. XII.
Bels arguments out of holy Fathers about the examination of Traditions an-
svvered.

Bel p. 117.
vntruth 98
vntruth 99

FIRST he saith, *That in S. Cyprians daies nether Tradition was a sufficient proofe of do-ctrin, nor the Popes definitiue sentence a rule of faith.* These be both vntruths For that Traditiō was a sufficient proofe of doctrin in S. Cyprians daies is euident by the testimony of his maister Tertullian, S. Ireney, and S.

Sup. cap. 4.
S. Augul. in.
12. de bapt.
c. 9.
Tripartit. l.
9. c. 38.
Vincent. Ly-
rin.
Socrates lib.
5. c. 22.
Te pacatum
reddat tra-
ditio. Basil.
hom. contr.
Sabellian.
Chrysost.
hom. 42. 2.
ad Thessal.
Cap. cit. pa-
rag. 6.

Dionis. before his tyme, and S. Basil, S. Chrisostom & others after his tyme before cited. And by his owne words before alleadged, and the decyding of two controuersies only by Tradition, the one in his owne tyme about the baptisme of heretiks, the other before his tyme about the tyme of Easter. Nether did he euer doubt that true Tradition was sufficient proofe of doctrin of which S. Chrisostom said. *It is Tradition, seeke no more*: but thought (and truly) that humane, and mistaken Tradition was no sufficient rule, as hath bene shewed before.

And

And that the Popes definitiue sentence in his tyme was a sufficient rule of faith is euident by his owne saying. *That false faith can haue no accesse to S. Peters chair,* and that *Heresyes, and Schismes rise not, but because it is not thought that there is for the tyme one Priest in the Church, and one iudge in Christs roome,* and by his owne subscribing at the last to the Popes commandement, though he thought it had bene contrary to Scripture. Nether did he euer withstand the Popes definitiue sentence. For P. Steeuen did not defyne as a matter of faith, but only commanded that such should not be rebaptized, but the Tradition obserued, as both S. Cyprian : Eusebius. Vincent Lyrinen : and others testify. And this command S. Cyprian did not at first obey, wherin he offended as S. Austin writeth though after he did. as the same S. Austin doth likewise testify. And no doubt but he thought as wel of the Popes decrees as S Hierom did, when he wrote to P. Damasus : *Decree I pray if it please you I wil not fear to say three Hypostases if you bid.* And requested him for Christs sake to giue authority, ether to affirme or deny three hypostases. And darest thou Bel make no account of the Popes sentence, when so great and holy a Doctor, so highly esteemed it, as without it he durst nether affirme, nor deny

three

Cyprian.lib. 4 epistol. 8. calleth Rome the Matrice and roote of the Catholique Church.
S.Cyprian.l. 1.epist. 3.
S. Augustin. l. 6. de bapt. contr. Donat c.2.
S. Cyprian. ep. ad Pompeium.
Euseb. lib.7. hist.c.3.
Vincent.Lyrin.
S. Augustin. lib. de vnic. bapt.cap. 13.
See c. 4. parag.7. & 8.
S. Hieroms account of the Popes decree.

three hypoſtaſes, and with it doubted not to do ether.

Bel p. 118.

2. After this Bel alleadgeth the practiſe of Fathers, who *when the Arians* (ſaith he) *wold not admit the word homouſion becauſe it was not in Scripture* (mark how he confeſſeth him ſelfe to imitate Arians) *the Fathers did not proue it by Tradition, nor ſay that many vnwritten things are to be beleeued.* This is not ſo. For S. Athanaſius ſaith that the Bishops of the Niꞏ cen Councel did not inuent that word, but ſet it downe *teſtimonio patrum* by teſtimony of their Fathers, and Euſebius though an Arian confeſſeth the same. And S. Gregory Nazian. writing againſt the Arians ſaith, that it should ſuffice vs that our Fathers thought not as they do ; and the ſame arguꞏ mēt vſeth alſo S. Athanaſius writing againſt the Apollinariſts. And how vntruly he afꞏ firmeth, that the Fathers did not ſay many vnwritten things are to be beleeued, I refer my ſelfe to their teſtimonies alleadged aꞏ boue cap. 4. But ſaith Bel S. Athanaſius proꞏ ued *homouſion*, becauſe though the word was not in Scripture the ſenſe was. A goodꞏ ly reaſon : He proued it out of Scripture, therfore not out of Tradition ; as if one should ſay. He proued it out of S. Ihon therꞏ fore not out of S. Paul.

S. Athan. aꞏ pud Theoꞏ doret. l. 1. c. 8. See epiſt. ad Epiꞏteꞏ tum. l. cit. Apud Athaꞏ naſ. & Theoꞏ doret. l. cit. S. Grego. Naꞏ zianz. orat. 2. de Theoꞏ log.

Bel p. 118.

3. Origen (ſaith Bel) hom. 25. in Math. and

and hom. 1. in 1. Hierem counſelleth vs to
try al doctrins by Scripture. This is vntrue. *vntruth*
For Origen ſpeaketh not of al, but only of 101.
our opinions, and doctrins. *Our opinions and* Origen.
expoſitions (ſaith he) *haue no credit without*
their teſtimonies. Againe: *VVe muſt alleadge the*
ſenſe of Scripture, for teſtimony of al the words
we vtter. Tertullian calling that truth which
is firſt, and falſe which is after, maketh nothing to his purpoſe. Next he alleadgeth S. S. Auguſtin.
Auſtin ſaying, *That we muſt not conſent euen* lib. de vnit.
to Catholique Biſhops error, or priuat opinion eccleſ. c. 19.
againſt Scripture. Error againſt Scripture is to. 7.
not to be followed. Ergo: nether Apoſtolical Traditions conteſted by the whole
Church. Surely Bel hath great facility in
inferring *quodlibet ex quolibet* : He brin- S. Chryſoſt.
geth alſo S. Chriſoſtom calling *Gods lawes a* hom.13.in 1.
moſt exact rule, and bidding vs *learn not what* Cor.to.4.
this, or that man thinks, and of theſe things en-
quire theſe points alſo out of Scripture. *Anſwer.*
S. Chryſoſtoms meaning is, that Gods word
is moſt exact in the matter whereof he talked: vz. whither pouerty be to be preferred before riches, in which matter *we ought*
(ſaith he) *to leaue the opinions of this, or that*
worldly man, who prefer riches, but ſeek what the
Scripture ſaith of it. And Bel to make him *Falſe tranſ-*
ſeeme to ſay, That al truth is to be ſought *ſlat.13.*
out of Scripture, tranſlated theſe words,

Deque his à Scripturis hæc etiam inquirite, thus:
Search the truth out of the Scriptures Englishing nether *de his,* nor *hæc.*

pag. 120.
Chap 5. pa-
rag. 5.

4. After S. Chrysostom he citeth two
sentences out of Victoria cited by him, and
answered by vs before. To whome he ad-

Canus l.3. de
loc.c. vlt.

ioyneth Canus teaching. That *Priests are not
to be heard vnles they teach according to Gods law.*
Certain: And then inferreth, That *Papists
teach plainly that no doctrine is to be receaued,
which is not tryed by Gods word.* True also, if

1.

it be rightly vnderstood, vz. of such doctrine as may be tryed, not of deuine, (as
Apostolical Traditions be,) which may not

2.

be tryed. And of Gods whole word, not of

3.

a part thereof (as the Scripture is. And that
expounded not according to the humor of
priuat spirits, but according to the vniforme consent of Fathers & Councels. This
most iust and reasonable rule of trying al

Concil. Tri-
dent. sess. 18.
in saluo cō-
ductu dato
Protestanti-
bus.

matters in controuersy the Councel of
Trent prescribed to the Protestants. But
they wil try deuine truth conteined not
only in Traditions, but also in Scripture,
& that part by which they wil try the rest,
they wil expound according to their owne
priuat spirits, which is to make them selfs
rule and iudges of al: wherfore vainly doth

pag. 120.

Bel professe to agree with the Pope in al cō-
trouersies if he wil be tryed by Gods word.
For

For vnles Bel be made iudge, and tryer both of Gods word, and of his meaning, or (as Proteſtants ſpeake) vnles he may iudge which is Scripture, and which is the true ſenſe, there muſt nether tryal, nor iudgement paſſe. For vnles Proteſtants may haue al the law in their owne hands they wil accept no iudgement.

5. But becauſe Bellarmin graunteth, that *ſinguli Epiſcopi* : al Biſhops ſeuerally may erre, and ſomtyme do erre, and diſſent one from an other, ſo that we know not which of them is to be followed : Bel thinketh that he hath a great catch. yet remembring him ſelf better, that though Catholiques graunt that euery Biſhop ſeuerally may erre, yet deny that they can erre al, when they are gathered in a Synode confirmed by the Pope, he taketh occaſion to make a long digreſſion about Councels.

Bellarm. lib. 2. de Concil. c. 52.

pag. 121.

Chap. XIII.
Of the authority of late general Councels.

GENERAL Councels in theſe our dayes are as certaine as before tymes. This is againſt Bel pag. 123. ſaying, *that in our dayes they are like a noſe of waxe , and as vncertaine as the winde.* And becauſe he denyeth

not, but that general Councels in some
times haue bene certaine (forsooth such as
defyned nothing contrary to Protestantisme) I wil only proue, that they are now
as certaine as euer. First because Christ pro-
myseth, that *he would be in the midst of them*
S. Math. *that are gathered in his name* Math. 18. v. 20.
That *the holy Ghost should teach vs al truth.*
S. Iohn. v. Iohn. 16. That *the gates of hel should not pre-*
13. *uaile against his Church.* Math. 16. v. 18. which
S. Math. promises are limited to no certaine tyme,
but are extended (as he saith Math. vlt.)
euen to the end of the worlde. Likewise Christs
S. Math. v. commaund of hearing his Church. Math.
17. 18. of hearing preachers sent by him . Luc.
S. Luc. 10. of obeying our Prelates and being sub-
S. Paul. iect to them. Hebr. 13. v. 17. bindeth as wel
in our dayes as before tymes. wherfore either the Church , Preachers , and Prelates
teaching in a general Councel in our dayes,
can not erre, or Christ in our daies commaundeth vs to beleeue heresy and lyes.

2. Secondly the present Church of our
daies hath authority to decyde controuersies in faith : Ergo , we be bound to obey
her decision: Ergo, it is no lye. The Ante-
Article 39. cedent is an article of Protestants faith.
art. 20. The first consequence I proue, because who
resisteth power in matters belonging to the
po**wer** *resisteth Gods ordinance, and purchaseth*
damna-

damnation to him selfe. Roman. 13. verſ. 2. 3.
which being true of temporal power, and
concerning wordly matters, much more
true it is of ſpiritual power, and in matters
of faith, and ſaluation : The ſecond conſequence is euident. For God who is truth it
ſelfe, and can not lye, can not binde vs (eſpecially vnder paine of damnation) to beleeue and follow lyes. Thirdly as Proteſtants except againſt the Councels in their
tymes, al hereticks may except againſt the
Councels of their tymes, and ſo none ſhal
be condemned as Hereticks, no Councel
certaine, but al things remaine as vncertaine, as if there had neuer been any Councel at al, which is to take away the end of
calling Councels. For if they can not make
things certaine, to what purpoſe are they
gathered. Finally Bel can giue no ſufficient
reaſon, whie general Councels be not as
certaine now as euer, as ſhal appeare by the
anſwer to this his obiection.

3. He obiecteth that Bellarmin lib. 2. de
Concil. cap. 11. writeth: that is the true decree of the counſel, which is made of the
greater part. But Canus ſaith lib. 5. de locis
cap. 4. q. 2. *That voices preuaile not with vs, as
in humane aſſemblies.* Againe, *theſe matters of
faith are iudged not by number,* but by waight.
And the grauity and authority of the Pope
is it,

See S. Gregory lib.1. epiſt. 24.

See l. Marciani. C. de ſum.Trinit.

Canus.

is it, which giueth waight to Councels. Ergo, (saith Bel) there can be no certainty in
Councels. A goodly reason, sutely: Two
Catholique writers agree not whether
should be accompted the decree of a councel, if the greater number of Bishops
should define against the Pope, and the lesser number of Bishops. Ergo no councel in
our dayes is certaine. As if nothing were
certaine, if two Catholiques disagree about
it. Wil Bel allowe mee to argue soe against
Protestants? I beleeue I should finde scarce
any one pointe of faith certaine amongst
them. But he should rather hane inferred:
Bellarmin, Canus, and al Catholique writers agree, that it is the decree of the Councel, and certaine truth, which the greater
part of Bishops defineth, and the Pope
confirmeth. Ergo general councels in our
dayes are certaine; Namely that of Trent,
in which the most, yea al (as appeareth
by their subscriptions) defyned, the Pope
confirmed.

4. I might omit a friuolous obiection,
which he maketh against Bellarmin of contradiction. Because Bellarmin saith, that
the assemblie of Bishops in lawful councels is an
assembly of Iudges, and their decrees laws necessa-
rily to be followed. And yet affirmeth that *it is*
al one for Councels to be reproued by the Pope, and
to doe

Bel *p.* 121.
122.

Bellarm. lib.
2. de concil.
c. 18.

Cap. 11.

to doe against his sentence : For though Bellarmin affirme Bishops to be Iudges, and their iudgement to be necessarily followed as law. Yet as himselfe explicateth cap. 11. it is not necessarily to be followed *antequam accedat sententia Summi Pontificis.* before it be confirmed by the Pope. As the Peeres in parliament are Iudges, and their acts necessary to be followed, but not before they be confirmed by the Prince, who in not confirming them, disannulleth them.

5. And because Bellarmin writeth, that one cause whie the Pope was neuer personally in any Councel of the East was, least he being then the Emperours temporal subiect should be placed vnder the Emperour. Bel inferreth both that the Pope is prowd, and that the East Church neuer acknowledged his supremacy. But as for pride it is none, to honour (as S. Paule did) his ministery, to challendge the place due to his dignity, and authority. For (as S. Gregory a most humble man said) *Let vs keep humility in mynde, and yet conserue the dignity of our order in honour.* No maruaile then if Popes being head and presidents of Councels, where matters of Church and faith are handled, and Emperours (as S. Gregory Nazianz: speaketh) but sheep of his flocke, and subiect to his power, and tribunal, did looke

to sit

Bellarm.lib. 2. de concil. c.19.

pag. 122.

Rom.11. v. 14.

S. Gregor. lib. 4. epist. 36. ad Eulagium.

S. Gregor. Nazianz. orat. 14. ad sub.

to fit there aboue Emperours. Yet the great Emperour Theodofius highly commended S. Ambrofe for putting him out of the Chauncel : And in the Nicene Counfel Conftantine that worthie Emperour entred laft, and after al the Bifhops were fett ; nor did not fit in a great throne befeeming his eftate, but in a low chaire, and that not before he had craued pardon, and asked leaue of the Bifhops, as Theodoret whom Bel calleth a Saint, Nicephorus, and others doe teftify. Albeit the Nouatian hereticke Sozomene, who lyeth much (as writeth S. Gregory) doe feeme to fay, that he fate at the toppe of the Councel, in a moft great throane.

6. As for the Eafterne churches acknowledging the Popes primacy, it is fo manifeft, as Iuftinian Emperour of the Eaft writeth. *No man doubteth but that at Rome is Summi Pontificatus apex : the toppe of the prieft-hood.* And if more witneffes need in fo euident a matter, certaine it is, that the general councels in the Eaft were called, and their decrees confirmed by the Pope. And the Councel of Calcedon profeffeth in plaine tearms, that *omnis primatus, al primacy belonged to the Archbifhoppe of Rome,* & the fame acknowledge the Grecians in the feauenth fynode in the Councels of Lateran, Lyons, and

Theodoret. lib.5.c.18.

Eufeb. lib. 3. de vit. Conftant.

Theodoret. lib.1.c 7. Nicephor. l. 3. c. 19.

Sozome.lib. 1. c. 19. Cregor. l. 6. epift.31. Nouel. 9. & C.de fumm. Trinit. lib. vltImo. Concil. Calced.act.1. Athanaf. apol.2. Socrates lib. 2.cap. 13. Sext. Sinod. act. 18. Theodoret. lib. 5.c.9. Euap. lib. 1. c. 4. Martian. ep. ad Leonem. Gelaf. ep. ad Epifcopum Dordon. Concil. Nicen.epift.ad Siluoft.

and Florence. Likewise some Patriarches of the East (to omit Bishops) were by the Popes authority created, as Anatholius of Constantinople by Pope Leo epist. 53. ad Pulcheriam, others deposed as Anthimus of Constant: Dioscorus, and Timothie of Alexandria, and Peeter of Antioche. Other being deposed or vexed appealed to Popes, as S. Athanasius and Peter of Alexandria, S. Paul, S. Chrisostom: and S. Flauian of Constantinople, Paulin of Antioch: which euidently proueth the Popes Primacy ouer them. Finally to omit the testimony of S. Athanasius, S. Basil, S. Chrisostom, Theodoret, and other Doctors and saints of the East church, both the Emperour and Patriarche of Constantinople did in S. Gregories time (as he witnesseth) daily professe the church of Constantinople to be vnder the Romane Sea.

7. Now to his reason. Bellarmin saith. The Emperour of the East would haue sate in Couucel aboue the Pope. Ergo, the East church neuer acknowledged his primacy. Who seeth not the manifolde weaknes of this reason. First I deny, that any religious Emperour of the East would haue sate aboue the Pope in Councel, as appeareth by the fact of the two great Emperours Constantin, and Theodosius before rehearsed,

and

Leo epist. 59. 60.61.
Conc. Constant. ep. ad Damas.
Concil. Calced. act. 16. 7. Sinod. act. 2.
Conc. Lateran. 13. c. 15.
Concil. Florent. in lit. vnionis.
Concil. Lugdun. in 6. tit. de election. cap. vbi poriculum.
Baron. 536.
Concil. Calced. act. 3.
Gelas. ep. ad Faustum.
Sozom. lib. 3. c. 7.
Baron. Ann. 371.
Baron. 342.
Chrysost. epist. ad Innocent.
Ex lit. Leon. & Valent. ad Theodos.
Athanas. ep. ad Felicem.
Basil. ep. 52. ad Athan.
Chrisost. ep. ad Innocen.
Theodoret. epist. ad Renatum.
Gregor. l. 7. epist. 63.

and by Iustinus humbling himselfe vnto
the Pope proftrate on the ground, Iufti-
nians lowly adoring, and Iuftinian the fecond his kiffing of his feeet. Is it likely that
thefe who fo honoured the Pope out of
Councel, would haue fate aboue him in
Councel? And albeit one grecian Emperour, after both religion, and reuerence
thereto was decayed in Greece, and the
whole nation fallen into Schifme and herefy, did in the Coûcel of Florence attempt
to fit aboue the Pope, yet the like is not to
be thought of other religious Chriftian
Emperours, whereof, diuers as Bel teſtifyeth art. 1. pag. 17. humbled themfelues,
and yeelded euen their foueraigne rights to
Popes. Yea the felfe fame Emperour, who
by fome euil fuggeftion would haue fate
aboue the Pope, would at his firſt meeting
with him haue kneeled vnto him. But fuppofe that the grecian Emperours, by reafon
of their temporal fuperiority, would haue
fitten aboue the Pope, Doe they therefore
deny his fpiritual primacy? No more furely
then a gentleman doth deny his paftours
fpiritual authority ouer him, becaufe he wil
fit aboue him. Did not the grecians euen in
the Florentin Councel, where they attempted to place the Emperour aboue the Pope,
defyne together with the Latins, that the
Bifhop

See Art. 1. c.
6. parag. 6.

Conceil. Flo-
rent. in ini-
tio.

Concil. Flo-
rent. fup.

In lit. vnio-
nis.

Biſhop of Rome hath *primatum in vniuerſum orbem*, primacy ouer the whole world.

8. In two other matters Bel iniuryeth *Bel p.127.*
the Pope, auouching, *that he would neuer shew his face in any Councel.* And *that he shamefully* *vntruth 102.*
abuſeth the worlde, becauſe he can not communi-
cate his ſupreame iudicial authority to his Legates, *vntruth 103.*
and wil approue nothinge decreed in Councel, vnles
it be agreable to that which he decreeth a part in
his chaire at home. For the firſt of theſe is a
manifeſt vntruth; becauſe the Pope hath
bene perſonally preſent almoſt in al the general councels helde in the weſt, as at Florence, at Conſtance, at Viena, at Lyons, at
Rhemes, at Claremount, and diuers councels of Lateran. In the other the Pope abuſeth the worlde no more, then doth the
Prince abuſe the Parliament, when ſending
thither the L. Chaunceller to ſupplie his
place, and præſeed in his roome, wil neuertheleſſe approue nothing what the Peeres
doe, or decree, vnles himſelfe iudgeth it
conuenient.

Chap. XIIII.
Of the oath which Biſhops vſe to make vnto the Pope.

BECAVSE Biſhops ſweare fidelity to
the Pope, and to keep and defend the
primacy

primacy of the Romane Church, and rules
of holy fathers against al men, and neuertheles as Bellarmin writeth, are not to obey
him, but when he commandeth according
to Gods law, and holy canons, and may not
withstanding their oath speake their minde
in councel, and depose the Pope, if he become an heretike. Bel inferreth diuers
things requisit to be answered: First, that
Bishops sweare the Pope can depose al Emperours
and Kings in the Christian wordle. Secondly,
that *they sweare to admit his decree, whome they*
freely graunt may be an hereticke: Thirdly, that
they sweare obedience to him in matters of faith,
whome they can depose for heresy: Fourthly, that
the Pope is not supreame Iudge of controuersies,
seeing Bishops may examyne and iudge, whether
what he commaundeth be agreable to Gods worde,
and the Canons. Lastly, that *they sweare flat re-*
bellion against their Soueraigns, seeing they sweare
to defend the Popes Primacy against al men
whomsoeuer.

2. Answer. As for the oath of Bishops
made to the Pope the lawfulnes thereof appeareth, because it is made withal Catholique princes consent, and meant only in
iust and lawful things, which are according
to Gods law, and holy Canons. And it hath
bene vsed aboue a thowsand yeare agoe, as
is euident by the like oath made by a Bishop
vnto

Bellarm.lib.
1. de concil.
cap.vlt.

pag. 125.
126.

vntruth
104.

S. Gregory the great. And S. Boniface the
Apoſtle of Germany, and worthieſt man
that euer England bredde, did ſweare when
he was conſecrated Biſhop *to concurre with
the Pope and commodities of his church.* And as
for the firſt poiñt which Bel inferreth, it is
vntrue, as appeareth by the anſwer to the
firſt article. The ſecond and third contayne
no inconuenience. For we muſt obey what
he decreeth, or defyneth Iudicially as ſitting in S. Peeters chaire, though in hart he
were an hereticke. As our Sauiour cõman-
ded the Iewes to follow what the Scribes
taught out of Moyſes chaire, but abſtaine
from their priuate leauen. If Bel can not
imagine how a man by Gods diſpoſition
may vtter truth cõtrary to his owne minde,
let him remember Balaam, and Caiphas,
and what hath bene ſaid before out of S.
Auſtin. Beſides we graunt not freely, as
Bel freely forgeth, that the Pope may be an
hereticke. For Bellarmin (*whoſe only teſtimony* ſaith Bel *is moſt ſufficient in al popiſh affaires*) defendeth the contrary And by that
which hath bene ſaid to theſe two points
appeareth the anſwer to the fourth. Becauſe
Biſhops muſt not examin the doctrine,
which the Pope deliuereth iudicially out of
S. Peters chaire, as ſupreame paſtour of Gods
church, but only that, wherein he vttereth

D d   his

S. Gregor. ▌
10. ep. 31.
baron. Ann.
723.

See Concil.
Tolet. 11.
can. 10.

S. Math. 23.
v. 3.
S. Marc. 8.
v. 15.
S. Math. 16.
v. 6.

Numer. 22.
Ioh. 11. v.
52.
Chap. 10.
parag. 9.
Bellarm. lib.
4. de Rom.
Pont. cap. 6,
& 7.
Bel p. 125.

his owne priuate opinion.

3. And as for the laſt point; Bishops ſweare no rebellion : Both becauſe they ſweare to defend the Popes primacie, only according to Gods worde, and holy Canons, which admit no rebellion. As alſo becauſe the defence which Bishops are to vſe, is not by inſurrection and rebellion, but by ſpiritual chaſtiſment, and correction. In which ſort S. Fabian deſended the orders of the Church againſt the Emperour Philip. S. Innocent: defended S. Chriſoſtom againſt Archadius, S. Babilas and S. Ambroſe puniſhed their Emperours without any rebellion at al.

The vvea-
pons of our
vvarfare
are not car-
nal. 1. Cor.
10 v. 4.
Euſeb. lib 6.
c. 25.
Gelaſ. epiſt.
ad Anaſt.
S. Chryſoſt.
lib. cont.
Gent.

pag 128.
Rhemiſts
Act 15.
vntruth
105.

4. After the foreſaid collections, Bel auoucheth an vntruth vpon the Rhemiſts affirming them *to tel plainely and rowndly, that the determination of Councels is needles, becauſe the Popes iudgement alone is infallible.* Where as they in that place which Bel cyteth write, that though the Sea Apoſtolique haue infallible aſſiſtance, yet the determination of Councels are neceſſary for many cauſes, as for ſearching out the truth, for the recouery of hereticks, and contentation of the weake, who not alwaies giuing ouer to one mans determination, yet wil either yeeld to the iudgement of al the learned men, and Bishops of al Nations, or els remaine

maine defperate,& condemned before God
and man. As the Apoftles (fay they) though
affifted by God, yet thought it neceffary to
cal a Councel , for decyding a controuerfy
ryfen in their daies. I omit three other
points touched here by Bel. *That the general* pag.128.
Councels is aboue the Pope, can, and hath depofed
him, becaufe he neither proueth them, nor
they concerne any matter of Catholique
faith. And are lardgely and learnedly handled of Bellarmin lib. 2. de concil. And thus
much of Bels feauenth article. *Be myndful* *Apocalip.*
therefore Bel from whence thou art fallen and doe
penance. Apoc. 2.

Dd 2   THE

THE
EIGHT AND LAST
ARTICLE OF KEE-
PING GODS COM-
MANDEMENTS.

CHAP. I.

*The possibility of keeping Gods comman-
dements explicated and proued
out of Scripture.*

ODs children can by his grace
keepe his cómandements. This
Bel absolutly denyeth pag. 143.
148. 149. and 152. though in the
very beginning of this article
he were a shamed to deny it plainly, but admitteth it (saith he) in a godly sence, and
in some sort, and only denyeth it in a Popish sence. But this godly sence is so vngodly, and the sort so sory, as he is ashamed
to vtter it. For as S. Hierom writeth of the
Pelagians, to haue discouered the opinions
of Protestants, is to haue ouercome them,
the blasphemy is manifest at the first : yet
may we gather his meaning by that he saith
pag. 149. That God hath giuen vs those
com-

S. Hieron. e-
pist. ad Cre-
siphontem.
Iren. lib. 1.
cap. 35.

commandements, which we can not poſ-
ſibly keep, and pag. 144. that euery breach
of them is of it nature deadly. The miſtery
therefore of his counſel is, that Gods children can not poſſiblie, euen with his grace
keepe his commandements, but that they
muſt needs oftentymes breake them deadly.
This kinde of keeping Gods commandements he tearmeth imperfect, and vnexact
keeping. But indeed it is no keeping at al,
nor a point of Gods children but of the diuels, and a true breaking of them. For how
are they Gods children, if they loue him
not, how loue they him, if they damnably
offend? If you loue me ſaith Chriſt Ioh. 14.   s. Ioh.
v. 15. keepe my commaundements; & how
can they keepe them, if they damnably, and
deadly breake them? can true keeping, and
true breaking ſtand together.

    2. God commaunded his precepts to be
kept, not ſo ſilily as Bel would, ſo as they
be oftentimes deadly broken; but as Dauid
ſaith *Nimis ſphodra* Pſal. 118. v. 8. *God* (ſaith   *Pſalm.*
S. Auſtin vpon that place conc. 4.) *hath very*   s. Auſtin.
much commaunded his precepts to be very much
kept. And according to S. Iames, *who offen-*   s. Iames 2.
deth in one is guilty of al. Wherfore deadly   v.10.
breaking of one of Gods lawes , can no
more ſtand with keeping them, then thefte
or murder can ſtande with keeping the

Princes lawes. Nor they, who oftentimes deadly breake Gods lawes, be his children whilest they doe so, more then theeues and murderers be good subiects. And as for the Popish sence, it is not as Bel falslie imposeth, that we can keepe Gods commaundements so perfectly, as we be free from sinne: For so (as S. Iohn saith) we should deceaue our selues, and as Bel confesseth we doe daily acknowledge our sinnes, but so as we be free from deadly sinne, which destroieth charity the end of the law, and keepe the commaundements in al great, though not in smal matters. For as S. Hierom saith we may be without *cacia*, though not *sina amartia*, or as S. Austin, and S. Gregory gather out of S. Paul *sine crimine*, though not *sine peccato*, that is without great sinne, though not without smal sinne, without mortal, though not without venial. And to keepe Gods commaundements in this sort, is substantially to keepe them, because we breake not the end of them, which is charity; and yet not perfectly, & exactly, as who stealeth but trifles keepeth the Princes lawes, though not perfectly; but if he steale great matters, he is said no more to keepe but to breake them. And in this sence, doe Catholiques defend the foresaid conclusion, which though I might proue many waies, yet

Luther. sermon. de natiu. B. Mariæ maketh al Christians as holy as the mother of God.

Bel p. 150.

The Apostles were cleane, and yet had need to haue their feete washed. Ioh. 13. ver. 10. 11.

S. Hierom. dialog. 2. cont. Pelag. S. Gregor. 21. moral. c. 9. S. Augustin. hom. 19. de temp. to. 10. lib. 1. contr. duas epist Pelag. c. 14. to 7. enchirid. c. 69.

1. Timoth. 1 y. 5.

yet wil I content my selfe with such proofes, as Bel vndertaketh to answer, and in
that order as he propoundeth them.

3. First therfore I proue it. because a
young man tolde Christ *he had kept al the* Math. 19.
commaundements from his youth. Bel answereth v. 20.
that S. Hierom saith he lyed, and S. Austin Bel p 150.
thinketh he spake more prowdly then tru- S. Augustin,
ly, neuerthelesse more probable it is that he epist. 89.
spake truly, because not only our Sauiour
did not rebuke him (as likely it is he would
haue done, if he had tolde him a lye) but, as
S. Marcke testifieth, *beheld him, & loued him,* Marc. 10.
and said, *one thing is wanting to thee, goe sel* v. 21.
whatsoeuer thou hast, and giue it to the poore,
and come, and follow mee. If the mans speeche
had bene a lye, it would not haue prouo-
ked Christs loue, but his offence; and if he
had broken Gods commaundements, Christ
would haue aduertised him whome he loued, rather of keeping the things which he
commaunded, then which he counselled,
as is the giuing al we haue to the poore.
Wherfore S. Chrisostome hom. 64. in Math. S. Chrysost.
saith, this man was *no dissembler.* And S.
Hierom. dialog. 2. contra Pelag. affirmeth, S. Hierom.
that Christ loued him, because he said he
had done al, *omnia fecisse se dicit, quamobrem*
& amatur à Domino: he said that he had
done al things, wherfore he was also loued

Dd 4 of our

of our lorde; which euidently conuinceth
that his fpeeche was true: for Chrift could
not loue him for a lye. Neither wil Bel I
hope maruel, that we expound S. Mathew
rather by S. Marcke, then by S. Hierome,
and S. Auftin, efpecially feeing S. Hierome
alrered his opinion, ad S. Auftin fpake but
doubtfully, faying *I thinke.* Neuertheles becaufe fome fathers haue thought that the
mans fpeeche was not true, Catholiques
rely not vpon this argument.

Rom. 2. v.
13.

pag. 151.

4. Secondly S. Paule faith. For not the
hearers of the law are iuft with God, but
the Doers of the law shal be iuftified. Ergo
there are fome Doers of the law, and it is
poffible to be done. Bel anfwereth that the
Apoftle fpake not abfolutly, but vpon fuppofal of a thinge, which (faith he) is impoffible, that there were doers of the law,
for fuch faith Bel, *should be iuftified by their
worke, though they could not glory in them.* But
that S. Paule fpake abfolutly, and not vpon
any impoffible fuppofal is euident. Firft becaufe in the firft part of the fentence he
fpake abfolutly of hearers, and not vpon
any impoffible fuppofal, when he faid *they
are not iuft.* Ergo: in the fecond parte he
fpake fo of Doers, when he faid *they shal be
iuftified.* Wherfore as wel may Bel fay there
are no hearers, as no doers of the law. Secondly

condly becaufe in the next verfe before, he *verf.* 12.
had faid abfolutly. *VVhofoeuer haue finned in
the lavv, shal be iudged by the lavv.* Which he
proueth faying. *For not the hearers &c.* Wherfore as the propofition which he proued is
abfolute, and vpon no impoffible fuppofal,
fo is that by which he proueth it. And in *verf.* 14.
the verfe next after he bringeth a proofe,
that the Doers of the law shal be iuftified,
though they heard it not, becaufe *Gentils
who haue no lavv, naturally* (that is without See S. Auftin
lib. 4 contra
inftruction of the law) *Doe thofe things which* Iulian. cap. 3.
are of the lavv : Behould the Apoftle auou- tom. 7.
ching that Gentils doe the law, & by their
example prouing the Doers thereof to be
iuftified.

5. And foe frequent it is in fcripture to *Pfalm.*
affirme, that there are Doers, and keepers
of Gods lawes, as it is auouched more then
twenty times in one Pfalme 118. *I wil keepe* 1.
thy iuftifications v. 8. *I haue fought thee in my* 2.
whole hart. v. 10. *I haue cleaued to thie teftimo-* 3.
nies Lorde. v. 31. *I haue runne the way of thie* 4.
commaundements. v. 32. *I wil keepe thy law in* 5.
my whole hart. v. 34. *I wil keepe thy law al-* 6.
waies. v. 44. *I haue not declined from thy law.* 7.
v. 51. *I haue kept thy law.* v. 55. *I haue not for-* 8.
gotten thy law. v. 61. *I am partaker of al that* 9.
keepe thy commaundements. v. 63. *I haue not for-* 10.
faken thy commaundements. v. 87. *I wil keepe* 11.
the

12. the testimonies of thy mouth. v. 88. *I haue for-bidden my feete from euel* way, *that I may keepe*

13. *thy* words. v. 101. *I haue not declined from thy*

14. *iudgements.* v. 102. *I haue sworne and determi-ned to keepe the iudgements of thy iustice.* v. 106.

15. *I haue not erred from thy commaundements.* v.

16. 110. *Deliuer mee because I haue not forgotten thy*

17. *lavv.* v. 153. *I haue not declined from thy testi-*

18. *monies.* v. 157. *My soule hath kept thy testimonies.*

19. v. 167. *I haue kept thy commaundements and te-*

20. *stimonies.* v. 168. *Seeke thy seruant , for I haue*

21. *not forgotten thy commaundements.* v. 176. What now is it to say that. there are no doers of Gods law, and it is impossible to keepe his commaundements, *but to sett his mouth against*

Psalm. 98.   *heauen.* Psalm. 72. and to giue God the lye.
3. Reg. 14.   I omit Moyses, Aaron, Samuel, Dauid, Io-
Act. 13.   sue, Zacharie, Elizabeth; and the Apostles,
Iosue 11. v.   who are said to haue kept Gods law , and
15.   some of them in al their hart. Only S. Paule
Luc. 1.   I can not omit., because Bel artic. 4. pag.
Ioh 17. v. 6.   48. graunteth that he was most free , and
Contradict.   innocent from actual sinne , therefore su-
19.   rely he kept Gods law perfectly : for if he brake it he sinned actually.

Math. 19.   6. Thirdly Christ said, if thou wilt enter
v. 17.   into life, keepe the commaundements. but entring into life is possible . Ergo: keeping the commaundements. Bel answereth, that Christ shewed not here, how one may at-

taine

taide to eternal life, but how perfectly they
who looke to be iustified by good works
muſt keepe the commaundements : *For
Chriſt* (ſaith he) *being asked what good a man
ſhould doe to attaine eternal life, anſvvered . If
thou wilt haue eternal life by doing good works,
then muſt thou keepe the commaundemēts , but this
is impoſſible* (ſaith Bel.) Here is moſt shameful abuſe of Gods worde, and this sheweth Bel to haue *a ſeared conſcience.* For neither in the mans queſtion, nor in Chriſts
anſwer, is there any worde about what
perfection of keeping Gods commaundements is requiſit to come to heauen by this
way, or that way: vz. by beleeuing , or by
working, or by both . But only about the
meane in general to come to heauen, what
that was, which the man ſuppoſing to bee
good , asked what good he should doe to
come thither (which queſtion of his is
common either to faith,or works, or both;
for al include doing good) And our Sauiour anſwered him , *If thou wilt enter* (not
this way, nor that way, but abſolutly) *into
life, keepe the commaundements.* As Dauid de-
maunding abſolutly , who shal dwel in
Gods tabernacle? anſwereth him ſelfe. *He
that walketh without ſpot, and worketh iuſtice.*
And as him ſelfe otherwere abſolutly ſaith.
Not euery one that ſaid Lord, Lorde shal enter into
the

Gods vvor-
de shame-
fully vvre-
ſled.

1. *Timoth.*
4. *v.* 3.

Pſalm. 14.
v. 1. 2.

Math. 7. *v.*
22.

the Kingdome *of heauen, but be that doth* the wil *of my father.* And furely if this man asking
Caluin. fimply, and of a defier to learne, as Caluin graunteth, had asked the way to heauen by an impoffible meane (as Bel imagineth) Chrift the author of truth, and who loued
Marc. 10. him, as S. Marke faith, wonld rather haue bidden him giue ouer that impoffible way, and taught him the true, then how he should proceede in his erronious, and impoffible way.

7. And though the man had asked Chrift particularly, how he should come to heauen by good works, whence hath Bel, that his meanes to come to heauen is impofsible? wil not Chrift fay in his laft fentence. Come you bleffed of my father, poffeffe the Kingdome prouided for you, from the conftitution of the world: becaufe I was Hun-
S. Math. grie and you gaue mee to eat &c. Math. 25. v. 34. 35. as wel as he wil fay, Goe you from mee you curfed into euerlafting fyer &c. becaufe I was Hungry and you gaue mee not to eate. v. 41. Are not good workes accounted the meanes, and caufe of comming to heauen, as the want of them the meane, and caufe of going to hel. Yea doth not Bel fay artic. 5. pag. 73. *that good*
Contradict. 20. *vvorkes are fo necefsary to attaine eternal life, as the* vfual*, ordinary, and* vndoubted *meanes*
(marke

(marke the worde) *by vvhich God decreed from eternity, freely for his ovvne name sake, to bring his elect to saluation.* And that *vvithout them none haue bene, are, or shal be saued.* How are they now become an impossible meane to come to heauen? how did the man enquire of an impossible way to heauen, by good workes? what neede this challenger any aduersary, who thus ouerthroweth him selfe.

8. Fourthlie I proue the conclusion: because Christ saith, *my yoake is svveete, and my burthen light.* And S. Ihon saith, *his commaundements are not heauy.* Ergo they are possible. Bel answereth that these wordes are meant not in respect of vs, but of Christ, whose keeping the commaundements is imputed to vs: which S. Austin (saith he) meant when he wrote. *Then are al the commaundements reputed as done, vvhen vvhatsoeuer is not done is forgiuen.*

Math. 11. v. 30.
1. Ioh. 5. v. 3.

Bel p. 152.

S. Augustin. lib. 1. retract. c. 19. tom. 1.

9. But this is easily refuted. For S. Iohn spake in respect of vs assisted by Gods grace, when he said. *This is the law of God, that we keepe his commaundements, and his commaundements are not heauie.* He saith not (Christ) but (we) must keepe Gods commaundements, & to animate vs thereto, he addeth. that they are not heauy vz. to vs. And cap, 2. v. 2. he giueth vs a signe to try if wee

knowe

Bel either keepeth Gods com‐ maunde‐ ments, or knovveth not God.

*Cap.*11.v.29.

know God: vz. if we keepe his commaun‐ dements, and v. 3. affirmeth, *that who keepeth not his cōmaundements knoweth not God:* wher‐ fore either Bel keepeth the cōmandements, or he knoweth not God. Likewise Christ meant his yoake was sweete, and his bur‐ then light to vs. For immediatly before he said Take vp my yoake vpon you, & learne &c. and you shal finde rest to your soules. For my yoake is sweet, and burthen light. To whom meaneth he it is light, but to vs, whom he biddeth take it vp? and whom he promiseth shal finde rest by it? or what rea‐ son had it bene for Christ, to exhorte vs to take vp his yoake, and tel vs we should finde rest by it, because it is sweet to himselfe?

S. Augustin. sup.to.1.

As for S. Austin he said our defectuous kee‐ ping is counted a ful keeping, when the de‐ fect is pardoned; which is a farre different thing from saying. That Christs keeping is counted our keeping. And he meaneth that our keeping is defectuous, because we keepe not the commaundements *ad vnum apicem* (as he saith) to the last ioat or title: But through venial sinnes haue need to say. Forgiue vs our trespasses, which venial trespasses being pardoned, we are accoun‐ ted to doe al Gods commaundements.

pag. 152.

10. An other answer Bel putteth in the margent, and in latine. That Christ mea‐ neth

neth not of the yoake, and burthen of the law, when he calleth it sweet, and easy, but of the Ghospel. That Christ meant of the law of the Ghospel, I graunt with S. Hierom dialog. 2. contr. Pelag, and is proued out of these wordes: *my yoake, my burthen.* But what is this to the purpose? Is Bel become a libertine, thincking as his father Luther did, that the tenne commaundements belong not to Christians, or that the Ghospel commaundeth only faith? Did Christ come to dissolue the law of nature, and to exempt vs from al law, but of belieuing in him? If Bel be of this minde, let him vtter it plainly, and say Christ came not to fulfil the law, but to dissolue it, that his faith establisheth not the law, but destroieth it. Or if he thinke that the law of the ghospel. Besides the precepts of faith, includeth at least the law of nature, let him confesse that the tenne commaundements, and al that God bindeth vs vnto, is not only possible, but easy, and sweet, vz. to such as loue God, as was Dauid when he said, *i haue runne the way of thy commaundements, when thou didst dilate my hart.* And *how sweet are thy speeches to my iawes, aboue hony to my mouth. The law of thie mouth is good to mee, aboue thowsands of golde and siluer.* For as S. Iohn saith 1. c.5. v.3. *this is the loue of God that wee keepe his com-*

maun-

S. Hierom.

Luther.

Math. 5. v. 19.

Rom. 3. v. 31.

Psalm. 118. *v.* 32. Omnia facilia sunt charitati cui vnl Christi farcina leuis est. Aug. de nat. & grat. c.69.to.7.see the place.
S. Iohn.

maundements. If Bel say that it is impossible
to loue God as we ought to doe. This is reproued, because he loueth God as he should
doe, who loueth him withal his hart, al his
soule and power. But Iosue so loued God,
of whome it is written. 4. Reg. 23. That he
returned in al his harte, in al his soule, and
al his strength. Likewise Dauid sought God
in al his hart. Psalm. 118. and followed him
in al his harte. 3. Reg. 14. And God hath
some seruants, that walke before him in al
their hart, with whome he keepeth his couenant, and mercy. 2. Paralip 6. v. 14. And
Deuter. 30. v. 6. God promiseth to circum-
cise the Iewes harts, that they might loue
him in al their harts, and al their soule. And
thus much for proofe out of scripture, now
let vs goe to the Fathers.

Deuter. 6.
v. 5.

4. *Reg.* 23.

Dauid.

verf. 8.

Chap. II.

The possibility of keeping Gods commaun-
dements proued out of Fathers
and reason.

MANY holy Fathers I might alleadge
for this verity, but I wil content my
selfe with two only, whome Bel obiecteth
against him selfe, and vndertaketh to answer. S. Hierom dialog. 1. contr. Pelag. we
confesse (saith he) God hath giuen possible
com-

S. Hierom.
See S. Hie-
rom in cap.
5. Mathei.

commaundements, left he should be author of iniuftce. Beholde our conclusion both affirmed, and proued. And Dialog 2. I say a man may be without vice, which in greeke is called *cacia*, but not *anamartyton*, that is without finne, which is as much as if he had faid. He can be without mortal, but not without venial finne. Againe: God hath not commaunded impoffible things, but hath afcended vp to fuch height of patience, as for their great difficulty he may feeme to haue commaunded almoft impoffible things. Againe: we curfe their blafphemie, who faie. That God hath commaunded to man any impoffible thing. This *pag. 153.* Bel alleadgeth out of his 3. & fourth booke againft Pelagians, whereas he wrote but one epiftle, and three bookes or Dialogues againft Pelagians. But it is in his epiftle to Damafus de expofit. fidei. And therein S. *pag. 149.* *S. Auftin.* Hierom curfeth this blafphemy of Bel: *God* *see S. Au-* *hath giuen vs thofe commaundements, which* we *ftin m Pfal.* *can not poßibly keepe.* Likewife S. Auftin fer. *56 tom. 8.* 61. de temp. God could not commaund any *vvhere he* impoffible thinge, becaufe he is iuft. The *faith the* fame he repeateth lib. de natur. & grat. cap. *did that* 69. and lib. 2 de pen. mer. & remiff. and in *charity,* pfal. 56. I can not doubt (faith he) that God *then the* hath neither commaunded any impoffible *vvhich,* thinge to man, nor that any thinge is im- *greater.*

E e poffipossible to God to helpe, wherby it may be done which he commaundeth.

2. For auoiding these authorities Bel deuiseth three shiftes. First, that Gods commaundements were possible to vs before Adams fal. Secondly, that they were possible to Christ, whose keeping them is accounted ours. Thirdly, that euen to vs they are now possible to be kept imperfectly, though not perfectly, which is (saith he) the doctrine of Aquinas: yet seeing that none of these shiftes would serue, he falleth to proue, that we may be iustly damned for not doing impossible matters; because Infants vnbaptized, are damned for original sinne, which saith he they could not possibly auoid. And in the margent calleth this a dilemma, which no Papist can auoid: But none of these shiftes wil suffice. For S. Hierome epist. ad Ctesiph. writeth, that the cōmaundements are possible to vs by Gods grace. And dialog. 2. cit. That they are so possible, as that Dauid we know (saith he) hath done them. If they be possible to vs, then not to Christ alone; and if Dauid did them, man after Adams sinne may doe them. And the reason which he, and S. Austin after him giueth of Gods iustice, conuinceth the same. For it is against his iustice, to commaund vs impossible things, as wel after

Adams

S. Thom. 2.
2. quæst. 44.
art. 6.
vntruth.

S. Hierom.

Adams finne as before. Likewife S. Auguftin after the Apoftle faith, that the iuftice
of the law is fulfilled in vs. Ergo not in
Chrift alone.

S. Auguftin.
fermon. 6.
de verb. A-
poftol. cap.
9. Rom. 8.
v. 4.

3. As for the thirde shifte. S. Thomas
faith indeed, that the precept of louing God
withal our hart &c. can not be perfectly
kept, but imperfectly, yet in a fenfe quite
contrary to Bel. Perfectly faith he is the precept kept, when the very end intended by
the commaunder is atchieued. Imperfectly,
when albeit the end be not attained, yet the
way vnto it is not left. As a fouldier fighting, and ouercomming, perfectly fulfilleth
the commaund of his captaine, bidding him
fight. And an other fighting, and doing nothing againft the duety of a fouldier, but
not ouercomming, fulfilleth it, but imper-
fectlie. Whereby we fee plainly, that though
S. Thomas deny, that the end, (vz. to bee
wholy vnited to God) for which he gaue
that precept of loue, be not poffible in this
life, yet he graunteth that we may fo fight,
or labour for the attaining it, as wee doe nothing againft the order commaunded by
God, or the duety of a fpiritual fouldier.
Which is indeed fubftantially to keepe the
precepts, though S. Thomas in refpect of
keeping them, and alfo attayning the end,
for which they were made, cal it imperfect

Ee 2 kee-

keeping. For seeing God commaundeth not the end, but only intendeth it (as S. Thomas saith) if the order and meanes commaunded be fulfilled, then surely the commaundement is fulfilled, though the end of the commaunder, which is only intended, not commaunded be not attayned.

4. And as for Bels dilemma it is easily answered, and therefore might haue bene better lefte out (as himselfe writeth in the margent) For though Infants after they haue sinned, and eaten the aple in Adam, cannot auoide the guilt thereof, but must needs contract it by origin from Adam. As a man after he hath committed adultery can not but contract the guilt of adultery : Yet because as Infants sinned in Adam, so they might haue not sinned in him, and so haue

Bel pag. 51. *art.* 4.

auoided the guilt of sinne, falsly doth Bel say they could not possibly auoide it. And

Contradict. 21.

I wonder why hauing taught before, that concupiscence (which is the effect of originall sinne) is voluntary, he wil now say that Infants could not possibly auoide originall sinne. But it is his custome to gainsay himselfe.

Reason.

5. By reason also it may be proued, that Gods precepts are possible. For besides, that if the law were impossible, sinne might be inuoluntary. I aske to whom Gods commaun-

maundements are impossible ? To man
alone ? and that is not the question nor denyed of any Catholique : or to man with
Gods grace? and that is contrary to S. Paule
saying *I can doe al things in him that strengthneth*   *S. Paul Phi-*
mee: and iniurious to Gods grace, making   *lip. 14 vers.*
it impotent, which S. Ihon maketh so po-   *13*
tent as he auoucheth, that he can not sinne,   *S. Iohn.*
in whom it remayneth 1. Ioh. 3. v. 9. why
did God say *suffecit tibi gratia mea* : *my grace*
sufficeth thee 2 Corinth 12. if his grace suffice   *S. Paul. 2.*
not. Likewise if God commaunded impos-   *9.*
sible things, he should be the Author of
iniustice, or vniust ; as affirme S. Hierom
dialog. 1. contr. Pelag. and S. Austin de nat.
& grat. cap. 69. and serm. 61. de temp. For
it is an vniust law which is impossible, and
to punish breakers were against right, and
equity. As Bel himselfe would graunt if
vpon paine of death he were bid to flie to
heauen, and executed if he did not. Wher-
fore S. Hierom epist. ad Ctesiphont : wri-   *S. Hierom.*
thus. we pronounce the commaunder vn-
iust, whiles we complaine, that the very
Author of equity, hath commaunded impossible things. And Simon Magus (saith
Vincent. Lirinen.) made God Author of   *Vincent. Li-*
sinne, in affirming vs to sinne of necessity.   *rin.*
Now let vs see Bels proofes to the con-
trary.

Ee 3   CHAP.

Chap. III.
*Bels arguments out of Scripture againſt the
poſſibility of keeping Gods commaundements anſwered.*

BEL proueth Gods commaundements
to be impoſsible. Firſt, out of S. Iames

Iacob. 3. v.
2.
Si quis in
verbo non
offendit, hic
perfectus
eſt vitæ. v. 2.

saying. *we al offend in many things.* Anſwer.
S. Iames meaneth of venial ſinnes, as idle
words are, whereof he ſpeaketh in the ſame
verſe. And though Bel replie, that he hath
already proued, that euery ſinne is mortal

Art. 6. cap. 6.

in it owne nature, yet neither is that true,
as before is ſhewed, nether though it were,
could it diſproue my anſwer. For it ſuffi-

Bel art. 6.
pag. 81.

ceth (which Bel denyeth not) that there indeed are venial ſinnes (whether they be
ſuch by their owne nature, or by Gods mercy) in the which iuſt men may offend, and
not breake Gods law deadly.

pag. 144.

2. Next he alleadgeth S. Paules wordes
Galath. 3. verſ. 10. *Curſed be euery one that ſhal
not abide in al things that are written in tke
booke of the law to doe them.* what can hence
be inferred to Bels purpoſe I ſee not, except that al men are curſed, or els freed
from al lawes of God, and true libertines.
But in truth it maketh more againſt him,
then for him. For S. Paules intention was
to proue,

to proue, that faith in Christ was to iustification, and that the works of the bare law
without faith were not sufficient. And
therefore hauing proued by Abrahams example, that faith doth concurre to iustificatiõ, in the tenth verse proueth, that workes
of the bare law suffice not. For whosoeuer
(saith he) are of the workes of the law (vz.
without faith) are vnder curse. For it is
written accursed be &c. Because such as
want faith, can not abide in al things of the
law, and consequently are vnder curse. But
what maketh this against those who haue
faith and grace. Such can doe al Gods wil
with Dauid: act. 13. Such erre not from
Gods commaundements: Psal. 118. Such can
fulfil al things, and let not passe one worde
of al Gods commaundements with Iosue.
cap. 11. Such are dôers of the law and iustifyed. Rom. 2. v. 12. 14. finally such because
the seed of God is in them neither sinne,
nor can sinne. 1. Ioh. 3. verf. 9. and confequently auoyd the foresaid curse. Neither
doe their venial sinns incurre the curse: for
it is pronounced only against heynous crimes, namely Idolatry, incest, murder, and
the like, as is euident by the 27. of Deuter.
from whence the Apostle reciteth the curse
But Bel who confesseth him selfe to incurre
the crime accursed by the law, must needs

Act. ves.
22.
Psalm.

Iosue.

S. Paul.

S. Iohn.

Deutr.

E e 4   con-

confesse him selfe to be vnder that curse, or say, that he is not bound to Gods lawes made against Idolatrie, Incest, murder, and the like.

pag. 144.

3. The like text he bringeth out of S. Iames. 2 v. 10. *whosoeuer shal keepe the whole law, and offended in one is made guilty of al.* This place also maketh rather against Bel. For it supposeth that al the law may be kept, as wel one point as the whole; and only teacheth, that the keeping of the whole law wil not saue, if one point thereof be deadly broken. But this is nothing against Gods children, who as long as his

S. Ioh.

seed abideth in them sinne not. Ioh. 3. v. 9. nor offend deadly in one point, but abide both in the whole law, and euery pointe thereof.

4. Diuers other places Bel alleadgeth to proue that al men are sinners, and that the iust doe sinne, which no Catholique denyeth, as Bel might learne out of the Tri-

Concil. Trident. sess. 6. cap. 11.

dentine Councel. But how followeth it thereof, that the Iust whiles they are Iust sinne deadly, or cannot auoyd al deadly

pag. 143.

sinne. This is the marque which Bel should shoot at, and hoped in the beginning of this article to hit the naile on the head; but

S. Hierom. dialog. contra Lucifer.

as S. Hierom said to a Luciferian: whiles he followeth his vaine of gainsaying, he hath

mist

miſt the queſtion, as ſome rather praters
then ſpeakers vſe to doe; who not knowing to diſpute yet ceaſe not to quarrel.

Chap. IIII.
*Bels arguments out of Fathers againſt
the poſſibility of keeping Gods commaundements anſvvered.*

pag. 145.

Firſt, out of S. Auſtin he alleadgeth,
that God commaunded vs to loue him
with al our hart, ſoule, and mynde, and
thereby left no part of our life vacant to
take fruition of any other thinge. But S.
Auſtin in theſe words meant nothing els,
but that wee muſt loue nothing as our end,
and for it ſelfe but God; for ſo he vſeth the
worde fruition, and therfore addeth which
Bel left forth. *But what other thing commeth
to our mynde to be loued, let it be carried thither,
whither the whole current of loue runneth.*

S. Auguſtin. lib.1. de doctrin. Chriſt. c.22.to.3.

2. Other words he citeth out of lib. de
perfect. iuſti. ratiocin. 16. but they are in
17. cap. 8. where S. Auſtin writeth. That
as long as there is any thing of carnal concupiſcence, which may be bridled by re-
frayning, God is not loued (*omnimodo*) altogether with al the ſoule. And yet though
none in this life haue that perfection it is
commaunded, becauſe it is not wel runne,
if it

pag. 146.

if it be not knowne whither to runne. Anſwer. What S. Auſtins meaning is herein himſelfe explicateth, ſaying, that the precept of louing God withal our ſoule is not *omnimodo* altogether fulfilled whilſt we haue inordinate motions. He denyeth not ſubſtantial fulfilling which auoideth ſinne

S. Auguſtin. tom. 3.

(yea lib. de ſpir. & liter. cap. vlt. affirmeth, that though wee did not loue God withal our harts, and ſoule, ſo as we had no motions of luſt: yet if wee did not obey them, we need not to aske God forgiuenes) but only denyeth *omnimodam impletionem,* which in the place cited he called moſt ſupereminent perfection of louing God, and ſaith not it belongeth to this, but to the next life, vz. to bee perfectly perfourmed. Wherfore when he ſaith ſuch perfection is commaunded in this life, he meaneth not that it is commaunded as a thing which we are bound to perfourme, but only as an end to

De perfect. inſtit. loc. cit.

which we ſhould runne. *For though* (ſaith he) *no man perfourme it, yet we runne not wel, if we knovv not vvhither to runne, and hovv ſhould we knovv if it vvere ſhevved by no precept.*

pag. 147. S. Thomas 1 2 q. 44. art 6

3. Next he citeth S. Thomas only becauſe he vſeth the words perfectly, and imfectly. But how contrary to Bels meaning hath bene before explicated, which reproueth his vntruth in affirming himſelfe to

teach

teach the selfe same doctrine with Aquinas.
What hath bene said to S. Austin, and S.
Thomas is to be applied to S. Bernarde, S. Bernard.
hom. 50. in
Cant.
when he saith in the like sort, that the precept of louing God can not be fulfilled in
this life. And that God in commaunding
impossible things made not men preuarica-
tors, but humble. For beside that S. Bernard, as himselfe, speaketh this only, if the
precept of loue be vnderstood of affectual
charity, or charity in worke, and graunteth
that so it is fulfilled, if it be perfectly obserued, as (said he a litle before) it may be
in this life by Gods grace. Besides this I say,
immediatly before the words which Bel
cyteth, he graunteth, that *initium perfectum-*
que the beginning and perfection of charity
may be experienced by Gods grace in this
life. If perfection be had, surely the precept
is fulfilled. For (as himselfe saith sone after)
doest thou not thinke is sufficient to the
fulfilling the precept of louing thie neighbour, if thou obserue it perfectly. And Bel
pag. 151. graunteth, that who perfectly obserueth the law shal be iustifyed.

4. And though he differ, or (as he speaketh) defend the consummation of charity
to the next life, and therefore accoumpt the
precept of charity impossible, as far forth
as it imbraceth the consummation, yet he
mea-

meaneth not, that it imbraceth consummation as a thinge needful to be perfourmed,
which (he faith) *shal be our reward in heauen,*
but as the end to which men ought to endeuour, *vt fcirent* (faith he) *ad quem iuftitiæ finem pro viribus niti oporteret,* that they might
know to what end of iuftice they ought to
endeuour withal their power. Behoulde he
faith not, that we ought to attaine to the
faid end, but to endeuour al that we can;
and therefore God in commaunding that
end in fuch fort as he doth, maketh men no
finners, thongh they attaine not to it.

*pag.*150.　5. After thefe fathers he bringeth two
reafons. The one out of our Lords prayer,
where we are taught to aske forgiuenes.
But where pardon is demaunded, ths law is
not exactly obferued. The other is out of
our daily confeffions, where we acknowledge our fault, and moft great fault. Anfwer; As the petition of forgiuing our finns,
doth euidently conuince, that we doe not
fo exactly keep the law, as we neuer fwarue
from it : So the other petition of doing
Gods wil in earth as it is in heauen, euidently conuinceth, that we can doe it without deadly breaking it. As for our confeffion, we doe not confeffe that our daylie
offences are moft great faults, but daily confeffe our moft great fault, whether it were
done

done then or before. Besides that humble
and penitent mindes accompt themselues
greatest sinners, and their offences greatest
faults. So S. Paul 1. Timoth 1 v.15 accoun- S. Paul.
ted himselfe the *chiefest sinner.* Yea *good souls*
(as S. Gregory saith) *acknowledge sinne where* S. Gregor. e-
none is, and with Iob, feare al their works. guft. Canr.
And as the same holy Doctour noteth, the cap. 10.
reprobate accompt great sinns litle, and the *Iob cap. 9.*
elect litle sinns great, and which before S. Gregor.in
they thought were light, straight they ab- nitent.
hor as heauy and deadly. And S. Hierom S. Hieron.
obserueth, that *it increaseth warines to take* epist.ad Co-
heed of litle (sinnes) *as if they were great. For* lant.
with so much the more facility we abstayne from
any sinne, by how much more we feare it.

6. And hence Bel may see, why we in dayly confessions confesse our most great fault,
which I would God he would imitate, and
both confesse, and amend his heynous fault
of sinning against the holy Ghost, and impugning the Catholique Church, which he
knoweth to be Gods Church. Otherwise
let him assure himselfe, that shame wil be
his end in this life, and endles punishment
his reward in the next. Wel he may beat a-
gainst this rocke, but like the waues, he shal
without hurting it, beat himselfe in pieces,
and be resolued into froth and foame. Let
him write books, let him spend himselfe,
and

and make nets with the Spider of his owne
guts, they wil proue only spider webbes,
apt to cath or holde none, but such as like
inconstant and fleshly flyes are carrayed a-
bout with euery mynde of new doctrine,
and following their carnal appetites, and
licentiousnes, seaze vpon fleshly baite. And
so Bel though he could become an other
God Bel, he should but be Beel zebub the
God of flies. *Be myndful therfore* (Bel) *from
whence thou art fallen, and do penance.* Apocalip. 2.

F I N I S.

Al praise to Almightie God.

A TABLE

Of the things cōteined in this booke vvherin a signifyeth article. c. chapter and parag. paragraph.

B.

Bels

of Po-

C.

art.

Chrift

giue

Gg   Iniqui-

Mariage

no do-

                                        chap.

Popes

Prote-

Reading

Sacra-

FINIS.